Migration in European History

The Making of Europe

Series Editor: Jacques Le Goff

The *Making of Europe* series is the result of a unique collaboration between five European publishers – Beck in Germany, Blackwell in Great Britain and the United States, Critica in Spain, Laterza in Italy and le Seuil in France. Each book will be published in all five languages. The scope of the series is broad, encompassing the history of ideas as well as of societies, nations and states to produce informative, readable and provocative treatments of central themes in the history of the European peoples and their cultures.

Migration in European History

Klaus J. Bade

Translated by Allison Brown

Blackwell
Publishing

First published 2003 by Blackwell Publishing Ltd.

Library of Congress Cataloging-in-Publication Data

Bade, Klaus J.
  [Europa in Bewegung. English]
  Migration in European history / Klaus J. Bade; translated by Allison Brown.
      p. cm. – (The making of Europe)
Includes bibliographical references and index.
  ISBN 0-631-18939-4 (alk. paper)
1. Europe – Emigration and immigration – History. 2. Migration,
Internal – Europe – History. 3. Europeans – Foreign countries – History.
4. Immigrants – Europe – History. I. Title. II. Series.

JV7590 .B3313 2003
304.8′4 – dc21   2002153201

A catalogue record for this title is available from the British Library.

Set in 10/12 pt Sabon
by Kolam Information Services Pvt. Ltd, Pondicherry, India
Printed and bound in the United Kingdom
by TJ International Ltd, Padstow, Cornwall

For further information on
Blackwell Publishing, visit our website:

http://www.blackwellpublishing.com

Contents

Series Editor's Preface

Europe is in the making. This is both a great challenge and one that can be met only by taking the past into account – a Europe without history would be orphaned and unhappy. Yesterday conditions today; today's actions will be felt tomorrow. The memory of the past should not paralyse the present: when based on understanding it can help us to forge new friendships, and guide us towards progress.

Europe is bordered by the Atlantic, Asia and Africa, its history and geography inextricably entwined, and its past comprehensible only within the context of the world at large. The territory retains the name given it by the ancient Greeks, and the roots of its heritage may be traced far into prehistory. It is on this foundation – rich and creative, united yet diverse – that Europe's future will be built.

The Making of Europe is the joint initiative of five publishers of different languages and nationalities: Beck in Munich; Blackwell in Oxford; Critica in Barcelona; Laterza in Rome; and le Seuil in Paris. Its aim is to describe the evolution of Europe, presenting the triumphs but not concealing the difficulties. In their efforts to achieve accord and unity the nations of Europe have faced discord, division and conflict. It is no purpose of this series to conceal these problems: those committed to the European enterprise will not succeed if their view of the future is unencumbered by an understanding of the past.

The title of the series is thus an active one: the time is yet to come when a synthetic history of Europe will be possible. The books we shall publish will be the work of leading historians, by no means all European. They will address crucial aspects of European history in every field – political, economic, social, religious and cultural. They will draw on that long historiographical tradition which stretches back to Herodotus, as well as on those conceptions and ideas which have transformed historical enquiry in the late twentieth and early twenty-first centuries. They will write readably for a wide public.

Our aim is to consider the key questions confronting those involved in Europe's making, and at the same time to satisfy the curiosity of the world at large: in short, who are the Europeans? where have they come from? whither are they bound?

Jacques Le Goff

Preface and Acknowledgements

The subject of migration is experiencing a negative boom in Europe. This has to do with global migration problems and European fears of growing 'migration pressure'. Current interests also raise questions regarding the history of migration to, from and within Europe, since twenty-first-century migratory processes can be better assessed if already completed – that is, past – processes are understood and the lines of development leading to present-day problems are known.

This book is intended as a contribution to that end. It goes beyond the narrower scope of migration research to reach a broader public concerned with migration in the past and in the present. I have therefore refrained from including an introductory discussion of the current state of international research and the different methodological approaches that have been adopted by scholars in the interdisciplinary field of social and cultural history research on migration.[1] Any of these aspects that are necessary for understanding the approach will be briefly explained in the text. I would, however, like to offer a few preliminary comments.

There has been a *Homo migrans*[2] for as long as *Homo sapiens* has existed, since migrations are as much part of the human condition as birth, reproduction, sickness and death. Migrations as social processes, with the exception of refugee and forced migration situations, are responses to more or less complex economic, environmental, social and cultural conditions of basic survival. The history of migration is thus always also part of human history in general and can only be understood against that background. This applies equally to the history of European migrations, yet the concept of Europe and its borders has changed over the course of centuries. The question that then arises – how European history should be perceived and written – has long been a subject of research[3] and is currently of great significance within the context of European unification at the beginning of the twenty-first century.

When researching European history, migration historians are confronted with an extraordinarily complex historical reality. For one thing, not only did people move over borders, but borders moved over people. Furthermore, even the attempt to 'order' historical migration processes is a very abstract and artificial exercise, since migration patterns,[4] like migration behaviour, assumed many different forms whose boundaries overlapped or were constantly shifting and blurred.

In geographical terms, despite considerable overlap it is possible to distinguish among, for example, emigration, immigration and internal migrations. It is also helpful to ask what were the causes, motivations and aims of these migrations. Economic and socio-occupational considerations, for example, can be further narrowed down, distinguishing between employment migrations as subsistence migration or betterment migration, and career migrations for the purpose of attaining further qualifications or training, or migration within branches of one company. Survival migrations, involving people for whom the late twentieth century coined the collective term 'environmental refugees', also took place owing to loss or destruction of economic means of subsistence and were thus ultimately also motivated by economic factors. Migrations for such reasons can in turn be viewed as separate from refugee or forced migrations on religious, ideological, political, ethnonationalist or racism-related grounds. These include the expulsions and forced resettlements of the twentieth century in which movements of people over borders were often the result of borders shifting over people.

Migratory patterns can also be sought, again bearing in mind the numerous transitions and intermediary forms, by distinguishing between local and circular, and between temporary (e.g., migration for work or training) and permanent (e.g., emigration and immigration). Transitions from temporary to permanent forms were usually marked by chain migrations. Migration traditions that developed through the migratory events themselves, together with the transfer of information between places of origin and destination via migration networks, accompanied and at the same time stabilized circular migration systems and emigration and immigration movements. In places of origin, they helped determine destinations and often led immigrants in their new regions into communities based on common origin, which greatly facilitated immigration and integration.[5]

This diversity of overlapping forms of mobility, behaviour patterns and collective motivations was even greater in the historical reality. It becomes yet more difficult to comprehend if historical change and changes in cultural and milieu-specific perspectives and contemporary descriptive forms are taken into consideration. 'Emigration', for example, was a central leitmotif in nineteenth-century Europe – with the exception of France – yet not in preceding centuries. Even within the nineteenth century, as we shall see, the ordinary person's dream that 'emigration' would bring happiness in the 'New World', despite pragmatic considerations and information from transatlantic networks, had little in common with a cosmopolitan businessman setting up a branch office in the United States as a better production location or market for his goods. In addition, scholars are only now beginning to consider gender-specific differences in emigration behaviour and coping strategies for migration.[6] Cultural, milieu- and gender-based differences as well as regional diversity and fluid boundaries in the course of epochal change raise particular periodization problems.[7]

For decades there have been demands for European history and even world history to be written as a history of migrations. These demands remained unsatisfied into the 1990s,[8] even for the European perspective, with the exception of Alexander and Eugen M. Kulischer's world history of migration,[9] E. M. Kulischer's European history of migrations during the world wars,[10] and a few edited collections[11] and stocktaking reports and syntheses geared to the second half of the twentieth century.[12] Efforts to approach this ambitious goal – beyond numerous offerings on the history of emigration or immigration of individual countries – usually restricted themselves to a particular time frame and were either specific in form and geographically non-specific, or specific in terms of geography and open as regards form. Subjects included certain types of migration in an extended area covering several countries, such as emigration from Europe[13] or labour migration in the Atlantic realm in the nineteenth and early twentieth centuries;[14] refugee migration to, from and within Europe in the twentieth century;[15] cross-border migration systems such as the North Sea system from the seventeenth to the early nineteenth centuries;[16] and all migration in a particular region and beyond its borders in longitudinal historical studies[17] or comparative international or intercultural histories of migratory and diaspora experiences and cultural identity issues.[18]

In contrast to those works, this book considers migration to, from and within Europe over a range of eras, countries and migration types. A relatively recent initial approach of this type is Leslie Page Moch's 1992 book *Moving Europeans: Migration in Western Europe since 1650.*[19] Focusing on economic and social history as well as cultural history, this pioneering study deals primarily with changes in the four aspects of landholding distribution, demand for employment, population and settlement structures and capital movements as material determinants in migratory events. The main time period under discussion is from the seventeenth to the nineteenth centuries, and the twentieth century is only briefly considered at the end. In contrast, the present book focuses on the nineteenth and twentieth centuries – apart from a retrospective discussion in chapter 1 and other comparisons that refer back to the eighteenth century – with special attention to the period following the Second World War and more recent problems at the close of the twentieth century. In addition to economic, social and cultural aspects, political factors will also be especially stressed.

This is due to the fact that the basic conditions of transnational migration have undergone significant change. The period of European migration history from the early nineteenth century to the eve of the First World War was dominated by 'proletarian mass migrations'.[20] It was determined to an unprecedented and never repeated extent by the freedom to migrate across borders. The subsequent 'century of refugees'[21] or of the 'homeless man'[22] was an era – continuing into the twenty-first century in this respect – in which migration movements in the European and Atlantic realms were triggered or forced, and at the same time regulated and limited, as never before by political developments and state-determined conditions. This epochal change in political and state conditions must be brought to bear in any account of twentieth-century European migration.[23]

The area under investigation ranges from Scandinavia to the Mediterranean and from the British Isles to east central Europe. Origin and destination regions outside this major area, such as the European part of Russia, will be included as necessary to explain migration contexts. This also applies, more or less, to selected non-European destination regions of migrations from Europe, such as the United States, in so far as this seems relevant in explaining the determining factors and underlying conditions that led to emigration.

Having considered several different criteria – chronological, systematic, typological – by which to structure the book, I rejected all of them in favour of a mixed form based on structure and epoch. In this way areas of overlap can be underlined without unnecessary repetition and contexts highlighted by means of cross-references. The book does not attempt to achieve encyclopaedic comprehensiveness, which is all but impossible, but presents typical examples and is not afraid to admit that gaps exist. This also applies to the notes and bibliography, which had to be kept as concise as possible.

In working on this book I received much assistance, for which I am very grateful. I would like to thank my life partner Susanne Meyer, who is also a historian and who accompanied me through the production of the manuscript from the outset, for her encouragement, patience and helpful criticism. The third part of the book is based essentially on the research findings of Jochen Oltmer. His suggestions, criticism, editorial revision of the manuscript, preparation of the index and clarification of questions for the translation were greatly appreciated. I received helpful assistance from Andreas Demuth with some of the final chapters. I would also like to thank the research assistants at the Institute for Migration Research and Intercultural Studies (IMIS) at the University of Osnabrück for their help in obtaining source materials, and Sigrid Pusch and Jutta Tiemeyer of the IMIS secretariat for their judicious supervision of the manuscript.

For their constructive criticism and reading of individual sections of the manuscript I would like to thank Michael Bommes, Pieter C. Emmer, Walter D. Kamphoefner, Klaus Manfrass, Rolf Meinhardt, Franz Nuscheler, Hannelore Oberpenning, Panikos Panayi, Günter Renner, Bernhard Santel, Ernst Schubert, Dietrich Thränhardt, Henk Wesseling and Michael Wollenschläger. For the English translation my thanks go to Allison Brown. The Deutsche Forschungsgemeinschaft (German Research Society) deserves much gratitude for granting me a sabbatical year in 1996–7, during which I was able to work in an unparalleled atmosphere of scholarly discussion at the Netherlands Institute for Advanced Studies (NIAS) in Wassenaar near The Hague.

Klaus J. Bade
Osnabrück

1

Migration during the Shift from Agrarian to Industrial Societies

1 MIGRATORY TRADITIONS AND SYSTEMS AT THE END OF THE EARLY MODERN ERA

Old Europe was a turbulent world on the streets of which itinerants, vagabonds and distinguished travellers encountered one another daily.[1] In the eighteenth century, the spectrum extended from young aristocrats aboard their coaches on a gentleman's excursion, to travel groups taking a grand tour to Italy, to travelling journeymen and heavily laden itinerant traders, right the way down to all kinds of riff-raff who never let foreign lands seem totally free of danger.[2]

A wide variety of migrant groups covered great distances in early modern Europe by sea or by land, either temporarily or permanently. There were employment migrations that included architects, artists and technical experts, seasonal labour migrants and itinerant merchants with a fixed residential base, transient labourers and traders without a residence, mercenaries, seamen, those working in colonial service and many others. There were settlement migrations, for example, to populate Prussia and Austria-Hungary, or to settle colonists in the Russia of Catherine the Great. Between overseas labour migration and colonial settler migration were the transatlantic migration of indentured servants, who worked in servitude in the 'New World' to pay their passage, at the end of which they often received a minimum start capital and/or a piece of land. There were also refugees and those expelled for religious reasons whose immigration was frequently viewed by the authorities of the receiving country as a welcome transfer of innovation and a strengthening of the country's industrious reputation, and in any case as an expansion of the working population and thus tax revenue. Huguenots and Waldenses in the seventeenth century and the Salzburgs in the eighteenth are the best known though by no means the only examples. In addition to the many temporary and permanent migrations over long distances, migrants, both men and women, also covered small to intermediate geographical distances between rural settlements or between the countryside and the growing cities with their enticing labour markets and their offer of 'freedom'. In virtually all areas of life and work, a large number of people covered ground and moved on, in one way or another, either voluntarily or against their will.

The diversity of forms encompassed by the word 'migration' in the highly mobile early modern age can hardly be ignored, and in some areas has not yet been adequately explored. The intention here is not merely to expand the list of works that offer orientation in this regard.[3] Let us instead choose two examples to create a bridge back into late Old Europe before the industrial age. We shall examine two widespread, long-established major forms from the area of employment migration: labour migration and itinerant trade. Both emerged largely against the background of a disproportionate relationship between population growth and available work options. This situation had been intensifying especially in rural areas since the mid-eighteenth century. In the demographic '*crise européenne*'[4] from the early seventeenth to the early eighteenth centuries, numerous wars, principally the Thirty Years' War in central Europe, and the accompanying yet also independently raging famine and epidemics, led in certain regions to a severe population decline. Not until 1700 had a population level around an estimated 115 million been achieved. Even before the mid-eighteenth century, the population started increasing dramatically, once again varying greatly from region to region. The population of Europe rose to about 185 million around 1800 and continued to climb, finally leading to the population boom of the industrial age.[5]

At first this population growth in central Europe essentially filled the gap left by the population decline from the period that became largely symbolized by deserted settlements, with their empty, plundered and dilapidated residences. For survivors, this might have served as a kind of crisis-related social compensation in which the redistribution of goods and opportunities in some regions even took on aspects of an economic miracle. But even in areas that continued to be affected by previous declines in population, the size of especially the landless population increased at the latest as of the mid-eighteenth century beyond the limits of available work. In rural areas, high natural fertility rate among these sub-peasant social classes acted in combination with their increase in numbers as a result of social decline due to exclusion from landholding. Manorial property structures as well as forms of cultivation limited the available agricultural land area. Inheritance rights in which an entire estate was transferred largely to one heir, usually the first-born, and division of land among all heirs had the same social repercussions in cases of high population growth: whenever offspring were excluded from inheritance or heirs could not subsist from the parcel of land they received, the growing army of those with little or no land continued to multiply through social decline.

In addition, another destabilizing factor, varying in degree from region to region, affected the precarious demographic-economic balance in areas with significant proto-industrial cottage production. These family-run home industries, which also included a large number of poor urban households, were mainly transplanted to the countryside by urban businesspeople and capitalist trade distributors and were ostracized by the urban guilds. They were tied to interregional and even intercontinental markets through trade by the distributors and wholesalers. Proto-industrial cottage production encompassed a broad spectrum of products ranging from linen and blended fabrics to haberdashery, wood, clay, copper and hardware products and all kinds of consumer goods for everyday use. Despite the frequently exploitative nature of the capitalist distribution system, in many areas it was often the only opportunity for those with little or no land to have a sole or additional family income that could remain fairly stable in good economic times. The comparatively secure, albeit low, income and the fact that children did not have to leave the house to work but could be used in the family's own cottage production had immense consequences for natural population developments. In many places, the population involved in cottage industries soon grew beyond the limits of what the domestic production system could absorb.[6]

Where even the proto-industrial domestic system could no longer resolve the disproportionate relationship between population growth and job availability, or if the population dilemma even intensified, the necessity for employment migration grew. If tools and production sites did not belong to the distributor or if credit financing or high debts led to an impossible situation of dependency, cottage producers turned to selling their own products. This usually involved itinerant trading in the local rural area or through sales at nearby city markets. When selling their own products over long distances, some family members became temporarily unavailable for cottage production. These early forms of overlap between independent production and travelling sales were maintained only in isolated cases, however. The situation was similar for labour migrants whose family income was still insufficient despite seasonal migration in summer, and who therefore strove to increase their income in the winter through the sale of cottage industry products. Usually, however, intensive proto-industrial domestic production represented a major wage-earning alternative to labour migration until it was pushed out entirely by machine competition in the early nineteenth century.

Labour migration and itinerant trade were the two most important forms of employment migration. They ranged from local movements to long-distance migrations of hundreds of kilometres. Both were stabilized by family or group-related migratory traditions, sometimes over generations. In contrast to the 'floating population' or traders and artisans without a fixed residential base and to other marginal migrant groups[7] who were mobile or even nomadic more or less as a means of survival, labour migration and itinerant trade refer to employment migration aimed at supplementing a basic – albeit insufficient – livelihood at a fixed location. It originated largely in rural areas, usually consisting of subsistence farming and/or proto-industrial cottage production. On this basis, labour migration was temporary work, preferably in wage-intensive regions with an additional demand for seasonal workers. Itinerant trade refers to the independent sale of goods produced in ('direct trade') or purchased from ('indirect trade') cottage industries, as well as non-self-employed travelling traders ('hired traders') or independent traders, usually established as an amalgamation of equal partners to form so-called trade companies. Rarer mixed forms of labour migration and itinerant trade included travelling sale of goods combined with service offers in the product range, such as tinkers who dealt with both new and used copper goods.[8]

This secondary supplement to an insufficient primary means of income in the place of origin could develop into a second main income source, depending on how much it contributed to the family income. In the absence of the husband as the main breadwinner, agricultural and/or cottage industry production was carried on by the rest of the family, under the wife's direction, who was then no less a main breadwinner. Labour migration and itinerant trade could also become the main income source. In such cases, agrarian subsistence production in the place of origin was downgraded to become a secondary business or subsistence gardening if the migrant labourers spent only the winter months at home, when there was no demand in the destination regions for their labour, which was usually in agriculture or outdoors. The same was true for itinerant traders if the main breadwinner was on the road not only during the spring and autumn months, which were generally favourable for sales since rural customers were more accessible, but was absent most of the year.[9]

In addition to migration by the main breadwinner in order to support the family, younger family members of working age also migrated, sometimes in combination with forms of apprenticeship migration, for the same purpose or to start up their own household. Apart from rural or agricultural jobs outside the home for young men and women, work was available in the trades or services in nearby cities, while domestic service provided an urban job opportunity especially for young women from the countryside looking for employment outside agriculture.[10] There were also diverse ways of relieving the burden on the family household by temporarily sending younger able-bodied family members off to fend for themselves outside the home. This was a side-effect of journeyman migrations, which in addition to their training purpose also served to exclude the individual for a period of time from the limited and inflexible local job market, in the system that required them to earn their 'honest bread'.[11]

There were also a number of regionally varied forms of exclusion from the household for the purpose of temporary self-sufficiency and modest supplementary earnings to the family income. Among these were numerous migratory traditions within the area of child labour, especially in barren mountainous regions. Up until the First World War this pertained, for example, to the so-called 'Swabian children' from Tyrol and Vorarlberg who went abroad to work each spring after attending a short 'winter school' at home. After several days' walk, the 'shepherd children', boys and girls from poor mountain peasant families, were offered for work in the countryside until autumn by their 'leaders' at the child markets in Upper Swabia, Friedrichshafen and Ravensburg. The girls generally cared for children and the boys usually worked as shepherds. Many also came alone or in groups to offer their services. Wages included free room and board, new clothing and possibly shoes, and a total remuneration that amounted to about 50–70 Reichsmarks in the late nineteenth and early twentieth centuries. Although this was a desirable additional source of earnings for the mountain peasant families, the main objective was to 'remove the children from the table'.[12] The situation regarding labour migration of children from northern Italy, Savoy and Ticino remained somewhat similar until the Second World War. Especially well known were the movements of 'Ticino chimneysweep children' to European countries north of the Alps from the sixteenth to the early nineteenth centuries within the scope of poverty-induced south–north child migrations.

Labour migration was often not a migration of skilled workers but was instead tied directly to processes of obtaining qualifications. Recent studies of pewterers of Italian descent who spread out throughout Europe, for example, have shown that there was no pewtering or pewterware trade in the small, clearly defined region west of Lake Maggiore from where they originated. Training as a pewterer was generally acquired through an apprenticeship migration, that is, after leaving the homeland. This was true also of brickmakers from Lippe, the leading brickmakers in north-western Europe. No notable brickwork trade had existed in the small principality of Lippe-Detmold, their place of origin. Over the course of generations the specific 'migrant occupation' of brick-maker was learned in the areas to which they migrated.[13] Aside from long-distance migrations, there was also a variety of forms of migrant movements over short or intermediate distances. This included countless migratory cycles between small and medium-sized cities and their rural surroundings, in which there was sometimes a blurring of the boundaries between apprenticeship, subsistence and employment migrations.[14] This diversity of migratory patterns will recede to the background in our examination of the two larger movements of employment migration. It should always be kept in mind, however, that alongside and even within major migration cycles, there were usually also many smaller active cycles.

With respect to medium- and long-range labour migration and itiner-ant trade, migration cycles could become consolidated into structurally stable, long-term 'migratory systems'[15] with firmly established migratory traditions that often continued over generations. Migration networks in and between the regions of origin and destination were extremely im-portant, not so much for their geographical dimensions as for their communicative and social aspects, which defined the direction of migra-tions and ensured the continuity of their traditions.[16] Selected examples from the history of labour migration and itinerant trade in Europe at the end of the early modern age will be used to discuss such major systems. In both cases, an overview of the general contexts will be presented first, then some systems will be considered in different European regions, and finally one example of each will be selected and described in detail. Both examples, the North Sea system (labour migration) and the *Tödden* system (itinerant trade), come from north-western Europe and have been chosen because they have been particularly well researched in all their complexity.

Labour migration

Common ground

In rural regions with heavy population growth and insufficient job opportunities, a wide range of labour migrations expanded in the early modern age, and especially since the mid-eighteenth century. Few statis-tics are available in this area for early modern Europe. A rare exception is the questionnaires on *migration temporaire* drafted towards the end of the period by the French interior minister Comte de Montalivet and used by the prefects under Napoleon. These questionnaires were designed to make it easier to recruit cannon fodder for the insatiable French army. In his classic study on systems of labour migration in early modern Europe, Jan Lucassen evaluated extant questionnaires in Paris with answers from the years 1808–13. His findings provide the basis for the following discussion.

From around 20 verifiable migratory labour systems around the turn of the nineteenth century in the European realm, Lucassen was able to reconstruct seven larger systems that had been formed significantly earlier. Around the turn of the century, more than 300,000 labourers migrated over distances up to 250–300 kilometres, even across national borders. The questionnaires on home regions and migration destinations enabled Lucassen to distinguish between movements out of 'push areas' and into 'pull areas' and to devise migratory labour systems of large groups with a work cycle determined by phases of fixed and distant residences, that is, by domestic and non-domestic phases. It was also possible to discern 'neutral areas' that were left untouched by the bulk of such systems or any migratory movement whatsoever. Lucassen worked at three analytical levels: macro (home regions/destinations), meso (work cycles) and micro (households). He modelled mirror-images between each of these to demonstrate the 'symbiotic' nature of migratory labour systems fixed by established migration traditions.[17] These findings, elaborated through further research and supplemented by other studies, lead to a kind of ideal typology of relationships between home regions and destination regions in migratory labour systems at the turn of the nineteenth century which reveals the following overall picture.

Home regions were generally characterized by structurally deficient options for work owing to environmental, economic, demographic and social factors; insufficient agricultural yield potential, in barren mountainous areas for example, yet also in lowlands with poor-quality soil; inefficient small businesses; excessive land prices; high rents for additional leased land that could be paid only through supplementary earnings; high population density with an upward trend due to high natural growth, and at the same time highly polarized land distribution with large fertile areas in few hands and small infertile areas in many. A decisive factor for seasonal labour migration with a fixed annual rhythm was the existence of a main, if insufficient, financial base in the place of origin with periods when one or more potential workers were available.

For poor subsistence farmers, the time between the end of the spring planting and the late summer harvest was just such a period, when stores were dwindling and food prices were rising. In terms of work yield, in the households of labour migrants the main income in the home region and the supplementary income in the seasonal destination properly balanced each other out, though as noted above the relationship could also be reversed. Sometimes small farms changed their forms of cultivation and crop rotations in order to improve availability for labour migrations. On the other hand, adapting one's own production to counter the seasonal cycle of large nearby farms with additional labour needs could also serve as an alternative to labour migration, such as in the north of Brabant province and the south of the provinces of Antwerp and Limburg. Sedentary small farmers near major grain farms that offered supplementary income focused on market production of vegetables and potato crops for their own consumption.[18]

The predominantly agricultural destinations of rural labour migrants were generally in fertile, high-yield flatlands where market production by large farms was mostly based on monocultures. For grain production and vineyards, for example, the need for year-round labour was limited, but at harvest time labour demand was very high. In order to cover this demand, farmers were willing to pay relatively high wages, which could rise to many times the wages paid in the regions of origin. Such major market-producing farms were frequently located near river or sea ports to facilitate export trade, or larger cities to provide markets. These offered labour migrants additional, often also seasonal, work opportunities, from construction to various services to market gardens.

Migratory labour systems were maintained through long traditions of seasonal migration. In the regions of origin there were additional needs for income which could be satisfied under poor wage conditions, if at all, and a seasonally available labour pool. In the destinations there was, conversely, a large additional seasonal need for labour and, as a rule, wages were clearly often many times higher than in the place of origin. The heart of this structural 'symbiosis' (Lucassen's term) was a reciprocal dependence through the labour market that had a different weight for each of the two sides. In the destination regions, which tried to lower their risks through planned labour recruitment, it was an economic question of yield for the family households; in the home regions, on the other hand, it was a matter of survival. Migratory traditions that became established often over generations led to fixed migration routes over long distances, frequently hundreds of kilometres, and just as fixed migration forms. The dominant form was groups or work brigades, many of whom stayed together in the destination, often under the direction of a brigade leader who knew the country and was an experienced negotiator.

To a different extent in the individual systems, there were often transitions from seasonal labour migrations to definitive immigration in the destinations, which in turn could trigger chain migrations. This was more the case with labour markets for urban trades than with agricultural labour markets, in which the additional need for labour and wages generally declined in the off season. The temporary nature of the high wages and the permanently high standard of living in the destinations were essential factors for the long-term continuation of seasonal labour migration. They provided the background for the notable fact – one that never ceases to provoke outraged incomprehension – that areas with the highest seasonal wages and temporary high numbers of labour migrants could simultaneously experience underemployment and social impoverishment among local labourers and their families.[19]

Based on the Napoleonic figures, we will review six of Lucassen's seven major western and southern European systems around the turn of the nineteenth century in synchronic cross-section as part of a brief *tour d'horizon*. We will then conduct an in-depth diachronic longitudinal examination of the North Sea system in order to follow the development of a migratory labour system starting in the early seventeenth century.

Regional examples

Aside from the North Sea system there were two other examples of migratory labour systems in north-western Europe around the turn of the nineteenth century, namely in eastern England and the Paris basin. In all three systems, a total of more than 100,000 male and female labourers migrated annually. At the same time there were four active migratory labour systems in southern Europe: in Castile (*c.*30,000) and on the Mediterranean coast of Catalonia, Languedoc and Provence (*c.*35,000). The system along the Po plain was considerably larger (*c.*50,000), and about double the size of that was the system in central Italy (*c.*100,000).[20]

Roughly 20,000 workers moved annually to eastern England, especially to the major grain farms in Lincolnshire and East Anglia that had a high seasonal demand for additional labourers. The labourers there assisted in the harvest; in the environs of London they also worked in horticulture, and in the city itself they were employed in a wide range of jobs, including municipal construction projects. They came from Scotland, Wales, England, and most of all from western Ireland, especially Connaught, where the agricultural industry was dominated by small potato farms whose oppressive and exorbitant rents could be paid only by earning additional income through labour migration. Lucassen determined that an Irish labour migrant earned about one-quarter of the entire household income in the grain season in eastern England, which fell between the sowing and harvesting of potatoes at home, while the rest of the family stayed behind and took care of the small estate. In the non-productive winter months, additional earnings were acquired through spinning, fishing and production of seaweed ash, which was high in potash and iodine and therefore important for field fertilizers and iodine extraction.

About 60,000, or three times as many labour migrants as in eastern England, came each year to the Paris basin and especially within the Paris city limits, where there was employment in public jobs, trading and services of all kinds. In addition the *départements* surrounding Paris, which secured the food supply for the metropolis as East Anglia did for London, were dependent on a supplementary seasonal army of labourers, especially in grain cultivation. A considerable portion of labour migrants to this area came from the Alps and western France, but most were from the Massif Central, or French central highlands, where grain production was insignificant and of mediocre quality. Small farms at higher elevations thus strove to improve their insufficient yields with milk products, chestnuts and turnips; those at lower elevations, with potato crops.

The destination of the third migration system was Castile, with its urban centre in Madrid. At least 30,000 labour migrants from regions with few work opportunities came each year. They found jobs working in the grain harvest on the Castilian plateau, or as construction workers in state and municipal projects, or as servants and maids in the capital. Most of them came from the mountainous region of Galicia where, in the second half of the eighteenth century, not even half of the agriculturally productive land was cultivated; besides, most of it was in the hands of large landowners, especially monasteries. Dwarfholdings (*minifundio*), with on average hardly more than half a hectare of productive land, required additional income from outside. Usually the husband went looking for work as a labour migrant in order to pay the rent and debts. The rest of the family, under the wife's direction, continued to operate the small estate, seeking to increase its meagre income with cottage industries, especially flax spinning.

Galicia was the classic home region of the labour migrants later referred to as *golondrinas* (swallows). Not without justification were they compared to birds of passage; every spring, men as well as single women formed migrant groups called *cuadrillas* (fixed group, community or working group), often along family lines. The stages of their migration followed climate-related differences in the harvest seasons. In early summer the *cuadrillas* harvested wheat in the environs of Madrid, Toledo and Guadalajara in New Castile. The harvest ended there on 25 July, St James's Day, which the *cuardrillas* celebrated even away from home, and then continued in Ávila and Segovia and ultimately farther north in the Old Castilian city of León. Later transatlantic seasonal migrants moved between Spain (and Italy) and Argentina, which also led to the term *golondrinas*. This migration became possible in the nineteenth century when steamers shortened the transatlantic journey time and lowered the cost so that harvest jobs could be taken in the Argentinian summer during the European winter (see chapter 2, section 2). Besides Galician workers in Castile and Madrid there were also labour migrants, although fewer in number, from other areas of northern Spain such as the mountains of León, Asturia and the Basque country, as well as from France.

Roughly 35,000 male and female labour migrants in the Spanish-French Mediterranean descended each year to the coastal regions between Catalonia, Languedoc and Provence to work, especially in the grain harvest for large farms but also in grape picking. On both the Spanish and French sides, the port cities of Barcelona and Marseilles seem to have attracted only a handful of the rural labour migrants who came to the coastal plains from Alpine regions and the Massif Central as well as from the Pyrenees. Here, too, the migratory labour system was kept intact owing to the seasonal dependence on supplementary labour, especially on the part of large farms in the plains, and the structural dependence on supplementary income on the part of dwarfholdings and cottage industries in the primarily mountainous regions of origin.

Similar conditions brought around 50,000 labour migrants, both men and women, to the Po plain from their mountainous home regions extending from the Bergamo Alps in the north to the Ligurian Apennines in the south. Work was also available in public construction and the service sector in cities such as Milan and Turin, but by far the largest portion of rural labour migrants worked in rice production on the western Po plain. This was carried out from planting to harvest almost exclusively by external labour, in which groups of six men and six women each worked as cutters and threshers, or in packing and storing.

The sixth and by far the largest migratory system, greatly exceeding even that of the Paris basin, was destined for central Italy and encompassed the southern part of Tuscany, Latium, Corsica and Elba. Around 100,000 labourers made their way to central Italy each year. A considerable portion sought work in construction and the urban service sectors, especially in Rome. Most of the labour migrants to central Italy were involved in agriculture, especially the harvest of grain and other crops, and in other areas of agricultural work, in part also in the winter months. The migrant field workers on the big *latifundios* came largely from poorer subsistence farming regions in the east and south. They offered their labour under the direction of a *caporale*, or work brigade leader, who negotiated jobs and wages. Sometimes boundaries became blurred between the destitute landless, who came in rags, and labour migrants from borderline subsistence farms. It was not uncommon for dwarf-holders or tenant farmers to end up in a kind of temporary indentured servitude with meagre supplementary earnings since profits from their small estates were insufficient to maintain their families, thereby forcing them to go into debt to purchase extra agrarian products and to pay off their debt by working in the harvest for large farms. A system of recruitment resulted that in some ways resembled indirect forced labour, and the agents who granted credits on behalf of the *latifundio* owners earned a premium for each labour migrant they mustered in this way. Harsh working and living conditions, intensified by climatic conditions and malaria, which was widespread, were the subject of repeated yet fruitless complaints by prefects in the destination regions in the largest migratory labour system of the time.

The North Sea system and the Holland migrants (Hollandgänger)

An extensive migratory labour system existed from the early seventeenth to the mid-nineteenth centuries in the coastal region of north-western Europe, with its centre – based on today's national boundaries – in the coastal areas of the Netherlands and north-western Germany and its areas of departure in Germany, Belgium, the Dutch interior and France. We shall now carry out a detailed longitudinal examination of what Lucassen called the 'North Sea system'.

The system's destination area was a commercial magnet, including one of the wealthiest trade and industrial areas in Europe, covering more than 200 cities; its tax revenue once brought the Spanish crown seven times the value of the silver it acquired from Central America. Rotterdam and Antwerp were the hubs of European world trade, with a total share of 50 per cent of all goods; Antwerp's stock exchange was also the centre for the European money market. During the prolonged Dutch war of independence against Spanish rule, which started in 1568 with the uprising of William I (the Silent, Prince of Orange) and ended in 1648 when Spain recognized the Republic of the Netherlands in the Peace of Westphalia, the centre of trade and commerce gradually shifted north to Amsterdam, especially after Spain's pillaging of Antwerp in 1585.[21]

The North Sea system developed in the final decades of the Netherlands' struggle for independence, in which the Dutch colonial empire also assumed firm structures through the founding of the Dutch East India (1602) and West India (1621) Companies. We shall return later to the Dutch empire with respect to its labour systems. Both the shifting of industry and commerce to the north and the global expansion of the Dutch labour market to include the colonies were definitive in establishing the migratory cycles of the North Sea system. The destination region of the North Sea system extended from Calais to Bremen; it had a number of sub-centres and continued beyond zones in between that were scarcely affected by the migration. By far the majority of labour migrants, male and female, in the North Sea system came from north-western Germany. There were also migrants from the Dutch provinces of Gelderland, Overijssel and Drenthe, from Flanders, Brabant and Limburg, as well as from the lower Rhine region and the environs of Lille.

Let us examine more closely the largest group of labour migrants, the *Hollandgänger*, or 'Holland migrants',[22] from north-western Germany. The first traces of 'Holland migration' in this area go back to the late Middle Ages, but a clearly defined migratory labour system did not develop until the early seventeenth century, when for the first time larger numbers of workers from the prince-bishopric of Osnabrück and the northern part of the bishopric of Münster migrated to Holland and West Friesland. After the Thirty Years' War ended in 1648 with the Peace of Westphalia, which was drawn up in Münster and Osnabrück, the Holland migrants' home regions in north-western Germany continued to expand. A similar situation occurred in the eighteenth century when the destination area along the coast expanded to the south-west and north-east.

The classic symbiotic character of labour market relations between a densely populated home region with insufficient work opportunities and destinations with a seasonal need for additional labourers that offered, in this case, wage levels four times higher at a piece rate also existed with respect to Holland migration. There were diverse other reasons for labour migration in addition to the dominant pressure to support the family through external supplementary income. Young, unmarried migrant workers, both men and women, wanted to earn the means to start their own family household, and the search for a spouse itself also played a role.[23]

The total proportion of Holland migrants in the regions of origin in north-western Germany was generally around 3 per cent, but in isolated cases it could also reach 12 or even 26 per cent. In evaluating the French figures, Lucassen discovered, on the one hand, major home regions in Westphalia and Lower Saxony; on the other hand, there were also 'neutral' areas with hardly any migration in either direction. This was the case, for example, in the Ruhr valley, which would later overtake the North Sea system in the course of industrialization, and in the Bielefeld 'corridor', Halle and Warendorf, as well as east of Tecklenburg. This was due to the great expansion of proto-industrial cottage production in these areas, which needed workers even outside the agricultural season. In addition to metalworking, other important fields were flax spinning and linen weaving, as in the Bielefeld (and Flemish) 'corridor'. There were about 50 looms to 1,000 inhabitants there, amounting on average to a loom for every fourth household, which, including setting up the loom, required at least four workers in the family. In addition, six to ten spinners were needed to supply enough raw materials for weaving.[24]

In the home regions, however, there were distinct differences between, and even within, villages with regard to the ratio of sedentary to travelling labourers, even in cottage industries providing supplementary income to the main agricultural work. This was presumably due to milieu-specific differences in cottage production. Intensive cottage production of linen, which was often a main source of income for non-landholding families or had become the main source of income where agricultural subsistence production was insufficient, seems generally to have been incompatible with labour migration for months at a time. Holland migrants, however, came predominantly from households whose supplementary income was earned not through weaving but through spinning. Unlike the cottage linen industry, spinning was possible without capital investment and was the more poorly paid cottage industry of poor households. It was carried out mostly in the winter and thus did not overlap with seasonal labour migration. This was significant, for example, for the tenant farmers who made up a large share of Holland migrants. In the early nineteenth century, they still cultivated barely more than an average of one hectare on their small leaseholdings. They were obligated to work on the farms that their leaseholds belonged to, but could arrange with their farmers to be available between planting and harvest to migrate to Holland in order to supplement the family income.[25]

Before the era of mass overseas emigration and the coal and steel industry or repeated and temporary shuttle migrations ('industrial hirelings') in the nineteenth century, small tenant farmers in rural north-western Germany who required supplementary income had several options. In addition to intensive cottage industry production and seasonal migration to Holland, another possible source of income outside the home was itinerant trade. Let us look more closely at this type of migration based on the *Tödden*,[26] itinerant traders from the northern Münster region, also a region of origin of Holland migrants. A report by District Councillor Culemann, who was commissioned by the Prussian king to travel through the Tecklenburg region in 1749–50, confirms that Holland migration and *Tödden* migration were significant and often completely distinct sources of income in the communities of origin in the eighteenth century. The report states that in towns with *Tödden* migration there was hardly any Holland migration, and vice versa.[27]

The North Sea system, spanning roughly three centuries, was primarily a rural, agrarian migratory labour system with a seasonal structure. This was particularly true for the Holland migrants from north-western Germany, more than three-quarters of whom worked in agriculture or peat bogs. Most of the agricultural workers did grass pasture work in dairy farming in Holland, West Friesland and the marshlands to the east. At first the north-west German grass workers went from farm to farm in Holland and West Friesland offering their services. Later there were often fixed employment agreements between the Dutch farmers and the brigades of grass mowers from north-western Germany who were summoned for the harvest period through a contact in the home region. Newcomers outside such groups still had to travel through the destination area offering their services themselves or going to municipal labour markets, referred to in West Friesland as *Poepenmärkte* (people markets), where a surplus of labour seekers could lead to severe wage competition. The relatively short work phase in the pastures in the destination region lasted from late May to early July, and the small yield from the second hay harvest in September was largely brought in by local labourers. Pasture jobs, mostly mowing and turning hay, were carried out under harsh conditions as piece work according to the rhythm set by the 'stroke'. Apart from Sundays, work continued from sunrise to sunset with breaks kept as short as possible; in June that meant up to 16 hours a day. Food was either made available by the farmers or brought by the labourers, who slept on hay in the barns.

Despite the back-breaking work, meagre provisions and unhygienic living conditions, the level of work-related sickness among grass workers was far lower than for the second-largest group of Holland migrants, the peat workers. Their areas of work were the bogs and fens in Holland, West Friesland, Overijssel, Utrecht, Groningen, Drenthe and East Friesland. Peat cutting remained one of the most significant economic branches until peat was superseded by hard coal as an energy source towards the end of the nineteenth century. Peat was the main source of fuel for domestic heating and for industries such as brickworks, distilleries, bleacheries, breweries and sugar factories, and it was also an important export product. Its extraction was combined with agricultural use, which is why it was doubly productive.

The peat season was twice as long as that for grass labourers. It usually lasted from two and a half to four months, beginning in March, when the cool damp weather in the coastal regions gave way to spring, and ending in July, when the heat on the fens became intolerable. Yet there were also Holland migrants who endured the bogs and fens from February to autumn, where the work – despite similar conditions as regards work hours and piece rates – was incomparably harsher and more dangerous than the already arduous piecework in the pastures. This applied in particular to the fens, where two-thirds of all Holland migrants who worked in peat cutting were employed. While the bogs were drained so that the peat could be cut, in the fens it had to be dug from the water using brute strength. In the fens that were far from settlements and accessible only by water, Holland migrants laboured in their boats for up to 16 hours a day, sometimes in stifling heat, engaged in extreme physical exertion. Their accommodation was in draughty peat huts on the work site, where they often slept in drenched work clothes. In addition to this health hazard, labourers were frequently malnourished since their food, partly brought with them and partly bought at exorbitant prices in their surroundings, was generally inferior in both quality and quantity. Among the risks presented by such working and living conditions were dangerous, often fatal or chronic diseases, ranging from rheumatism and gout to lung disease and mosquito-transmitted fever diseases, such as the notorious malaria known in the Holland migrants' home regions as 'Ems region malaria'.[28]

One in four Holland migrants worked outside agriculture as labour migrants in trades or crafts and in maritime work. Those employed in trades and crafts included especially brickmakers and the building trades, such as stonemasons, bricklayers, carpenters and plasterers, but there were also weavers, bleachers, gardeners, servants, maids and employees in other service sector occupations. Construction labourers and brickmakers, including the Lippe brickmakers who were esteemed as specialists far beyond the North Sea system, and most other Holland migrants who had non-agricultural outdoor jobs were still seasonal labour migrants, since there was little or no work in the destination region during the winter. This situation applies only partially if at all to urban domestic personnel; there was a long tradition of labour migration of German maids to the Netherlands that started in the early seventeenth century and lasted until the mid-1930s, and even experienced a revival after the Second World War.[29]

Seasonal maritime labour migrants in the North Sea system included the domestic crews of Dutch and East Frisian whalers and herring boats. Also called 'Greenland drivers' after the fishing grounds of their fleets, they usually left their villages in February or March for seven or eight months. This form of labour migration at sea reached its height in the eighteenth century. It was severely restricted in the late eighteenth and nineteenth centuries by various naval wars and ultimately by the Continental system from 1806 to 1814. Increasing once more after the Wars of Liberation, it never again reached the level it had attained in the eighteenth century, although there was even a German nautical school in Mühlen (Vechta) for maritime labour migrants from the interior in the nineteenth century.[30]

In the Netherlands, foreign sailors within the range of the North Sea system were also used in intercontinental merchant shipping, especially on board the East Indian vessels of the United East India Company or those of the West India Company and other shipping companies operating in the Atlantic region. This was true of the Dutch naval warships involved in numerous wars at sea in the seventeenth and eighteenth centuries (for example, against England 1652–4, 1665–7, 1672–1714, 1780–4). At least they had one thing in common with merchant shipping companies: low pay, poor working conditions and a high mortality rate. A macabre gauge of the share of foreigners aboard Dutch ships in the eighteenth century could be expressed as: 'The bigger the ships and the longer the voyages, the lower the remuneration and the higher the percentage of foreigners.' For the Dutch East India Company, with its own war fleet, for example, about 40 per cent of its sailors in the seventeenth and eighteenth centuries were foreigners, at least half of whom were from Germany. The proportion of German seamen on Dutch ships declined significantly in the nineteenth century. Being hired on board an intercontinental sailing vessel was like having a temporary contract job and, because the overseas passage depended on seasonal wind and weather conditions, it was seasonal as well. But sailors' expectations of returning to the home village after a long journey at sea with a tidy sum of money saved from their pay were often disappointed. Frequently, pay and possessions returned home unaccompanied, since one-third of the seamen aboard Dutch East Indian vessels in the eighteenth century perished during the voyage.[31]

The status of foreign mercenaries with Dutch military forces at home and in the colonies resembled that of foreign seamen aboard Dutch merchant marine and navy ships more than that of North Sea system labourers in agriculture, the trades and commerce. Mercenary soldiers, unlike sailors, came from the northern areas of the Holland-migration sphere, and from Westphalia, the Rhineland and southern Germany. Recruitment of foreign soldiers and civilians for the Dutch army, which continued until the early nineteenth century, reached its zenith during the combative reign of governor-king William III (William of Orange) around the turn of the eighteenth century, when the Dutch army numbered some 100,000 men, most of whom were foreigners. The area from which foreign soldiers were recruited for the colonial army also lay largely within the sphere of the North Sea system. Recruitment of colonial mercenaries of foreign origin was organized from the seventeenth century by the East and West India Companies, which made direct efforts to enlist them, and in the early nineteenth century by the Colonial Enlistment Depot on Harderwijk on what was then the Zuider Zee.[32]

Holland migration reached its greatest intensity in the second half of the eighteenth century, when each year more than 40,000 labour migrants from a catchment area of up to 300 kilometres found work in the North Sea coastal areas. The only comprehensive and detailed statistical record that exists is from the aforementioned survey conducted by the French administration in 1811, when the North Sea system was already in gradual decline. In 1811, approximately 35,000 labour migrants in the North Sea system were registered, of whom about 21,000 worked in agriculture mowing grass, turning hay and harvesting grain; about 10,000 were employed in peat cutting; and another 5,000–6,000 worked in a wide range of trades. For the maritime labour migrants, however, their work sphere had almost totally disappeared during the time of the Continental system.[33]

Interregional movements of tens of thousands of seasonal Holland migrants, most of whom worked in the grasslands and peat bogs, led to fixed migratory routes in the North Sea system that in turn also became significant in terms of seasonal work, especially for innkeepers, transport companies and ferrymen. Based on our present state of knowledge, this applied less for the southern regions of the North Sea system, where migration distances were relatively short, generally within at most three days on foot, and where there were hardly any natural barriers forcing the routes to join together. In the northern and eastern catchments of the North Sea system, on the other hand, distances were far greater and migratory routes were characterized by natural obstacles, especially bogs and fens, which were passable only at a few locations. Fixed routes thus developed in the migration tradition of the Holland migrants with virtually ritual resting habits at particular sites marked by cliffs, trees, forests or inns. There was a northern route for Holland migrants from East Friesland and the northern Ems region, northern Oldenburg and Bremen-Vörden, and a far more travelled southern route from the Osnabrück region, Lingen, Meppen, South Oldenburg and Diepholz and the adjacent regions of origin to the east and south-east.

In the destinations of the Holland migrants, not only seasonal wages but living costs as well were up to four times higher than in the areas from which they came. In order to spend as little as possible of their savings in their place of work, labour migrants brought with them not only equipment such as scythes and their work clothes as well as a skein of linen to sell at their destination, but also a considerable quantity of food that would keep for some time. The heavy baggage was transported over considerable distances on special wagons in lengthy convoys, of which up to 900 supposedly stood ready at times in Lingen in the Ems region. Transport of the Holland migrants' baggage was also an important source of business for ferry operations at the Ems River and for shipping along the Vechte River to the port cities on the Zuider Zee. There, the baggage was reclaimed and the journey by sea on livestock carriers set off in different directions, for example to Amsterdam, where the paths branched further after a night spent in a *Moffenbeurs*,[34] a trade centre for Holland migrants. The peat diggers travelled on by boat to the fens; the grass mowers continued north on foot. The journey was long and meant a loss in wages and additional costs for food along the way. For this reason, the Holland migrants were always in a hurry along their foot marches, which could lead to rough brawls at bottlenecks at the ferries and riverboat docks.[35]

The Holland migrants' seasonal migratory cycle was of interest not only for innkeepers, transporters by land and sea, employers in the destination region and the labour migrants' households. Other businesses in the places of origin were also affected, since their own sales were subjected to a kind of secondary seasonal dependence by the seasonal Holland migration. Consider, for example, the textile city of Bramsche in the Osnabrück region, which became known for 'Bramscher Red', a plain, hand-woven red woollen fabric that was used for the uniforms of both the Hannover and English armies as well as for everyday clothing in the region. Local sales were influenced not only by the agricultural season in the countryside of the Bramscher clothworkers, but also by the Holland migrants; seasonalization was so severe, in fact, that state intervention seemed necessary.

In the 1780s, the clothworkers' guild in Bramsche complained that the peak sales period for the red fabric had narrowed down in the region to the months from September to February, 'because in autumn farmers as well as tenant farmers got money from linen or crops, etc., or earned money in Holland and so they were then in a good position to buy and pay for the clothing they needed'. The cloth producers of Bramsche thus faced a lean period between the buying season for wool in spring and the season for selling the fabric woven from the wool in autumn and winter. To compensate for this delay, the prince-bishopric government in Osnabrück established a storehouse in Bramsche that served a dual function. First, the wool, the raw material used by the Bramscher clothmakers, could be bought up in larger quantities at more favourable prices, stored there, and then bought as needed. Second, the woven fabric could be stored at low cost until the sales season in order to keep the price stable. Such mercantile intervention by the Osnabrück government had its origins in the secondary seasonalization of the goods market in the home region due to the labour migration of the Holland migrants.[36]

As the authorities in the places of origin disapprovingly noted, seasonal labour migration also influenced the ways of thinking of the Holland migrants and of the itinerant traders who also preferred to work in the Netherlands, who will be discussed below. Not only did they dare to violate the ban, issued in 1742 in the county of Lingen, on the 'careless and dangerous smoking of tobacco', a fashionable habit at the time; they also openly flaunted more liberal patterns of behaviour that they had adopted elsewhere. This was regarded as civil disobedience in the regions from which they came, as District Councillor Culemann reported in 1749: 'The people live like the Dutch. They become accustomed to a casual lifestyle and they care little or nothing for order and authority. Young men of draft age avoid being mustered into the Prussian army by going abroad for an extended period of time – sometimes even for good. These people have a natural inclination for freedom and a life of peddling. As soldiers they are useless.'[37]

The Holland migrants' migratory tradition achieved an almost ritualized stability that continued to exert a trend-setting influence on migratory patterns even at a time when industrial options for supplementary and even main income sources in the place of origin were increasingly becoming available. At the time when the North Sea system, and thus also Holland migration, fell into decline, there were reports that labourers from far afield had to be recruited when Georgsmarienhütte was established in the 1850s as a centre for heavy industry in the rural environs of Osnabrück, while in the rural areas in the immediate vicinity of the site the predominant source of supplementary income among tenant farmers was still the journey to Holland.[38] Only gradually were the seasonal agricultural migrants replaced by 'industrial hirelings' who shuttled between the agrarian surroundings and the expanding coal and steel industry while their wives stayed at home, as in the days of Holland migrants, and, along with the rest of the family, took over the running of their small estates.

Itinerant trade

Systems of travelling sales and those of labour migration in early modern Europe overlapped in many ways in their geographical movements. In the regions of origin, however, the two kinds of systems were generally alternative forms of non-domestic employment migration. Pedlars from many different backgrounds selling a wide range of products were part of everyday town and country life throughout Old Europe.[39] Their sometimes mixed offer of wares and services occasionally blurred the distinction between them and 'vagabonds' or traders without a fixed residential base. The issue that interests us here, as mentioned at the outset, is travelling sales as a supplement to a sedentary, albeit insufficient, subsistence.

Similar to labour migration, a great increase in regional, interregional and cross-border systems of itinerant trade could be observed in rural society as of the mid-eighteenth century as a response to the drastic gap between population development and work opportunities. The roots of such trade are older, however, usually dating back to the seventeenth century and probably back to the late Middle Ages in many cases, although sources from this period are rare. It can be documented this far back for travelling traders from the Belgium–Netherlands borderlands, known as Teutens, and those from northern Italy, Savoy and Gottschee (Kočevje). Itinerant trade systems were integral elements of business life in many regions of early modern Europe. Hannelore Oberpenning recently conducted a large-scale regional case study of travelling trade in Europe since the eighteenth century which, using a similar approach to Lucassen, also determined common ground among European itinerant trade systems.[40] Let us follow her findings in a brief overview of the basic structures of itinerant trade in early modern Europe in order to outline selected systems, as with labour migration, before examining one of them more closely in an in-depth longitudinal analysis.

Common ground

Like those of labour migration, the geographical origins of itinerant trade lay in economically depressed marginal zones of old European agrarian society. This pertained, among others, to mountainous and other agriculturally low-yielding regions where proto-industrial cottage industries developed and occasionally became a nucleus around which travelling trade grew. Items that were sold were not so much luxury goods as articles for everyday use. Some were self-produced; others were acquired elsewhere. This included especially household utensils of wood and clay, but also textiles and iron and steel goods, whereby among the textiles some semi-luxuries were also sold, such as lace. Itinerant trade as a system of sale of cottage industrial products functioned especially in places where cottage production was not commissioned work for municipal distributors. Oberpenning therefore described itinerant trade and proto-industrial market production as 'two interrelated, if not interdependent, systems in the pre-industrial production and circulation process'.[41]

Itinerant trade had many faces. It could be seasonal mobility in the off season of agrarian subsistence production for small agricultural landholders or tenants who could not produce enough to support the family. It also existed as the husband's permanent main occupation outside the home in cases of agrarian subsistence production and, more rarely, in the winter months in addition to domestic or cottage industrial supplementary production by the rest of the family under the wife's direction. The inevitable division of labour could have a geographical and temporal dimension such that members of the family only rarely saw each other for longer periods of time throughout the year – yet another reason why further research is necessary on the history of women on subsistence farms. Though less frequent and existing more as an early form, some cottage industrial producers arranged their own sales through travelling members of the family. Following from the group of travelling traders was a diversity of enterprises with fluid boundaries between long-distance trade and a putting-out system and, finally, there were also many low-earning hired pedlars known as 'packmen', whose families in the place of origin also lived from their earnings.

Forming the structure for each individual system of travelling trade were manifold interrelations: between periods in addition to, or outside, the work season in the rural sales areas when customers were more accessible; between their own production and sales; and among types of goods, forms of transport and range of business, with the basic rule that all itinerant trade crossed the boundaries of their range of business whenever travel costs or costs for interim storage came too close to the market value of the goods. The larger itinerant trade systems in eighteenth-century Europe were marked geographically by their having regional concentrations of several neighbouring travelling trade villages with interregional ranges of business that sometimes extended throughout or even beyond the borders of Europe. These businesses generally specialized in particular products and traded long distance with goods that were no longer self-produced but purchased interregionally from producers and wholesalers. Their structures were influenced by business or entrepreneurial forms of organization that had developed by the eighteenth century. They ranged from agreements – which were informal, more or less secret and decipherable only through a system of codes which the respective authorities viewed with suspicion – to formal associations in trade societies called 'companies' with binding product and market arrangements.

As developments continued from the early nineteenth century to the age of industry and mass markets, these structures were dislocated or destroyed. Successful businesses that had already become relatively prosperous in the regions of origin moved permanently to their sales areas and adapted to the rapidly changing market conditions by growing into urban trading houses, some of which still exist today. Those who remained in the barren places of origin were the 'labourers' or 'boys', in other words, the hired pedlars who had no family connections with the 'companies' enabling them to obtain permanent positions at the new company sites or their sales offices, and who were soon to be replaced by modern means of transportation. Many packmen also stayed behind, as well as small, self-employed itinerant traders. They increasingly lost their markets to small urban competitors who had expanded into the countryside, but especially to competition from large branch stores, which were growing along with developments in transportation and trade, leaving only niche and bargain sales for rural and urban travelling traders alike.

But events could take a completely different turn, since itinerant trade developments were as diverse as the responses to market expansion in the industrial age, which some pedlars earning low to moderate incomes were able to handle flexibly. Improved transportation could temporarily extend the radius covered by travelling traders and even lead to a rise in their numbers. Regional specialization in current or even new products could increase chances for survival. There were isolated instances of new 'pedlar communities'. Alternatives open to those unable to take advantage of the changing situation were to return to seasonal labour migration in agriculture, shuttle migration, permanent migration to the expanding urban-industrial world or exodus to the New World, where many hoped to regain the Old World they had lost.

Regional examples

From a vast number of traditional itinerant trade systems in early modern Europe, we shall discuss some of Oberpenning's regional examples from the Belgium–Netherlands borderlands, France, Italy and Germany, most of which reached their greatest expansion in the eighteenth century.[42]

The origins of the travelling Brabant and Loon pedlars known as Teutens from the Kempen region of the Belgium–Netherlands borderlands presumably go back as early as the fifteenth century, yet their history has only been documented since the sixteenth century. Towards the end of the eighteenth century, their home region encompassed about 40 villages with a total of 500–800 travelling traders whose traces stretch from the Netherlands in the west to Russia in the east. A peculiarity of the Teutens was the combination of travelling to offer their services (tinkering, haircutting or animal gelding) with sales of goods they acquired through their services (trade in copper, hair and livestock), on the one hand, and/or buying and selling textile and copper products not related to their services or the door-to-door sale of junk. 'Hair Teutens' cut the women's hair that was needed for wig production and traded it for textiles and haberdashery; exceptionally, this was also done by women, who otherwise stayed home to run the rural household. They generally travelled each year from February to the middle or end of the year, sometimes even longer, and sometimes even for years at a time if warehouses or sales locations had to be supervised in the destination areas. This travelling occupation was born of necessity, yet most Teutens remained economically tied to their rural origins for a long time or permanently; only a minority could support themselves entirely though travelling trade. The more successful among them later moved to their sales areas, from Alsace-Lorraine to French Flanders and Luxembourg to Friesland, Denmark and eastern Germany, where some had long before established storage depots or small shops. Itinerant trading by the Teutens did not disappear entirely until around the turn of the twentieth century.[43]

Itinerant traders in France in the eighteenth century came largely from poor mountainous regions in the Alps, Pyrenees, the Massif Central and the Jura mountains. Seasonal travelling trade, which started there as a result of insufficient agricultural subsistence production and long remained tied to it, could also be connected with home production and itinerant services. They were predominantly dealers in haberdashery, tinkers or copper goods dealers and itinerant cobblers who were normally on the road from October or November for a few months or until the next year's harvest. Destination and sales regions for itinerant selling, which reached its greatest scope from the mid-eighteenth to the mid-nineteenth centuries, were almost all regions in France, though there were also destinations outside the country, from Belgium and the Netherlands in the north and Germany in the east to Spain and the Balearic Islands in the south. At first mostly haberdashery or household and cooking utensils were sold, as well as cloth and small textile items. These were later supplemented by semi-luxury items such as copper engravings, prints and books from the printing works in Troyes, Caen, Limoges or Toulouse. Pedlars offered their wares from door to door or at markets; some also had shops in the destination regions where they offered merchandise and repairs. Success or failure in the travelling trade led to social advancement or decline. Some travelling traders managed to become leaders (*maîtres*) who directed work brigades (*équipes*) of hired traders (*domestiques*) in purchasing, sales or warehouse supervision; others descended into vagabondage and crime. The decline of itinerant trade in the late nineteenth century meant the end of economic subsistence relief for some; for the successful it simply meant shifting from itinerant to sedentary trade in the form of settling down as merchants in French cities.[44]

In addition to travellers of high standing and, for example, northern Italian labour migrants such as chimneysweeps, stonemasons and construction workers from Alpine valleys and especially Lombardy, evidence of northern Italian travelling traders has been documented as far back as the late Middle Ages and as far afield as Switzerland and southern and western Germany. This was the case from the Thirty Years' War, especially regarding southern fruit dealers. The latter were the largest group in Germany, where they were called *Pomeranzenkrämer* (bitter orange

sellers) or *Comenser*, since most of them came from the economically
depressed region around Lake Como and the other Lombardy lakes.
Dealers in silk and fashion accessories who had been coming since the
eighteenth century, primarily from Savoy and Piedmont and farther
north, clearly enjoyed a higher social standing than the *Comenser*. There
were also dealers in plaster sculpture, especially from the Duchy of
Lucca, rug dealers from South Tyrol, dealers of devotional objects, pictures
and copper engravings, especially from Milan, and cosmetics dealers
mainly from South Tyrol, Verona and Venice who were known as 'tray
vendors' in Germany because of the sales trays they carried around their
necks. Thus most of these small pedlars offered what were considered
luxury goods at that time. As early as the seventeenth and especially the
eighteenth centuries, many of them settled down in their destination
areas, in Germany mostly in the cities along the central Rhine and the
Main rivers, where records show that at that time about 1,400 Italians
immigrated there for the first time. From here, many managed to advance
both economically and socially to become wholesalers and long-distance
traders or industrialists dealing in chocolate, tobacco (Bolongaro in
Höchst) or cologne (Farina in Cologne).[45]

Since the *Tödden* system in the northern Münster region will be
presented in detail below, we shall limit our discussion of Germany
here to some key terms regarding other systems that existed at the same
time in western and southern Germany. Aside from the *Tödden*, in the
seventeenth century at the latest there was another itinerant trade system
in Westphalia that was equally well established in the neighbouring
upper Sauerland, where trade was mostly in purchased products. The
individual travelling trade towns in the Sauerland specialized in various
goods, especially woollen, wood and hardware products that were produced nearby in cottage industries up to the second half of the nineteenth
century. After repeated changes in the selection of goods, they sold
mostly iron and steel products made by manufacturers in Bergisches
Land, east of Cologne, and Mark County; travelling sales were of central
significance for the sale of these items. Itinerant trade in the Sauerland
was one of the systems that expanded when transportation improved in
the nineteenth century; its widest range reached from the Netherlands to
Russia and from Schleswig-Holstein to Hungary. The goods carriers
referred to as 'labourers' or 'helpers' by the work brigades stocked the
warehouses in the destination regions. From the early nineteenth century,
these depots sometimes developed into shops, and consequently a
number of pedlars became sedentary merchants in the destination
regions.

In southern Germany there were numerous itinerant trade communities and systems, of which only two extreme examples will be

mentioned here. One of the most well known and successful were the Black Forest watch and glass dealers who in the first half of the eighteenth century formed strictly hierarchical companies held together through family relations to organize sales using a division of labour. At the lowest level were the labourers, followed by the mid-level *Ruhkamerads* and, at the top, the *Gutkamerads*, equal partners who in turn united to form trade societies for common invoicing and profit sharing based on level of investment. The widest range encompassed not only almost all of Europe but included even an intercontinental sales network of watch dealers from Denmark to Egypt and from North America to Russia.

Among the poorest of the settled poor in itinerant trade were travelling trade villages in eastern Swabia such as Unterdeufstetten and Matzenbach, which emerged in the eighteenth century as a result of population measures to start new settlements, especially by vagabonds. Since they did not own land, the villagers' only alternative to migrant labour was a combination of domestic production (pottery, owing to a nearby clay pit) and travelling trade, whereby the production season took place during the winter and the sales season normally started on 2 February (Candlemas) and lasted until 1 November (All Saints' Day). After a short period of prosperity with intermediate wholesale trade (especially porcelain and stoneware), the villages once again became extremely poor settlements in the nineteenth century.[46]

Unlike the pedlars who moved around selling only or mostly their own products, indirect dealers (*Fremdhausierer*) who bought their goods from other producers or wholesalers often served important functions, not only for market developments in their sales areas but also for commercial developments in their purchasing areas. This was true also in southern Germany, where for example in Württemberg many craftsmen's towns owed their successful development into trade centres to the wide-ranging sales of their goods by travelling traders. As a consequence of industrialization, traditional itinerant trades declined dramatically in the southern German trade communities. Over time, however, in the nineteenth century it led temporarily to a great expansion of new forms of travelling sales in the developing industrial trade centres. Dealers came less and less from poor peasant classes and increasingly from urban lower classes; and trade was linked to a general shift towards a fixed range of goods because of the availability of ready-made goods from factory production. The marked combination of itinerant trade and proto-industrial cottage industries that emerged from rural poverty and often served as collective subsistence relief for entire villages of pedlars was replaced in the industrial age by itinerant sales of industrial products as an individual solution to ensure subsistence.

The Tödden *system*

The itinerant trade system we will examine in depth in a longitudinal analysis originated in the northern Münster region in the western borderlands of the present-day German states of North Rhine-Westphalia and Lower Saxony. The first evidence for the travelling traders known in the part of Westphalia from where they originated as *Tödden* or *Tuötten* dates back to the time of the Thirty Years' War. This system of trade increased in the late seventeenth century into the beginnings of one of the biggest European itinerant trade systems, which Oberpenning, echoing Lucassen, referred to as the '*Tödden* system'.[47] Its core regions were in the North Sea system, but the *Tödden* cannot simply be subsumed into the group of Holland migrants, who in part came from the same geographical regions. The travelling trade of the *Tödden* reached considerably farther in its continental dimensions, especially to the north and east. The places of origin of the labour migrants in the North Sea system extended, as noted above, up to 300 kilometres into the hinterland beyond the destination region along the coastal strip that was up to 50 kilometres wide. In the *Tödden* system, however, travelling distances of 500 kilometres were by no means unusual, sometimes extending even twice that far.

The *Tödden* system, like most of the European systems of labour migration and travelling trade, emerged when extreme growth of the smallholder and non-landowning classes intensified the lack of a sufficient economic subsistence base in a rural home region where there was a high proportion of dwarf- and smallholdings on relatively low-yielding land. Cottage textile production as an adequate source of supplementary income was evidently not an option for the *Tödden* and the Holland migrants, although the neighbouring Tecklenburg region became one of the centres of the proto-industrial domestic system in north-western Germany. Oberpenning had good reason to assume a connection between small tenant farm holdings and the cottage weaving industry, on the one hand, and dwarfholdings and labour migration or itinerant trade, on the other. Small tenant farm holdings could guarantee subsistence if supplemented by cottage weaving production. Itinerant trade and labour migration emerged especially in cases where the tenant farm holdings were so small that it was impossible to plant even hemp and flax in addition to the already insufficient cultivation of crops for the family's own subsistence. The Holland migrants' custom, mentioned above, of carrying a skein of cloth into the destination region along with their baggage should not be viewed as a form of travelling trade but as a means to reduce the costs of the journey and their stay during their labour migration.

In addition, the Holland migrants worked in their destination regions primarily in agriculture or as peat labourers, thus remaining tied to their insufficient agricultural income base in their place of origin and migrating in accordance with seasonal cycles determined essentially by that base. As the *Tödden*'s itinerant trade system expanded throughout Europe, however, many of them increasingly detached themselves from the context of the family subsistence economy operated by their wives and families as a supplementary source of income. The *Tödden* usually spent nine or more months a year in their distant sales areas, where many later set up a second household. In many cases they returned home only twice yearly, as a rule on Christian holidays in the summer (St James's Day) and winter (Christmas), when they also stocked up on new merchandise. Some also returned at harvest time, though this was less to supervise the small subsistence operations run by the rest of the family than because their rural customers in the sales area had no time to discuss sales during the harvest. When the sales season resumed after the harvest, this apparent seasonal cycle, too, had less to do with the households in the place of origin than with sales opportunities in the destination regions; in other words, after selling the harvest, farming customers had more money to purchase goods. Moreover, the schedules of the trade fairs where trade goods were bought had an influence on migratory cycles. In contrast to most Holland migrants, therefore, many *Tödden* were not at home in one place and foreigners in another, but locals and foreigners in a number of places at the same time.

Centres of *Tödden* pedlars were the parishes in Lingen County and the Hopsten parish in the prince-bishopric of Münster, with more than one thousand registered pedlars around 1750. Of these, 213 came from the community of Hopsten alone, with a population of about 2,000; the town was significant beyond the region due to the fact that the wealthiest wholesalers among the *Tödden* could be found there. Travelling trade remained the predominant sector of community business life in the county of Lingen and in Hopsten into the nineteenth century.

In contrast to many other, generally similarly structured, European itinerant trade systems, the wholesale and retail companies of the *Tödden*, also organized by family associations, were very complex and hierarchical as early as the seventeenth and eighteenth centuries. This is why even the Prussian General Directorium spoke in 1797 of the *Tödden* having a 'trade system'. It was notable that particularly lucrative vertical concentrations developed because individual wholesalers became involved in retail trade as well through an extensive sales network of pedlars hired for a wage. Travelling, working and living in groups, the *Tödden* had mutually aligned or separated sales areas within their itinerant trade system covering north-western, northern and north-eastern

Europe. The sales areas were passed down from generation to generation, developing into permanent migratory traditions in the family associations. The range of the itinerant trade network of the *Tödden* from Hopsten was the most extensive: from northern France to Sweden to Russia. Organizational structures of *Tödden* trade were flexibly adapted to conditions in the respective destination regions. Thus the restrictive mercantile dirigism in the part of Prussia east of the Elbe River differed greatly from the long-standing, relatively free development opportunities that let the Netherlands develop into a kind of itinerant trade paradise.

Textiles and metal goods were the two main areas of proto-industrial market production. These dominated in *Tödden* trade, which was characterized by extreme specialization in the selection of goods offered. The *Tödden* from Hopsten, for example, dealt exclusively with textile products, especially cloth, and notably Bielefeld linen produced in the county of Ravensberg. Conversely, the knife vendors of Lingen were known for a wide variety of metal goods, especially hardware products. Different conditions and regulations in the destination areas influenced not only the specific selection of goods offered, but the purchase of goods as well. Prussia in particular sought to instrumentalize *Tödden* trade through a mixture of concerted market demands and restrictions in the interest of its mercantile trade policies.

Social stratification in the *Tödden* system, like many other European itinerant trade systems, resembled a large business and social pyramid within which numerous smaller pyramids existed. Differences that applied in the large pyramid emerged owing to an enormous differential in economic status and social standing. Anchored at the top were the roughly two dozen families whose wholesale companies dominated the wholesale and itinerant trade market in the county of Lingen and in Hopsten, in some cases for centuries. This social group was prominent through its lifestyle of conspicuous consumption, and even today we are reminded of them through numerous impressive *Tödden* concerns in the communities where they originated. Names of companies either in cities in the greater area of origin or in the pedlars' former destination regions are known beyond the region, throughout Europe and even worldwide. The best-known example is the 'C & A' company, named after the two company founders, Clemens and August Brenninkmeyer; the company has been in Dutch hands for generations but was originally from the *Tödden* community in Mettingen in the northern Münster region.

Smaller pyramids that overlapped at diverse points protruded from the broad base of the large business and social pyramid in the *Tödden* system. Within these, medium-sized, small and very small retailers with largely self-sufficient smallholding and leasehold subsistence livelihoods strove upwards, so that the social standing of the lowest of these often overlapped with that of the hired pedlars who worked for a wage. At the top of the small pyramids, in turn, were independent company or work brigade supervisors, some of whom managed to establish small businesses that developed a long family tradition, whereas the climb from the broad base of hired pedlars working for a wage appears to have been extremely difficult. Statistics dating back to 1780 show that in Lingen, about 75 per cent of travelling pedlars belonged to the sub-peasant class of tenant farmers and landless, among which the landless dominated with 52 per cent, all of whom were unmarried. About 19 per cent had dwarf- or smallholdings (*Kötter*, or cottagers, new farmers, and *Brink-sitzer*, or land-poor at the town's edge); only 4 per cent came from peasant backgrounds.

However, the income of retailers in itinerant trade who came from the group of smallholders or non-landowners was incomparably higher than any possible returns from alternative sources of income in their home region. The annual earnings of a well-paid agricultural labourer in the county of Lingen, for example, were about 14 Reichstalers in 1750, and that of a journeyman tradesman about 18 talers. The mean yearly income of an average pedlar was about 150–200 talers, or more than ten times as much. For those able to make the difficult break out of the dependent status of travelling traders working for wages and become independent pedlars, this led to an income range that broke the conventional social order. Their wealth and consumption level in their place of origin had far greater economic significance than that of the Holland migrants among the Bramsche clothmakers. In addition, there was a dual entrepreneurial function at work regarding the *Tödden*. On the one hand, they were buyers from wholesalers in the place of origin, from cottage industry producers or at trade fairs; on the other hand, they were 'market creators' in the rural areas and towns of their destination regions.

In the destination and sales areas of the *Tödden*, situations repeatedly arose that threatened their livelihoods. Such threats came not only from state regulations on itinerant trading. Justus Möser, an Enlightenment thinker from northern Germany, for example, had filed a 'complaint against the packmen' which both attacked and, in some ways, defended them. As pedlars gradually moved from rural trade into the cities, there was also a threat from obstructions by city merchants fearing competition caused by the pedlars' greater flexibility and cheaper wares. Many *Tödden* traders knew how to avoid such risks, especially in the Netherlands, by acquiring civic rights and joining guilds, often only on paper. Owing to other circumstances, the primary income earners' centre of economic subsistence as well as their main living base had often already moved to the sales areas in any case, but this further contributed to shifting the weight in that direction, although the place of origin never-theless remained the family's residence and home community for gener-ations.

The long-term and fluid transition that started in the late eighteenth century from itinerant trade with long periods of absence, ultimately interrupted only by short stays in the home region, to definitive emigra-tion and immigration processes was reinforced when Dutch trade regu-lations were made more stringent. They required the *Tödden* registered there as residents to set up households liable to taxation starting in the late eighteenth century. In Prussian sales areas, an ordinance aimed at strangling itinerant trade had the same effect. A licence for an 'open store' was required along with obtaining civic rights and abandoning itinerant trade. Step by step over the course of the nineteenth century, while itinerant trade continued and municipal trade centres became estab-lished in destination regions, businesses and ultimately families gradually moved to the destination areas from their places of origin, albeit without breaking off contact with their former home. Many returned to their previous home communities after retiring from active business life in order to spend their old age and be buried there, while the next gener-ation continued the business in the pedlars' former destination region.

In the late eighteenth century, travelling trade by the *Tödden* had already passed its peak, and by the mid-nineteenth century it had decreased to a minimum. Various factors combined to create a hopeless crisis situation in the place of origin for most wholesale and retail businesses. Aside from the restrictions in the destination regions noted above, obstacles to long-distance trade connections arose on account of the European wars that continued almost without interruption from 1792 to 1814. Yet the Napoleonic Continental system also served to protect the trade products of cottage industries from English competi-tion.

With peace in 1815 came the end of what had been a favourable border situation for *Tödden* trade in the place of origin, since the parish of Hopsten was incorporated into the Prussian county of Tecklenburg, to which the *Tödden* parishes of Mettingen and Recke had already belonged since the eighteenth century. More importantly, inexpensive English textile products started flooding the market in 1815, and in the 1830s this was followed by industrial products from continental European competition. The end finally came when cotton, which was generally less expensive, began pushing out linen and other traditional fabrics of the proto-industrial domestic system, the ultimate collapse of which meant the loss of major items of *Tödden* trade, especially linen.

Tödden practices became lost in economic and social contrasts. For many *Tödden* families whose economic standing was strong at the top of the large and even the smaller social pyramids, prevailing circumstances accelerated the transition that was in the offing from rural itinerant trade to urban entrepreneurship in the destination regions. Acquiring civic rights and setting up businesses in the cities cost money, a commodity that was in short supply for small, independent retailers, with their falling profit margins, and non-existent for wage-dependent hired pedlars. But many wholesalers and medium-sized *Tödden* businesses who had remained in the home regions in the hope of better times ultimately missed their chance and collapsed with huge debts in a wave of bankruptcies. The wholesale community in Hopsten suffered an economic nose-dive that had disastrous social consequences; within a short period of time, it was transformed from a well-off rural wholesale trading centre into a farming village with bankrupt commercial enterprises. A business registry of 1811 from what had become the French *arrondissement* of Lingen suggests that there were only about five wholesalers in the entire *Tödden* region.

The entire region of origin and its environs got caught in a devastating spiral of crisis. As a result of agrarian reforms, tenant farmers lost their small auxiliary incomes from the collective use of common land. The collapse of *Tödden* trade, on the one hand, and, on the other, the decline in domestic industry in the eastern part of Tecklenburg County and adjoining areas (not discussed here) buried traditional ways of countering the disproportionate relationship between population growth and available work, and increased the mass poverty known in pre- and early industrial times as 'pauperism'. Poverty turned to squalor when in 1846–7 the *'type ancien'* (Ernest Labrousse) agrarian and trade crisis – the last in Germany – erupted and the former *Tödden* villages turned into a depressed area that encompassed the communities of Recke, Mettingen and Ibbenbüren. These were to become rural centres of revolution in 1848.

In response to crisis, distress and the decline of their economic base, the communities in proto-industrial regions differed from those in which *Töddengang* and Holland migration had been more prevalent. The areas with a disappearing proto-industrial domestic system in the north-eastern Münster region became out-migration areas for increased overseas emigration. During parts of the nineteenth century, they were among the regions in Germany with the highest migration intensity (ratio of emigrants to total population). In the former *Tödden* villages, however, the picture was one of reagriculturization and a stepwise shift to the coal and steel industry that was expanding in the greater vicinity and to the growing cotton-processing textile industry in the German–Holland borderlands. Areas that had traditionally concentrated on Holland migration continued this primarily agricultural seasonal migration into the

1850s, though with a generally downward trend in the first half of the century. Aside from those who emigrated overseas, the migration trend from the 1860s then finally turned around from agricultural to labour migration in the coal and steel industry, which for a time remained determined by agrarian seasonal cycles for 'industrial hirelings' with small subsistence landholdings.

The magnets for labour migration in north central Europe changed totally in the mid-nineteenth century, and the directions of movement in some cases turned around completely. The North Sea system, with its declining attractive force, was replaced in importance by the Ruhr system based in the coal and steel industry. As regards the agrarian seasonal migrations in north central Europe, on the other hand, the decline in Holland migration in the west was replaced by a rise in Prussia migration in the east (see chapter 2, section 1).

2   Economic Development, Population Growth and Urban Areas of In-migration in the Process of Industrialization

The 'long nineteenth century' in European history lasted from the end of the Napoleonic wars to the First World War.[48] In terms of migration history, it was marked above all by proletarian mass migrations that were largely free to take their own course in the age of liberalism in the European and Atlantic realms. These mass migrations came as a consequence of the critical shift from agrarian to industrial societies in Europe, the development of the Atlantic economy, and the pull of the New World.

The historic change in the material culture of Europe in the nineteenth and twentieth centuries is usually described as a transition from an agrarian to industrial to post-industrial age (or the age of services), or as the path from primary to secondary to tertiary civilization. The paradigm outlined by Jean Fourastié and usually discussed in Anglo-Saxon scholarship as the Fisher-Clark model[49] applies only for the economic and social history of Europe, however. Only in Europe did the long road from agrarian to service societies lead through such a clear-cut intermediate stage capable of being described as an 'industrial society', in which the proportion of workers in the industrial sphere more than outweighed those in the agrarian and service sectors.

The European path from an agrarian to an industrial society was characterized by a wide diversity of economic, population and migratory developments. At one end were countries in which the industrial 'take-off', the sudden rise in net investment rates in industry to a level that remained at that high plateau, came early on (England and Wales around

1820, Germany around 1850) and led to a dominance of highly developed industrial structures with corresponding opportunities for employment. At the other end were countries such as Italy, Spain and Greece where this shift did not take place until after the First or even the Second World War.

Yet even within individual developing industrial states in Europe there were sometimes regional differences in development. In France, for example, there were distinctions between the more industrialized east and the regions west of the Cherbourg–Marseilles line, where agriculture and small trade continued to dominate; in Italy, between the entire south and the industrial regions of the north, especially in and around Milan, Turin and Genoa; in Germany among, for example, the urban-industrial conurbations in western and central Germany, the mixed agrarian-commercial regions of south-western Germany, and Bavaria, which was primarily agrarian.

Based solely on total figures relating to changes in occupational patterns in nineteenth- and twentieth-century Europe, according to which the agricultural sector was still just about the main area of work even in the period following the Second World War, the 'epoch of the European industrial society' lasted only from the 1950s to the 1970s.[50] Such a perspective would even out much of the tension between different levels of development within the process of industrialization. Yet this is precisely what led to the determining forces that defined economically and socially motivated migratory processes, both interregional and international, that radically changed the face of the European professional and social worlds within only a century.

Employment structures, population developments and migratory forms

Employment structures

As the leading sectors in the industrial revolution, the textile and coal and steel industries were the driving migratory forces. The textile industry pushed out cottage textile production, in some regions as early as the late eighteenth and early nineteenth centuries, in others not until the decades after the mid-nineteenth century. This forced people who had previously supported themselves partly or even entirely from domestic textile production to seek a new basis for subsistence. In the second half of the century the coal and steel industry moved progressively to the foreground. Its rapidly expanding centres for mining and iron and steel production became magnets for migratory movements. The construction industry also developed strong attractive forces. In civil engineering it was railroad construction, which was closely tied to the coal and steel industry, as well as road and canal construction. In structural engineering it was the truly explosive rise in residential and factory construction in the rapidly growing industrial cities. These cities attracted labour migrants who built or expanded them and worked in their industries, in urban working and living environments that gradually became the permanent residences of the emerging industrial proletariat.

Based on the development of employment and real net output, in Germany for example there was a transition from an agrarian state with a strong industrial sector to an industrial state with a strong agricultural base between 1889 (employment share) and 1904 (net output share). This shift in the period of high industrialization was connected to a high level of migration.[51] Political economist Werner Sombart imaginatively described the situation as an anthill into which a hiker thrust his walking stick.[52] With respect to Germany, Steve Hochstadt has observed that geographical mobility increased from a high level in the pre-industrial era to a peak during the process of industrialization, only returning to the high pre-industrial plateau in the course of the twentieth century.[53]

A highly mobile phase of 'industry-intensive employment' (Horst Matzerath) could be observed in this form only among the leading European political economies, in particular England and Germany. It was not very pronounced in the economic history of various other European countries, such as France, and did not exist at all in the Netherlands, Norway, Sweden, Denmark and Greece.[54] With the population growth of the nineteenth and early twentieth centuries, the absolute number of those working in rural and agricultural spheres also grew, while their proportion of total employment already started to decline. Not until the twentieth century did the deagriculturization of the labour market in absolute figures follow, in which again the European states that were farthest along in the industrialization process led the way.

The shift from the agrarian to the industrial age was not a one-way street, however. Instead, it displayed a diversity of paths, stages and transitional forms. On the one hand, as we have already seen in the context of the history of labour migration and itinerant trade in early modern Europe, even during the agrarian age there were already significant proto-industrial regions dominated by cottage industry production. Their economic forms and the corresponding main and secondary bases for earning a subsistence income were pushed out early on by less expensive factory and machine competition in some areas. Elsewhere, they did not disappear until after a varied transitional phase that sometimes lasted into the second half of the nineteenth century. In both cases this served to mobilize a potential labour force. On the other hand, working-class households in the industrial age were characterized by a varied mixture in the composition of their household income, with portions coming from employment in the primary, secondary and tertiary sectors. The link was, aside from cottage industries, usually intersector shuttle migration. Even the major shift in employment structures in the process of industrialization, often misleadingly described as 'countryside–city migration', tended to have the character of a definitive direct migration from rural to urban working and living situations only in exceptional cases. In fact, as will be shown, it took place as a rhythmic or rotating process, an animated transition in which personal life histories often went through multiple temporary movements back and forth until permanent settlement finally occurred.[55]

In natural population developments in Europe, the transition from agrarian to industrial to service societies was determined by changes in generative structures. This 'demographic transition'[56] started with population structures associated with agrarian societies, characterized by high fertility rates, that is, large families, but also high infant and child mortality rates. It ended with a prolonged low reproduction level associated with structures of modern industrial societies in the national welfare states of the twentieth century, in which provisions for old age were no longer dependent on having large families. In between lay manifold transitions.

Changes in generative structures followed those in economic structures, but with a phasal shift. They started in different European industrial states at different times, progressed at different speeds, and took different courses. In France, for example, the start of the transition came early and forcefully in the early nineteenth century; after a relatively long transitional phase it was concluded at the end of the century. In Germany the process did not come to an end until the 1920s.

The interconnections between agricultural economy and population developments that were typical for agrarian society began to break down during the transition to the industrial age. Population structures associated with agrarian society in Old Europe showed high birth and death rates that could counteract each other under the pressure of perpetual cycles of famine, epidemics, and especially *type ancien* agrarian and trade crises. This 'old type' of crisis usually began after crop failure as a crisis of scarcity and rising prices in agriculture. Trades were soon drawn into this spiral, since all money had to be spent on food. Ultimately, anyone lacking material goods or savings was affected by starvation, desperate attempts to survive through migration and, not infrequently, hunger riots. The early modern state tried to anticipate this situation by opening granaries and strictly enforcing exportation bans and price limitations, which in turn intensified the crisis for the producers, since the only way for them to cover their own obligations in the face of low harvest yields was to raise prices.[57]

In the 'hungry forties' in Ireland, death through starvation, social poverty, overseas emigration and the already prevalent migration to England, Wales and Scotland became mass experiences; in Germany they culminated in the crisis of 1846–7. This was the last of the 'old' agrarian and trade crises, which was then superseded in central and western Europe by economic developments that were decisive for the emerging industrial age. Improvements in nutrition, in medical, sanitary and public hygiene, and especially the decline in epidemics initially led to a lowering of the mortality rate in the nineteenth century. Cities usually led the way, especially those which had a strong service sector. The combined impact of declining mortality rates and, lagging a short way behind, decreasing birth rates led to a rapid rise in population starting in the mid-eighteenth century, despite mass overseas emigration of more than 50 million Europeans in the nineteenth century. This was due not to more babies being born but to their living longer as infant, child and childbed mortality went down and average life expectancy rose.

In the 'industrial population explosion' (Wolfgang Köllmann), the population of Europe grew approximately 43 per cent in the first half of the nineteenth century, and around 50 per cent in the second. It rose – in spite of the mass overseas exodus – from around 187 million in 1800 to about 266 million in 1850 and roughly 468 million in 1913. The distribution of population growth was varied: the average annual growth rate by country from 1800 to 1910 was highest in Britain, where the population quadrupled. The rates at this time were also high in Denmark, the Netherlands and Finland, where the population increased threefold, whereas in Germany, Sweden, Austria-Hungary and Belgium the populations doubled. Only two countries experienced unusually low growth rates or even a population decline: in France the population figure for 1910 was one and a half times what it had been in 1800; and Ireland, which had a population of 5 million in 1800, registered only 4.4 million in 1910.[58]

The demographic–economic relationship was dependent on regional options for employment. Thus its impact in Ireland and Italy, for example, was considerably greater than in Germany, which experienced an abrupt rise in employment options in the last three decades of the nineteenth century. Overseas emigration and emigration and labour migration within Europe – for example, Irish going to the United States, England, Wales and Scotland, or Italians going to the United States, South America, Germany and France – long offered only limited social relief.

France was a special case where development progressed more smoothly. From 1789 to 1870 the population grew from 24.8 million to 38.4 million (about 154 per cent), which was clearly below comparable values in neighbouring countries. Up to 1911, the year of the last pre-war census, the population had increased to only 39.6 million. Nowhere else in Europe were the birth rates so low. This was due to a voluntary birth limitation that was unique in Europe; in the course of the nineteenth century it spread to more and more social classes. Those who were first and most affected were small families in the French middle class. Birth rates were especially low among salaried workers, who tried in this way to improve their social advancement and that of their children. Compared with them, the birth rates of the working class as well as those of the economic middle class and the elite initially remained high. In the course of the nineteenth century, the middle-class ideal of the small family spread downwards and upwards in the social pyramid. Starting in the late eighteenth century, the child mortality rate also began to decline as a result of medical and public hygiene measures. Children were increasingly seen as individuals in need of care; their upbringing appeared more important and expensive, so that birth control was considered the flip side to responsible parenting. The average number of children in a French family in 1896 was 2.2; in 1911 it was only 1.9. The French defeat in 1870–1 and the large increase in the population of their enemy in the war, Germany, led to widespread public discussion centred around fears of a general population decline.[59]

Forms of migration in the process of industrialization

In the period of early industrialization, the disproportionate gap between population growth and employment options that induced migration initially increased to a decisive degree. While the population grew, a number of critical factors that varied from region to region choked off sources of work. From enclosures in England to peasant liberation in Prussia or land reform in Sweden, agrarian reforms brought to an end all kinds of dependency. However, the increasing concentration in land distribution literally took the ground, and thus the means of support, from under the feet of subsistence smallholders and leaseholders. The advancement of capitalist agrarian operating structures and intensive forms of production created agricultural labour markets with high employment during the season and shortages of employment in the off season. The process of industrialization, on the other hand, initially influenced labour opportunities more negatively than positively. The victory march of cotton and the advancement of industrial mass production sent manufacturers' prices crashing for household products such as woven and knitted wares or hardware products. Consequently, many proto-industrial subsistence bases and income combinations were destroyed. Over time this intensified pre- and early industrial pauperism, which had been caused by the accelerated growth in population. Despite the social safety valve of mass overseas emigration, the gulf between population growth and employment options opened ever wider. With the exception of France, where there were also no waves of mass overseas emigration, it added further fuel to the Malthusian nightmare of an accelerated decline in the ability to obtain sufficient food relative to population growth (see chapter 2, section 3).

The tension of supply and demand on labour markets was often not reversed in central and western Europe until the period of high industrialization. This was the background leading to the increase in transnational labour migration within Europe that was soon to affect millions, especially in the south–north and east–west directions, which will be discussed later in greater detail (see chapter 2, section 1). Within this basic threefold pattern of development of industry, population and migration during the evolution from agrarian to industrial societies, dramatic differences also existed among the most rapidly advancing countries of central and western Europe.

In the British Isles there was generally high population growth; England and Wales went through an early and rapidly accelerating process of industrialization with a strong attractive influence on migration and, at the same time, a high level of overseas emigration during the era of high industrialization prior to the First World War. But the greatest interregional and transatlantic mobility was experienced in Ireland. Ireland's population declined during the 'hungry forties' from 8.2 million in 1841 to 6.5 million in 1851. Between 1845 and 1855 about 2.1 million people left the island, 1.5 million of them emigrating to the United States and roughly 300,000 to Canada. During this time approximately 200,000 to 300,000 Irish went to England, Scotland or Wales; their main destinations were the industrial regions in western England or south-western Scotland. In 1851 there were almost 730,000 native Irish living in England, Scotland and Wales, the number rising to 806,000 by 1861 and then dropping back (1901: 632,000). It has been estimated that between 1840 and 1914 about 5 million Irish migrated to other parts of Britain. In 1914 two-thirds of all Irish-born were living abroad.[60]

Germany also experienced increased population growth, although its industrialization process did not start until later. From the early 1840s until the early 1890s millions went overseas in a mass exodus. In the era of high industrialization in the late nineteenth century, overseas emigration became increasingly replaced by massive internal migrations from rural, agrarian areas of work to urban industrial areas, which made up the 'greatest mass movement in German history' (Wolfgang Köllmann). Starting in the 1890s, there was also dramatic growth in the employment of foreigners, making Germany in the decade prior to the First World War the 'greatest labour-importing country in the world' (Imre Ferenczi), after the United States.

In France, as mentioned, there was no such tension between population growth and employment options resulting in mobilization for migration, since the industrialization process there did not progress quite as hectically. The agrarian basis remained stable for longer and the population grew relatively slowly, which is why no mass overseas emigration took place. Starting in the mid-nineteenth century, however, immigration from abroad into France grew at a magnitude comparable to the Irish migration to England, Scotland and Wales. It began in the 1840s with a flow from Flemish-Belgian areas that had been hard hit by the collapse of the linen industry, crop failures and famine. Flemings migrated at first to work in French agriculture on the harvest, and then increasingly to the industrial centres of northern France.[61] In the mid-1880s there were roughly half a million Belgians living in France. As we shall see, the labour migration of Italians and finally also of Poles grew parallel to these developments (see chapter 2, section 1).

Labourers were attracted or even recruited to travel ever-greater distances in Europe, increasingly across national borders, starting in the last three decades of the nineteenth century. The advancing 'internationalization of the labour market'[62] applied not only to secondary and tertiary areas of work, in which a divided labour market with a clearly defined higher 'national' level and a strongly 'international' lower one quickly developed, but also to the agricultural labour market. It came about as a result of the sizeable number of foreign workers who not only undertook seasonal labour, but also substituted for local labourers who went to work in industry or in better-paid agricultural jobs or who emigrated overseas. Before the emergence since the late nineteenth century of national welfare states that distinguished between their 'own' and 'foreign' workers in terms of benefits and job offers, a sort of unregulated European labour market had developed in the age of liberalism. Labourers crossed national borders with fewer restrictions than merchandise did, with the exception of the anti-Polish migration and labour policies in Prussia, to be discussed later (see chapter 2, section 4).

A new topography of cross-border migration thus emerged in Europe in the late nineteenth and early twentieth centuries. The main regions of origin were in southern, eastern and south-eastern Europe, especially Italy, the Russian partition in central Poland and Galicia in Austria-Hungary, and to a lesser extent also Belgium, the Netherlands and Sweden. The main destination regions for migrants were in central and western Europe, above all Germany (especially Poles and Italians, followed by the Dutch and Ruthenians) and France (especially Italians and Flemish Belgians, followed by Poles); to a lesser extent they went to Denmark (mostly Poles) and Switzerland (Italians).[63]

European migrations within the process of industrialization over-lapped in many ways and, as we shall see, were closely tied to Atlantic migration history. As a rule, events were not determined by individual, clearly distinguishable migratory movements; instead, areas of move-ment were highly complex and changing, with diverse, overlapping subsections, subsystems, and secondary and counter-streams that were both large and small, and constantly growing or shrinking. There were diverse cause-and-effect relationships among them, in which migrants and migrant groups encountered one another on the labour market, serving substitute or supplementary functions or temporary buffer func-tions in the fluctuation of crisis and upswing.

Urban-industrial migration destinations

The most powerful expressions of this interaction between changes in employment structures and geographical population movements were urban growth and the increase in urban-industrial economic conurba-tions. The process of urbanization in nineteenth- and twentieth-century Europe comprised many elements; of particular relevance were the growth and consolidation of old and newly founded urban working and living spaces through migration to and between cities, the different forms of natural population growth within their borders, and the exten-sion of these borders through administrative reforms.[64]

The rapid increase in urban magnets in the secondary and tertiary sectors in the industrialization process is reflected in local, regional and national figures. At a local level there was accelerated growth of towns to small cities and then to major cities and metropolises, while at the same time new cities emerged from industrial settlements and 'indus-trial villages'. In 1800, there were 23 major cities in Europe with popu-lations over 100,000; a total of 5.5 million people lived in them. A century later, there were 135 major cities with a total population of over 46 million. In a European comparison, the cities of the Ruhr valley showed dramatic growth rates; in the six decades from 1850 to 1910 the population of Essen grew from 9,000 to 295,000, and that of Düsseldorf from 27,000 to 359,000. While there had been only two genuine German metropolises in 1800 (Berlin and Hamburg), in 1910 there were no fewer than 45.[65] In regions with growing urban aggregations, major urban landscapes grew together in a process that Leslie Page Moch has fittingly described as 'mushrooming'.[66] In Germany this applied above all to the Ruhr valley area, the Saar and Berlin-Brandenburg regions, and Silesia and Saxony. In England it applied to the large conurbations around London, Manchester,

Birmingham, Leeds and Sheffield; in France to Paris, Marseilles, Lyons and Bordeaux.

At a national level, the proportion of people living in cities grew constantly during the process of industrialization. In 1801 in England and Wales, about 31 per cent of the population of 8.9 million lived in communities with a population over 2,000, only 16.9 per cent in cities over 20,000, and only 9.7 per cent in cities with populations exceeding 100,000. The population had grown explosively to about 36 million by 1911, with the corresponding figures of 78.1 per cent in towns over 2,000, 60.6 per cent over 20,000, and 37 per cent in cities over 100,000. Roughly 15 per cent of the total population lived in the Greater London area around the turn of the century. In Prussia, where the population shot up from about 10 million in 1816 to about 40 million in 1910, there were only 11 cities with populations of 20,000–100,000 in 1817, but 155 in 1910, comprising 4.1 per cent of the total population in 1817 and increasing to 14.7 per cent in 1910. In 1817, Berlin was still the only Prussian city with a population over 100,000 (1.8 per cent of the total population); in 1910 there were 33 such cities, in which 22.5 per cent of the total Prussian population lived.

In France the population growth from 1811 to 1911 was comparably moderate, from around 29 million to roughly 39 million. The percentage of those living in communities with over 3,000 inhabitants was 14.3 per cent in 1811, increasing to 34.9 per cent in 1911 (the share of the population living in communities over 2,000 in 1911 was 44.2 per cent). The Netherlands showed a clearly different growth pattern; because of its much earlier urbanization process with strong tertiary work areas concentrated mostly in trade and shipping, 28.5 per cent of the total population of 2.6 million already lived in communities with populations over 20,000 in 1830. By 1909 the population had increased to about 5.8 million, of which 40.5 per cent lived in cities over 20,000. If we assume the statistical definition of a city as a community with a population of at least 2,000 as an indicator for urbanization, then almost 80 per cent of the Netherlands was urbanized in 1869, increasing to 90 per cent before the start of the First World War.

The general population growth in the course of industrialization definitely served the cities far more than it did the countryside. But urban growth parallel to general population growth does not necessarily mean migration from rural areas in the sense of depopulating the countryside. Instead, as previously noted it can be traced back to the diversified interaction of migrations from the countryside, increasing interurban migrations and natural population growth through an urban excess of births over deaths. The differences that thus arise can be exemplified here based on research by Horst Matzerath in a comparative overview of Prussia, Sweden and France.

In Prussia the ratios of urban and rural populations to the total population at the turn of the century were entirely reversed; the urban population grew from one-third in 1867 to two-thirds in 1910. More than half of this urban growth can be traced to an excess of births over deaths in the cities from 1875 on, almost one-third to gains due to in-migration and the rest due to administrative changes, such as incorporations. Developments in Sweden were very different, where the rural population of about 2.2 million in 1805 increased to 3.9 million in 1890. The urban share of the population grew only from 10 to 19 per cent in the same period, though there was a rising excess of births over deaths in the cities and urban in-migration gains outweighed out-migration losses in the countryside, not to mention heavy overseas emigration. The situation was again very different in France, where population developments in the second half of the nineteenth century were characterized across the board by high out-migration from the countryside, that is, high in-migration to the cities, especially Greater Paris. From 1891 to 1898, for example, the population growth of French cities was almost entirely due to in-migration surplus (1.1 million), which also took up the natural population growth from rural areas, the population of which dwindled to half a million. With a continued trend in 1901–6, urban growth here was in fact due to internal migration from the countryside to the cities.

It is generally true that in-migration gains in major cities or cities with peak growth, and especially in the newly formed industrial areas, were highly significant. Only 15 per cent of the aforementioned growth in the population of Paris from 1821 to 1890 can be attributed to an excess of births over deaths. Aside from incorporations (21 per cent), in-migration was the most significant factor (57 per cent). In the Silesian city of Breslau, in-migration was responsible for an even larger share (79 per cent) of total population growth. And in Berlin, too, only 27 per cent of its population increase was due to an excess of births over deaths. St Petersburg is an extreme example with a 27 per cent excess of deaths over births, which meant that population growth was attributed entirely to in-migration and incorporations. On the other hand, no less than 85 per cent of the population gain in Greater London from 1850 to 1890 was due to natural growth. And in Copenhagen, the ratio of in-migration and incorporations to natural growth was almost balanced; 57 per cent of the city's population gain from 1801 to 1890 could be traced back to in-migrations and 43 per cent to excess of births over deaths.[67]

In comparing different cities in the urbanization process, Horst Matzerath and Leslie Page Moch[68] have distinguished between three urban development types in weighting growth due to migration or to an excess of births over deaths. Service cities had low birth rates and growth due mainly to in-migration; the share of women was dominant owing to the number of domestic servants. Textile cities had high birth rates – decreasing after 1870 – and in-migration mostly from the direct vicinity with an extremely high proportion of women. Coal and steel cities had the highest volume of migration, with high male in-migration and high birth rates. These distinctions are purely for heuristic purposes and should not be confused with historical reality, as evidence of exceptions is just as plentiful as that which proves the rule. Even this ideal type differentiation might appear problematic, since while there were textile cities that lacked major coal and steel industry areas and vice versa, there were no cities without service sectors; and as the Dutch example shows, trade and service cities existed which totally or largely lacked industrial areas.

Growing cities and urban-industrial conurbations with their expanding secondary and tertiary employment options functioned as magnets of varying ranges, attracting labour migrants and permanent immigrants. Assuming the old rule of thumb, recently reaffirmed by Page Moch, the range of the attractive force was largely related to the size of the city and the dynamics of its growth. Small to medium-sized rural cities attracted labour migrants and immigrants from the villages of the local and regional vicinity; medium-sized to large cities had regional to interregional radii of pull; and major cities and national metropolises had an interregional, national and, increasingly, international range. Among European metropolises, London grew 340 per cent in the course of the nineteenth century; Paris, 345 per cent; Vienna, 490 per cent; and Berlin a staggering 872 per cent. In the late nineteenth century, 68 per cent of Paris's population had been born outside the city; in Vienna, 65 per cent; and in Berlin, 59 per cent.[69] The attractive pull of temporary and permanent urban work options corresponded with mobilizing forces in the regions of origin, especially the collapse of cottage industry subsistence bases and of combined agrarian and proto-industrial subsistence, and the advancing proletarization of the agricultural labour force.

The most dramatic urban growth in Europe took place during the industrialization process in the Ruhr valley. As James H. Jackson and Steve Hochstadt have shown,[70] it resulted from migration – from rural places of origin – that became permanent, although initially intended as only temporary. In fact, for a long time there had been diverse smaller or larger migratory cycles between rural and urban regions, in which labour migrants spent increasingly longer periods of time in the cities, ultimately staying there permanently. These migratory cycles ranged from neighbourhood commuter migrations to regional labour migrations of intermediate distance to long-distance interregional migrations. The length of time migrants stayed for work in the destination regions varied, sometimes only weeks or months, sometimes a season or even years. Migrants often went through a number of different migratory cycles. There were also different forms of migrations in stages or phases from and one job to another, and increasingly also from one place of residence to another, often in a progression from village to the closest town to a city and from there further on to other cities or major urban conurbations.[71] In cases of interregional long-distance migrations, first-generation pioneer migrants sometimes returned to the rural environment in their old age, in order to realize the dream of a better life in traditional surroundings with savings from 'the city', while the next generation that was born or raised in the urban-industrial world found its home there.

The stages of such transitions, sometimes over generations, can be more clearly described with respect to interregional long-distance migrations than for shuttle migrations and movements over short distances. By examining three migrations to urban-industrial and tertiary sectors of work, we can gain a better understanding of these contexts. Example 1 depicts long-distance internal migrations; example 2, a transnational immigration to the metropolis of Paris; and example 3 shows east–west long-distance migrations to the Ruhr valley, specifically dealing with the 'Ruhr Poles'.

Example 1

Migration from the Auvergne region developed from temporary labour migration to chain migrations to permanent settlement. It played a significant role in migration to Paris in the nineteenth and early twentieth centuries. Intensive exchange and migratory relationships to the rural home regions continued in many cases even after the family residence and main living base had long since moved to the metropolis. Little by little such migration networks of rural families with a second generation working 'in the city' developed into urban families with parents or grandparents who remained 'in the countryside' or who returned there when they retired.

At first it was primarily male labour migrants who came, while their families remained at home in the Massif Central to run their small farms. Gradually they remained for longer periods in the city, and chain migrations developed. In the course of the first half of the nineteenth century, large numbers of self-employed small merchants and their wives from the Auvergne also started arriving in Paris. But the goal of migrating to the city was for many still to return home with savings. Children were often sent back to the home region for their schooling and did not return to Paris until they had reached working age. Work stays in Paris were increasingly prolonged, so that visits to the 'old home' appeared as a limited interruption of work. In the second half of the century, the Paris-born children of the pioneer migrants started remaining in the city and visiting their parents during school vacations, although the first generation of Paris migrants often still dreamed of returning to the Auvergne region, if no longer to farm the land, then at least to retire in the homeland of their youth. Not until after the First World War was the integration process complete; *Auvergnats* had become permanent residents of the metropolis, generally with close family ties to the rural place of origin.[72]

Example 2

At the same time in Paris up to the 1880s, there was also a working population of sub-proletariat to petty bourgeoisie who had migrated from Germany. Contemporaries estimated that there were about 50,000 Germans living in Paris in 1825, and more than 100,000 by the 1850s. German labour migrations to France, especially Paris, led to a stable lower- to lower-middle-class social environment for several generations, starting in the Bourbon Restoration period (1815–30). This differed from the famous Parisian colonies of German furniture makers in the eighteenth century and their descendants, as well as from the Germans in earlier courtly and later bourgeois environments, which partially overlapped with the political refugees from the Germany of restoration and reaction (see chapter 2, section 4).

A kind of temporary foreign sub-proletariat lived in Paris, working for the lowest of wages and in the worst of working and living conditions. There were street-sweepers from Darmstadt in Hesse; factory, construction and excavation workers, as well as rag-and-bone dealers from the Palatinate; and German and Alsatian maid servants. As early as 1845 a status report by German clerics sent to care for this wretched migrant group declared that 'no railroad or canal is built where there are no German day labourers and workers streaming in *en masse*. All the streets from Germany to Paris are alive with German emigrants and travellers'. Most of the sub-proletarian Germans in Paris had intended to come only for a limited time. They settled in various German colonies, sometimes according to their place of origin. Those from Rhineland-Palatinate lived at the Barrière Fontainebleau, where they worked in the surrounding quarries; the Hessians from around three dozen upper Hessian villages initially lived in the St Marcel quarter between the Panthéon and the Val-de-Grâce and later also in northern Paris. Many had come to work and live in the most pitiful conditions in order to save money to improve their even worse living conditions in their home region. These movements increasingly developed into chain migrations. Small businessmen and salaried workers also started to arrive, from the upper Hessian village of Burggemünden, for example. Letters from Paris to the home villages formed a kind of informational bridge and stabilized the transnational migratory tradition. Genuine integration problems began to emerge across the generations, as the German clerics reported: the first generation of migrants spoke little or no French, whereas their children soon spoke better French than German.

The history of the sub-proletarian German colonies in Paris came to a relatively abrupt end in the 1880s; in the Franco-Prussian War of 1870–1, the French government issued a decree after the battle of Sedan demanding that all German men leave the city within three days. The Hessians returned to Paris from the mid-1870s, but in the 1880s French street-sweepers were hired in place of Germans against a background of economic crisis, and soon only French were allowed to perform municipal services. Most Hessian street-sweeper families, who were the poorest of the poor among the Germans in Paris, returned to their homeland, where their paths then partly continued on either to the Ruhr valley or the United States.[73] But small businesspeople, salaried workers and traders also returned to Germany from Paris. In some cases this completed interregional and international migratory cycles, for example for the Lichtenfeld and Sehrt families from the Hessian villages of Roda and Burggemünden. The son, Heinrich Lichtenfeld, could not inherit the farm in Roda im Burgwald and migrated in the 1870s from his village to the rapidly expanding industrial city of Essen. He became a blacksmith for the Krupp company, where two of his brothers already worked, moved up to a supervisory position in his field and returned to his village after his retirement, where in 1915 he bought a farm and the accompanying estates with the money he had saved. One of his sons, who shared his father's first name, stayed in Essen with his brothers and married Maria Sehrt, who had returned from Paris to the upper Hessian town of Burggemünden as a child. She was the daughter of a small businessman who had migrated further to the Ruhr valley with his family after migrating back from Paris.[74]

Example 3

In a curious intermediary between interregional and transnational migration, the story of the 'Ruhr Poles' emerged in the urban coal and steel migratory region of the Ruhr valley. In some ways they were related in terms of labour migration, chain migration, colony formation and definitive immigration. But the history of the Ruhr Poles from East Prussia also showed remarkable peculiarities; it was about the integration of a national, cultural minority in a true immigration situation, not in a legal sense but in a social, cultural and psychological one.

The history of the Ruhr Poles started shortly after the Franco-Prussian War of 1870–1, when the first miners were recruited from the Polish minority in eastern Prussia, especially Upper Silesia.[75] This was part of an effort to import strike-breakers during the boom of rapid economic and industrial expansion that took place in Germany from 1871 to 1873, a period also characterized by politicized strikes. Under the pressure of the economic crisis that began in 1873 ('*Gründerjahre*'), strike activities came to an abrupt end; in the mid-1870s, there were lay-offs for the first time in the coal and steel industry and in-migration initially began to flag. The first phase of this international 'trend period of economic growth disturbances' from 1873 to 1896 (Hans-Ulrich Wehler) had been overcome by 1879. A second crisis followed from 1882 to 1886, and the third, the weakest of the three in Germany, from 1890 to 1896. In the 1880s east–west migration heading from East Prussia to the Ruhr valley was already growing steadily, at first through deliberate recruitment and then through subsequent chain migrations. It encompassed not only miners from Upper Silesia but increasingly Polish agricultural labourers as well, especially from East Prussia, West Prussia and Posen (Poznań). About 500,000 people from eastern Prussia made up the Polish-speaking minority in the Ruhr valley on the eve of the First World War. They were generalized simply as 'Poles' in the coal and steel industry of the west, although they also included about 150,000 Mazurs (discussed in chapter 2, section 1) from southern East Prussia. The Catholic, Polish-speaking Ruhr Poles, who were suspected of having 'anti-Reich' Polish national ambitions, settled in relatively isolated works colonies set up by the companies. They were allowed yards for small domestic animals and vegetables for some subsistence planting, but plant managements also increased social controls, in that the cheap accommodation was dependent on the place of work. Despite the tension between integration and segregation, the Ruhr Poles increasingly became integrated prior to the First World War, though Polish clubs, the Catholic church, their own press and even their own union also played a significant role. From 1906 on, there were also Prussian-Polish representatives in individual city and local parliaments in the Ruhr valley.

The end of the First World War, the re-establishment of a Polish state and the option to choose between German or Polish citizenship provided for in the Versailles Treaty marked a deep break in the integration of the Ruhr Poles. Christoph Kleßmann has assumed that out of a total of approximately 350,000, two-thirds either returned to the new Polish state or migrated further to the coal-mining areas in northern France, while a third remained in the Ruhr valley. With firm and lasting connections to the home region in the east, the integration process continued despite violent oppression during the Second World War. By the 1950s the only obvious reminders of the former Ruhr Poles' background and the significance of club life for their integration were the many names ending in 'sky', especially those belonging to successful football teams.

The migration of the Prussian 'Poles' in the late nineteenth and early twentieth centuries to the Ruhr valley with its coal and steel industry was part of the powerful internal east–west migration during the imperial period that grew into a mass movement in the 1880s.[76] It first pushed forwards to the industrial centre of Berlin, reached the industrial areas in central Germany in the 1870s, and to a lesser extent the Rhineland and Westphalia as well. The 1880s saw the beginning of massive coal and steel labour recruitment on the agricultural labour market in the region of East Elbia, while the railroads brought inexpensive mass transport. Since then, and especially since the 1890s, internal intersectoral east–west movement was characterized by long-distance migration to the Ruhr valley from the eastern Prussian provinces.

German long-distance migration from east to west was synonymous with a mass transformation of sub-peasant classes from the rural into the industrial proletariat. With the concentration on mining work and semi- and unskilled industrial work, 86 per cent became part of the secondary sector labour force in the Rhine Province and 94 per cent in Westphalia. East–west long-distance migration from the north-eastern regions of Germany represented the most clear-cut socio-historical break in the shift of lifestyles during the transition from an agrarian to an industrial society in imperial Germany. It developed into a kind of internal counterpart to overseas emigration, in terms of acculturation and assimilation problems in the destination regions, and was more similar to overseas emigration in some ways than to other forms of internal migration.

In the parallel history of immigration to the United States, certain settlement regions and areas of work could be related for the most part to certain national immigrant groups. This largely applied also for the settlement and labour structures of the German-born immigrant population, whose family members were soon known in their home country as 'Americans', but, owing to their lifestyles in the new country, they were often still regarded as 'Germans' there, even in the third generation. The immigration process in the United States led to colony-building not only because of language barriers, but also because of socio-cultural discrepancies in the broadest sense between the countries of emigration and immigration. During the immigration process, which was at the same time a process of identity crisis and ethnogenesis, common ground shared by the 'immigrant aliens' as regards material culture, lifestyles and outlook was revealed all the more clearly; in many cases, immigrants became aware of this common ground for the first time. And yet immigrant groups were by no means as homogeneous in their settlement priorities as it might have seemed from the outside. Apart from internal social stratification, this could be expressed within the German-born population in the United States in the clear-cut local separation of settlements according to regions of origin. The regions of origin or 'home towns' in the Old World kept their ties to the New World, sometimes for generations, through networks based on transatlantic migration traditions and a corresponding form of transatlantic communication ('emigrant letters').

There are numerous examples proving that intersectoral long-distance east–west migration led to a genuine immigration process in the destination region, based on the form of settlement and employment as well as on the structure and level of job offered to the sub-peasant classes streaming in from the east. The choice of town, occupation and even place of work for 'newcomers' in the Ruhr valley and especially the Emscher region, as in the Germans' main overseas immigration destination, had features of stable colony-building that sometimes continued into the 1920s ('Westphalian Eastern Marches', 'Little East Prussia', 'New Mazovia', 'Little Allenstein'). This continued to hold together the second generation of migrated 'East Prussians', whose parent generation had already been considered 'Westphalians' in their place of origin. Just as Gelsenkirchen, for instance, was the domestic New York for the East Prussians, serving as the 'East Prussian distribution centre', the 'new arrivals' who landed there by mass transport 'on recommendation' went straight to 'their' districts of the city and 'their' plants of the coal and steel industry. Certain East Prussian regions populated certain urban districts in the Ruhr valley in the course of long-distance east–west internal migration, while certain eastern provinces still sent workers to particular coal mines in the 1920s. Whereas the earlier migrants or those from areas closer to the industrial sites had achieved their social advancement in a literally spatial sense, that is, out of the coal seams, the 'new arrivals' also came in, literally, 'at the bottom', that is, underground, or began as unskilled industrial labourers at the lowest, least respected levels of heavy industrial work. On the other hand, old-established or older migrant groups and migrants from the direct vicinity of the industrial sites frequently worked, as in the United States, as group or brigade leaders, as foremen, masters and pit foremen. These levels were just as hard to attain for unskilled 'eastlings' without means – for reasons of language (Prussians 'Poles') as well as finances (mining school for pit foremen) – as was advancement to tertiary spheres of work.

The designation of 'Polish colonies' or 'Polish mines' in the Ruhr valley of the late nineteenth and early twentieth centuries was more of a generalized assessment by the settled outside populace than an accurate description of the actual internal structure of colonies or workforces at mines – similar to perceptions of immigrant colonies in major American cities. 'Newcomers' from 'the east' were often, with sceptical reserve, simply considered 'Poles', and at first were generally avoided as such in settlement areas and workplaces. Mazurs, who migrated from eastern Prussia, however, responded with hostility to the derogatory as well as historically and linguistically incorrect label 'Polack'. Similarly, Germans from the eastern Prussian provinces who immigrated to the United States during the time of the rising 'new immigration' from eastern and south-eastern Europe did not like being mistaken for 'East Europeans', which they were not, although the groups might have seemed related based on their lifestyle, way of thinking and heavy accent. What for US trade unions – who pushed for organization, control and, ultimately, severe immigration restrictions – were the mostly rural, unskilled immigrants in the era of high industrialization were, for German industrial unions, the *'wulackers'*,[77] 'wage-cutters' or even 'scabs' from the eastern provinces of Prussia. While migrant groups from the same eastern provinces were separated on the coal and steel labour market of western Germany into 'Prussians' and 'Poles', they were thrown together on the industrial labour markets on the east coast of the United States. Urban-industrial development dynamics in the Ruhr valley, and especially the Emscher region, took on 'American' proportions in migratory processes, and so the area became a kind of domestic immigration country with all the characteristics of a socio-cultural melting pot. During industrialization it brought about what Wilhelm Brepohl described as the 'creation of the Ruhr people in the course of the east–west migration', which was an internal migration and yet at the same time a kind of internal emigration and immigration.

The strength of the Ruhr valley's attraction for migrants can be understood if we look at Lorraine, France's coal and steel centre, whose swift expansion started in the late nineteenth century. The rapid growth there with minimal regional labour force potential led to an increasingly urgent labour shortage. The number of foreigners rose. At first many Belgians were taken on in the coal and iron mines, but they often left these jobs in the summer to work in agriculture or construction. In their efforts to obtain a regular workforce, companies tried to recruit other foreign labourers. Recruitment aimed especially at Poles and Italians proved unsuccessful, since German competition from the Ruhr valley, as well as the German part of Lorraine and along the Saar River, won the battle for jobs with the offer of higher wages. Only a few hundred Poles came at first to the Lorraine industrial region. The number of Italians recruited mostly at the Franco-Italian border was higher, but here too after a short period of time many of those recruited went across the border to Germany. After the First World War, however, when the economic situation in France was favourable and German competition lost its significance, the Lorraine coal and steel industry finally became an important destination region for Polish and Italian labour migrants.

None the less, some urban-industrial conurbations with a large number of foreign workers also developed in Lorraine, in particular Longwy. This rapidly expanding centre of the northern Lorraine iron ore basin near the Belgian and Luxembourg borders had the highest concentration of foreigners in France prior to the First World War. The impetuous boom of the iron and steel industry in Longwy, which did not have the advantage of an adequate regional labour pool, entailed severe social problems: miserable living conditions, high mortality, epidemic diseases, alcoholism and violence. Gérard Noiriel described this situation in the boomtown of Longwy as France's 'Wild West'.[78]

Urban immigration regions such as the Ruhr valley, Lorraine and the Paris basin offered constantly growing, permanent employment options, even over long distances, during the process of industrialization and urbanization. Temporary work and labour migration became less significant in the face of permanent employment and definitive immigration. The major cities and urban agglomerations created more than just growth of a permanently working populace. In the course of building and expanding them, as well as providing for their inhabitants, temporary industrial labour migration and agrarian seasonal migrations also increased.

2

Migration in Nineteenth- and Early Twentieth-century Europe

1 LABOUR MIGRATION AND BUSINESS TRIPS

In the nineteenth and early twentieth centuries, 'proletarian mass migrations' increased considerably in intensity, fluctuation and range. Starting in the last three decades of the nineteenth century, they led to an accelerated interregionalization and internationalization of labour markets, not only for industry but for agriculture as well. The basic conditions for this were the rapid expansion – mainly based on labour migration – of the infrastructure and the resulting concentration of transportation networks, shorter travel times and lower travel costs. The sections that follow start with an overview of this increased transnational labour migration in examples provided by France, the Netherlands and Germany, Italy and Poland. The most important forms of industrial labour migration and agrarian seasonal migration in the nineteenth and early twentieth centuries will then be presented.

Places of origin and destinations of labour migration

France

There was simultaneous continuity and long-term change in the configuration of places of origin and destinations throughout France. All the migration centres that could be observed in France around the turn of the nineteenth century still existed in generally the same distribution a century later, in the Paris basin and in southern France, in Lyons and Bordeaux-Toulouse. Migration volumes and distances, however, had increased considerably. This was true especially in the case of Paris, where, according to the calculations of Abel Chatelain, annual labour migrations that focused on construction and services climbed from about 30,000–40,000 in the early nineteenth century to about half a million in the early twentieth century.[1] Temporary interregional labour migrations shifted step by step in that time to chain migrations and then to permanent migration, such as the example of migration from the Auvergne to Paris discussed in chapter 1.

In the 1870s and 1880s, immigration by Italians to France started to increase and finally surpassed Belgian immigration. In 1851, there were 63,000 Italians registered in France; a decade later there were 77,000. By 1881, the number had risen to 241,000, growing to over 330,000 in 1901 and 419,000 in 1911. Whereas in 1851 Belgians still made up one-third of all foreigners, by 1911 more than one-third of all foreigners in France came from Italy.[2] There were clear regional and field-specific differences with respect to the proportion of foreigners hired in France. The figure was especially high in the industrial areas of the north and east, as well as in Paris. In the secondary sector, aside from employment in construction, it applied particularly to metalworking with 18 per cent and the chemical industry with 10 per cent foreign workers. In 1907 the police prefect of Paris reported that 20 per cent of all construction workers were Italian or Belgian, and 40 per cent of labourers for demolition firms and 40–50 per cent of the labour force in sugar factories and the glass industry were Italians. The rural environs of the metropolis, on the other hand, showed a large increase in seasonal agricultural migrants, also with a growing proportion of foreigners since the mid-nineteenth century. Moreover, foreigners working in agriculture were used mostly in locations where seasonal labourers were needed in large numbers.

The Netherlands and Germany

The development of labour migrations in the region of the earlier North Sea system was marked by a decline in old migration centres and a rise in new ones. This was based on the collapse of the North Sea system with its centre in the Netherlands, which Lucassen put down to the attraction of new industrial magnets within its range, especially the competition of what he described as the 'Ruhr system,' the new migration destination in western Germany that offered higher wages and year-round work.[3] Places that had earlier been destinations of seasonal agricultural migrations developed growing labour shortages at planting and harvesting times as a result of the competing draw of industrial wages. Not only did this situation bring about a drop in Holland migration from north-western Germany and other former areas of out-migration such as the

Dutch provinces of Gelderland, Overijssel and Drenthe; ultimately, it withdrew even Dutch agricultural workers.

As the North Sea system died out and new migration centres emerged, the typical direction of migrations within the system's former range turned around. Instead of 'Holland migrants' from Germany, there was an increasing number of Dutch 'Prussia migrants', especially to the industrial Ruhr valley. Starting around 1870, labour migration to Prussia increased abruptly, especially to the rapidly expanding western German industrial cities such as Oberhausen and Essen. In the late 1880s, around 20,000 men and women in Limburg alone sought work across the border each year, primarily in the western provinces of Prussia, but also in Belgium.

The Prussian district council kept records from 1906 to 1914 on the 'arrival', 'departure' and 'number' (at year end) of foreign workers, though these were about 10–20 per cent higher than the actual figure because of occasional double-listings. According to these records, the number of male and female 'foreign workers' from the Netherlands had already reached almost 100,000 (99,376) in 1907 in Prussia alone, the main destination of Dutch labour migrants. Except for a slight decline after the economic crisis in 1907–8, the number climbed steadily to over 115,735 in 1911, reaching its peak of 118,390 in 1912 (1913: 116,602; 1914: 111,115). From information compiled by the French administration concerning 20,000 German 'Holland migrants' in 1811 to the Prussian records about Dutch 'Prussia migrants' in the years preceding the First World War, transnational labour migration movements in the German-Dutch sphere had thus completely reversed.[4]

There were also significant changes in Switzerland. Into the late eighteenth century workers left Switzerland, but starting in the mid-nineteenth century there was increased migration to Switzerland. From the late 1880s, net migration figures revealed growing in-migration, especially in the years leading up to the First World War. In 1910 almost 15 per cent of the total Swiss population were foreigners, as compared with 2.7 per cent in France, 3.1 per cent in Belgium and 1.7 per cent in Germany. Almost 17 per cent of the total Swiss labour force around this time came from abroad, mostly from southern Germany and northern Italy. Germans and Italians made up relatively equal proportions and together comprised almost 80 per cent of all foreigners in Switzerland. The main area of their employment was construction, followed by the textile industry, trade, tourism and domestic service.[5]

Labour migration also increased in Denmark, initially from northern Germany, later also from Sweden, and finally from Poland. In Spain, too, there was large growth in labour migration in agriculture as well as in public works and services in the nineteenth century. Barcelona's industries, construction trades and service sectors became magnets for hundreds of thousands of migrants. In 1877, 40 per cent of the population of 249,000 were immigrants; in 1920, the population had almost tripled (710,000), and the proportion of foreigners had risen to 53 per cent. In the late 1870s, one-third (in 1920 one-fifth) of migrants came from the Catalonian environs. Other important home regions were the neighbouring province of Valencia and Andalusia, in southern Spain. Catalonian migrants, including a disproportionately large amount of skilled labourers, tended to move into higher-level career positions.[6]

In the late nineteenth and early twentieth centuries, European labour migrations generally started expanding, and extended ever farther over national borders. This led to a new migratory topography, as discussed above, with areas of high foreigner employment in industry and agriculture in central and western Europe, and out-migration areas in southern, eastern and south-eastern Europe with a high degree of European as well as transatlantic labour migration and emigration. This can be confirmed by looking at Italy and Poland.

Italy

In addition to Poland and Ireland, Italy[7] developed into one of the most significant emigration regions in the European and Atlantic economies (see section 2 in this chapter). In addition to out-migration, however, there was also extensive internal migration with clearly defined changes in direction. In 1910, there were around 600,000 temporary labour migrants working in agriculture alone within Italy's borders, especially in the traditional migration destinations in northern and central Italy, but also in individual regions in southern Italy. Various changes in migratory patterns can be observed. Corsica, for example, which in the first half of the nineteenth century was still part of the central Italian region that attracted migrants, transformed into an out-migration area starting in mid-century for labour migrants who went first to south-eastern France and then, towards the end of the nineteenth century, primarily to the Paris basin.

Transnational labour migration from Italy to other European countries, which was not yet very pronounced in the early nineteenth century, swelled in the second half of the century into a mass movement. In the early twentieth century, about 250,000 workers annually left Italy, largely from the north, for other parts of Europe; they worked in construction, road-building, as quarry workers and brickmakers and, as had been common for generations, selling ice cream and making plaster figures. Only about 10 per cent stayed permanently in their European destinations, dominated clearly in the late 1870s by France (46 per cent), followed by Austria-Hungary (24 per cent), Switzerland (16 per cent) and Germany (9 per cent). A clear change had taken place by 1906–10, the last census period not affected by the war. The total number of Italian labour migrants in Europe was increasing, and the proportion in Switzerland was now the highest, at 31.1 per cent, followed by Germany at 25 per cent, slightly ahead of France at 24.2 per cent. The share of Italian workers in Austria-Hungary had gone down to only 15 per cent.

Regional patterns of northern Italian migrations in Europe can be clearly discerned. Labour migrants from Piedmont and Tuscany went mainly to France; those from Lombardy, to Switzerland; and Venetians, especially to Germany and Austria-Hungary. Between 1872 and 1915, almost two-thirds of all Italian migrants who went to Germany were from Venetia; in the late 1880s and early 1890s, the figure even rose to over 90 per cent. According to the occupational census of 1910, most Italians in Germany worked in construction and the directly related stone and soil industry, followed by coal and steel. A distant third was the textile industry. Two main groups can be identified among the construction jobs: in civil engineering, especially major projects such as railroads, roads, canals, fortifications and docks, the 'mobile' construction sites took above all migrants from the Po basin who, as agricultural labourers, were not qualified for industrial work. In structural engineering, however, especially skilled Italian tradesmen such as bricklayers, stonemasons and plasterers were hired, predominantly from the mountainous regions of the Udine and Belluno provinces. Brickmakers, on the other hand, largely came from Friuli.

More than half of all Italian 'emigration' overseas, which attracted between a quarter and half a million annually in the early twentieth century, was actually labour migration, which will be discussed later (see section 2 of this chapter). In 1870–80, most transatlantic labour migrants came from northern and central Italy; in the late nineteenth century their place of origin shifted to southern Italy. Clear distinctions between northern and southern Italy can be discerned in this context. Whereas almost a million migrants within Europe from northern Italy were counted for 1906–10, the number of northern Italians who went to the United States was only a third of this figure. The ratio was reversed for southern Italy. About 1.4 million southern Italians went to the United States, but fewer than 100,000 to parts of Europe. Lucassen estimated the total number of internal, continental and transatlantic labour migrants from Italy around 1900 at about 1 million per year, but this figure is probably too low, as he himself wrote that within Italy alone there were about 600,000 agricultural migrants. Including the number of emigrations abroad, the total number has to be assumed to be far above 1 million. René Del Fabbro estimated the number of Italian cross-border migrants around 1913 at almost 873,000.

Poland

Over the course of the long nineteenth century, labour migration and emigration from Polish areas grew on just as massive a scale in the European and Atlantic economies. This was true for all three regions of Polish territory, partitioned among Prussia, Russia and Austria-Hungary. From 1870 to 1914, over 2 million Poles left their homeland permanently and settled overseas or in other European countries. Another 300,000–600,000 Poles annually worked as seasonal labourers in western and central Europe in the last decade before the First World War. The total number of Polish internal, European and overseas migrants between 1860 and 1914 was over 10 million, that is, more than one-third of the Polish population of 29 million (in 1914).[8]

It must be assumed that in the early twentieth century a quarter of all Poles in the partitioned territories were financially dependent on income from labour migration. About 85–90 per cent of all Polish labour migrants from the Russian and Austro-Hungarian partitions who went to western and central Europe were 'Germany migrants' ('*Deutschlandgänger*'), especially 'Prussia migrants' ('*Preußengänger*'). A comparable percentage of all overseas migrants went to the United States, although this migration flow amounted to only about one-third of the magnitude of those who migrated to Germany. Ewa Morawska has determined, for instance, that in 1913 there were 643,415 labour migrants from the Russian and Austro-Hungarian parts of Poland in Germany and, at the same time, a total emigration of 174,300 from all three partitions to the United States. Adding the Ruhr Poles from the eastern Prussian provinces, the figure for 1913 would have to be well over 800,000 Polish labour migrants in Germany. Restrictive Prussian policies towards Poles forced Polish labour migrations from Russia and Austria-Hungary to assume the form of annually fluctuating seasonal migrations (see section 4 of this chapter).

Industrial labour migration

If large groups of labour migrants in urban-industrial migration areas remained in stable, temporary migratory cycles despite the trend towards permanent immigration and employment, this was primarily in cases of seasonally dependent jobs. The large service sector that was needed to supply the rapidly growing urban populations was attractive in this regard, and its outdoor jobs were seasonally dependent. This also applied to the large field of construction work, which drew not only semi- and unskilled workers but also qualified artisans into the building trades. Temporary labour migrants came from the greater urban vicinity as well as over long distances to the cities. As noted, cities were expanded in the course of nineteenth-century urbanization to a large degree by labour migrants, a growing number of whom remained in the cities.[9] Finally, the large agricultural supply regions in the hinterlands of metropolises and conurbations stimulated temporary labour migrations. This was true for Greater Paris as for Berlin and London. Starting in the 1880s, for example, production in Essex was increasingly geared to work-intensive products such as potatoes and milk to supply the London population.

There were also mobile industrial labour migrants who travelled great distances, often increasingly across borders, in stable migratory cycles that linked industrial destinations with remotely located home regions where family subsistence could only be ensured or expanded through additional income. Temporary migration destinations included centres of the coal and steel industry as well as mobile secondary work opportunities, especially in construction. Continuity in the structures of migratory cycles did not necessarily mean continuity in individual migration practices, since a number of alternative destinations also existed for individual labour migrants within these cycles.

The labour migrations noted in chapter 1 of the roughly 150,000 'Ruhr Mazurs' from southern East Prussia to the Ruhr valley in the late nineteenth and early twentieth centuries are an example of temporary intersectoral long-distance migrations between agricultural home regions and destinations in the coal and steel industry. These migrants were often regarded as Poles on account of their Old Polish dialect, although in contrast to the Ruhr Poles, who were Catholic and frequently had Polish nationalist leanings, the Mazurs were Protestant and adopted a strict Prussian, monarchical stance. While the Ruhr Poles in western Prussia shifted from being labour migrants to chain migrants to permanent immigrants – except for the above-mentioned return and further migrations after the end of the First World War – a considerable portion of the Ruhr Mazurs initially remained in structurally stable migratory cycles. Mazurs who had dwarf- or smallholdings shuttled to the Ruhr valley during the agricultural off-peak seasons to earn additional income in order to supplement or expand the income from their low-yielding subsistence smallholdings. But the boundary between temporary labour migration and permanent immigration was blurred for the Mazurs, too; they became better integrated in the Ruhr valley than the Poles and experienced greater upward social mobility.[10] Such forms of temporary labour migration in the (coal and steel) industrial centres also existed in other European countries. Italians, for example, went to the Lorraine coalmines, and Flemings to the textile industry in northern France. This was a seasonal trade to the extent that there was generally such little work from July to September that the workers returned home or sought jobs in agriculture.[11]

Another major source of secondary income within the scope of stable temporary labour migration was construction, with its sometimes highly mobile workplaces. This included, beginning with urban-industrial migration destinations, civil and structural engineering jobs building factories, apartment buildings and roads in the rapidly expanding city centres and industrial zones. In a broader sense, however, it also included all stonework – from semi- and unskilled quarry workers to trained stonemasons and construction workers. In addition to native labour migrants, there was also an increasing number of foreign work brigades beginning in the last three decades of the nineteenth century, who worked under the direction of a brigade leader, or what Italian labourers called the *capo*, who often spoke several languages. They either were recruited abroad or offered their services as they were travelling. North Italians worked in the quarries or as stonemasons in southern Germany, and a small segment also worked in the Rhine-Westphalia industrial area. Italians also made up a large share of the workforce in Switzerland. Especially in Swiss cities the proportion of foreigners, primarily Italians, was extremely high in the construction trade. In Switzerland's 23 largest cities, almost 85 per cent of all masons in 1910 came from abroad; among stonecutters the figure was 60 per cent; brickmakers, 57 per cent; and painters and plasterers, 50 per cent.[12] As suppliers, brickworks also belonged to the construction field in a broader sense; they were occasionally operated as a supplement to agriculture. After the decline of traditional brickwork brigades such as the Lippe brickmakers, it became a specialized field of Italian and Polish labour migrants in central and western Europe.[13]

Another major area of work for temporary labour migrants included, in the secondary sector, mobile, seasonally dependent jobs building railroads and roads, tunnels, bridges and canals, for which permanent settlement was in any case not an issue. In addition, the extremely heavy labour, usually piecework that was carried out under permanently provisional living conditions, attracted labourers interested in earning as much as they could in as short a time as possible, the money to be spent elsewhere and thus involving minimal costs during their stay. This was generally to supplement the family income at the distant residence; sometimes it was to finance emigration or to get started in the New World.

Europe's major construction sites of the nineteenth century, with their fluctuating populations of interregional and international labourers, were regarded with suspicion by the bourgeois world, who associated them with immorality, crime and brutality and often saw them as a potentially dangerous source of social revolution.[14] This was partially due to the fact that, in addition to the typical migrant labourer who sometimes lacked a fixed residence and thus lived on the large construction site, who was native to the country and yet 'foreign', there were also many workers who spoke foreign languages. In expanding the rail as well as road and canal networks, foreign worker brigades were very often hired: Irish in England, Italians and Belgians in France, Italians and Poles in Germany.[15]

In this context, railroad, road and tunnel construction were of major importance. Pride of place goes to the railroad, that epochal symbol of the industrial age that emerged when the steam engine was mounted on wheels. This brought about a uniquely reciprocal relationship with migratory events. Railroad construction created numerous jobs in the coal and steel industry, many additional stationary jobs in the areas where suppliers were located, and, at the same time, hundreds of thousands of mobile jobs all over Europe. The expanding rail network in turn offered faster and less expensive transportation for workers, even over long distances, and was simultaneously an instrument of market expansion since it accelerated and lowered the cost of haulage. Expansion of the market in turn facilitated increases in production, which led to additional demands for labour. In the individual states of the German Confederation, over 25,000 kilometres of track were laid from 1835 to 1870; during the German Empire another 6,500 kilometres were laid in the period 1871–5 alone. According to some estimations the number of workers involved also rose steadily. In 1841, there were an estimated 30,000 people working directly in railroad construction; in 1851, the number had already risen to 90,000; in 1860 it was 171,000; and finally, in 1875 there were 541,000 railroad workers in Germany. At this time, more people were employed in railroad construction in Germany than in the entire coal and steel industry.

Railroad construction sites generally extended over kilometres and at times there were more than 15,000 labourers simultaneously at work on any one site. After the peak in 1875, the number of kilometres of track laid each year and the number of railroad workers gradually declined, but the network of track in Germany nevertheless continued to grow from over 34,000 kilometres in 1880 to over 61,000 kilometres in 1914. The European rail network expanded to the same degree. In 1840 there were over 3,000 kilometres of railroad track in Europe; there were already 20,000 kilometres in 1850; over 170,000 in 1880; and, finally, in 1913 there were 350,000 kilometres. In a European comparison, the most extensive rail networks were in Belgium, Britain, Switzerland and

Germany. Not only rail networks expanded rapidly; so too did road networks. The total length of paved road in Prussia, for example, grew from 1837 to 1895 from about 13,000 to almost 83,000 kilometres.[16]

Tunnel-building was a specialized aspect of railroad and road construction. Italian specialists from particular areas long remained leaders in the field. Railroad and tunnel construction was the major draw bringing Italian migrants to Switzerland. Some segments were built almost exclusively by Italian labourers. They constituted by far the largest proportion of the labour force that built the 15–kilometre-long tunnel at the St Gotthard Pass (1872–82), in which more than 2,600 Italians simultaneously worked from both ends during the main building phase. The situation was similar for the construction of the Simplon Tunnel (1898–1906), measuring almost 20 kilometres in length. One-third of all Italians working on this project brought their families with them, so that mobile colonies of labour migrants developed. The last major tunnel project before the First World War was the Lötschbergtunnel: 3,250 workers were hired, 40 per cent of whom were from southern Italy, 30 per cent from central Italy, 12 per cent from Lombardy, and 15 per cent from Piedmont. Local labourers made up only 3 per cent of the total workforce.[17]

The large canal-building projects in Germany were also largely completed with foreign workers. In the construction of the Dortmund–Ems Canal (1892–1900), sometimes more than half the workers in the northern sections towards the North Sea were foreign labourers, especially from the Netherlands. There were clear-cut hierarchies that fluctuated over time; tradesmen, technicians and machinists were almost exclusively German labourers, and the Dutch were used only as unskilled navvies to do the heavy excavation work. The subsequent construction of the first section of the Midland (*Mittelland*) Canal, which lasted until the outbreak of the First World War, was, in contrast, carried out almost entirely by Polish workers from Russia and Austria-Hungary. Their employment in the construction of the Dortmund–Ems Canal had been prohibited since foreign Poles were not allowed to be hired in the central and western provinces of Prussia except in agriculture (see section 4 of this chapter). This ban was specifically yet only partially lifted in the interests of agrarian employers near the canal sections, who feared losing their farm labourers to the canal construction sites. However, foreign labourers in canal construction were hired not just to do unskilled excavation work. Unlike the construction of the Dortmund–Ems Canal, building the Kaiser Wilhelm Canal (now the Kiel or North Sea–Baltic Sea Canal) connecting the North Sea with the Baltic shortly before the First World War involved a large number of highly trained Dutch technical specialists for the dredging work. Two-thirds of all these labourers came from abroad. Most of the unskilled labourers, too, were recruited in the Netherlands. They were exploited, largely by Dutch specialist companies, sometimes working 16–hour days and receiving relatively low wages with one week's holiday after three months of continuous work. German unions raised bitter protests but were unsuccessful in bringing about any change.[18]

In the nineteenth and early twentieth centuries, migratory cycles involving movements of industrial labour migrants over long distances, especially transnationally, brought together a number of out-migration areas with large destination regions, within which specific destinations often changed with the greatly increasing degree of mobility on the labour market. One such home region was Friuli, where an 'emigration system' with different destinations emerged. The densely populated highland region in the northern Italian Friuli region showed an extraordinarily high number of seasonal migrants, which could make up 20 per cent of the population in individual towns. The work season in the destination region lasted from March/April to September/October for most Friulian migrants who worked in their main destination areas in southern and south-western Germany, especially in the building trades. However, they also found jobs in the Ruhr valley and in Austria, Switzerland and France.[19]

Polish industrial workers and miners from beyond Prussia's eastern border involuntarily remained temporary industrial labour migrants starting in the late 1880s, since they were permitted to work only in the eastern, but not the central and western, Prussian provinces and, except when given special authorization, had to return each year for a minimum length of time.

Agrarian labour migration

Seasonal agricultural migrations in the nineteenth century experienced shifts in destination areas, increasing seasonal concentration and growing migration distances.[20] There were complex reasons leading to these changes. The urbanization process increased the seasonal migrations to agricultural hinterlands that supplied the nearby urban-industrial destinations. Agrarian modernization in the nineteenth century accelerated seasonal migrations; agrarian reforms supported the concentration of rural land capital and agricultural production areas and permitted the number of people with little or no land to rise. The intensification of land cultivation by means of new farming and fertilization methods, increased monocultural market production, the advancement of capitalist agribusiness structures and agro-industrial forms of cultivation all led to an increased seasonal demand for agricultural labourers, and in turn to a corresponding decrease in that labour demand during the off season. In addition, a capitalist agribusiness mentality developed with an interest in high producer prices and low operating and, especially, wage costs. This corresponded on the labour side to the formation of a rural proletarian worker consciousness with a virtually diametrically opposed interest in high wages and low market prices for agricultural products. Combined with continued population growth, the collapse of home economy structures and growing attraction of the secondary and tertiary employment sectors, which often offered permanent employment and higher wages, the result was a general mobilization of rural and agricultural labour potential.

The continuing seasonalization of the agricultural labour market became an essential driving force in agricultural migration, especially in the expansive centres of capitalist agribusiness production, such as the provinces of East Elbia, northern France and the Dutch provinces of Holland and Friesland. It led to the highest wages during the shortening season and underemployment at moderate to poor wages or even unemployment during the off season. Steam threshing machines put threshers in the grain industry out of work in the winter, from the 1840s in England, the 1850s–1860s in Belgium and the early 1880s in East Elbia. Similar repercussions were experienced in other production areas by agro-industrial root crop cultivation (especially potatoes and sugar beet), with its high proportion of female labour migrants. Especially as regards sugar beet, there were extreme seasonal peaks but no employment opportunities at all outside the season. This led to a decline in permanent employment for locally resident labourers and a rise in seasonal employment for labour migrants, who were generally hired only for the harvest piecework. Some of them travelled long distances, increasingly across national borders beginning in the last third of the nineteenth century. In regions with heavy seasonal employment this initially led to growing internationalization of the labour force, on the agricultural labour market as well. Labour migrants had to compete with one another for jobs with high seasonal wages; those who generally stood the best chance were labourers who worked hard, mostly at piece rates, to bring home the largest possible amount of money and who had regard only for the level of wages, paying no heed to the severity of the working conditions.

An especially dramatic example of these developments was the agricultural labour market in East Elbia. In the late nineteenth and early twentieth centuries, the scarcity of agricultural labourers threatened the very survival of agrarian production, as the eastern Prussian provinces were among the most significant out-migration regions in the period

1880–93. In parallel there was also strong internal migration from agriculture in an east–west direction, targeting either non-agricultural areas of work or the western agricultural areas that offered higher wages.

The labour market and labour migration in East Elbia had been influenced since the 1880s by the aftermath of intensified land cultivation and rationalized production methods and business structures. This was the path described by Max Weber from the traditional 'intensive interest community' of a large agricultural estate economy and a bound labour force to agro-industrial operations with antagonism between the business interests of agrarian capitalism and the rural proletarian self-image. Especially significant was the grain cultivation crisis under the pressure of international price competition on the global agrarian market, the consequences of which were barely kept in check by German protective duties.

Many agrarian producers therefore saw better chances of profit starting in the 1880s in the cultivation and processing of root crops. This applied to potato crops and distilleries and the export of potato spirits, and especially the cultivation of sugar beet for beet sugar production and export, which was first developed in Germany (first beet sugar factory in 1798), but in contrast to France was not expanded until the 1830s. The planting of beet was independent of the size of the farm and was therefore pushed to the same extent by both large-scale producers and small beet farmers. The main beet regions in Germany were, in addition to Braunschweig and Anhalt, at first also the provinces of Saxony, Silesia, Hanover and Schleswig-Holstein. Once new methods of fertilization were implemented, beet production was no longer dependent on high-quality soil. The predominantly grain-producing economic areas in the East Elbian provinces started intensive crop rotation (first year beet, second year grain, third year beet, and so on), with increased root crop cultivation as the final stage in a long-term transition from the traditional three-field system to crop rotation (four- or five-year turn).

Both steam threshing and sugar beet production led to an increased and, at the same time, greatly seasonalized need for labour. The advance of the steam threshing machine, which replaced the horse-drawn thresher and flail in large-scale production districts, led to a progressive flattening out of the need for agricultural labour outside the harvest season. Conversely, the expansion of root crop and especially sugar beet cultivation caused a sharp increase in labour needs during the season, with no guarantee of work afterwards. The combined impact of both factors, intensive crop rotation and root crop cultivation, led in the months of the peak season to labour shortages and overemployment at the highest piecework rates; in the winter months it led to under- or unemployment at low wages.

All of this shifted the constitution of agrarian labour and threw into upheaval vast areas of the social constitution at the base of the agrarian social pyramid. Max Weber analysed survey findings to determine the 'conditions of rural labourers in East Elbian Germany' for the Verein für Socialpolitik (Society for Social Policy) in 1892–3. He observed a general 'destruction of the labour constitution in the east' and concluded that 'in material terms two major disorganizations cause this deterioration in the most obvious manner, one – the less important – is the threshing machine, and the other, the sugar beet'.[21]

Intensified seasonalization of work options in East Elbia led to a strong mobilization of workers, especially independent agricultural day labourers whose labour increasingly became an available seasonal commodity. Those who were not willing to go hungry through the winter on farms offering meagre wages were forced to take on temporary work in industry and the trades wherever secondary agricultural jobs such as fishery or forest work, or even road, canal or fortification construction, did not offer any short-term substitute in the direct vicinity. Therefore, they successively entered the stream of internal migration from rural areas or sank into the marginal social group of itinerant workers with no fixed residential base, whose fates were at the forefront of contemporary discussions on how to organize welfare for the itinerant poor. Even part-time subsistence smallholders, who were indispensable in the summer season on their own dwarf- and smallholdings and who had worked in the autumn and winter on neighbouring large farms as threshing labourers paid by the day, had to resort to migrant labour over large distances, often outside of agriculture, to earn the much-needed supplementary income. Consequently, the small family production community essentially lost its core, psychological attachments to the insufficiently productive land were loosened, and a latent willingness to migrate permanently within the country or to emigrate overseas grew.

'Reaper processions' to the grain harvest were joined, and increasingly replaced, by 'beet migrations'. This form of seasonal agricultural work migration was also called '*Sachsengängerei*', or 'going to Saxony', after one of the first and most important destinations. The migration started out from East Elbian Germany to the main beet regions to the west, where foreigners had been employed early on. Among them, for example, were Swedish labourers in the agriculture of Schleswig-Holstein from the mid-1860s. They were largely replaced from the 1890s by Poles from the Russian partition in central Poland, and later by Polish and Ruthenian rural labourers, male and female, from Austro-Hungarian Galicia. This shift occurred especially because the Swedish economy began to offer more jobs at higher wages, but also because 'foreign labour migrants' from the east were 'cheaper' and 'more eager' (*billiger und williger*), since living conditions in their home regions obliged them to go west and accept the least appreciated working conditions.[22]

As intensive crop rotation and root cultivation expanded, the draw of high wages unleashed its potential to induce migration, even within East Elbian agriculture. As a result, a severe wage war for labour ensued, which was ruinous in some areas, between districts with an extensive corn economy offering continued permanent employment, but at low wages, and districts with intensive crop rotation and considerable root cultivation that offered the highest wages but only seasonal employment. The chief president of the province of Posen issued an alarming warning in 1890, predicting that increasing intrasectoral wage competition would cause 'extensive farms to be slaughtered by their compatriots who switched to intensive operations. . . . Farmers in the eastern provinces who practise intensive cultivation are thus ruining their compatriots who practise extensive cultivation and will soon be ruined themselves because of their inability to raise wages to a level common in the west'.[23]

This was the background that led to the employment of 'foreign labour migrants' from the east which had begun to soar in the early 1890s in agriculture in the East Elbian provinces. Almost half the agricultural reserve army of 'root pullers' and 'potato diggers' referred to as 'labour migrants' from countries to the east was generally comprised of women and girls. 'Foreign labour migrants' replaced local 'reapers' and 'sugar beet migrants' who migrated westward during the season, at first in their home regions and soon in their destination areas as well. Traditional local seasonal labour migrations thus decreased almost in inverse proportion to the increasing employment of labour migrants from countries to the east. The brigades of seasonal agricultural workers from abroad also included self-employed landowners with farms operating at the very limits of economic subsistence, in addition to the landless and land-poor. They were not at all differentiated by employers in the destination areas; all were viewed and treated simply as 'foreign labour migrants'.

The hiring of foreigners extended westward from East Elbian agriculture, increasing abruptly beginning in the 1890s and swelling to a mass movement in the decade prior to the First World War. All together there were 605,339 foreign labourers registered in 1906 in Prussia. By 1913 the number increased by 50 per cent to 916,004. Except for a small decrease after the 1906–7 economic crisis, the figures increased year on year. From the outset, employment in industry (1906: 369,271; 1913: 551,371) dominated over agriculture (1906: 236,068; 1913: 364,633). The largest group of foreign labourers in Prussia were Poles from Russia and Austria-Hungary (1906: 210,692; 1913: 270,496). While most foreign workers were men (1906: 484,415; 1913: 712,453), there was a clear-cut differentiation depending on area of work. The ratio of men to women in agriculture in 1913 was 55 per cent to 45 per cent (203,076 to 161,557), whereas men made up 93 per cent of all foreign labourers in industrial jobs.[24]

Prussia's anti-Polish 'defence policy' (see section 4 in this chapter) contributed to limiting the rise of Poles among the total number of foreign workers. There were also efforts, albeit relatively unsuccessful, to recruit ethnic German labour migrants and settlers living in countries to the east instead of foreign Poles. More successful were attempts to favour other non-German labourers from the east over foreign Poles; this included especially Ruthenians, who often lived in conflict with Poles in Galicia, and who gave the ministerial labour market strategists in Berlin hopes of 'pushing out' the unpopular Poles, especially since Ruthenians often demanded far lower wages than Poles did. In 1906 there were only 22,733 Ruthenians in Prussia; by 1913 the number had increased almost fivefold to 102,158. Poles and Ruthenians worked mostly in Prussian agriculture. Italians and the Dutch, on the other hand, who together amounted to up to 120,000 workers in Prussia prior to the First World War, worked predominantly in industry.

The late 1890s brought an end to the agrarian crisis that had troubled Germany since the mid-1870s and which had affected the major grain producers in the eastern Prussian territories hardest of all. Hans Rosenberg aptly referred to it as a 'structural agrarian crisis', because it was jointly caused by an economic crisis resulting from international pressure on producer prices and a corrupt economic structure.[25] The agrarian upswing that continued until the First World War pushed producer prices back up and many large farms switched to labour-saving equipment, especially sowing and harvesting machinery. There were two main reasons why the employment of foreigners still did not decline.

First, a considerable portion of farms – 44.7 per cent in West Prussia, for example – were in debt, sometimes owing more than 50 per cent of the total operating capital. These were often non-productive debts from investments not in operations but in the private living standard of the landowners, who had leased their facilities and kept track of the economic situation on their estates only by their Berlin bank accounts. From an economic perspective this was extremely dangerous since, according to Prussian law, farm mortgage liability was against the entire land capital. It was therefore impossible to sell individual pieces of land, and in cases of hopelessly excessive debts entire estates had to be sold at a rock-bottom price.

Second, farms existing at borderline operating returns lacked the capital to invest in labour-saving equipment. Yet even in those farms with good yields, machinery sometimes did not supersede the employment of foreigners, since foreign labourers, the demand for whom could be calculated exactly, were sometimes less expensive. Machines required high start-up investment, maintenance in the off season and repairs during the season. Travel and placement costs paid by the employer for use of foreign work brigades were incomparably cheaper. Non-productive costs were eliminated, not only in the off season but in the peak season as well, since workers suffering long-term accident or sick-ness-related disabilities were transported back to the border and replaced by other foreign labourers. Under the terms of the contracts with the partly state-run German Labour Agency for the placement of foreign workers in Prussia, even pregnancy was viewed as an offence under labour law and women were charged for the cost of their transport back to the border, since they were considered at fault.[26]

Related developments, with greatly fluctuating annual seasonal migra-tion or increasing use of labour-saving equipment, could also be observed in other European agricultural regions, especially with the advancement of root crop cultivation. This can be seen in a comparative view of the situation in France, the Netherlands, Denmark and England.

France

Seasonalization of the agricultural labour market through intensive cul-tivation, agro-industrial production methods and capitalist agribusiness structures had already begun in northern France in the nineteenth cen-tury, much earlier than in the eastern Prussian provinces. The expansion of sugar beet production, with its extreme seasonal peaks, served a pioneering function. The flip side of this was the structural depopulation of the countryside in the Paris basin.[27] The growing labour demand attracted labour migrants, both men and women, from more and more distant regions and also led to a rise in transnational labour migration. It started in the 1820s with the migration of harvest workers from Belgium to work in the grain harvest. Labour migration to France experienced a great rise with the collapse of the Flemish linen industry in the 1840s, and seasonal employment of agricultural workers increased with the devel-opment of agro-industrial sugar beet production. Around 1913 there were 40,000 Flemings, mostly women, working in northern France culti-vating and harvesting sugar beet. The first 400 agricultural labourers were recruited in 1908 in the *département* of Meurthe-et-Moselle in eastern France through a placement agency in Warsaw. The following year they were joined by Poles from Austro-Hungarian Galicia. From 1908 to 1914 there were a total of 20,000 Polish labourers from Galicia working in agriculture in north-eastern France.

Agricultural seasons became tighter everywhere, with higher employment peaks, ever-greater migration distances and an increased level of foreigner employment. This could be observed for the grain harvest as well as the grape harvest, for which about 20,000 men and women from Spain were employed as seasonal workers in France prior to the First World War. There were similar developments for fruit, olive and chestnut harvests, as well as flower cultivation for the perfume industry. About 18,000 Italian labourers worked in the lavender and flower fields of Provence in 1912, including jasmine pickers from the province of Cuneo from July to September.

The Netherlands

Labour migrations shifted to new destinations with the decline of the North Sea system and the tension between supply and demand intensified the agricultural labour market at the expense of employers. They responded flexibly to the fluctuating and ever-dwindling supply of labour by using labour-saving equipment, especially harvest machinery (grass reapers and hay turners). The expensive machines remained idle as long as a sufficient and cheap labour force was available; when it was not, the mechanical harvest aids took to the fields. Another component of change in the agricultural labour market came at the end of the century, when here too sugar beet cultivation was expanded, with its extremely high labour needs filled especially by women, for a limited season.[28]

Denmark

Sugar beet cultivation was expanded in the second half of the nineteenth century in Denmark as well. In the last quarter of the century, transnational seasonal migrations increased dramatically. The dominant group in the period 1874–1900 was Swedish women and girls. Starting in 1893, they were increasingly replaced by Polish women and girls; at first there were about 400 migrants, but in the years prior to the First World War the number rose to about 13,000 each year. After the Polish state was re-established and under pressure from restrictive Danish admission policies, Polish workers were gradually replaced by labourers from Jutland until they totally disappeared by 1929.[29]

England

Grain production in England always dominated root crop cultivation, which never gained the significance here that it had in Germany or

France. In 1841, 57,651 Irish harvest labourers boarded a ship destined for England. From mid-century until the mid-1870s a total of about 100,000 labour migrants in all areas of work may have crossed the Irish Sea annually. This was a response to famines in Ireland and the growing demand for labour in England's grain cultivation. The mechanization of reaping and threshing and the inadequate development of agricultural wages as compared with those in industry led to a considerable drop in the employment of Irish harvest labourers in the last quarter of the nineteenth century, especially in central and southern England. Around 1900 only 32,000 Irish harvest workers were still registered in eastern England. Aside from these long-distance migrants, there was certainly also a considerable number of English – often urban – labourers who took on temporary seasonal work in agriculture.

In contrast to the large-scale agricultural operations, regions with primarily family-run farms – that is, those with total production limited by the work capacity of the family – contributed the least to the need for agricultural seasonal workers, except for the hiring of individual foreign workers during the season. These family farms, which were still dominant by far among German and French farms prior to the First World War, thus formed a kind of flexible intermediate stage, though relatively immobile from the perspective of labour migrations. Beyond their upper limit, as the size of the farm and the amount of cultivated land grew in the course of agrarian modernization, there was a growing tendency to hire seasonal workers. Beyond their lower limit were those with small- or dwarfholdings who operated virtually subsistence production; family members were all the more dependent on taking on seasonal work on farms larger than family-run operations.

Functions of transnational labour migration

In the decades leading up to the First World War, Hungarian economist Imre Ferenczi regarded Germany as the 'second-largest labour-importing country in the world', after the United States.[30] Based largely on the German example, therefore, we will trace the contours of transnational labour migration to European destinations in the late nineteenth and early twentieth centuries, distinguishing among economic, social and cyclical business functions.[31]

(1) Economically, employment of foreigners served various supplementary and substitute functions. It offered additional and replacement labour in employment areas whose working, wage and living conditions were less accepted by local labourers in view of the availability of better alternatives. It also balanced out disturbances in the supply–demand

ratio on the labour market that were triggered by migration losses, and at the same time covered the increasing demands for additional seasonal labour in agriculture. In places where net earnings and working capital did not yet permit a transition to intensive cultivation and labour-saving machinery, the large supply of cheaper foreign labour and the subsequent savings in non-productive costs of wages during the off season allowed farms operating at the break-even point to continue extensive cultivation until capital-intensive modernization became possible. Here, too, employment of foreigners played an important role; their use could be calculated specifically at the fluctuating limit of operational labour capacity, without any off-season costs. Therefore, foreign labour could – not only in agriculture – greatly increase the flexibility of the cost factor for labour. It could also relieve the pressure to rationalize and over time facilitate a rise in yield even without modernization, indirectly via a relative decrease in labour costs. Availability and calculability of the business cost factor of labour thus reached an unprecedented level.

(2) Foreign labourers dependent on wage payment transfer often preferred working in areas and under conditions that were relatively wage-intensive since these jobs, including pulling beet and digging potatoes as harvest pieceworkers, were often eschewed by native workers. A stratification developed with foreign labour having lower status than native labourers, not only in agriculture but also in other fields, especially the building trades. These 'jobs are strenuous, frequently taking their toll on health, often dirty and repulsive', reckoned German economist Sartorius von Waltershausen in 1903 with regard to Italian labourers in civil engineering jobs. This is why Germans 'preferred to reject [such jobs] if it were at all possible to find something more pleasant'. These jobs were therefore increasingly taken on by the sub-proletarian, foreign, 'second-class workers' who satisfied similar functions as 'the Negroes in the eastern states of North America, the Chinese in California, the East Indian coolies in the British West Indies, the Japanese in Hawaii, the Polynesians in Australia'. This was confirmed by a 1913 memorandum on unemployment and foreign employment in Germany: 'The fact that unemployed nationals are available should by no means always exclude the introduction of foreigners from the outset. There are certain hard and dirty jobs, in underground work for example, that the national labour force is incapable of doing in the long term, and which they accept either only temporarily or not at all.'

On occasion, foreign labourers were deliberately placed in a stratum below native workers by employers, or stratification was introduced as a response to growing criticism in order to justify the hiring of foreign labourers. According to a 1911 report issued by the Breslau central mining authority, the hiring of foreigners had been hitherto carried out with 'strict' adherence to certain 'principles', namely, that 'foreign labourers, since they are untrained and not intelligent, are to be used exclusively for the more poorly paid jobs that require little or no skill; nationals, on the other hand, are to be given the more profitable jobs, and those requiring superiority and greater dexterity'. It was noted in passing 'that bringing in foreigners to do exclusively more simple and thus poorly paid jobs results in native labourers being hired for better-paid jobs at a relatively young age and thus having greater earnings and acquiring a more favourable position in material terms'.

There were also barriers in Germany that made it more difficult for foreign labourers and non-German-speaking minorities in various areas of work to advance either socially or professionally. Consequently, the opportunities for native labourers were indirectly improved. This applied, for example, to the so-called language clause that was added to the Prussian mining code of the 1890s. It tied the assumption of qualified duties to competence in written and spoken German. Thus, on the one hand, it served operational safety; on the other hand, it made it harder for foreign labourers, as well as for the non-German-speaking Prussian Polish minority, to be promoted. It was up to the coal and steel industrial plant and the respective foreman in each case to assess level of competence. This in turn increased workers' dependence on their bosses, and thus also what native workers complained of as the 'grovelling' obligingness and 'obsequiousness' of the 'stupid Poles'. The language clause thereby intensified the unequal opportunities that existed on the internationalized lower stratum of the double labour market. Unskilled German-speaking labourers were regarded as a kind of trained German speaker and therefore had a considerable head start in front of the unskilled labourers who spoke a foreign language.

(3) A third problem area in the employment of foreigners included their buffer function in situations of economic fluctuation. In 1895 the Prussian ministry of trade and commerce assessed that 'industry has finally achieved a certain expansion option with respect to the number of workers in the transition from an economic high to a low'. He continued: 'If industry hires only native workers, an economic decline would leave a large number of employees without work, thus increasing the discontented elements. In such a case, however, it is possible to dismiss foreign labourers without a second thought.' The Royal Central Mining Authority in Breslau confirmed in 1911: 'To the extent that a reduction of the labour force turns out to be necessary at certain times or in certain branches of industry, the first step is to dismiss only the foreigners.' But even in Prussia it was possible to 'dismiss the foreigners' only to a certain degree, with the exception of foreign Poles, who lost their residence permits along with their work contracts. Other foreign

workers who were dependent on wage income, whatever the conditions, tended to change fields if they were laid off. Sartorius von Waltershausen described this with respect to the industrial workers in underground work, predominantly Italians, who were dismissed in the 1900–2 crisis: 'From 1895 to 1900 the demand for labour could not be satisfied with the native labour force; the Italians were sought at increasing wages, and could not harm the local labour market. The situation was different when business started to become slack. The entire industry began laying off workers, many of whom were then pushed to do underground work, if they were continued at all, as day labourers. Now, as soon as the undercutting started, the competition of the Italians was felt.'

Tension and sometimes violent conflicts ensued among native labourers, but especially among local workers, interregional and, above all, transnational labour migrants regarding not only wage issues, but also labour struggles for permanent improvement of wage and working conditions. At their core was a confrontation between labourers tied to the area or dependent on earning additional income nearby and labour migrants who had travelled long distances, attracted by high wages and dependent on work regardless of the conditions, as well as those hired by employers for strike-breaking brigades. This situation even led the Italian foreign office to complain that in the construction trades 'Italians are considered to be virtually synonymous with scabs', and that this 'breeds hatred and rejection of Italians among foreign labourers'. All this acted as a thorn in the side of the national employees' organizations and impelled the Free Trade Unions in Germany to increase agitation against the 'exploitation' of foreign workers as 'wage-cutters', 'dirty competition' and 'scabs', especially in industry but in the building trades as well. In Germany, as a 'labour-importing country', unions fluctuated between proletarian internationalism and national worker representations with respect to the demand raised at the Stuttgart Congress of the Second Internationale (1907) for equal treatment of foreign and national labour.

These conflict situations on the labour market could also be observed in other countries with cross-border labour migrants. In Prussian Germany they did not yet lead to protectionist intervention before the First World War, but this was implemented in Germany after the war in the form of 'priority for nationals'. A similar development took place in other industrial nations in Europe, with France representing an exceptional case: there conflicts between native and foreign (again, especially Italian) labourers in public works triggered restrictions as early as the late nineteenth century, which will be reviewed later as part of the discussion of the relationship between nation-states and cross-border migration in the late nineteenth and early twentieth centuries (see section 4 of this chapter).

Labour migration and technology transfer: Training migrations, business trips, industrial espionage

Migration was and is always also a transfer of abilities and skills. This is especially true regarding the mobility of enterprises, businesspeople and skilled technical know-how. Our context concerns the relative weighting of the relationship of ends to means, in other words, whether innovation or technology transfer was merely a side-effect of the migration, or its main purpose. Flight or expulsion for religious reasons in early modern Europe, for example, brought a transfer of technology and innovation that was a highly valued side-effect in the host countries. It increased acceptance of the migrants to the point that they were invited to come.[32] The mobility of highly specialized labour migrants and travelling traders long contributed to such a transfer of innovation. They earned a living from the itinerant application of special skills that were uncommon or unknown elsewhere. All traces of them disappeared, with isolated exceptions, by the late nineteenth century and sometimes even much earlier. Some of these itinerant specialists ultimately became victims of the transfer process they had initiated. Travelling craft specialists, tradesmen and merchants with migratory traditions going back generations sometimes settled down with their own businesses and stores in fixed locations, such as the Italian plaster figure-makers and grocers in their transalpine destinations or the *Tödden* from the northern Münster region in their sales areas in the Netherlands (see chapter 1, section 1).

The decline in traditional labour and trade migration overlapped with the rise in migration of a new kind of mobile specialist, who played an important role in introducing new – mostly English – techniques in the textile industry, mechanical engineering and heavy industry.[33] Such labour migrations were among the economically 'purest' forms combining migration and technology or innovation transfer. Those migrants were predominantly highly qualified skilled craftsmen who had been trained in the progressive industrial centres. Commanding top wages over more or less extended periods of time, they were either recruited or worked independently as travelling developmental consultants. In the opposite direction of transfer, this also included the business trips of entrepreneurs with espionage intentions ('the rewards of travel')[34] and of others, often disguised as private or even state-subsidized technology scouts, following the famous 'path of Peter the Great'. Finally, this area also included technology transfer through migration for the purpose of study and training.

Let us examine these contexts using four examples: (1) the reaper in early agricultural industrialization; (2) the self-acting spinning machine in textile production; (3) the puddle process in accelerating pig iron conversion for mechanical engineering; and finally (4) Swedish examples of the blurred boundaries between migration for training purposes, technology investigations and industrial espionage.

Example 1

In the nineteenth century, a decisive stepwise technological development in early agricultural industrialization brought far-reaching consequences for rural populations. It started with the reaping machine, which put reapers in grass and grain cultivation out of work, and with the steam threshing machine, which replaced the threshers in grain cultivation. It finally led in the twentieth century to a combination of both inventions to form the reaper-thresher, or combine harvester, which reduced the still high seasonal peak employment of harvest workers down to only a few. Though this path started with the invention of the reaping machine, invention and implementation were in fact two very different things. The background to the 'emigration' of this patent from England to the United States follows.

   In the late eighteenth and early nineteenth centuries, the intensification of English agriculture progressed far more rapidly than did mechanization. Harvests were always completed under incredible time pressure; ripeness of the crops and weather conditions set the timetable. There was no scarcity of mechanical inventions but the surplus of cheap labour still made it unnecessary to implement them. A contest was held in 1783 in England to mechanize reaping. After several experiments that proved unfavourable for the grain, Cyrus McCormick developed his cutting machine, which would quickly initiate a technological breakthrough in machine reaping. For the reasons noted above, however, it remained an 'invention in reserve' in England. Disappointed, McCormick emigrated to Chicago in 1847 and founded a factory there. The vast plains of virgin soil in the prairies of the US midwest made possible the time-lapse mechanization of agriculture, a process that lasted about a century in Europe. McCormick returned to England in 1851 to attend the London World's Fair with his mowing and reaping machines, which were based on the standard machine still under English patent. The machines yielded huge profits on the wide American prairies, especially since the volume of grain produced grew with use of the machine. Against this background, it is understandable that an English Member of Parliament recommended in 1859 that British emigrants should 'not take with them more than a suitcase of clothing', since they would 'find better tools in Illinois than in England'.[35]

Example 2

The significance of the mechanical reaper for agriculture corresponded to the role of the self-actor for spinning, but its use in England, where it was invented, did not progress quite as hesitantly. As early as the late eighteenth century, fully mechanized spinning and weaving mills were busily humming throughout central England. In France, Germany and the territory of present-day Belgium, in contrast, a mercantile mindset still predominated in precisely these fields. There were a few progressive centres, especially in western Germany and western Belgium around Verviers. In Flanders, Limburg, Saxony, Bohemia and Moravia, on the other hand, there were great reservations against introducing newer and faster spinning and weaving processes, which at the same time was 'negative evidence of a surplus of labour' (David Landes). Finally, in Prussia of the 1780s, the otherwise reform-friendly Friedrich II, in the final years of his reign (d. 1786), prevented the use of spinning machines, which were known through industrial espionage. Fearing the impoverishment of labourers in the putting-out system, he allowed machinery to be used only in the production of military fabrics. Here, too, the surplus of labour was an obstacle to mechanization. As long as hand spinning by women, children and servants appeared less expensive, the introduction of the 'English machinery' was not encouraged.[36]

In view of England's tremendous head start in development, many entrepreneurs in other countries did not see themselves in a position to start up modern textile factories without English technology. For this reason, the new weaving and spinning machines were systematically spied upon in England and complete imitations were used on the Continent. Unlike the intermediate stages in modernization that took place in mechanical engineering and heavy industry, in textiles home production leapt straight to factory work.[37] Lieven Bauwens, who had spent most of his time in England around 1797–8 in order to smuggle out state-of-the-art technology, introduced the semi-automated spinning jenny in 1801 in Flanders, thus founding the powerful cotton industry in Ghent. This machine, the first model of which was smuggled out of England in its entirety, is today still considered a symbol of the industrial revolution in Flanders and even led to the foundation of an industrial museum in Ghent.

An even bolder step was taken by Johann Gottfried Brügelmann from the small western German duchy of Berg. He set up the first German cotton spinning mill in 1784 in a village named Ratingen, east of Düsseldorf, and cheekily gave it the name 'Cromford', after the site of the prototype of the cotton spinning mill in the British Midlands where

Richard Arkwright had begun in 1771 with his patented water-driven spinning frame. Brügelmann managed to acquire the entire technology from Cromford in England. Fearing justifiably that the technology would again be copied, he forced his workers to stay put under threat of imprisonment and to keep the factory secret.[38] Ironically, when a textile museum was being built on the Cromford site in Ratingen some 200 years later, English technicians were called in to prepare reproductions of the 1780 machines that had been copied from England.

Bauwens and Brügelmann were not alone. On the contrary, virtually every middle-class and aristocratic entrepreneur, craftsman and technician on the road in England was there for the purpose of learning and copying, sometimes with the sanction of the state, with subsidies or even with escorts. As early as 1800 Britain had tried unsuccessfully to prohibit foreigners from viewing the country's factories. Copies and spin-offs were often not used until English mechanical engineers, spinning masters or weavers came along with the application. This was also the case in the coal and steel industry, as the third example shows.[39]

Example 3

While inventor Cyrus McCormick emigrated with his English patent designs in his luggage, and travelling businesspeople from the Continent copied English spinning machines based on their observations and sketches, the puddle process for pig iron conversion could only be passed on by the migrating specialists themselves. In terms of technological history, puddling was a process that fell between craft and industry. The puddling technique was decisive for the emerging field of mechanical engineering. Until the Bessemer process was discovered in 1856, puddling was the only – albeit still very costly – way of preparing at least small quantities of high-quality wrought iron and even small quantities of much sought-after steel. In the puddling process, pig iron was brought in contact with air; the subsequent oxidation allowed carbon to escape, which made the iron less brittle. Developed in England, the process 'migrated' first to Belgium and thence to France and Germany, where it was in use from 1824. In all three countries on the Continent, the puddling technique was brought over by skilled English specialists.

The trips that Belgian, French and German iron industrialists and technicians made to Britain, the 'Mecca of the Iron Industry', and later to Belgium were not sufficient to enable them to use the technology. English specialists had to be recruited, as previously in copying spinning and weaving machines in the textile industry; this was the only guarantee that the process could successfully be introduced into factories. In addition, the performance of English puddlers was unsurpassed in terms of minimizing consumption of fuel and pig iron. To safeguard the English lead in development, British laws of 1718, 1750, 1782 and 1785–1824 banned skilled English workers from emigrating. Of course this offence was punished consistently only for a short time, while those who recruited them from abroad risked high penalties. The prohibition was circumvented in a number of ways, especially since iron industrialists on the Continent offered English puddlers up to three times their English wages.

This extremely resilient elite was lured away not only by higher wages but also by bonuses, financial inducements and apartments; and they knew their price. The economic speculation behind their migration sometimes saw them shuttling from Belgium to France to Germany in search of the highest wages in exchange for their know-how. No textbook or engineer could replace them since their knowledge was based solely on experience, as puddling was a skilled craft. Puddlers usually migrated in groups, within which they constantly shared technical expertise. The first migratory movement started within Britain, and Wales was the main supplier of puddlers into the second half of the century. As a skilled elite, puddlers remained in contact with each other even when they went abroad, first to Belgium and France. They finally came to the German iron industry where they were soon replaced by Belgian and French puddlers who had since been trained. At the end of this technological cycle, each country had its own puddlers. Here, too, a familiar fate met the traditional migration of specialists; in other words, the transfer of technology through migration tended to make the migration of the experts themselves unnecessary. When the 'west–east differential' in skilled workers ended around mid-century, so did this 'travelling circus' (Rainer Fremdling) of technology transfer. The puddlers returned home, since wages abroad were no longer high now that their technical know-how had become widespread. When the new molten steel process (Bessemer, Thomas or Siemens-Martin process) was introduced in the 1880s, the profession of the highly specialized puddler with wanderlust was no longer in demand anywhere in Europe.

Example 4

The developmental history of temporary labour migration of skilled industrial workers, technicians and engineers from Sweden is a well-documented national example. It was examined early on by Torsten Gardlund and later expanded and studied more precisely by Claudius Riegler.[40] The labour migration of skilled industrial workers and technical know-how evolved with fluid transitions out of traditional artisan migrations. In contrast to the situation in England, Germany and

Belgium, it did not assume clear contours until the last three decades of the nineteenth century, but had already been of considerable importance in the breakthrough phase of Swedish industrialization (1850–70). Even more significant than industrial exhibitions – especially the 1876 World's Fair in Philadelphia – were the training periods, often lasting several years, that Swedish skilled labourers, technicians and engineers spent in foreign companies. They went first to England and, after around the 1860s, especially to the United States. That is where the 'new methods' – not only in mechanical engineering but also in efficient plant organization – that played such an important role in the 'Americanization of the Swedish engineering industry' were partly discovered on the job and partly researched intentionally. Scholarships for temporary labour migrations fostered technology transfer, which was often willingly supported though frequently also unwittingly facilitated since it was impossible to know whether new employees would remain in the country as immigrants or return home after sounding out the company. In Sweden, too, there was a great deal of transatlantic return migration, which was significant with respect to the importation of migration-related innovation.

From 1861 to 1907 about 12,000 applications were filed for assistance for training periods, especially in other European countries, generally by people in permanent positions in Swedish industry or the skilled trades. Of 23,000 Swedish mechanical engineers who were surveyed around the turn of the century, almost 5 per cent (1,043) had worked abroad for more than a year – in neighbouring Scandinavian countries (690), in the United States (437) and, ahead of England (47), in Germany (176) as well.

Interest in technology transfer was occasionally nothing more than blatant industrial espionage. In 1905, for example, a 25-year-old 'machine technician' from Härnösand in the province of Jämtland applied to the Kommerskollegium (commercial training institute) in Stockholm for a stipend to travel to the United States for a four- to five-year stay in Brooklyn, Boston, Chicago and San Francisco in a starting position deliberately below his own qualifications in order to gain an insight into the technology and plant organization from the bottom up, that is, from the lathe to plant optimization: 'I imagine that I would start as a cutter and filer in an American (machine) workshop in order to have more intimate contact with the detail workers there so I could study how the work is carried out by the labourers. After sufficient practice I thought I would seek a position in a drafting office in order to study the practical and theoretical work done there.' The applicant also intended 'to study American working methods, contract work and a suitable systematization of the latter for our Swedish conditions, in order to increase production performance if possible and at the same time reduce the number of workers'.[41]

Training migrations in trade and commerce also gained significance in late nineteenth-century European migration history. There was already a strong tradition, which increased further in the nineteenth century, especially regarding the circulation of international personnel for training purposes in and between larger commercial enterprises in the European and Atlantic realms, from sales trainees to mid-level employees to executive employees with entrepreneurial responsibilities. Some well-known businesspeople of this kind in the nineteenth century were, for example, the Godeffroys in Hamburg, whose company had been founded by Huguenot immigrants, and the Sinkels in Amsterdam, who came from the north German linen industry. Department stores, business firms, retail chains and networks of branches emerged with internal labour markets worldwide; at the same time, the global network of Euro-colonial, international temporary migrations within the same company also developed.

When considering the 'proletarian mass migrations' of the nineteenth and early twentieth centuries, it should be kept in mind that the area of economically motivated migrations also covered elite migrations with just as far-reaching consequences. The geographical mobility of entrepreneurs, salespeople and technical experts, the relocation or interregional and transnational expansion of company premises and the related movements of capital increased job opportunities in the destination regions of mass migrations and, at the same time, benefited from these mass movements through the markets.

2 THE MASS EXODUS TO THE NEW WORLD

Overseas emigration as a historic social movement accompanied the European path from an agrarian to an industrial society. This mass exodus was possible as a result of the revolution in transportation technology during this era. Yet the prerequisite for its rapid rise came before the onset of the industrial age, through the transatlantic bridges established by human, goods and capital movements. They enabled development between Europe and the New World to unleash its migration-inducing potential. This is the subject of this section. The first part illuminates developments from colonial emigration to mass exodus to the New World in the nineteenth and early twentieth centuries. The second part examines regions, scale and forms; the third attempts to find regional differences in migratory events and migration behaviour. Finally, the social release function of this mass exodus in the critical transition from the agrarian to the industrial age is questioned.

From the redemptioner system to mass emigration

Overseas emigration from the emerging industrial societies of Europe followed the Euro-colonial migratory traditions that had become established since the time of early European overseas expansion. Intense overseas emigration with the formation of Euro-colonial societies was continuous across the centuries only in the Spanish colonies in South and Central America. Economic forms, especially in plantation and mining production, were initially supported largely by the enslavement of indigenous populations, which had already been reduced to less than half their original size in the sixteenth century under the triple burden of forced labour, cultural oppression and imported infectious diseases. The collapse of traditional economic and social structures whose existence had greatly facilitated the Spanish take-over and control thus became predictable in some areas. As a result of the growing labour shortage, the Spanish began to import African slaves at an early stage; the Portuguese did so in Brazil from the very beginning.[42]

In the Dutch, French and English Caribbean and the southern colonies of North America, on the other hand, instead of African slaves, European indentured servants or 'engagees' were contracted, as well as convicts and Scottish and Irish prisoners of war transported from England.[43] In addition to free settlers, who paid their passage and settlement costs themselves, and employees of the state, church and/or settlement societies, indentured servants made up a considerable portion of emigrants from north-western Europe bound for America in the sixteenth and seventeenth centuries. Indentured servitude was a broad, socially differentiated system of employment. Indentured servants, male as well as female, were usually unskilled workers with insufficient or no means, although some were also skilled and a few coupled an overseas job with a contract for training. They pledged their labour with the contract dealer or ship's captain and worked off the cost of their overseas passage over three to ten years, depending on the contract. At the end of the contractual period, they were usually offered payment in kind or a corresponding sum of money and a piece of land; in Barbados in the seventeenth century, for example, they were offered either 200 kilograms of sugar or tobacco or ten pounds and ten acres of land. Contracts were sold or auctioned overseas by contract dealers or ships' captains to the highest-bidding employer, and the contractual partner had no say in the matter.

The auctioning of binding labour contracts was the auction of contract work for a period of time, and thus ultimately the auctioning of the contract labourers themselves. Breach of contract by 'running away' was considered a legal offence leading to pursuit. In some areas, indentured servitude was therefore a system of temporary slave labour. It was not identical to slavery, because the employer owned only the labour of the contractual partner for a set period of time, not the person outright. In extreme cases, however, the system could lead to servants being worked even harder and sometimes punished more severely than slaves, with whom they often worked. Employers treated their own private property – slaves and their offspring – with greater care since the servants' labour belonged to them only for a period of time, after which they owed the servants – if they survived – remuneration of some kind. But things did not always get that far. Up to 80 per cent of indentured servants died after the ordeal of the passage since they were unable to adapt to the climate or they died shortly after their arrival from tropical diseases. In addition to this, initially, 50–75 per cent of servants did not survive the harsh working conditions in the Caribbean, exacerbated by climatic problems and undernourishment.

After numerous revolts by indentured servants in Barbados in 1661, for example, manifestly deplorable conditions were regulated by a law that guaranteed servants a higher status than slaves, yet employers still had the right to transfer, rent out, sell or gamble the labour contracts of their indentured servants and thus the servants themselves. Indentured servitude could therefore still lead to slavery-like forms of forced labour, as a result of which there were a large number of breaches of contract in the form of escape, which was pursued and severely punished. This applied also to migrants who were lured into the contract system under false pretences or kidnapped outright. Sometimes they signed a contract while intoxicated after a night of drinking and found themselves in one of the harbour depots, in a contract dealer's informal private jail in the back room of a cheap inn, or else already onboard a ship. Recruitment for contract labourers sometimes took place under similar conditions as military service recruitment.

Reports about employers' non-compliance with contract conditions and about brutal exploitation and high mortality of European contracted servants in the New World brought about a decline in this form of migration, which forced employers to make concessions; their costs in the system of indentured servitude rose, so that this, too, led to an initial shift from contract labour to slave labour. The shift in the Caribbean took place relatively abruptly within one decade in the mid-seventeenth century. In the southern plantation colonies of the North American mainland, where immigration of indentured servants continued for longer, it took place around the turn of the eighteenth century. Basic elements of indentured servitude continued into the early nineteenth century in the modified and more flexible form of the redemptioner system.

In the North American colonies, the indentured servants' working conditions in the seventeenth century were determined less by deliberate intentions to emigrate than by a continuation overseas of job searches that had been unsatisfactory or totally unsuccessful in Europe, except for the above-mentioned examples of coercive migration and deportations of criminals released into the 'freedom' of overseas indentured servitude.[44] Most indentured servants remained in the country after working off their debt and became *de facto* immigrants, due to the fact that the system was generally a one-way ticket overseas, in contrast with temporary contracts to work in trading posts in the tropics, which included – if the person survived – return transportation at no charge.

The redemptioner system, the earliest traces of which go back to German immigrants to Philadelphia in the late seventeenth century, was a system of credit to finance transatlantic passage that emerged in the eighteenth century, partly in parallel with (as in Ireland) and partly replacing (as in Germany) the system of indentured servitude. It was aimed no longer primarily at those seeking work but at those desiring to emigrate. Immigrants in the redemptioner system were also obliged to repay the cost of their passage overseas through labour, either their own or their children's. But at the end of the transatlantic voyage, they were no longer faced with arbitrary auctions where their labour contracts, and indirectly they themselves, were offered to the highest bidder. Redemptioner servants, also called 'free-willers' to distinguish them from indentured servants and deported prisoners, were instead given about two weeks after arriving onboard to negotiate with employers or their agents a way to repay their debt, either by drawing up a work contract of their choice, having the debt paid off by a guarantor, or seeking help from friends and relatives. These efforts took place onboard, increasingly from the 1720s and as a general practice from the 1740s, after many redemptioners had initially 'run away' as soon as they disembarked. However, the willingness or material means of relatives or friends to pay off the redemptioners' debts or to vouch for them was often grossly overestimated. If no solution was negotiated within the time limit, the contract dealer or captain could sell the redemptioners or, as a proxy for them and for a longer time, a member of their family for the corresponding period as an indentured servant. This was the risky point, even after the American Revolution, at which individuals could plummet out of the new contract system back into the old one.[45]

Despite its clear improvements over indentured servitude, there were good reasons why the redemptioner system was referred to by contemporaries such as Isaac Wald, an English traveller to America, as the 'white slave trade'.[46] This is demonstrated by a report by Gottlieb Mittelberger, a Württemberg traveller who arrived in 1750 in Philadelphia:

When the ships have landed at Philadelphia after such a long journey at sea, no one is allowed off except those who pay their sea passage or offer good guarantors; the others, who cannot pay, must stay on the ship until they are sold and are taken from the ship by their buyers. The sick have the greatest hardship, since the healthy are always preferred and therefore sold first, and the wretched sick ones often have to stay another two or three weeks at the shore and often die. On the other hand, any one of these, if he could pay his debt and were let off the ship directly, could escape with his life.... If you can come to an agreement, it happens that grown people oblige themselves in writing to work for the sum, depending on their strength and age, for three, four, five or six years. The very young people between 10 and 15 have to serve until they are 21 years old. Many parents have to negotiate and trade their own children like livestock, so that if the children take on the burden of the parents, only the parents get to leave the ship free.

Passage costs that had to be worked off for those who died en route or who could not be referred for work due to illness had to be assumed by other family members. Families were often separated since members had different labour agreements; children under 5 who disturbed the labourers had to be given up to be raised by others, and they themselves had to work until they turned 21.[47]

The redemptioner system was the means by which ordinary people could emigrate, that is, the proletarian and landless classes who had nothing to sell to finance their dreams except a few years of their labour and their lives. In the seventeenth century, at least three-quarters of the Chesapeake Bay colonists had financed their passage with the help of labour obligations of some sort. In the eighteenth century, this was true for around half of all Europeans headed for British North America. Redemptioners made up about 50–60 per cent of all German immigrants up to the War of Independence. The redemptioner system still existed in the first two decades of the nineteenth century before abruptly disappearing with hardly a trace around 1820.[48] This background is part of the history of the rise in transatlantic mass emigration from early nineteenth-century Europe.

The transition that was apparent beginning in the 1720s from indentured servitude to the redemptioner system had clearly improved the legal standing and scope of action of most of those immigrants who could not finance their passage to the New World with their own means. However, it did little to change the 'horrors of the sea voyage' well into the nineteenth century.[49] Sailing vessel crossings remained risky and exhausting; emigration agents, redemptioner brokers and captains, who all profited from the number of 'freights', overloaded the provisionally built 'tween decks with densely packed passengers in spite of the protective, albeit undoubtedly vague, regulations passed as early as 1750–1 for

Pennsylvania. 'Ships normally used for transport weigh 150–300 tons', according to a report from 1750 on travel conditions, which already no longer corresponded to legal requirements but were by no means unusual. "Tween decks are added for this purpose, which are divided into 6–foot squares. This is the space provided for five people to sit and sleep, since they cannot stand, as the space is only 3 feet high. Additional space for children is not provided for and it is often the case that eight or more children are crowded close together with the five persons in the afore-mentioned space of 6 feet wide and 3 feet high. Thus it is easy to see that this inhumane treatment during the journey necessarily leads to a great number of passengers inevitably dying. In addition, the poor provisions should also be mentioned, made up of old and spoiled stocks. These are bought up at the lowest possible price, since controls are non-existent.'[50] On top of all this, passengers to the Americas were sometimes essentially robbed onboard, for example, when drinking water was sold by the half-litre at exorbitant prices. This served to increase the debts that had to be repaid or worked off through indentured servitude on arrival.

The average death rate of white passengers as opposed to slaves on eighteenth-century transatlantic passages was about 4 per cent for adults and more than double that figure for children. Another almost 4 per cent of passengers survived for only a short time after arrival (debarkation morbidity).[51] In the early nineteenth century, the mortality rate for the transatlantic voyage had declined by 50 per cent, but the great crush of emigrants led at the same time to catastrophes such as the deadly voyage of *The Good Intent* in 1751–2. The ship had boarded more than 200 passengers in Rotterdam and was scheduled to dock in Philadelphia in the autumn of 1751. However, it did not reach the US coastline until after the onset of winter and had to set course for an island in the West Indies after making several futile attempts to steer through the frozen Phila-delphia harbour. When *The Good Intent* finally anchored in Philadelphia in June 1752, there were only 19 passengers on board. The rest, including a few crew members and the captain, had not survived the odyssey.[52] On 6 March 1818, three Dutch ships arrived in New Orleans; 1,100 passengers, mostly redemptioners, had boarded in Den Helder, 503 of whom perished en route, having 'died, starved to death, or been driven to jump overboard by despair or fever or insane thirst'.[53]

In the years following this tragedy, the number of redemptioners appeared to drop sharply until reaching a low in 1821. Theories abound in the relevant literature as to the reasons for the apparently abrupt end to the system, whereby an organized Atlantic labour market that had lasted for almost a century and a half had totally collapsed within a few years.[54] The image of a sudden end was particularly reinforced by a final upsurge in the number of redemptioners from south-western Germany in the period directly preceding the collapse. This was part of the mass flight from the agrarian crisis of 1816–17, which we shall explore in more detail. Especially hard hit by this crisis was the southern Rhineland. This was a classic emigration region, the home of the immigrant population from south-western Germany known in colonial North America as the 'Palatines'. The Napoleonic Wars brought about great disruption and general poverty in this area. Military units of different combatant nations repeatedly marched through south-western Germany, leaving a trail of devastation and impoverishment in their wake.[55] After coming to a temporary standstill, emigration grew after the wars into a wave that had been steadily building up in this region. The pressure of the severe agricultural crisis in 1816–17 then turned it into a regional mass exodus.

The crisis of 1816–17 came in the aftermath of the cold, wet year of 1816, which resulted in minimal harvest yields throughout Europe. In London there was snow in August during this 'year without a summer', when John Quincy Adams declared that there was 'not one evening and scarcely a day in 1816 when a fire would have been superfluous'. The grape harvest came later than ever, the summer was the coldest since temperature records were kept, and 1816 was the wettest year since the 'minor ice age' of the mid-1670s.[56] As we now know, these climatic conditions were triggered by the eruption of the Tambora volcano on Java in 1815, which caused a kind of 'nuclear winter' in the 'summer' of 1816. While most depressed areas were able to avert the spectre of famine in the winter of 1816–17 by importing grain from elsewhere in Europe and overseas, the crisis turned into a catastrophe in the southern Rhineland. Summer rains led to disastrous flooding and unusually poor harvests, grain stores had been exhausted since the final years of war, and early frosts and harsh weather conditions delayed grain imports via Baltic ports until the spring. Food shortages and famine drove prices through the roof. The inflation was followed by a crisis in the crafts and trades. Crop failure and famine were bad tidings for agrarian societies; followed by inflation, under- and unemployment and general impoverishment, they set in motion the 'old type' of classic crisis spiral in agriculture and trade that Germany would face for the last time in 1846–7.

Traditional continental and transatlantic migratory paths turned into escape routes from these crisis areas. Desperate masses headed for Russia along the continental west–east migration routes and to the Habsburg territories in the Balkans.[57] Most emigrants moved down the Rhine, however, seeking an escape 'to America' as redemptioners via Dutch ports. Almost two-thirds of emigrants from Württemberg headed towards eastern and south-eastern Europe, while most of those from Baden went to the United States. This was not just because of the growing pull of the New World, but also had to do with the transportation and geographical aspects of migration traditions. The journey down the Rhine offered people from Baden a convenient connection to northern seaports, while the trend among Württembergers was still towards the continental west–east migratory route and thus the Danube shipping route. Transportation geography was more significant in these cases than religious affiliation, which would have sent the emigrants in precisely the opposite directions – the Protestants from Württemberg to the British colonies and the Catholics from Baden to eastern and south-eastern Europe.[58]

Because of the mass of people wanting to emigrate, conditions in the overseas ports on both sides of the Atlantic were catastrophic. The redemptioner system was not an instrument for absorbing mass migration; instead, it was a system of transportation on credit, dependent on demand in the destination region and thus on the market. Consequently, the sudden surplus ruined chances for profit when selling the labour contracts of passengers who did not have the wherewithal to finance all or part of their passage and who had no relatives or friends to pay off their debts. The collapse of the contract market began as early as 1817, when emigration from Baden and Württemberg was still developing with a dynamic of its own. Although impoverished travellers to the United States were turned back at the borders, soon thousands wanting to emigrate were stuck in Dutch ports. A greater number of ships' captains refused to take passengers under redemptioner conditions, demanding prepayment that would-be emigrants either lacked or no longer possessed, since they had spent everything in getting to and waiting in the port cities. The poor who were refused passage were obliged to return home as beggars. When they finally arrived, in a wretched state, they were often treated unsympathetically and even ridiculed, since many had begun their journey down the Rhine with defiant songs of emigration and loud protests against their pitiful living conditions.

In 1817, the overcrowded redemptioner ships brought the highest annual volume thus far of German emigrants to the United States. In Baden alone, 16,361 legal emigrants – that is, having official emigration authorization – were registered by early May 1817. By July there were 17,216 in Württemberg, more than half of whom headed for Russia and the Habsburg Empire, yet around 6,000 had given 'America' as their destination. Friedrich Kapp spoke of a total of 'over 20,000' immigrants to the United States from south-western Germany in 1816–17. They usually arrived in just as miserable a state as those unsuccessful emigrants who returned to their German hometowns. Henry Fearon described the landing of German redemptioners at the piers of Philadelphia in the autumn of 1817: 'Their clothes, if rags deserve that denomination, actually perfumed the air. Some were without shirts, others had articles of dress, but of a quality as coarse as the worst packing cloth. . . . Their countenances fell to that standard of stupid gloom which seemed to place them a link below rational beings.'[59]

Many of those who had someone to pay their way out of the threat of indentured servitude could not find a job to work off their debts. Those who were able to finance their passage but arrived without means and without a job were in similarly dire straits. Both groups added to the urban sub-proletariat in Philadelphia, who were kept under the watchful and increasingly suspicious eyes of citizens and authorities to the extent that they were not, as a German businessman living in the city wrote to the king of Württemberg in 1817, 'lucky enough to become part of the local corps of municipal street-sweepers, all of whom have been such German adventurers'.[60] German-American societies sounded the alarm in view of such circumstances, less for reasons of philanthropic empathy than from outrage at the harm done to their group's reputation in the New World through the 'flood' of social 'dregs' from the Old World.[61]

The collapse of the contract market in the United States under the pressure of the 'emigration wave' of 1817 was merely the final nail in the coffin of the redemptioner system.[62] Since the second half of the eighteenth century, there had been various legal albeit vague and, especially with respect to the 'tween decks, easily circumvented regulations from the American side regarding the maximum allowable number of passengers, depending on cargo space, and limitations on the duration of indentured servitude. These regulations reduced the profit margins of contract dealers and captains and made it harder to sell contracts. This led to corresponding risk surcharges (approximately 15 per cent) and often also to a further deterioration of transport conditions as well as cheating of passengers by all manner of tricks. Such deplorable conditions continually worsened the reputation of the system and encouraged would-be emigrants all the more to find other secure ways of prefinancing their overseas passage.

The misery of redemptioner landings during the immigration peak in 1816–17 quickly led to protective regulations, first for the passage, then for indentured servitude, and finally also for imprisonment for debt, which was limited and later totally abolished. As a result, contract dealers and captains saw their chances for profit dwindle even further while employers' costs continued to rise. Various shipowners and redemptioner brokers went bankrupt. Interest in emigration to the New World even declined for a short time in south-western Germany, especially since the US economic crisis of 1818–19 made immigration conditions even worse. At the same time, the European agrarian upswing resumed after 1819, including in the southern Rhineland.[63] Would-be emigrants were also lured by alternative offers, not only in eastern and south-eastern Europe but also in Brazil. Here, the '*parceria* system' (sharecropping system) developed, which in some ways resembled indentured servitude. Workers, especially Germans and Swiss, were exploited in a form of servitude that resembled temporary slavery with despotic working conditions and time regulations. It ultimately stirred the Prussian government in 1859 to issue a general yet relatively ineffective ban on emigration to Brazil through the 'Von der Heydtian edict' that remained in force until 1896.[64]

When European emigration to America grew from the 1830s into a historic mass movement, the redemptioner system had already disappeared, while the organizational and transportation-related conditions of transatlantic migration were entering a period of far-reaching change. Financing the passage after arrival (the redemptioner system) was increasingly replaced by prepayment, or remittance, prior to the voyage. A prerequisite for this system was the transatlantic networks that developed as a result of chain migrations.[65] Increased transatlantic communication in the form of letters from would-be emigrants to previously emigrated friends and relatives (kinship market) facilitated prefinancing of the passage, of which prepaid tickets ('prepaids') would become the most popular form. After the end of the Napoleonic Wars, the concentration of the networks was greatly enhanced by the increase in transatlantic travel, trade and bank connections, which made money transfers and prepayment arrangements much easier than the extremely risky route of agents and private messengers. The remittance system was widespread among the Irish as early as the 1820s, and in 1834 it made up one-third of Irish sailing vessel passages from Belfast, which was a higher share than that of financing passages through labour obligations in the 1770s.[66]

Other changes influenced the volume of travel and price structures. When European mass emigration climbed in the 1830s, the main structural changes to transatlantic travel were already in full swing and continued to accelerate through the rising demand. This brought about the transition to larger, faster ships built primarily for passenger and postal transport, and especially the general advancement of steam navigation on the transatlantic routes in the 1860s. The German Hamburg-America line (HAPAG) also abandoned the use of sailing vessels for the transatlantic journey in 1867. In the same year, the voyage from Europe to the United States under sail took on average 44 days, but only 14 by steamer. In the 1880s, New York could be reached from northern Europe within ten days, and after the turn of the century, within a week.[67] With the reduction of the transatlantic passage and price wars between ship-owners leading to a drop in price for transatlantic tickets, it became increasingly possible for people to finance their journeys with their own savings. Europe's destitute, however, with no means to afford even the reduced prices or have their passage prefinanced, had virtually no chance of emigrating once indentured servitude and the redemptioner system came to an end, and especially once the United States began to require a minimum start capital as a condition of entry.[68]

The changes in volume of traffic and prices for transatlantic travel facilitated the rise in Atlantic mass migrations of the nineteenth and early twentieth centuries. They must be seen against the backdrop of deeper-rooted economic and commercial developments.[69] The abandonment of mercantilist restrictions and advancing liberalization in the century of the bourgeoisie brought down barriers to emigration and trade. In the British Isles, the most significant area of emigration, the path to free trade went through a succession of stages from relaxing the customs tariff in 1819, liberalization of the Navigation Acts beginning in 1822 (and their repeal in 1849) to the end of grain duties with the repeal of the Corn Laws in 1846 and the lifting of controls on grain importation in 1849. In the second most significant emigration region, Prussian Germany, it took the route from the liberal Prussian Trade and Tariff Act of 1818 to the German Customs Union of 1834.

The result of this and other forms of foreign trade liberalization was an explosive expansion of European and intercontinental commodity trading and capital export. Britain led the way once the focus of European business finance had shifted to London following the Napoleonic Wars. After the end of the slave trade, transatlantic transfer of goods, capital and emigrants replaced the classic Atlantic triangle of trade in the seventeenth and eighteenth centuries. Export of capital, finished products and human resources from Europe corresponded especially to the parallel importation of raw materials (such as cotton, grains, tobacco) in the other direction. Capital export financed the development and expansion of overseas agricultural production and, with respect to the United States, industrial production as well. European markets opened their borders for products from overseas, while mass emigration abroad answered the need for labour and at the same time created an emerging mass market.

A visible symbol of the connection between the flows of goods and of people was the aforementioned 'tween decks, avoided by better-off emigrants and transatlantic travellers. The ever-growing cargo shipments transported from the New World to Europe led to a surplus of cargo space on the return voyages that served to transport emigrants. The 'tween decks that were provisionally added to the cargo space offered an additional source of transport income, and virtually the only cost was that of their installation. Conversely, European emigrant ships that had been converted in this way were transformed for the return journey into freighters with a few cabins for the better-off passengers. 'Tween decks finally fell out of use with the advent of purely passenger ship navigation, with its respective ticket classes corresponding largely to class society. The definitive acceleration in the growth in European mass emigration came when the steam engine was mounted on wheels and ship planks. The railroad and steamship eased travel in two ways: the network of overseas passages became increasingly faster, better developed and more comfortable and at the same time less expensive; and overseas ports were linked to the expanding inland navigation and rail networks on both sides of the Atlantic.

Aside from temporary drops in emigration after the American War of Independence and throughout the Napoleonic Wars, transatlantic migratory traditions developed beginning in the mid-eighteenth century and became firmly established in the early nineteenth. In addition to 'emigrant letters' from friends and relatives, which were often passed from hand to hand, commercial means of communication also played a part through the network of emigration agents and shipping company representatives that was rapidly expanding in the nineteenth century. Moreover, there was a wealth of informative literature, partly commercial and partly independent, with practical tips on routes and financing methods, as well as opportunities and risks of overseas emigration.[70]

This served to satisfy what in many respects was a unique accumulation of the basic prerequisites for the free development of migratory movements in the Atlantic economy in the first half of the nineteenth century: the desire and freedom to emigrate in the home regions, the need for immigrants and the still largely unconditional acceptance of immigrants in the accessible destination regions, the heavy flow of information and calculable costs with a high level of transfer as a result of the integration of migratory, capital and goods flows.[71] Once it got going, the transatlantic mass movement developed its own dynamic up to the First World War, until post-war migration controls and limitations strove to subdue it (see chapter 3, section 2).

Regions, scale and forms

The 'classic' home regions of nineteenth-century overseas emigration were – with the exception of France, which hardly experienced any mass emigration at all – the areas in Europe that had a clear head start along the path towards the industrial age until the late 1880s. Only a small portion of mass overseas emigration from these areas of western, central and northern Europe came from the industrial centres themselves, however, which were in turn destination areas for interregional migration. Emigrants came primarily from peripheral regions that were often also regions of origin for internal migrations, such as Ireland. The most significant destinations of overseas emigration until it declined considerably in the late nineteenth century were in North America, and here especially the United States clearly ahead of Canada. From the 1860s Australia and New Zealand gained ground, joined in the 1870s by immigration countries in South America, which had had mixed populations since the colonial period. Argentina and Brazil were of particular importance for emigration from southern Europe (especially Spain and Portugal), which had been growing prolifically since the 1880s and 1890s. Correspondingly, the share of emigrants to the United States dwindled, from about 80 per cent of all European emigration prior to 1850 to about three-quarters in the period 1851–90 to roughly a half after that.

As job opportunities in Europe grew in the course of industrialization, the migration-inducing tension between the United States and the developing centres in western, central and northern Europe decreased, and overseas emigration declined dramatically in the 1890s, except in Britain. Emigration from southern, south-eastern and eastern European regions – referred to as the 'new immigration' in the United States – emerged with even greater force starting in the 1880s and especially the 1890s, corresponding by and large to the north–south and west–east differentials in the industrialization process. In the first decade of the twentieth century, European emigration experienced its most intensive period of development. A total of only about one-third of all emigrants came from Great Britain and continental north-western Europe, within which the previously large share of German emigrants had sunk to about 2 per cent. Roughly two-thirds of European emigrants now came from southern Europe (41 per cent) and eastern, east central and south-eastern Europe (approximately 25 per cent).[72] These were often simultaneously regions of origin for labour migrations within Europe, so that a dual centre–periphery dichotomy emerged: to transatlantic as well as western, central and northern European destinations. Up to 1880 US immigration statistics showed fewer than 150,000 emigrants from Austria-Hungary and tsarist Russia. In the 1890s, the figures had already risen to 593,000 and 602,000, respectively. In the first decade of the twentieth century, when the new immigration reached its peak, US statistics registered 2,145,000 immigrants from Austria-Hungary and 1,597,000 from Russia, including a total of 976,000 Jews and 874,000 Poles.

Emigration from eastern Europe via German seaports to the United States makes up a special chapter referred to in Germany as 'transit migration' (or transmigration). As German overseas emigration began to wane in the early 1890s, the Hanseatic transatlantic lines became desperate for transit migrants from eastern, east central and south-eastern Europe; the result was a bitter competition, in which international overseas shipping companies tried to crowd each other out. Transit migrants were recruited and ruthlessly prodded in their home countries by an army of legally and illegally operating agents.[73] From 1894 to 1910, only 11 per cent (380,907) of overseas emigrants from German ports were German, while 89 per cent were other nationalities (2,752,256). In order to fill the German emigrant ships, agents for German shipping lines in eastern, east central and south-eastern Europe began to employ tactics for which North American emigrant recruiters in Germany in the nineteenth century had been criminally prosecuted. They were no less successful and no less unscrupulous in their recruitment methods, and were therefore similarly scrutinized by the governments of emigration countries in eastern and south-eastern Europe. Even Heinrich Wiegand, director of the North German Lloyd line, felt obliged to concede that '[i]n Galicia we work with the scum of humanity', referring to his agents and human smugglers.[74]

The burgeoning new immigration from southern, south-eastern and eastern Europe met with growing rejection in the United States from the 1890s. This was especially true after the economic crisis of the 1890s, which reduced this mass immigration only insignificantly. Rejection was due to economic and social fears and nativist xenophobia, combined with religious rejection, political and ideological differences and racist prejudice. It was an explosive mixture, at the centre of which were serious misunderstandings.

Except for the Jewish immigration from eastern Europe, 90 per cent of all new arrivals between 1899 and 1909 from economically less developed home regions in southern, south-eastern and eastern Europe were unskilled labourers. Their only work experience was often in agriculture using antiquated production methods. The social and career structures of these new immigrants corresponded to the economic and social structures of their home regions; this was misunderstood in nativist US discourse as a kind of negative social and career selection. On the other hand, the much-cited counter-image of 'classic' immigration from north-western Europe was clearly exaggerated. At least by the final third of the nineteenth century, this had long since become a 'mature' migration movement, with sophisticated social and career structures that sometimes corresponded more to the demands of the destination region. This had partly to do with the decline in socio-economic developmental tension between north-western Europe and the United States. According to the Dillingham Commission Report of 1911, only 30 per cent of German immigrants to the United States had any industrial experience.

British immigrants were the group with by far the most experience in industry, and they remained virtually alone.[75] The heavy transatlantic fluctuation and the high level of return migration of especially southern Europeans, which will be discussed later, was not a characteristic specific to new immigration and was certainly not an expression of a lack of willingness or even 'ability' to become integrated in the New World. It simply reinforced a general trend and was able to develop more clearly from the outset with respect to new immigration precisely because this mass movement evolved at a time when frequent, inexpensive and fast transatlantic passages limited wage losses due to travel time.

In addition to this aggressive equation of less advanced development in their places of origin with inferiority, migrants were identified as being insufficiently loyal to their new country on account of their high level of return migration. Nativist and racist sentiments intensified basic economic and social fears about the mass new immigration into the United States, since migrants accepted working conditions that American social reformers and trade unions had long been fighting against. Starting in the 1890s, demands for immigration restrictions became increasingly louder and reached a peak in the debate on the report issued in 1911 by the Dillingham Commission following a three-and-a-half-year study. This report became an important milestone in immigration discourse and led to legislation instituting restrictive quotas in the 1920s. According to a main recommendation of the commission, it was important that immigration did not hinder the 'assimilation process', whereby 'assimilation' was used to mean 'Americanization'.[76]

Comprehensive data on the volume and course of Atlantic mass migrations in the nineteenth and twentieth centuries are available everywhere and yet the figures are unreliable. Even in the age of official emigration, immigration and census data, official figures on overseas emigration are questionable even at a national level, let alone for all of Europe, although overseas emigration was presumed to be easily controllable since everyone had to move through the narrow passageways of overseas ports. Methods of collecting data varied from place to place; terms such as 'emigrant' and 'immigrant' were often defined insufficiently and in a number of different ways, sometimes including visitors or business travellers or failing to subtract those who returned to Europe. Corrections on the basis of passenger lists from the countries receiving overseas emigrants are possible only to a limited extent since they have their own problems, from using incomplete, misunderstood or falsely transcribed data given by the immigrants themselves to incorrectly identifying immigrants' country of origin by registering them according to their native tongue.[77]

In Germany, for example, one of the main countries of European emigration, even after the German Empire was founded in 1871, there were neither any statistics on transatlantic returnees[78] nor comprehensive statistics on emigration in the strict sense. The only statistics available were on emigration via German seaports. However, a considerable portion of German emigrants left Europe in the first few decades of the nineteenth century via other western European ports, especially Antwerp, Rotterdam and Le Havre. This was not only because German transatlantic passenger navigation was not as developed as elsewhere; with respect to French ports, it also resulted from the predominance of overseas emigrants from south-western Germany during the first half of the century. As of mid-century, Hamburg and especially Bremen, with its direct rail connection from Leipzig and Cologne, became by far the biggest departure ports for German overseas emigration. Yet the proportion of foreign ports used by German emigrants remained significant, fluctuating around 20 per cent in the period from 1880 to 1910.[79] This was also largely due to 'clandestine emigration' by those aiming to evade the compulsory three-year military service in Prussia. Dutch agents in the late nineteenth century explicitly advertised offers to help those eligible for military service to escape by emigrating via Rotterdam, which was prohibited by law in Prussia.

In the late nineteenth and early twentieth centuries, in turn, in European countries of emigration with a high level of transatlantic labour and shuttle migration, for example from Italy to Argentina, transatlantic labour migrants were often registered more than once as 'emigrants'. For some this amounted to more than a dozen emigrations within a lifetime. Because the cost of overseas passage fell so drastically in the last three decades of the nineteenth century, the boundaries between definitive emigration and transatlantic labour migration became increasingly blurred. It was not uncommon for people really to experience multiple emigrations, for instance if emigrants reconsidered their decision because they were disappointed, or if they were enticed by news from the former homeland to return to Europe, only to 'emigrate' later, again perhaps not for good. In other words, what in retrospect might seem like temporary transatlantic labour migration might have been planned and experienced by the actual emigrant as a permanent emigration or return.[80]

In 1996, Walter Nugent compared recent studies estimating the volume of European overseas emigration in the nineteenth and early twentieth centuries. One of them assumed that from 1846 to 1924, a total of about 55 million people left Europe (gross emigration), one-quarter of whom later returned (return migration, or repatriation), so that the actual number of emigrants was 41 million (net emigration). A second estimated a total number of 55–60 million Europeans who crossed the Atlantic westward in the period 1820–1930; a third referred to 65 million gross and 50 million net for the 1800–1914 period.[81] Leslie Page Moch cited Magnus Mörner's figure of roughly 52 million gross for the 1824–1924 period, of whom about 37 million (72 per cent) were destined for North America (United States and Canada), 11 million (21 per cent) for South America and 3.5 million, mostly of British descent, for Australia and New Zealand.[82] This corresponds approximately to the partly extrapolated total figures that had been calculated from official statistics around 1930 by Imre Ferenczi and Walter Willcox, according to which a total of about 55 million Europeans (gross) emigrated overseas between 1820 and 1924.[83] There is much to support Dudley Baines's estimate that the actual number of Europeans who emigrated overseas from 1815 to 1930 is closer to 60 million.[84] Heiko Körner, too, came to the conclusion that a total of about 63 million gross and 50–55 million net emigrated overseas between 1820 and 1915.[85] His 1990 international comparison was based on earlier estimates.

Standard descriptions of European overseas migrations of the nineteenth and early twentieth centuries refer to the image of wavelike movements.[86] Overseas emigration in the first third of the nineteenth century remained relatively low, with an average annual volume of about 50,000 emigrants (gross). As in the late eighteenth century, individual countries of emigration sometimes experienced short periods of mass emigration as a result of domestic crises, as in 1816–17, for example, in south-western Germany. The first European emigration wave began in 1846. Compared with preceding decades, the average annual volume of emigration from 1846 to 1850 had already climbed fivefold (256,000 gross), and in the 1851–5 period almost sevenfold (342,000 gross). Up to the start of the First World War there was a steady rise, despite spasmodic interruptions. The final level of each wave was always higher than the starting level so that the curve increased overall.

From 1856 to 1860, which included the 'first world economic crisis' (Hans Rosenberg) of 1857–9, European emigration sunk to an annual average of 201,000, which was still four times higher than the annual average in the first three decades of the century. The American Civil War (1861–5) did its bit to put a temporary stop to the rise in emigration. With a renewed economic upswing and following the Homestead Act of 1862 to promote settlement in the United States, a second wave of European emigration started after the war (1866–75). From 1871 to 1875 it brought an annual average of 372,000 emigrants overseas. In the middle of the first phase (1873–9) of the Atlantic period of economic growth disturbances (1873–95/96), this second wave dropped back to a relatively high plateau from 1876 to 1880, from which an even steeper emigration wave (1880–90) emerged. It arched over the less pronounced second critical phase (1882–6), and from 1886 to 1890 it brought a yearly average of 779,000 Europeans overseas, primarily to the United States.

The first Atlantic crisis (1873–9) hit north-western Europe, which was still the predominant region of emigration, and the United States, the main country of immigration, almost equally hard. On the other hand, the third critical phase from 1890 to 1896, with its peak in the panic of 1893, hit the United States far harder than it did the economic area of north-western Europe. Overseas emigration from there had been steadily decreasing since the 1880s relative to emigration from southern, south-eastern, east central and eastern Europe, which became the central focus of transatlantic migration. This new immigration to the United States fell off after the end of the third phase of economic crisis in 1896 to a yearly average in the period 1896–1900 of only 602,000; it then developed into the fourth and final – and also the largest – European wave of emigration from 1900 to 1915. From 1906 to 1910 an annual average of 1,389,000 Europeans emigrated overseas, and from 1911 to 1915, despite the outbreak of war in 1914, an average of 1,345,000 continued to emigrate. The migration tailback during the war reduced the annual average for 1916–20 to 431,000. In the early 1920s another wave of overseas emigration that peaked in the first half of the 1920s again reached the high level of the third wave after 1880; following the 1929 stock market crash and the Great Depression, it dwindled to a trickle.

Describing emigration patterns as 'waves' might be vivid, but it has often led to misunderstanding when at the same time it is assumed that there were direct, parallel 'migration causes'. This applies, for example, to attempts to explain the occasionally abrupt rise of an emigration wave on the basis of a presumed increase in particular, parallel driving forces (push–pull combinations), or even the one-sided intensification of a crisis situation in the emigration country. It is problematic to explain abrupt fluctuations in emigration curves on the basis of changes in 'migration causes' presumed to be simultaneous, apart from critical events that actually did have a direct impact, such as in 1816–17 in south-western Germany. This is because emigration was not an isolated event but a medium- or often long-term process. It spanned from developing a latent inclination to emigrate to the decision to emigrate, which was often event-related, to actually emigrating at a point in time when the decision itself, its deeper-seated 'causes' and actual triggers, might go back a long time, even years. In regions with a stable emigration tradition and intensive transatlantic communications, on the other hand, as shall be shown, disturbing influences ('intervening factors') in the destination regions could lead to abrupt changes in collective migratory behaviour that had nothing to do with changes in 'emigration causes'.

In the history of German overseas emigration, for instance, from the emergence of the mass movement in the early 1840s to its end in the early 1890s, there was basically only one major 'emigration wave' with a number of peaks and event-related troughs. A tailback caused by obstacles to migration could, after the obstruction had been cleared, abruptly release a powerful onrush that then appeared as an independent 'emigration wave', although it had been affected in part by decisions to emigrate that might have been made years earlier. This was the case during the American Civil War, for example, which caused such a tailback of prospective emigrants from 1861 to 1863 in Germany that a second nineteenth-century German emigration wave emerged in 1864, even before the war ended, during which more than 1 million people emigrated within the following ten years. Similar examples are the decline in the German emigration curve at the beginning of the crisis period from 1873 to 1879 and its renewed ascent in 1880 to form the third and largest wave of German overseas emigration in the nineteenth century, which then ended suddenly in 1893. In this context, the severe economic crisis in the United States in the early 1890s, with its peak in 1893, was only one of several triggering factors, as German emigration did not climb again even after the crisis was over. The reasons lay in the prolonged and intense growth of the German economy in the late nineteenth and early twentieth centuries. The disparity between population growth and job opportunities was entirely turned around, and Prussian Germany changed from a country of emigration to a 'labour-importing country'. My own assessment that the wavelike fluctuations in emigration from nineteenth-century Europe were basically one single, large emigration wave interrupted by various obstacles has also been supported recently by Heiko Körner.[87]

If economic and migration movements throughout the history of European emigration are compared, clear parallels can be drawn from the 1850s to the severe decline in overseas emigration from western, central and northern Europe – with the exception of Britain – in the 1890s. The progress of economic activity was less a causal than an intervening factor; economic crises in destination regions usually caused emigration to fade in the short or medium term. Subsequent phases of economic recovery or prosperity with a renewed rise in job opportunities generally also brought about a renewed increase in emigration as the potential that had been blocked during the crisis was all the more forcefully unleashed. This could clearly be observed with respect to the economic crises of the late 1850s, 1870s and early 1890s. One problem with interpreting migration processes with an eye to economic history is in how to deal with highly aggregated data on migration from major regions with different economic and social structures. The western, central and northern areas of Europe from which the 'old' emigration movements set out were, in some respects, similar in many ways to the United States. Though the United States progressed from agrarian to industrial society more rapidly than these parts of Europe, they were nevertheless related in terms of structure and course of developments. This comprehensive picture of the Atlantic realm was eclipsed from the 1890s by the new immigration from southern, south-eastern, east central and eastern Europe, which, for example, hardly reacted at all to the economic crisis in the United States in the early 1890s.

Emigration regions and transatlantic networks

Baines has succinctly characterized the basic structures of overseas mass emigration from nineteenth- and early twentieth-century Europe: 'The most important characteristic of European migration was diversity.'[88] It is clear that we actually know very little about the driving forces behind the transatlantic exodus by the mere fact that the vast majority of Europeans stayed in Europe and did not leave behind the very conditions that research has assumed to have driven people to emigrate. By far most Europeans remained in the Old World, adapted to its conditions, tried to change them within the bounds of possibility or escape them by migrating within Europe.

A series of changes took place in the structure of transatlantic migration from the early nineteenth to the early twentieth centuries. Emigration from western, central and northern Europe changed from what was sometimes still religiously and socially motivated group migration in the late eighteenth and early nineteenth centuries to family and then to individual migration. Relatively parallel to this was a shift in the migration outcome from rural settlement migration to industrial labour migration. There was also a shift in migration behaviour from definitive emigration or immigration to a great increase in temporary labour migration and even transatlantic shuttle migration.

Theses changes in structure, movement patterns and migration behaviour were partly weakened and partly strengthened from the 1890s by the emergence of transatlantic migration from southern, south-eastern, east central and eastern Europe. The gradually increasing proportion of transatlantic emigration and labour migration from urban-industrial regions, for example, was eclipsed in the overall picture by 'new' emigration from rural areas. As a result of the change in occupation structures in the United States as receiving country, there was a rise in the tendency towards unskilled work in the urban-industrial sphere and temporary transatlantic labour migration, which made up about 40 per cent of migration from southern Europe after the turn of the century.[89]

Beyond real, often mostly general employment and socially oriented individual reasons, goals and plans, the motivation to emigrate as reflected in popular contemporary reading ranged from ideas about greater personal freedom and opportunities, to better chances on the marriage market, to the idea that everything in the New World was somehow 'bigger and better'. This is why labourers who migrated to the expanding industrial centres within Europe occasionally referred to the settlements they built up from scratch as 'Little America'.[90] Early surveys of emigrants, such as the survey conducted by Friedrich List, former Royal Württemberg audit councillor and later political economist, attest to this complexity of reasons. List was commissioned by his king to poll emigrants at the time of the mass emigration from southwestern Germany in 1817. From 1825 to 1832, List himself lived as a farmer, editor and businessman in Pennsylvania, from where he later returned to Leipzig as an American consul. Among the most frequent responses he received in 1817 was long suppressed discontent with economic and social conditions, intensified by military events, and as the final straw, the severe agrarian crisis. All of this, combined with the notion that they had reliable sources of information about the road leading 'to America', sealed the emigrants' decision to leave their homelands. In addition to this, a variety of motivations that could be viewed as psychological might also have played a role, such as a kind of personal settling of accounts in respect of restrictions or degradation that had been experienced, with emigration being used as a form of social protest.[91]

In the nineteenth century, too, the dream that had underpinned the colonial migratory cycles of the seventeenth and eighteenth centuries still existed to some extent; this was the dream of becoming rich, or at least attaining a degree of prosperity overseas, and investing the money back home or living off it abroad in a life of conspicuous consumption.[92] The fact that the intention to return was rarely put into effect in the first half of the nineteenth century was one consequence of the attraction of the New World and the new relationships formed there. More than that, as noted above, until after the mid-nineteenth century it was a result of the costs and conditions of transatlantic voyage. For those who had invested all their savings to finance their journey and for redemptioners who had to pay off the costs of their passage through years of labour, return migration was hardly an option in so far as any prospects at all opened up in their new home. Over the course of the nineteenth century, opposing trends developed: the more emigration led to leaving Europe permanently and successfully starting a new life overseas, the more the New World became a recognized alternative to the Old World. At the same time, however, as transatlantic passages became more frequent, shorter and less expensive, it became financially possible for mass emigration to develop into circular migration.[93]

The difficult, older or 'pre-industrial' rural migration with family settlements showed the lowest amount of return migration. Return figures were much higher for 'modern' or 'industrial' migrations that tended to end in secondary or tertiary urban sectors and were more individual. These increased considerably in the late nineteenth century, apart from training migrations or business travel to branch offices, which were intended as temporary journeys from the outset. The highest level of return migrations was among economic, speculative individual migrations. These followed concrete, albeit fluctuating, socio-economic opportunities or the lure of high wages, and increased in the early twentieth century. This overall picture of development trends in the shift from 'rural' to 'urban-industrial' migration behaviour is broken by national and regional emigration potential from very different social structures and milieus, especially as European emigration shifted from the north-west to eastern, east central and south-eastern regions.

When reports of successful emigrations led to chain migrations and then to transatlantic migration networks, decisions to emigrate lost some of their radical character. Even minor reasons were sufficient to decide 'to travel to America'. In other words, where comparing life situations or opportunities had become a basic pattern for developing life plans, or rather life dreams, in which emigration was not only possible but had become a common pattern of behaviour, then emigration in any life situation could be seen as a key to solving problems or opening up solutions, even if under some circumstances it might only be an escape from inevitable decisions to distant substitute or would-be solutions. With such a dynamic of transatlantic and cross-border migratory processes developing within Europe, it is fitting to speak of self-driving factors or 'multiplier effects'. Even people who were not sufficiently motivated to emigrate could find themselves being pulled along as if by a chain reaction. The contagious swelling of migration movements often prompted contemporary observers to use sickness metaphors such as 'migration fever'.[94]

Any attempt to infer intentions to emigrate by drawing comparisons between the economic structure of the home region and migration outcomes in the destination region poses problems. Intention and outcome of migration often diverged. For example, for emigrants who had little or no land in the home region, the lure of the 'frontier' notion of homesteading on government land in the United States can hardly be overstated. US census data on the occupation and settlement structures of the immigrant population reveal astounding discrepancies between migration intentions that could supposedly be attributed to rural background (land acquisition, independent agricultural production) and actual outcome of the emigration (work in urban industry or service sector). Before the 'frontier' movement gave way to other currents of internal migration within the United States, the settlement focus of the US-born offspring of immigrant groups encouraged them to move westward, freeing space that would later be taken up by new immigrants. This was the case not only in agriculture and rural businesses, but also in urban secondary and tertiary sectors. 'Even if individual immigrant groups in certain periods took an active interest in settling the land', observed Alexander and Eugen Kulischer, 'most of them played a rearguard role in the American colonization movement, both geographically and economically. They provided the labour for industry that developed on the east coast based on the growth in the market that resulted from the expanding westward colonization.'[95]

The dream of a free homestead settlement on government land in the American West bore little comparison with the harsh reality of the 'frontier', and in the late 1880s it often came to resemble a romantic agrarian utopia. Many emigrants from rural areas might still have been drawn to the New World by the hope of regaining the rural 'Old World' that was threatened or had already disappeared at home. But for many, emigration represented precisely that step into modernity that they had wanted to avoid by going overseas. Alternative options for taking this step were increasingly being offered by the growing urban-industrial labour markets of Europe, which could easily be reached by rail simply by purchasing reduced labourer tickets that were often paid for by the new employer.

Regional studies show that at the time of the European mass exodus, some Atlantic migratory systems exhibited fluid boundaries between intercontinental and interregional migration.[96] Emigrants were recruited partly from regions and social environments that also had heavy interregional mobility. Transnational and interregional migration movements could be interconnected, but they could also be relatively unrelated, running parallel to each other. Interregional mobility could also be a preliminary step to overseas labour migration or emigration by stages, in which migrants 'worked their way towards' regions of overseas emigration or overseas ports. Studies on emigration from port cities show, for example, that many male and female emigrants who originated there according to the statistics had actually only migrated there a short time earlier or had merely worked there to save money for emigration or for a new life overseas. Because there is a particularly strong corpus of data, such stage migrations can be documented above all for Scandinavia. This pattern appears to have been highly significant for young female emigrants. After migrating from the countryside to the cities, they could work as maids to earn money for their passage to a fresh start overseas. No assessment has been made of the extent to which such transitions between European labour migration and overseas emigration were the result of long-term migration plans, or whether they arose out of dissatisfaction with the interregional labour migration while simultaneously allowing the migrants to become familiarized with the idea of emigration.

Regional studies also show that occasionally clear-cut priorities were established or that European and transatlantic migratory movements existed as unrelated parallel alternatives. Interregional and transatlantic migratory traditions led to clear distinctions among the respective home regions in which European and transatlantic movements followed each other step by step, replaced each other or overlapped; or they were juxtaposed as parallel alternatives. For the region of 'old' European emigration this can be demonstrated by British-Irish and Prussian-Germans; for 'new' emigration, by Poles and Italians.

Britain and Ireland

In a European national comparison, the British Isles had the most emigrants up to the First World War, with clear distinctions in migration behaviour between migrants from England, Scotland and Wales, on the one hand, and Ireland, on the other. About 60–70 per cent of English, Scottish and Welsh emigrants headed in the late nineteenth century for the United States; the rest went to the British colonies. The scales started shifting in the early twentieth century. From the turn of the century until the First World War, only about 37 per cent of emigrants went to the United States. In the last four years before the war, Australia, New Zealand and Canada surpassed the United States as a destination for emigrants from England, Scotland and Wales. Parallel to this shift in destination countries, there was also a clear rise in the return migration rate, due especially to the high rate of return from the colonies. This was a product of the growing significance of overseas labour migration, which increased here earlier and to a greater degree than in all other European out-migration countries. As early as the 1840s, industrial labour migration by individuals emerged alongside rural settlement migration by families. In the 1880s, the return migration rate was already 35 per cent of total emigration, reaching 60 per cent in the 1890s. From 1885 to 1888, the number of men emigrating alone to North America was eight times the number of those who crossed the Atlantic with their families. Sixty per cent of overseas migrants from England at this time came from urban-industrial areas. In the 1880s, 35 per cent of English emigration came from London, the western Midlands and Lancashire; another 25 per cent came from other industrial conurbations.

The much greater Irish emigration offers a stark contrast. The highest return migration rate of the English compares with the lowest among Irish overseas migrants. For them, transatlantic labour migration was far less important, especially because there was always the internal alternative of going to find work in England, Scotland and Wales, which were in turn also emigration regions. Ireland was influenced by emigration more than any other region in Europe in the nineteenth century. In a century in which the whole of Europe experienced heavy natural population growth, the population in Ireland declined from 8 million in 1846 to only 4.5 million in 1901.

The Irish population grew considerably into the first half of the nineteenth century. Increasing amounts of pastureland were broken up and leased in ever-smaller parcels by large landowners, who in 1869 comprised just 1 per cent of the population while owning 80 per cent of the land. They allowed subsistence but not market production; the primary crop was potatoes for personal consumption. High leasehold rents could often only be paid by carrying out secondary cottage industrial production, especially spinning and weaving. However, Irish leaseholders could not compete with English industrial textile production, which gained a foothold in the early nineteenth century. About 1.5 million Irish emigrated as early as 1815–45, most of whom (*c.*900,000) went to North America, and most of these to the United States. The others went mainly to England, Scotland and Wales. Chain migrations and migration networks stabilized transatlantic and internal migratory traditions.

When the potato blight destroyed the agricultural basis for subsistence as well, the only choice that remained open to millions was between emigration and starvation, which was the fate of almost one-quarter of the total Irish population between 1846 and 1848. About 80–90 per cent of Irish emigrants were small tenant farmers, agricultural labourers or farmhands. Overcrowded, unseaworthy ships equipped with insufficient food and water left Irish ports. Disease spread in epidemic proportions. In 1847, en route to Canada, no less than 17 per cent of all passengers perished, not to mention those who died of exhaustion or disease after putting into port. In the eight years from 1846 to 1854, 1.75 million Irish emigrated to North America, one-fifth of the total population. By the end of the century, the number of Irish emigrants had risen to almost 4 million. North America as a destination continued to gain precedence over England, Scotland and Wales. From 1876 to 1921, 84 per cent of all Irish emigrants went to the United States and only 8 per cent to England, Scotland or Wales. Transatlantic migration chains had asserted themselves over their internal counterparts.[97]

Prussian Germany

German overseas emigration, 90 per cent of which in the nineteenth century was directed to North America, reached its century maximum in the third emigration wave from 1880 to 1893. While the first wave of emigration around mid-century was still concentrated around the traditional emigration regions in south-western Germany, the third wave was dominated by the mostly agrarian north-eastern regions. From 1880 to 1883, almost 1.8 million Germans emigrated to the United States alone. It was internal migration over greater distances, however, that developed in the course of rapidly accelerating urbanization during the period of high industrialization into the 'largest mass movement in German history'.[98] East–west migration from the rural proletariat of the primarily agrarian north-eastern regions to the industrial proletariat of central and western Germany was especially pronounced. As noted above (see chapter 1, section 2), it thus became an internal counterpart to transatlantic emigration, since here again chain migrations and migratory networks served to establish stable migratory traditions.

At the time of the third emigration wave of the nineteenth century, emigration from the urban-industrial and service sectors increased only gradually. It already assumed some aspects of individual, wage-oriented migration behaviour that might also lead to transatlantic shuttle migrations with longer periods of stay for work purposes. A more cumbersome comparison, and one that was slow to react to disturbances in the destination areas overseas, was family emigration from rural regions, which was still the dominant form during the third emigration wave. For organizational, family-related reasons, family emigration often had to be prepared longer in advance and may have been impossible to call off or even postpone. This was the case, for example, where a dwarf- or smallholding was sold to serve as start capital in the immigration country, or where a family did not want to leave behind a son who was nearing the age of compulsory military service. In Germany, and especially in Prussia with its long period of military service, family emigrations were often planned so that conscription was sufficiently far off not to threaten the official 'emigration authorization', if the son had not already been sent on ahead for this very reason or emigrated 'secretly' via a foreign port, parallel to the rest of the family.

Two examples from the rural north-eastern regions of Germany illustrate that even rural regions with strong emigration traditions had some flexible forms of migration behaviour, even with respect to family emigration. The eastern Prussian provinces, predominantly agrarian in structure, were affected by overseas emigration and internal migration out of agriculture in different yet ultimately similar ways. The background to both movements was the above-mentioned agricultural crisis in eastern Prussia that began in the mid-1870s, and the increasingly underdeveloped agrarian structures in East Elbia that offered poorer wages and working conditions than those in the west. The eastern provinces all experienced severe losses to emigration in the decades prior to the First World War. Wherever overseas emigration was not very pronounced – as in East Prussia – losses through internal migration were all the higher. Tradition and communication via transatlantic and interregional networks played an important role in this regard, as can be seen in a comparison of Mecklenburg and East Prussia, at the western- (Mecklenburg) and easternmost (East Prussia) peripheries of the north-eastern German territories.[99]

Overseas emigration was extremely high in Mecklenburg during the first (1846–57) and second (1864–73) German emigration waves in the nineteenth century. A transatlantic migratory tradition had become firmly established and initially continued to have an impact in the third emigration wave (1880–93). Mecklenburg had the best-developed communication system in the north-eastern German emigration region. In 1892, Franz Lindig, a government clerk from Schwerin, reported on emigration movements in Mecklenburg that 'today, particularly from rural population circles, there are only very few families that do not have relatives or acquaintances living in America'.[100] This high degree of communication made it possible for potential emigrants to weigh up the options, in objective, realistic and comparative terms, as can be seen from the emigration curve, which reacted sensitively to economic changes in the United States. Susceptibility to vague rumours about the supposedly endless possibilities 'in America' was kept in check. Instead, people in Mecklenburg demonstrated objective forward thinking which already displayed some aspects of economic, speculative migration behaviour rarely encountered anywhere else in the north-eastern territories during the third emigration wave.

Overseas emigration and internal migration became viable alternatives, especially since, in addition to a transatlantic tradition, Mecklenburg had an equally active and stable tradition of internal migration, especially to prospering Prussian regions and Hamburg. In direct competition to the lure of the United States, the growing attraction of internal industrial trade options was able to develop. Mecklenburg was clearly ahead of the other emigration regions in north-eastern Germany in its early transition from transatlantic emigration to internal migration. The shift here took place earliest, in the mid-1880s, in the emigration region that had the strongest emigration tradition in north-eastern Germany and the best-developed system of transatlantic communication.

The situation in East Prussia was very different from that in Mecklenburg. East Prussia had no comparable transatlantic migration tradition or communication system, and internal long-distance east–west migration developed instead of overseas emigration. Emigration volume and intensity were incomparably lower in East Prussia, making the simultaneously high losses through internal migration all the more apparent. While only 35,237 people emigrated overseas from East Prussia in the three decades from 1881 to 1910, overall migration loss amounted to 629,449, of which 218,269 were registered in 1910 in Rhineland and Westphalia alone – more than six times the total amount of East Prussian overseas emigration from 1881 to 1910.

Therefore, this was not a matter of a shift from overseas emigration to internal east–west migration. East Prussia had a comparably low intensity and late development of transatlantic emigration, and therefore did not play any role in the third German emigration wave. Instead, it linked directly into the internal east–west migration, thereby developing an interregional migration tradition and communication system that were decidedly comparable to the transatlantic tradition in Mecklenburg. In East Prussia starting in the 1880s and 1890s, the 'prepaid ticket' came not from the United States but from the Ruhr valley.

This highly flexible migration behaviour assumed clear contours in urban-industrial as well as rural home regions with long emigration traditions and well-developed transatlantic communication. At the same time, in rural districts lacking information networks and the corresponding transatlantic communication, deceptive lures 'to America' by emigration agents could still, in the late nineteenth century, trigger 'migration fever', which was known but hardly encountered any further in Germany. Authorities sought to combat this 'fever', usually to little effect, by pursuing the agents or by using deliberate counter-propaganda. In 1845 a rumour spread throughout East Prussia that the Prussian king wanted 'to establish an empire in America'. Preparations were made everywhere for emigration, until a cabinet decree of 17 October 1845 put an end to this serious hoax. Another rumour emerged a short time later in Pomerania and was in circulation until 1852, according to which 'a Prussian prince' had obtained estates 'in America and Australia' and was offering free passage and support for Prussians wanting to emigrate. 'As a result, all of Prussia is experiencing a lively emigration movement; the unfortunate are leaving their homes, sometimes without any means, and are trying to make their way to Bremen, where the prince would take care of them.' Behind this imaginary 'king' or 'prince' was probably an overseas or German emigration agent or overseas labour importer with prefinanced emigrant passages to be worked off in the country of immigration.

Phenomena such as this reappeared at the time of the third German emigration wave in the nineteenth century. They immediately shed light on gross differences in mentality and social and protest behaviour among the industrial proletariat in the western immigration areas, the objective migration behaviour in rural home regions with long migratory trad-itions and intensive transatlantic communication, and sub-peasant envir-onments in home regions with insufficient access to information. In 1889, when public debate was dominated by the serious miners' strike in the Ruhr valley, yet another Prussian prince had supposedly acquired 'estates in Brazil' and called upon the Pomeranians – among whom there had been heavy emigration to Brazil since the 1860s – to emigrate. This was all the more remarkable since recruitment for emigrants to Brazil had been made punishable by law due to the exploitative '*parceria* system' of plantation labour. Once again, the response was so great that it needed a royal decree of February 1890 to counter it.[101]

Poland

Between 1860 and 1914, probably more than one-third of the total population of almost 30 million in the Polish territories was familiar with different forms of migration as part of their everyday working lives, whether short- and long-distance migration in rural districts, rural–urban migration, or continental and overseas labour migration and emigration. In the first decade of the twentieth century, a quarter of the population earned their livelihood directly or indirectly through labour migration.

Mass overseas emigration from the Polish territories, which belonged to Russia, Austria and Prussia after the partitions of 1772 to 1795, began very late in comparison with western, central and northern Europe. Political refugees had emigrated to North America in the first half of the nineteenth century, but the total number of emigrants did not start to increase gradually until the late 1850s. Here as well, there was a clear shift in emigration regions, in this case from west to east. The Polish emigrants of the 1850s to 1880s mostly came from the Prussian part of Poland. Over 400,000 Prussian Poles emigrated to the United States, 90 per cent of them between 1850 and 1890. The peak of Prussian-Polish emigration was situated in the third German emigration wave of the nineteenth century (1880–93), supplied primarily from the north-eastern German territories. These figures decreased along with the general decline in German mass emigration in the mid-1890s. Up to the First World War, only another 50,000 Prussian-Polish emigrants left for the United States. In the two eastern partition regions of Poland, on the other hand, emigration did not really get started until the 1890s. Austrian-Polish emigration commenced earlier than Russian-Polish emigration and was heavier before the turn of the century. Around 400,000 people emigrated to the United States from the Austrian partition of Poland in the 1890s, and just as many followed up to the First World War. From the Russian partition in central Poland, there were also roughly 800,000 people who emigrated, though of these only about 170,000 had left the country before the turn of the century.

All in all, about 1.8–2 million Poles emigrated to the United States between 1870 and 1914. The curve of annual emigration climbed from about 30,000 in 1890 to 50,000 around the turn of the century to up to 130,000 in 1910. The rise took place parallel to the general increase in new immigration to the United States from eastern and south-eastern Europe. Nevertheless, in the last 15 years before the First World War, Polish overseas emigration, 85–90 per cent of which was headed for the United States, did not reach a level of more than one-third of Polish continental migration, of which 85–90 per cent went to Germany.

Characteristic features of Polish migratory traditions to Germany and the United States were migration agents, chain migrations and migration networks. Agents who recruited agricultural and industrial labourers in Germany competed with agents from shipping lines who sought passengers for their large ocean liners after the severe decline in German emigration in the early 1890s. Ewa Morawska has been able to carry out detailed research into the establishment of chain migrations once agents became involved in the process, based on the situation in Maszkienice, a village in central Galicia in the Austrian partition. Beginning in the 1880s, the community was visited regularly by agents working at first on behalf of Austrian mines, later for Prussian landowners, and finally for German shipping companies. In 1899, 40 per cent of all young, able-bodied men worked as labour migrants outside the village. After the recruitment campaigns of the shipping line agents, however, emigration figures to the United States grew increasingly from the turn of the century. By 1911 continental labour migration had lost significance, while the number of migrants bound for the United States rose fourteenfold. At this time, 20 per cent of all labour migrants from Maszkienice went to the United States and another 20 per cent to Germany; 27 per cent worked in the Bohemian-Moravian coal and steel industry in Ostrava, and the remaining third in various Galician cities. The ten surrounding communities that were also studied showed a similar breakdown: 27 per cent of labour migrants had left their villages in 1911 for the United States, 15 per cent went to work in agriculture in East Elbia and 10 per cent in Denmark. Another 10 per cent worked in the coal and steel industry in Ostrava, and 38 per cent were seasonal workers in agriculture or industry in Galicia.

Long-distance continental and overseas migration was not that important in all areas of Poland. Some regions with less advantageous transportation services, especially in eastern Poland, were left untouched by the pull of mobility. Here too the population often had to rely on earnings from labour migrations, but these remained limited to traditional harvest migrations over short or intermediate distances. In many areas of central Poland and Galicia there were traditions, sometimes going back to the mid-nineteenth century, of seasonal agricultural migrations to East Elbia. They often remained intact until the First World War, unaffected by the rise in transatlantic migration. In Maszkienice, too, it took an entire decade after the arrival of the first shipping company agents before emigration to the United States took hold. At first villagers stuck fast to the old migratory paths leading to Prussia and Moravian Ostrava, until these were superseded by overseas migration traditions. In 1898 the first villager went to Pennsylvania, returned, and the following year took two relatives with him to the coalmines of the north-eastern United States. An increasing number of residents from the village and surrounding area soon followed, and a new emigration tradition had begun. Within a decade, settlement colonies appeared with common hometown communities, in which the 'Americans' from Maszkienice were concentrated in four cities directly prior to the First World War.

Except for the special case of the Russian and Galician Poles in Prussia, who had to leave the country each year (see sections 1 and 4 of this chapter), Poles in both the United States and Germany formed strong urban immigrant colonies even though almost two-thirds of Polish emigrants had come from rural backgrounds and were small leaseholders or agricultural labourers and about one-third were subsistence farmers. The network structure determined settlement forms and areas of work. In the Ruhr valley, Poles formed immigrant colonies mostly in the cities with coal and steel industry such as Bochum, Gelsenkirchen and Dortmund. In the early twentieth century, half of the total Polish immigrant population in the United States lived in seven industrial centres: Buffalo, Chicago, Detroit, Pittsburgh, Cleveland, Milwaukee and New York. Ninety-five per cent of Polish immigrants in the United States who worked in industry had positions that required few special qualifications. Three-quarters of Polish men worked in coal production or metal or meat processing. In Germany, the occupational levels of the Ruhr Poles who worked in industry were very similar; however, because of the bans restricting their employment options in Prussia, which was the main in-migration region, only 40 per cent of Poles in Germany worked in industry, while 60 per cent worked in agriculture, primarily in the eastern provinces of Prussia. There was a large proportion of return migration among Polish overseas migrants, as was also the case among Italians, who will be discussed next. Among Polish emigrants to the United States, probably about 60–70 per cent returned within the first two or three years. Shortly before the First World War, 40 per cent of Polish migrants coming back from the United States were not going back to Poland for the first time.[102]

Italy

From the early 1860s to the late 1920s, Italy was the second most important European emigration region, after the British Isles; at the same time, it was a major region of origin for labour migrants bound for other parts of Europe. Almost 18 million people left Italy in these six decades. From 1871 to 1914 alone, the figure was 14 million. Roughly one-third went to the United States, 24 per cent to South America, 44 per cent remained in Europe, and several tens of thousands went – mostly temporarily – to Italy's colonies in North Africa (see chapter 3, section 2). Of the 7.3 million overseas migrants between 1871 and 1914, more than half (4.2 million) headed for the United States, followed by Argentina with 1.8 million (13 per cent) and Brazil with 1.2 million (9 per cent).

As was the case with German and Polish emigration, there were characteristic shifts in regions of origin depending on the industrialization differential, in this case from north to south. Emigration and migration were initially concentrated almost exclusively in northern Italy. As the north became progressively industrialized, central and southern Italy gained importance. The shift in regions of origin was simultaneously a shift in migration destinations, because migration from northern Italy was more marked by seasonal European migration, whereas southern Italians went primarily to North America. In 1880 only 5 per cent of cross-border Italian emigration went to the United States; by 1914 the figure was 43 per cent.

Northern Italians who made their way across the Atlantic, however, went mostly to South America. This was owing to specific migration traditions. The severe agrarian crisis in Venetia tended to reinforce the direction of northern Italian transatlantic migrations towards South America, and coincided with the abolition of slavery in Brazil in 1888. More than 250,000 Venetians were recruited from 1891 to 1897 to work on Brazilian plantations, indirectly as a substitute for slaves, and were transported across the south Atlantic from Genoa. Most of these emigrations were supported by the state of São Paulo; a total of 82–99 per cent of all overseas passages in the period 1889–93 were subsidized. Owing to the pioneering function of recruitment, a migratory tradition targeting Brazil developed in Venetia through recruitment patterns which soon became pronounced for certain plantations and through emigrant letters. This tradition remained unbroken, despite harsh measures taken by the Italian government in 1902 to counter mass emigration. At about the same time, Genoese and Ligurian migration traditions became established in Argentinian agriculture.

North America's attractiveness for migrants from southern Italy lay mostly in the inexpensive and rapid transatlantic line from Naples to New York. Southern Italian agricultural workers, who had little money even relative to other Italians, tried to earn their livelihood in North America's industry and service sector doing semi- and unskilled jobs. Because South America was largely settled by immigrants from the Mediterranean and other Romance-language regions – from 1854 to 1924, 77 per cent of all immigrants in South America came from Italy, Spain and Portugal – it offered better conditions for rapid acculturation. North America could be reached faster and at a lower cost, however, and had much larger labour markets with a wide range of employment options for unskilled workers at relatively high wage levels. Despite these clearly defined migratory patterns, southern Italians especially remained highly mobile and flexible as compared with other Europeans in terms of country of destination and areas of work.

Like Italian migration within Europe, Italian migration to North and especially South America was to a large degree temporary seasonal labour migration. Half of all Italian immigrants, for example, returned to Italy from the United States within one or a few years. Many young men crossed the Atlantic every year in the spring, worked in the United States until autumn, and then returned to Italy in the winter. One group of transatlantic labour migrants with a highly distinctive migration pattern, which is widely known for that reason, were the *golondrinas* ('swallows' or 'birds of passage'), whose estimated numbers grew from about 25,000 in 1880 to about 100,000 in 1914. *Golondrinas* took advantage of the opposite seasons in the northern and southern hemispheres. They worked on the harvest in Italy until late autumn and arrived in Argentina in late spring for the planting season. Then they left South America after the grain and fruit harvests in the autumn in order to return to Italy in time for the spring agricultural tasks. This required a constant improvement in transatlantic navigation, which led to shorter and shorter travel times and reduced costs. After 1880, for example, a passage from southern Italy to North or South America cost less than the rail journey from northern Italy to northern Germany.[103]

Regional examples of transnational and transatlantic 'proletarian mass migrations' encompass a wide range of forms. Based on available data, general structures can be identified in retrospect; as for local case studies, even detailed structures can sometimes be made out. For the actual men and women who migrated, however, these structures were understandable only within a limited framework based on their respective living sphere. The rationale behind individual decisions to migrate should therefore neither be confused with the structural rationale of migratory processes that can be concluded retrospectively by migration research, nor did it represent different individual decision making within the migratory process that appeared to result from a survey of all simultaneous options for migration. Information bases, points of reference and latitudes for action were limited and different for each individual and they varied from situation to situation. Nevertheless, it is possible to identify – as far as the available information allows – an *animal rationale migrans*, who used his own (albeit limited) life experience to derive selection criteria and standards for assessment, in order to make migration decisions, evaluate the outcome and possibly modify those decisions as a result. It was this tension between 'global and local perspectives' (Dirk Hoerder/Leslie Page Moch), between 'local life' and 'Atlantic world' (Georg Fertig), that determined such decisions. In the social sphere of the 'proletarian mass migrations' surveyed here, migrants were not global actors, even as regards decisions on intercontinental migration alternatives. In the late nineteenth and early twentieth centuries as in the early modern period, they transported the small world of their home regions in their mental maps as the standard by which to evaluate the wider world they experienced.[104]

A recurrent theme in scholarly debate is that the European mass emigration of the nineteenth and early twentieth centuries was primarily due to demographic and economic 'pressure' as a result of the imbalance between population growth and job opportunities. There is comprehensive literature on the determining factors for emigration and on the history of transatlantic movement and its consequences for the emigrants and the receiving societies overseas. The converse question, what were the consequences of emigration for the societies left behind, has received only scant attention. Frank Thistlethwaite's famous call for research to wade through the 'saltwater curtain' and uncover the overall process of transatlantic migration caused something of a stir, but has produced very little, very late.[105] This 'saltwater curtain' often still separates works on the history of overseas emigration from those on the history of continental and transatlantic labour migration in which the home region more often remains in the field of view as a site of migratory consequences.

Using Heiko Körner's estimate that from 1820 to 1915 about 63 million gross (and 50–55 million net) Europeans emigrated overseas, a comparison of these figures with population developments in Europe reveals the following picture. The European population grew from about 180 million in 1800 to about 266 million in 1850, roughly 328 million in 1882, and about 428 million in 1910. This represents a growth of 140 per cent (248 million) over 110 years. If we take the segments of the population that emigrated and their potential natural fertility rate in

Europe (which was lower than in the United States because of fewer chances of finding a spouse and higher child mortality) in the same time period, hypothetical growth could have been more than 200 per cent.[106] What would have been the historical consequences for society if this 'emergency exit' overseas had not existed for about 60 million emigrants and the much larger number of those who did not actually emigrate, but who always imagined it as an attainable life choice?

Within the developing regions of western Europe which made up the first main regions of origin for overseas mass emigration in the nineteenth century, if overseas emigration had not been an option there would have been no release even for severe internal tensions that developed, since the receptiveness of the emerging industrial labour markets remained limited for a long time. Even in general terms, overseas emigration offered an alternative for those in the shadow of the historic path from agrarian to industrial society who sought a place to escape their economic and social problems. This was true for farmers' sons born without opportunities in the countryside, who considered the industrial route to be social decline, for the land-poor and landless, and for petty bourgeois and proletarian environments, from which many impoverished small master craftsmen and journeymen without prospects strove to leave the overcrowded old trade as emigrants to the New World.

Apart from the mass flight of the Irish from the crisis of the 'hungry forties', the move 'to America' in the nineteenth century might have been a question of physical survival for very few, but it was a question of social survival for many. Not until the period of high industrialization in the decades before the First World War did job opportunities in western European development centres increase suddenly. Emigration declined in importance – except in Britain, where it remained high, and in France, where it was never high – as compared with internal migration to the expanding urban-industrial areas of employment. At this time, however, a considerable portion of the labour surplus that had already gone overseas would not yet have been able to earn a sufficiently secure subsistence during the harsh decades of transition to industrialization in the developing centres of north-western Europe.

Overseas emigration served as a safety valve even beyond the borders of the home regions. After the disparity between population growth and job opportunities had been balanced out by economic growth during industrialization, additional losses caused by overseas emigration and internal migration to more industrially advanced emigration countries created a growing demand for substitutes on the labour market. Moreover, in the period of industrial growth prior to the First World War, there was an increasing labour demand due to expansion as well as additional seasonal needs in areas with high agrarian modernization. The substitute, expansion and additional demands that arose in the central and western European centres as a result of the combination of migration and modernization processes could be covered to a large extent by labour migrants from southern, south-eastern, east central and eastern European areas. At the same time, these migrants replaced those from western Europe in overseas emigration.

For these southern, south-eastern, east central and eastern European regions of origin of overseas emigration and transnational labour migration in the late nineteenth and early twentieth centuries, however, there would probably have been no other ways to resolve the problems resulting from deficient development and structural and economic crises. For the rural-agrarian and urban-industrial labour forces of western Europe as well as for those in the growing urban service sector, in turn, labour migrations from southern, south-eastern, east central and eastern Europe brought social relief, despite tension and conflict on the labour market. These labourers took on the working and wage conditions that locals were increasingly unwilling to accept, and they also served a buffer function in the fluctuation between boom and crisis. Without them, the road to industrial society would not have been very different but would probably have been much harder. The transatlantic flip side of this social relief through overseas emigration was the increase in elasticity that European immigrants brought to the labour market on the hectic 'American' road to the industrial age.

Basic ideas that were widespread at the time of the 'industrial population explosion' in most developed European industrial countries with – except for France – high population growth were fear of social revolution and the notion of a kind of balancing out of social pressure through the safety valve of overseas emigration. How great the balancing effect of overseas mass emigration from nineteenth- and early twentieth-century Europe might have been in this regard can only be hypothesized, as the extent to which fear of revolution had a basis in reality cannot be measured using superficial econometric means by the degree of disparity between population growth and job opportunities. This kind of assessment, if any is possible, would need to take into account ideational, political, cultural, psychological and many other material and conceptual factors.

Assuming Albert O. Hirschman's alternative of 'migration or contradiction', emigration was a kind of silent social protest for many emigrants. They voted with their feet against the poor living conditions in their home countries, which they could escape easily by leaving the country rather than fight for change.[107] But what if dozens of millions of emigrants had not been able to leave nineteenth- and early twentieth-century Europe? What if all those who could have emigrated but stayed behind had not had the escapist vision of the New World as a viable alternative to fighting for better living conditions? Might what in retrospect was the false expectation of Karl Marx and Friedrich Engels, that a successful international social revolution would follow the failed political revolutions of 1848–9 in Europe, not generally have been less of an illusion?

3 EURO-COLONIAL MIGRATION IN THE AGE OF HIGH IMPERIALISM

The idea that social problems could be overcome through colonial expansion and migration was, in addition to power rivalries and economic or trade interests, a third essential component of imperial thinking in nineteenth- and early twentieth-century Europe. Power relationships within the colonial empires targeted by these concepts had changed in many ways since the first phase of European overseas expansion that had followed the age of exploration. The first part of this section provides a brief overview, while the second traces the ideas and reality of this Euro-colonial concept of migration, which to some degree became historical reality in the case of Britain, while remaining largely an illusion with respect to Germany.

Colonial migration between liberalism and imperialism

European colonial empires survived the age of liberalism, which for a long time was wrongly considered simply as a period of colonial disinterest, or even as marking a change of course to an anti-colonial setting. Ideas concerning the colonial policy of *laissez faire*, colonies as 'millstones about the neck of the mother country' and the 'anti-colonialism' of the mid-Victorian period were enduring legends of Britain's imperial history in the epoch of liberalism.[108] They were not shot down until the mid-twentieth century by the famous attack of historians John Gallagher and Ronald Robinson, with their reminder that around the mid-nineteenth century Britain had still clearly expanded its 'informal empire' as well as its formal, direct territorial rule overseas.[109]

As the European colonial empires developed from the age of exploration to the age of high imperialism in the late nineteenth and early twentieth centuries, there were fundamental changes in imperial inventories of possessions as well as in the relationships between European metropolises and colonial periphery. In addition to and ultimately displacing Portugal, Spain and the Netherlands, England and France had become colonial powers. In the decades preceding the First World War, Italy made its debut as a new European colonial power, with colonies in Libya, Eritrea and Italian Somaliland; Germany did the same, with its 'protectorates' in Africa (German South-west Africa, Cameroon, Togo, German East Africa) and the Pacific realm, and with Tsingtau (Qingdao) as a German concession in China from 1898. As the final carving up of the world began in the 1880s, a large number of new overseas territories were incorporated into the colonial empires: in Africa, in the Pacific realm and as a result of the Eurasian expansion of the multi-ethnic Russian empire, which is beyond the scope of this book.

The European colonial empires overseas in the late nineteenth and early twentieth centuries encompassed a diversity of types of rule, from direct territorial rule to commercial regimes to indirect control through local elites. Most of the old Spanish and Portuguese colonies in Central and South America had become immigration countries. The United States, the most significant country of immigration for Europeans, whose liberation from colonial dependence had come only a century earlier, was already pursuing its own expansionist policies, not only through the Monroe Doctrine on the American mainland and in the Caribbean but also much further afield, especially in the Pacific realm.

After the end of the slave trade, there were approximately three main areas in the history of colonial migration of the nineteenth and early twentieth centuries: (1) colonial service and settlement of Europeans overseas either temporarily or permanently; (2) further migrations of non-European locals within the colonies, triggered by European colonial expansion; (3) 'relocations' of non-European labourers and population groups within or between European colonies and regions of interest.

(1) European colonial service and the Euro-colonial labour market had not changed fundamentally in terms of structure and functions since early modern times, as far as it concerned groups circulating in Euro-colonial migratory cycles who remained for a more or less limited period of time. This included not only European ship and port personnel, but also military, administrative and mission staff and the employees and supervisors of European companies or those that had since been established in the colonies. Older settlements and bases overseas developed into or were replaced by new colonial metropolises with extensive hinterlands, such as Batavia (1619–1949), which later became Jakarta. They expanded Euro-colonial labour markets considerably, often offering outstanding employment opportunities compared with what was available in the European 'mother country'.

Euro-colonial emigration apart from labour migration with more or less limited sojourns aimed at different types of settlement colony. There were pure settlement colonies, such as Australia and New Zealand for

Britain. There were also white settler colonies whose economy was dependent on an indigenous labour force, such as Algeria for France, Rhodesia, Kenya and South Africa for Britain, and, to a far lesser extent, South-west Africa for Germany and, in the twentieth century, Libya (Tripoli/Benghazi) for Italy. Dutch Indonesia assumed an intermediate position. In 1930, about 80,000 Dutch were living there. They were not settlers in the strict sense but worked mostly in administration and trade or as employees of branch offices of Dutch firms. Even with respect to Euro-colonial settlement migration, there was sometimes a high return or circular migration rate between Europe and overseas.

(2) Triggered by European expansion, subsequent migrations of non-European populations within the European colonies included migration and recruitment of an indigenous labour force from other regions to the European settlement and commercial districts, such as farm and mining workers in Rhodesia and South Africa. Economic coercion to this kind of geographical mobility was prevalent, for example, where migrations by locals to districts settled by Europeans were in reality return migrations of former producers to work as hired labourers in regions from which they had previously been forced out. This was the case for the burgeoning local production of cocoa in German Cameroon, which had been stifled by the domination of large colonial concession companies around the turn of the twentieth century, or later for indigenous coffee production in British Kenya, which had been banned by white settlers. Another example of economic coercion was the devastation of the traditional subsistence base of local nomadic livestock breeders in German South-west Africa, when geographical mobility was restricted and the pasture-land of the Hereros was destroyed in the interests of German farmers. These and similar measures forced many nomads to become agricultural wage labourers after the social and cultural disaster of the rinderpest of 1897 and the population losses of genocidal proportions during the German colonial war against the Herero and Nama peoples from 1904 to 1907. An indirect form of economic coercion that had a similar effect was the levying of duties to be paid in European currency, which forced workers to take on wage labour. This was the case with the 'hut tax' in German East Africa. There are just as many examples of direct extra-economic coercion in respect of colonial production in nineteenth- and early twentieth-century European colonial history. In Africa, for example, there was forced labour on German plantations in Cameroon and in Belgian mines in the Congo.

(3) There was sometimes a fluid transition from these kinds of intra-colonial movements to intercolonial and intercontinental 'relocations' on the part of non-European labourers and population groups. These organized mass transfers were often accompanied by coercive measures and

represented the end of a progression that has already been discussed: they led from the slave trade and extremely varied systems of forced labour and compulsory work for a certain time to the export and import of colonial contract labourers, who in the second half of the nineteenth century primarily took over the plantation work that had been done by slaves. Contract workers were used in about 40 countries by all of the big colonial powers. The system was extraordinarily complex, especially since some areas received labourers transported from different territories, and, moreover, migrations or transfers also took place between these receiving areas. British colonial authorities thus recruited about 1 million people on the Indian subcontinent between 1839 and 1917 for plantation work in Trinidad, Guyana and other places in the Caribbean, and for plantation work, mining and railroad construction in Malaya and East Africa. Dutch authorities employed Chinese worker brigades in their East Indies colonial territories until the system of contract labour was abolished in the Dutch colonies in 1941. Contract workers were often cheaper than slaves. They were paid a pittance and worked in the most dreadful conditions without their employers' incurring a purchase price or unproductive costs such as sickness and old age benefits. Even where working and wage conditions appeared more tolerable, there was often indirect pressure to work; for return transportation over long distances, if contractually provided for at all, was dependent on fulfilment of the contract, as was the case for Chinese coolies in German Samoa. Contract work was also performed by Japanese in South America, for example, and by Chinese and East Indian contract workers in the Caribbean in the nineteenth and early twentieth centuries, not to mention the Chinese contract workers used in building the railroads in North America.[110] This kind of colonial or post-colonial migration by non-European labourers in and between extra-European territories will not be discussed further here since our focus is Euro-colonial migrations.

Empire settlement and imperial 'social policy': British experience and German illusion

In the decades prior to the First World War, the British Empire continued to grow considerably in the age of high imperialism that began in the early 1880s with the 'scramble for Africa'. At the time of its greatest expansion in 1933, it covered almost 32 million square kilometres, almost 24 per cent of the earth's surface, and had a population of almost 502 million, nearly a quarter of the global population. The parts of the British Empire that retained their orientation towards London were India, the dependencies, some of which were under direct territorial rule and others under informal rule, and the crown colonies that grad-ually became self-governing dominions while retaining ties of loyalty to the crown, including the former settlement colonies of Canada (1867), Australia (1901), New Zealand (1907), Newfoundland (1907) and the South African Union (1910–61), as well as Ireland (1921–49) in Europe.

Emigration and settlement were central themes in nineteenth- and early twentieth-century debate on the British Empire. Not until the early twentieth century, however, did the empire evolve into the main desti-nation for the continuing heavy stream of emigrants from the British Isles. In the period 1884–1903, less than half of British emigrants trav-elled to the British overseas territories, as John Atkinson Hobson noted in his study on imperialism.[111] Since the early nineteenth century, various 'imperial social' perspectives have run through British colonial history against the background of the respective economic, social and political histories. Even beyond the idea of promoting colonial settlements by moving in war veterans, for example, the notion of using the colonies to relieve the national and local budgets of the 'mother country' by moving people living off the state out of the metropolises and into the colonial periphery was not new. There had been a long tradition of deporting prisoners and workhouse inmates and even children from homes and orphanages to the colonies. As early as 1618, a British sailor brought 100 children to colonial Virginia.

Quite apart from the relief that ensued from getting rid of social cases who were unwanted because of their cost, what was new was the idea, spurred by visions of threats to society, of using 'empire settlement' as a way of resolving or at least lessening social problems. These ideas formed the core of British social and colonial discussions that overlapped in the first half of the century. They were reiterated whenever a crisis emerged, especially in the 1880s, in the period before, during and after the First World War, and even during and after the Great Depression. In the late nineteenth and early twentieth centuries, social reform and empire settle-ment were competing, even occasionally overlapping, concepts, until in the end, instead of fundamental reform, the argument of social policy in a national welfare state won out against the colonial export of social problems, which had been preached more than it had been practised.[112]

Early industrial mass impoverishment, or pauperism, fear that social revolution would erupt, and the high rate of immigration from Ireland intensified fears in England that the situation would get dramatically worse. Against this background, attention was focused on the gloomy prospect of drastically diminishing food reserves, with a population growing in geometric progression while means of subsistence could only be multiplied in arithmetic progression. The theory had already been outlined in the late sixteenth century by Giovanni Botero (*Della ragion di stato*, 1589); in the eighteenth century it was rediscovered and expanded, and finally became known worldwide through the treatise by Thomas R. Malthus.[113]

Among social imperial perspectives up to mid-century, the search for solutions led to two major schools of thought, the first of which dominated into the early 1830s, when it was superseded by the second. The first focused on the journalistic and parliamentary discussion of what Charles Buller referred to as 'shovelling out your paupers', that is, exporting the poor by promoting emigration, preferably though not necessarily to British colonies. The burden of the poor would decrease, wages would rise, and the threatening spectre of an all-devouring social revolution would be averted. Sir Robert Wilmot Horton, undersecretary for war and the colonies from 1823 and president of the parliamentary emigration committee from 1826 to 1827, and his followers, dubbed 'Hortonists', were leading representatives of this school. Even Malthus saw this as an interim solution, since high temporary emigration could bring relief to the labour market and some improvement in the situation faced by the rapidly expanding lower classes; thus, the prospects of his theories would also be improved. Malthus assumed that voluntary birth control through 'moral restraint' by the lower classes, who had a high birth rate, presupposed a minimum of experience in developing a 'taste for conveniences and comforts'.

Starting in the early 1830s, the Hortonists' relatively simple ideas for exporting paupers were eclipsed in journalistic and parliamentary debate by the far more complex politico-economic concept of 'systematic colonization', which encompassed economic, social and colonial policies. 'Colonial reformers' from the circle surrounding utilitarian social and legal philosopher Jeremy Bentham were early contemporary expansion theorists in this context. These 'philosophical radicals' devised the basic principles of political economy long before Karl Marx arrived in London in 1849, and generations before the critique of imperialism of Hobson and Marxist theorists. They developed programmes with instructions for imperial practice that later became the central arguments of critical imperialism theory. Critical of the restrictive mercantilist 'old' colonial system, they also provided for the elimination of contradictory strategies and inhibiting restrictions. At the same time, however, they supported plans for the intensive settlement and development of Australia and New Zealand. They were thus neither critics of nor apologists for colonialism alone, but in a flexible way they were simultaneously both.

The philosophical radicals were no longer content with the concept of exporting paupers overseas to secure job opportunities and social peace. With their political and economic analysis of how modern capitalism functioned, they had already by the 1830s developed the concept of a threefold export offensive of goods, capital and human labour: pushing goods export through formal colonial and informal overseas market expansion; overseas export of surplus capital that was forcing down profit rates; and export of surplus, and therefore cheaper, labour that could be used in colonial production. This imperial way of thinking was based on an awareness of Britain's then undisputed global leadership position in industrial production, foreign trade and on the global capital market. The philosophical radicals also felt that formal direct colonial rule was necessary where investments and market conditions were particularly in need of safeguards and protection. But they propagated an 'informal empire' that was as far reaching as possible. Cultural and psychological connections were supposed to hold it together, as was the material binding power of capital transfer and continual exchange of agrarian products for British industrial products. If this necessary overseas expansion of the field of production were to fail, then a social revolution that would destroy Britain's economic and social structures would finally have to be reckoned with.

The most important theorist of this group was Edward Gibbon Wakefield, the impetuous son of a London property broker. While serving a three-year term in Newgate prison for attempting a fraudulent marriage to a wealthy heiress, he had time to analyse colonial issues in depth. The result was the concept of systematic colonization, which was soon well known and overshadowed his other ideas. He introduced the economic core of systematic colonization in his 1829 book *A Letter from Sydney*, and embedded it into the political and social backdrop in *England and America*, published in 1833. Among representatives of the 'Wakefield school' were not only well-known contemporary spokespeople such as political economist Robert Torrens, who was not part of the Bentham circle; they also included John Stuart Mill, the most significant economist of the Bentham school, who used central arguments from Wakefield's writings. Marx was mistaken when he remarked later that the 'bourgeois' Wakefield inadvertently revealed the secrets of capitalist exploitation of the working class. Wakefield had openly presented action-oriented drafts for a 'general theory of the empire' (Bernard Semmel), which focused on the demand for an 'expansion of the production sphere'.

Hortonists were concerned first and foremost with exporting unemployed workers suspected of having social revolutionary potential. The goals and utility of their settlement overseas were only of secondary importance. Among the guiding principles of the Wakefield school, on the other hand, in addition to the central focus on capital export, was the idea of redirecting British emigration from the United States, which was a competitor on the world market, to the British colonies or areas of interest, where their settlement could have economic utility. The Horton-ists and followers of Wakefield shared a common interest in the welfare solely of the 'mother country' and not of the 'surplus' sub-peasant and proletarian lower classes who were to be sent overseas.

Central to Wakefield's ideas was a profitable system for exporting labour, capital and goods that would be largely self-financing through the labour of exported settlers: previous attempts at colonization had often failed because of bottlenecks of labour and capital. Emigrants became owners in the colonies too quickly, and all too often fell victim to their own inexperience as independent producers. At the same time, there was insufficient labour to build up a profitable colonial economy, which is why the export of surplus capital from the British domestic market for the purposes of colonization did not get properly off the ground. In other words, a sufficient pool of inexpensive labour to develop and operate productive colonial estates would secure job oppor-tunities and social peace in the 'mother country', stimulate capital export to the empire and yield huge profits for the system's financiers. Wake-field's solution centred on one main idea, which also adopted elements of the redemptioner system: those willing to emigrate should be resettled in exchange for an obligation to work for a number of years – three, according to Torrens's proposal. Only after fulfilling that obligation should they be allowed to acquire land, and even then it should be at a 'sufficiently high price', which would enable the financiers – among whom Wakefield hoped to count himself – make considerable profits from investment and speculation. Remarkably, Wakefield saw slavery as the only alternative to this system, although at the time his first book was published (1829) slavery was already publicly condemned, and in the publication year of his second book (1833) it had been abolished once and for all.

The threefold export of goods, capital and labour was to offer a flexible means of control to cope with crises of overproduction and secure lasting economic growth and sufficient job opportunities in the 'mother country' as well as profitable economic development in the British colonies and other interests and their firm connections to the home country. The socio-political function of systematic colonization was primarily as a social safety valve against a social revolutionary 'explosion'. For Torrens it was already clear in 1817 that 'a well-regu-lated system of colonization acts as a savety-valve [*sic*] to the political machine, and allows the expanding vapour to escape, before it is heated to explosion'.[114] Many contemporaries supported these ideas, which in the wake of the Chartist risings in Birmingham and Newport in 1839, and finally under the impact of the revolutions on the Continent in 1848–9, had virtually been seen as something of a socio-political panacea.

Starting in 1880, the period of high imperialism brought first the 'scramble for Africa', and then, under the growing pressure of foreign competition around the time of the Boer War, a shift from 'free trade colonialism' to 'liberal imperialism'.[115] Beyond this change, the concepts for solving social problems at a national and imperial level were once again competing as of the 1880s in debate on the empire. In 1868 Sir Charles Dilke spoke of 'the World [that] is rapidly becoming English' in his book, *Greater Britain*. John R. Seeley demanded a planned 'expansion of England' in 1883, while Rudyard Kipling propounded the 'white man's burden' as a primarily British colonial idea of mission. The newer English colonial movement that was discussed from the late 1860s defended the value of the empire against its liberal critics and resumed the old arguments for emigration in a more elaborate form. This time there were two main objectives. Cohesion with the colonies should be reinforced by means of 'imperial and colonial partnership in emigration'. The 'educational investments' and production and consumer strength of emigrants should no longer be ceded to the United States but retained for Britain. Moreover, in view of disturbances in global economic growth and thus the related economic and social problems in England as elsewhere, the old idea of emigration as a way of regulating social crises was introduced afresh.[116]

As of the 1880s, the discussion of 'empire migration and social reform' became consolidated into concepts and concrete programmes. After deportations of prisoners to Australia and Tasmania had come to an end in 1853, concepts for 'empire settlement' included a wide variety of elements in addition to the traditional promotion of emigration and settlement and the forced sending off of children from homes and orphanages as well as other young people. They ranged from proposals to balance out the gender ratio – surplus of women to Britain and surplus of men to the dominions – to encouraging the emigration of women, to the urbanophobic or socially critical idea that emigration to the settlement colonies would function as a kind of 'new baptism, washing away the sins' of the urbanization process.[117]

The implementation of such ideas was initially taken up by numerous non-governmental relief organizations, some of which later worked together with state institutions. Among trade unions that tried to promote the emigration of the unemployed or of members who were dissatisfied with their work situations, the National Agricultural Labourers' Union supported the emigration of more than 40,000 members and their families from 1872 to 1881. The efforts of some philanthropic and charitable organizations in counselling and promoting emigrants especially with little or no means went back far earlier than the nineteenth century; the Migration and Settlement Department (founded in 1903) of the Salvation

Army had advised and supported about 80,000 emigrants by 1914, and more than 250,000 by 1938. The British Women's Emigration Association and other similar organizations assisted more than 20,000 women to emigrate between 1884 and 1914.

English philanthropist and physician of the poor Thomas Barnardo played a pioneering role in organizing children's transports to the colonies. Also called the 'Father of Nobody's Children', he started setting up homes, schools and hospitals for homeless, needy and afflicted children (Barnardo Homes) in London and other English cities after the devastating cholera epidemic of 1865. These were joined together in 1899 to form the National Association for the Reclamation of Destitute Waif Children. Barnardo condemned the slums of East London in 1870 as 'pestilential rookeries', where children lived 'in such conditions of abominable filth, atmospheric impurity and immoral associationship' that made the 'maintenance of virtue' impossible. Around the turn of the century, caretakers of the poor sent about 1,000 children to Canada each year through the children's relief organizations founded by Barnardo. Aid organizations for the emigration of children and young settlers assisted in the emigration of about 80,000 children, usually up to 14 years of age, to Canada between 1868 and 1925. Transport of home and orphanage children, which usually took the form of a compassionate yet compulsory deportation, and fostering the emigration of youthful settlers were also organized to South Africa and Australia. Kingsley Fairbridge, the son of a British colonial surveyor, promoted and implemented children's transports to South Africa to increase the British stock with respect to the Boers. An admirer of Cecil Rhodes, Fairbridge founded the Child Emigration Society, which continued its efforts with royal support until the period following the Second World War. Fitting into the concept of the 'White Australia' policy, British ('white, not yellow') children from institutions were sent to Australia until after the Second World War as well, the last known transport having taken place in 1967.

In the late 1990s a House of Commons select committee on health looked into the matter of the 'lost children of the empire' in Australia, some of whom are still alive. The findings were received with shock and outrage. No British authorities had ever concerned themselves with the fate of these young emigrants. Institutionalized children were sometimes subjected to 'quite exceptional depravity' in their new homeland 'that terms like "sexual abuse" are too weak to convey it'. Roger Singleton, chief executive of the children's relief association founded by Barnardo, admitted to the committee, once the later perversions of Barnardo's ideas of rescuing the children for a 'virtuous life' through emigration became known, that: 'It was barbaric; it was dreadful. We look back on it in our organisation with shock and horror.'[118]

Although non-governmental aid organizations can claim to have transported about 10 per cent of the empire migration from 1910 to 1913, the true significance of their work was more in mobilizing long-lasting public pressure on the government, which nevertheless remained unresponsive for a long time. Mobilization activities were finally successful after the First World War, though they reached their peak in 1910, when the Royal Colonial Institute convened a conference of representatives from 50 emigration organizations, which came together to form a standing committee. In view of the continued high rate of British emigration and against the background of this public pressure, the state gradually intensified the dual course of national and imperial 'social policy', which had initially been accepted only reluctantly in the 1880s. As a result of economic crisis, unemployment and the feared social and domestic repercussions, both courses were pushed after the First World War. The 'empire settlement' argument secured its pre-eminence with the Empire Settlement Act of 1922, which provided for up to £3 million annually to support emigration. Between 1922 and 1935, 405,242 people received emigration assistance within the scope of this act. The 1922 act was revised and extended for another 15 years in 1937; in the 1950s and 1960s it was extended a number of times.

A total of more than 21 million people emigrated from the United Kingdom from the early nineteenth to the early twentieth centuries (1815–1912). In the late nineteenth and early twentieth centuries, the figures increased from almost 1.1 million in the decade from 1871 to 1880 to 1.8 million from 1901 to 1910. Over 1.8 million emigrants were also registered in 1920–9. From 1930 to 1938, when Britain, like Germany, experienced increased in-migration and return migration, the figures dropped dramatically to only 334,467. From 1871 to 1880, only one-third of emigrants went to the overseas territories of the British Empire. By 1901–10 about half did so, and from 1920 to 1929 almost three-quarters chose to emigrate overseas within the British Empire. In the heaviest phase of emigration, from 1923 to 1929, more than 31 per cent of these emigrations were assisted. Initiators and organizations that promoted and subsidized emigration and directed it toward the empire, with the full weight of public opinion behind them, attributed this shift in emigration destinations essentially to their efforts. Nevertheless, it could not be ignored that the restrictive immigration policies of the United States after the First World War had also contributed greatly to these developments.

Despite their efforts, the intensification of empire settlement policies did not reach the level imagined by their proponents, for several reasons. For one thing, the receiving capacity of the dominions had been greatly overestimated. In addition, they had in the meantime become sovereign states and had long established their own immigration policies aimed at control and regulation, so there were generally more Europeans who wanted to immigrate than were accepted. Furthermore, the development of a national welfare state took place at the expense of the prospects for imperial social policy. For the relief organizations and state institutions working to support emigration, it became obvious that 'the evolution of the domestic social reform program was in fact inhibiting the imperial strategy'.[119] Finally, the radical change in generational structures as modern industrial society developed increasingly removed the basis for media agitation for organized emigration to release potentially revolutionary 'population pressure'. The decline in birth rates from the 1930s even led to fears of an ageing population and labour shortages. The export industry, too, warned that British emigrants working in the processing industries in the dominions could help them seize overseas markets from the 'mother land'. Even if individual measures in the empire settlement tradition still existed into the 1960s, the competition of development lines between 'national' and 'imperial' social policy clearly ended in the 1930s at the latest with a victory paving the way to the national welfare state.

If the visions of German expansion invoked by publicists and colonial agitators of the late 1870s and early 1880s had become reality, the German colonial empire would have become an imitation of the British Empire, competing with what was both its model and its worst nightmare. Its orientation towards British models ranged from the goals of the colonial movement to Bismarck's largely unsuccessful attempt to use non-governmental chartered companies to administer the German protectorates. But things were to turn out differently. The short-lived German colonial empire lasted only three decades, and after the First World War it had already been consigned to history. From the outset, the socio-imperialist perspective lived far more in its propaganda than in the reality of imperial expansion.[120]

All its plans remained illusionary. The protectorates of the German colonial empire in Africa and the Pacific, which was founded in 1884–5 and was already in decline during the First World War, were totally unsuited for mass immigration, as had been demonstrated back in the 1880s. Furthermore, attempts to move to the German colonies and become settlers, farmers or small traders remained tied to a substantial start capital, which the feared 'proletarian population' did not in any case possess. On the eve of the First World War, the number of Germans in the colonies (including administrative and military personnel who were there only temporarily) was still under 20,000. In 1912 there were only a total of 18,578 Germans in the colonies of German East Africa (3,579), German South-west Africa (12,135), Cameroon (1,359),

Togo (316), New Guinea (897) and the Pacific Islands (294). On the other hand, in the three decades from the commencement of German colonial expansion to the outbreak of the First World War (1885–1914), almost 1.5 million (gross) people emigrated overseas from Germany, of whom more than 1.3 million headed for the United States, so that even the idea of 'redirecting' emigration from North to South America remained a chimera. Propaganda for 'German' settlement colonies even had a sometimes counterproductive effect on the immigration policies of South American destination countries. In Brazil, where there were fears of a German state within a state, for example, measures promoting German immigrants were sometimes temporarily discontinued; other immigrant groups, especially Italians, were deliberately settled in strongly German areas. German emigration to South America did not rise considerably until the time of the Weimar Republic, when no other German colonies were still in existence. This essentially had to do with restrictive US immigration policies and administrative impediments to procedures by consulates; they acted as such a strong deterrent that German emigration to North America did not even take full advantage of its allowable quota in the 1920s (see chapter 3, section 2).

In the 1920s, fears of overpopulation were gradually replaced by ethnonationalist complaints about the decrease in the birth rate as a 'question of survival of the German people'.[121] In Nazi Germany prior to the Second World War, population growth increased as compared with the 1920s, a situation which was used by Nazi propaganda to grant ostensible demographic legitimacy to agitation for new *Lebensraum*, or living space. The gain had in fact less to do with Nazi population policies aimed at increasing population growth than with the fact that net German migration following the world economic crisis was in the black, since return migrations (about 300,000 in 1933–9) far outstripped emigrations (roughly 120,000).[122]

4 NATION-STATES AND INTERNATIONAL MIGRATION BEFORE THE FIRST WORLD WAR

From the French Revolution to the First World War, the idea of the nation developed from being a guiding light of national revolutionary movements to 'Europe's most powerful legitimizing concept'.[123] The flip side of this development was the history of persecution and flight for political reasons. The nineteenth century, into the second half, was an era of state opposition to revolutionary national, liberal and democratic movements. It created the political refugee, who was defined by the persecuting country as well as for support and control purposes in the country granting asylum, and thus became institutionalized. Lines of development and examples will be presented in the first part of this section. This thread will be taken up again later on, when in the third chapter of the book the consequences of ethnonational thinking in imperial nation-states will be highlighted with respect to flight and refuge in the twentieth century. The discussion will concentrate on forced migrations and flight by national minorities in conflicts involving nation-states and as a result of the establishment of new nation-states following the decline of the multi-ethnic Ottoman and Habsburg empires.

The development of the nation-state also had serious consequences for the history of cross-border labour migrations: they became 'international' migrations, while the development from national revolutionary ideas of the early nineteenth century to the ethnic nationalism of the late nineteenth and early twentieth centuries created collective definitions that distinguished between members of one's 'own' and 'other' 'nationalities'.[124] At the same time, the late nineteenth and early twentieth centuries formed an important transitional phase between a liberal era of relative freedom from state controls in European migrations of the nineteenth century and one of protectionist state migration and labour market policies between the First and Second World Wars. The second part of this section presents an overview of the basic structures of this transition and traces national lines of development by comparing France, Germany and England. A case study then follows, dealing with Prussia's anti-Polish migration and labour policies in the decades prior to the First World War. As a partly state-implemented variant, it was a distinct special case which simultaneously bridged the eras of relative freedom from state controls and state regulation of transnational migration and employment of foreigners on national labour markets.

National revolution and political asylum

The history of flight for political reasons is as old as political history itself. Yet the terms political refugee and political exile first became established in nineteenth-century Europe, which began to define and institutionalize political refugees by attributing to them specific refugee characteristics. At the end of the *ancien régime*, a type of refugees emerged that was part of the political consciousness of the time, less because of their numbers than their having a particular political bias, which divided the whole of Europe along political rather than national lines.[125]

This is one thing that political refugees of the nineteenth century had in common with the religious refugees of early modern times. But the change from flight for reasons of faith to flight for political reasons was not simply a change in the sense of different reasons for persecution; it was also a change in other criteria for choosing a country in which to seek asylum, in so far as such a choice even existed and the flight was not just to escape acute danger. Whereas religious refugees generally sought a permanent host country that would allow them to develop a lasting religious and cultural community, political refugees often sought a temporary place of exile. They were not always forced by persecution to go into exile. Many looked for a place from where they could continue unhindered or even more effectively to influence political developments, especially in their home countries. This is why the United States, which offered the greatest personal security for persecuted refugees from Europe, was by no means desired as a place to live in exile. Political refugees instead usually preferred to seek asylum in European countries, such as France, Belgium, Switzerland and England. Furthermore, these countries enabled refugees to maintain a certain degree of communication – Switzerland for Germans, France for Poles, the southern Netherlands for the French.

The reasons for these significant political movements into exile lay first and foremost in the unresolved constitutional and territorial issues of countries that had previously been under Napoleonic rule. The Congress of Vienna had created a system of equilibrium among the major European powers in 1815. The 'remainder of Central Europe' (Reinhart Koselleck) remained largely unformed and disputed in Vienna. Especially in this region, constitutional efforts and national and social movements were viewed as threats to the European balance and therefore decisively repressed.[126] The suppression of uprisings and revolutions caused the number of political refugees to rise dramatically. The period from 1830 to 1848–9 thus became the epitome of the epoch of political exile in the nineteenth century. Extant information on the number of refugees is very scarce and imprecise, especially since police identity registers did not exist or contained many gaps.

At the same time as refugee criteria were starting to be assigned, the search for the 'genuine' refugee also began. This pure form existed in the past just as seldom as it exists today. In the nineteenth century, there were several types of political refugees or refugees for whom political motives and goals were more or less predominant in their decision to go into exile. There were royalists who were partly chased out and partly voluntary emigrants; revolutionary fighters for national, liberal or democratic ideals; irregular volunteers; soldiers or officers. There were also, often overlapping with the above, political intellectuals who fought with their pen for national, democratic, socialist or even anarchist goals, from the critical journalist who occasionally traded his pen for a weapon to the career politician or career revolutionary. There were travelling craftsmen, from the politically educated revolutionary with a background in the trades to the casual transporter of revolutionary flyers. Moreover, what was considered as 'political flight' or 'political asylum' by the governments of the persecuting and receiving countries did not necessarily coincide with the understanding of those personally involved, since it was the former that wielded the power to define refugee traits.[127]

Movements of nineteenth-century political refugees occurred in several waves. At the beginning was the emigration of royalists from France after the 1789 Revolution. A second wave followed from 1815 into the 1820s during the Bourbon Restoration; and a third was provoked by the unrest, revolutions and uprisings that began in 1830 in the aftermath of the July Revolution in Paris. A fourth wave followed the revolutionary events of 1848–9. Bourgeois nationalism and proletarian socialism encountered each other in the emerging parties as well as in exile. Much smaller political emigration waves included those who had fought in the Paris Commune of 1871 and, in the 1880s, socialists from the time of the German anti-socialist law (1878–90).[128]

The major European countries that offered asylum in the nineteenth century were France, Belgium, Switzerland and England. They differed in their respective traditions, procedures and alternating willingness to accept refugees. Here we shall limit our discussion to the period from the early 1830s to the late 1850s, when for the first time the four most significant host countries articulated their political and legal opinions on asylum issues, reducing them to pragmatic policies on forms of treatment that would be formative also for the second half of the nineteenth century.

France

In France it had not been unusual for political refugees to be taken in as early as before the revolutionary period. Among the numerous foreign nationals who served in the French army were persecuted exiles from various countries. Thousands of Dutch patriots whose constitutional and democratic demands had failed in 1787 fled their country and requested asylum in Brussels and in France. The same was true for Irish patriots and Geneva revolutionaries who fled to France in the 1780s and 1790s. During the years of the revolution, France itself experienced a mass emigration for political reasons that was unique in its history. It included royalist nobility, priests, middle-class citizens and even peasants, especially from the borderlands. The royalists usually left the country not as political refugees but as representatives of an ousted ruling class, partially in order to organize the struggle against the revolution from other royal courts in Europe. Figures from the period 1789–1815 are not reliable, especially since many emigrants temporarily returned several times in the 1790s, only to leave the country once again. Estimates range from a maximum of 60,000, to 100,000–130,000, to 180,000 French emigrants.[129]

Most refugees to France after 1815 came from Germany, Italy and Spain. After the Carlsbad Decrees of 1819, national-liberal patriots came from the German Confederation, whose system of police informers spanned central Europe. Italian refugees from Sicily, Piedmont, Lombardy and Venetia followed after 1821, fleeing Habsburg weapons and persecution after the failure of their movements for national unity and a liberal constitution. Spanish liberals arrived in 1823; they had lost power and influence after defeat by, ironically, the French army and were ruthlessly oppressed and then driven out by Ferdinand VII, who had been installed with France's aid.

Refugees lived in France without any official assistance, surviving through their own work or the charity of others; only the poorest among them received support. The situation did not change until the mass emigration after 1830, when the term the 'Great Emigration' was coined with respect to the Polish refugees of 1830–1. The July Revolution in Paris had triggered a chain reaction of uprisings and unrest. The spark spread to the southern Netherlands, Switzerland, the central German states and on to Poland and central Italy. Success or defeat depended on the openness of individual countries to constitutional reform and on the power play of the major powers.[130] After the rebellions were quelled and suppressed, thousands from throughout Europe requested asylum in France, a country that had never before taken in more than a few hundred political refugees at one time. During the July Monarchy (1832–51), France took in far more asylum seekers than any other country. For the first time, the mass of refugees led to talk of a 'refugee problem', and the coming and going of refugees did not cease until the Second Empire.[131]

The Great Emigration of the Poles in 1830–1 was great not only in terms of numbers but also in terms of its intellectuals, such as composer Frederic Chopin and Polish national poet Adam Mickiewicz, whose *Ode to Youth* written in 1820 later became the hymn of the November Uprising of 1830–1. The conservative and irreconcilably anti-Russian Polish prince Adam Czartoryski took up residence in the Hotel Lambert on the Île Saint Louis, from where he led the aristocratic camp in Paris. Joachim Lelewel, a history professor, did so for the Democratic Society of the Polish opposition in Brussels.[132] Up to 12,000 Poles crossed through Europe from east to west. Two-thirds of them ultimately sought refuge in France.

In the 1830s the number of political refugees in France had reached an estimated 20,000 (Grandjonc), including roughly 10,000 Poles and 'a few thousand each of Portuguese, Spaniards, Italians and Germans'. Lower estimates assume about 13,000 (Noiriel), and the lowest, slightly more than 10,000 refugees (Schieder).[133]

For French republicans, there was no question but that France should open its borders to revolutionary fighters after their failed revolutions: 'To let the consequences of the revolution be halted at the border is denying France's mission and instinct for the spreading of civilization.' The ambiguity of the position of the new 'bourgeois king' Louis Philippe, however, was apparent in his symbolic policies, his 'gestures to the French public and the parliamentary rostrum',[134] on the one hand, and his satisfaction at being recognized by other European rulers, on the other. The treatment of refugees in France after the July Revolution thus spanned a large and often contradictory spectrum. It ranged from financial assistance and employment integration to expulsion, and from support for emigration to being sent to the Foreign Legion. Refugees during the time of the Great Emigration were totally dependent on the government of the host country and its political decisions, not only in France but in Switzerland and Belgium as well.[135]

A basic concept for the treatment of political refugees did not yet exist in France in the first half of the nineteenth century. Being granted asylum was considered a state privilege and was not regulated by law, as the famous right to asylum in the constitution of 1793 never came into force, a fact that is often overlooked. However, individual aid from the populace and local communities for refugees, especially the Poles, was overwhelming. It corresponded to the wave of national enthusiasm for the Poles who passed through Germany in late 1831 and early 1832. After eagerly taking in Polish refugees from 1831 to 1837, the French government authorized a total of more than 20 million francs for aid to refugees over six years, most of which was financed through credits. Relief for the Poles was thus far higher than it was for Italians and Spaniards. The French government's treatment of political refugees was still obviously influenced by estates thinking. This treatment did not follow the republican ideal of equality but the norms of Christian charity. It assumed that different social environments had different needs and was therefore geared towards reconstructing the home country's social hierarchies in the receiving country.[136]

Refugees were treated as if they were an escaped revolutionary army. Their civilian careers were assigned military ranks and refugees' pay level was determined according to the respective pay of soldiers. The first major wave of newly arrived refugees were put in reception camps at the borders and sent to different barracks. In principle, however, refugees in France were free to practise any profession, in the arts and sciences as well as trade, commerce and industry. In 1837, 4,000 of 6,130 refugees receiving support worked in these areas. Of 1,000 Polish refugees who were registered according to their occupation in 1839, there were 500 clerks' assistants, 270 medical students, 135 pupils at elite schools, 100 teachers and about 50 doctors.

The challenge presented by the growing influx of Polish and other refugees led in 1832 to the beginnings of a legal definition of political refugees in France. The law described them as people 'without the protection of their country, without a passport or any connection to a diplomatic mission in France'. They were required by law to show evidence of a permanent residence. That in turn made it necessary to organize their distribution within the country. In order to ensure that they arrived at their destinations, travelling refugees received their 'pay' stage by stage. In order for them to receive their assistance, personal identity cards were introduced in 1837. Destination towns and routes were selected on the basis of domestic and foreign policy security needs. Paris, for example, with its German colony of about 20,000 residents and its radical trades associations, was definitely excluded. The same was true for *départements* on the border in the south and south-west, in order to prevent contact with the homeland and attack.

France's policy towards refugees after the July Revolution was generally one of unrestricted integration. This included, first of all, the establishment of the Foreign Legion in 1831, which was intended to combine ideals with budgetary interests. Behind the idea of a legion of foreigners under French leadership was the goal of 'honouring' the soldiers among the foreign refugees by having them fight alongside French soldiers; at the same time, it would reduce the costs of refugee support and the number of refugees by transforming them into legionnaires. In the subsequent years and also after 1848, France was constantly trying to decrease the number of foreign refugees with the help of the Foreign Legion.

Rising numbers of refugees, high support payments, and cooperation between German and French radicals in south-western Germany led France to move away from integrative refugee policies by 1834. New ways to reduce the number of refugees were to turn them back at the border, require them to join the Foreign Legion, and introduce policies of state-promoted emigration and expulsion. Extradition of political refugees had become an everyday practice during the Bourbon Restoration period. At the time of the July Monarchy, the French government generally refused to extradite refugees to a country of persecution. However, refugees who were politically active were confronted with expulsion, especially those from Germany, because cooperation between German and French radicals was considered particularly dangerous. Refugees were also expelled if they left the town to which they had been assigned or disturbed the 'public peace'. Another measure was to incarcerate them in certain places. Refugees were only guaranteed asylum in France if they lived inconspicuously and abstained from all political activity.

After the Revolution of 1848 French refugee policies became even more restrictive and defensive. They now aimed to allow as few refugees as possible into the country, which hit German refugees especially hard. Asylum that was still granted was restricted under the premise that large segments of the French labour force suffered deprivation and had to be given priority. 'True' political refugees were still to be accepted, but their status as refugees had to be reviewed by prefects, for which French diplomats or foreign authorities were also to be called in. Assignment of the corresponding criteria remained wholly dependent on decisions by governments, which were clearly influenced by foreign policy considerations and the desire to protect their own national interests.

Refugee policy using the Foreign Legion was sometimes exploited for foreign policy purposes or as power politics through aid to neighbouring countries. In 1849, France offered Switzerland to take in refugees, no matter what country they came from, for the Foreign Legion. After the suppression of an uprising in Baden that year, the Baden government sought to find a home for the numerous non-Baden revolutionaries who had been arrested, at first unsuccessfully offering them to the Dutch government to join their colonial troops. Their offer to send them to France for the Foreign Legion in Algiers was more successful. In 1849, Austria too sent requests to France in respect of insurgent Hungarian soldiers. Seven hundred people from Baden were recruited in Switzerland for the French Foreign Legion in 1850. At the same time, England established its Foreign Legion and openly recruited in Switzerland – with the toleration of the Swiss authorities – mustering 3,300 foreign revolutionaries for the British Swiss Legion to serve in the Crimean War, though they arrived too late. The Foreign Legion was thus used as an instrument to reduce the number of refugees or to find a place for unwanted refugees from their own or other countries.[137]

Aside from requiring refugees to enter the Foreign Legion, other methods of keeping their numbers down in France were to discontinue financial assistance and to support their efforts to move to Belgium or England or to emigrate to the United States. Finally, even before Louis Napoleon seized power in 1851, his intensified persecution of domestic adversaries also made the situation more difficult for refugees in France. During the Second Empire from 1852 to 1870, the total number of asylum seekers and refugees dropped significantly. France under Napoleon III was no longer a country that offered asylum.[138]

Belgium

Belgium demonstrated a more consistent position after the Revolution of 1848 than did France. The nation-state that emerged from the 1830–1 revolt against the United Netherlands had chosen its own king, and instead of a monarchical claim to hold legitimate power, it brought a national, revolutionary sense of monarchy. This and the image of progressive, aspiring Belgian industry after 1830 determined the country's reputation as '*terre d'accueil*' and '*Belgique hospitalière*'. The Belgian constitution of 1831 was considered a model of asylum-friendly politics in western Europe, but within Belgium itself its far-reaching conception and unforeseen consequences brought growing uncertainty.

In the Bourbon Restoration period from 1815 to 1830, political refugees from France and Italy had already come to the kingdom of the Netherlands, especially to the south and to Brussels, in the region that later became Belgium. They were guaranteed freedom of the press and the right to political action. The French sought refuge in the French-speaking southern Netherlands from 1816 to 1818, or they were exiled there. Most of them were Bonapartists who fled in ever-greater numbers after 1815, during Napoleon I's Hundred Days, and especially in response to the arrests and censorship following the murder of the Bourbon heir to the throne in 1820.[139]

Italians fled, as noted above, to France, England, Switzerland and, after 1821, mostly to the Netherlands. A 'centre of moderate politicians, refugees and artists' was established after 1821 in Gaesbeck Castle near Brussels. Lord of the castle was Giuseppe Arconati-Visconti, a Lombardy count condemned to death in Italy by the Habsburg government, who enjoyed the protection of William I. Some Italian refugees served in 1830 as volunteers in the Belgian revolutionary army; others were politically active outside Belgium.[140] In the Belgian army, high-ranking positions were sometimes filled by Poles in exile after 1833. This was true in all European national movements, in Belgium as in Italy, Germany and Hungary; and in all anti-Russian conflicts participants included experienced Polish officers and sometimes entire Polish legions, all coordinated remotely from the Polish centre of exiled aristocrats in Paris's Hotel Lambert.[141]

The number of political refugees in Belgium can also only be approximated. As in the rest of Europe, after 1830 most political refugees were Poles. In 1846, there were a total of about 95,000 foreigners living in Belgium. Most were French (*c.*34,600), followed by Dutch (*c.*20,500) and Germans (*c.*13,000). The fact that the German Workers' Union in Brussels only had 100 members in the period 1847–50 shows that the significance of political refugees depended not on their numbers but on their role as a voice of the opposition abroad. The abundance of their writings and the activities of their groups and clubs convey the image of lively populations of political exiles, but it easily leads to an overestimation of their numbers as compared with immigrants for other, especially economic, reasons. The German press in western European emigration countries included about 50 political journals and newspapers in the period from 1830 to 1848, although the number of political refugees in the strict sense among all Germans in western Europe prior to 1848 was only about 1 per cent.

Karl Marx and Friedrich Engels had been living in Brussels since 1846, after being expelled from Paris under German pressure. Marx had left Germany in 1843. At that time he was part of a group of exiles who did not initially go abroad as political refugees but assumed that status while in exile. He belonged to the circle of journalists and writers who hoped to be able to avoid censorship by working abroad.[142] After being expelled from Belgium, Marx moved on to England in 1848. The Communist Correspondence Committee, the Communist League and the German Workers' Union were all active in England at that time. The branches and networks of the democratic and communist organizations in the period leading up to the 1848 Revolution were broad and complex, reaching Paris, Switzerland, Brussels, London and Germany.

In 1847, Marx still praised Belgium as the country where 'there is free discussion, freedom of association and the sowing of humanitarian ideals can take place for the best of all Europe'.[143] The fact that he was expelled a short time later reveals one facet of Belgian policies, according to which political refugees – as in France and Switzerland – were strictly prohibited from political activity. On the other hand, however, liberal Belgian policies offered liberties for all political refugees: freedom of the press, freedom of association even for the Communist League, guaranteed privacy of the post, and democratic clubs and the press watching out for every case of expulsion.[144] Above all, there was general protection against extradition. The extradition law passed in 1833 was a model for other European countries that granted asylum, although they did not adopt this unrestricted form until later: the Netherlands in 1849, England in 1870, Switzerland in 1892. In all other countries, the decision to extradite remained – into the twentieth century – a matter of government discretion. Belgian law prohibited extradition not only in the case of a political offence but also for *crimes connexes*, crimes connected with a political action, from confiscation to robbery to politically motivated murder.[145]

This refusal to extradite was *de facto* the true right to asylum in Belgium. The relative non-violence of the Revolution of 1830–1 and the large number of intellectuals and university graduates among the refugees, as well as the acceptance of using violence against reactionary systems, for example in Poland, created the backdrop of experience leading to the broad regulation of Belgian protection for refugees. After at first generously taking in and even financially assisting unemployed refugees, however, Belgium, too, soon steered a more restrictive course in its refugee policies. The main objective was now to reduce the number of refugees by expulsion or by moving them to other countries, especially England.

While France pursued anti-asylum policies after Louis Napoleon seized power in late 1851, Belgium still remained – in addition to Switzerland – the most significant asylum-granting country on the Continent, even if it initiated numerous measures to resist the flow of refugees, some in cooperation with other countries. In order to reject refugees at the border, the Belgian government received refugee lists in 1849 from German governments. In 1850, Belgium requested from Switzerland a list of refugees who were willing to go to England or the United States via Belgium. In 1852, the Belgian government then banned French refugees coming from Switzerland via German states from passing through Belgium, in order to prevent their infiltrating France. In 1849, 34 Italian and Hungarian refugees were turned back at the border since they had already been taken in by another country – this was in historic anticipation of the 'first country of asylum' clause that would play a central role in the asylum policies of European countries at the end of the twentieth century (see chapter 4, section 4 and chapter 5, section 1).

Belgium became an important country for granting asylum after 1848, especially for the French. There were 2,400 applications for asylum from 1848 to 1853 in Belgium, 1,572 of them from French after Louis Napoleon seized power. However, probably only a small percentage were finally granted asylum, and from 1848 to 1852 the Belgian government also expelled almost 700 refugees. Since Belgium, like Switzerland, had not been affected by the Revolution of 1848–9 and remained politically neutral, their asylum policies came under increasing pressure, from the French government in particular.

After the failed assassination of Napoleon III, the *crimes connexes* clause was watered down in 1856 regarding extradition in cases of assassination of heads of state and capital crimes such as murder. Except for Switzerland and England, almost all European countries adopted the new assassination clause. The Belgian government thus legalized what it had long been practising: a greater intolerance of violent revolutionaries, representatives of the labour movement, opponents of the liberal state and members of anarchist movements.

Switzerland

Neutral Switzerland, too, disappointed many refugees with its asylum policies, which at the time of the Revolution of 1848–9 seemed to consist primarily of transferring an army of revolutionaries made up of thousands of refugees either back to their home countries or to England and the United States. Here as well there were restrictive definitions of who was considered a refugee. Only those who were persecuted in their native country for political crimes and could not return because of threat to life and limb would be acknowledged as refugees. Political asylum in Switzerland, as in France and later in Belgium, was never more than a humanitarian concession which, for political considerations and without any basis in law, could be refused or revoked at any time. After the major European powers acknowledged Switzerland's perpetual neutrality in 1815, the land-locked country was put into a dilemma: refugees who had already been taken in could not be expelled or allowed to exit the country or pass through other countries in transit without the agreement of neighbouring countries. Dealing with asylum law therefore remained a perpetual balancing act of trying to reconcile the regulations that assured a European equilibrium with Swiss asylum law without violating either.[146] Nowhere was the definition of political refugees and their treatment so dependent on the general foreign political climate as in Switzerland.

However, from the 1820s conspiracy and revolutionary propaganda were organized from Switzerland's secure base more than from any other European country that granted asylum. This would lead to severe restrictions in the asylum law by the Swiss Confederation. The first groups of political refugees to go to Switzerland, as elsewhere, were Germans, Italians and Poles. Again, there was a wave of support for Polish emigrants, who either went directly to Switzerland or, starting in late 1832, received transit passes from the French government, if they so desired, to pass through France on their way to Switzerland. Almost exclusively, officers went to Switzerland in this way; estimates fluctuate from 500 (Bonjour) to 380 (Reiter). The refugees had taken a detour via Frankfurt am Main, where they arrived too late to participate in the revolutionary Frankfurt riots, the so-called *Frankfurter Wachensturm* of 1833. They joined the Italian national revolutionaries surrounding Giuseppe Mazzini, who from his exile in Switzerland had prepared an invasion of the kingdom of Sardinia (the Savoy campaign), which failed miserably.

The asylum law was restricted in 1836, at first to avoid its 'abuse' by foreign refugees. Refugees were to be expelled, not only from the asylum-granting canton but from all of Switzerland, 'if they in any way disturbed or could still disturb the relations of Switzerland with other countries or if they intervened in the internal affairs of the country'. Pressure by the big powers ultimately led to a general ban on foreign refugees' participation in any organization. Political work was then only possible when carried out clandestinely, and the number of secret associations rose dramatically. For example, after founding Young Europe in Bern in 1834, with Young Italy, Young Germany and Young Poland sections, the revolutionary Mazzini even called for the foundation of a Young Switzerland from his Swiss exile.

The list of political refugees expelled from Switzerland offers insight into their background and social class. A total of 156 refugees were expelled in 1836, of which 8 were from Poland and 12 from Italy. All the others were from the German Confederation, including 22 university graduates and students and 77 craftsmen, which was the largest group. Some of them had probably not been politicized until after going to Switzerland, and so they entered the country as travelling journeymen and left it as political refugees.

The greatest influx of political refugees to Switzerland took place during the Revolution of 1848–9 after the uprisings in Italy and the south-western region of the German Confederation. The canton of Ticino became the base for Italian revolutionaries. After the defeat of the Milan uprising, about 20,000 refugees, among them not only soldiers but civilians including women, children, the elderly and infirm, crossed the border to the Swiss cantons of Graubünden and Ticino. The Baden uprisings in the south-west of the German Confederation from April 1848 to May 1849 resulted in a total of 10,000–12,000 refugees entering Switzerland. The first to flee to Switzerland with their families were Baden civil servants and officers referred to as 'monarchists'. After the democrats were defeated in the summer of 1848, defeated troops of over 9,000 men as well as war supplies entered Switzerland. The refugees were distributed evenly among all cantons; they received daily support of 15 centimes and were closely monitored. Foreign pressure by France, Prussia and Austria grew, culminating in the demand to expel all refugees immediately. Switzerland responded without delay, disbanding 16 revolutionary German Workers' Unions, expelling their members and deporting the revolutionary Mazzini. It negotiated with the home countries about amnesty or at least emigration to England or the United States. With that, the number of refugees started to drop dramatically.

From then on, a rapid decrease in the number of refugees became the main objective of Swiss foreign policy, which deployed various ways and means towards that end. The Council of Ministers no longer considered it sufficient grounds for asylum or for opposing the deportation of refugees to their native countries if the possible impending sentences were only a few weeks in prison, payment of fines, revocation of civic rights and similar penalties, even if in reality more severe punishment was to be expected. Refugees wanting to escape such penalties had to provide proof either that they had received a serious sentence or that a corresponding investigation had been opened with a foreseeably serious outcome. Even being 'work-shy' became grounds for expulsion.

Another method was to expel leading political figures and military superiors of the Baden-Palatinate uprising, which initially involved 47 people and later another 34. This measure was vehemently disputed; behind it was the expectation that without leadership, the refugees would instigate no further plots and might even follow their leaders to other countries. The European powers cooperated very closely towards the goal of deporting political refugees, who were disliked by all sides, from the Continent altogether: England and the United States became host countries for expelled German revolutionaries. France allowed them transit permission and even offered to assume the travel costs for non-French refugees. Through this French–Swiss collaboration, 462 refugees emigrated to the United States. The German states in turn declared themselves willing to grant transit permission to French and Italian refugees en route to Belgian or Dutch ports. Remarks were to be entered into the passports of the refugees in transit identifying them specifically as political refugees in order to facilitate their surveillance. With that, the assignment of refugee status turned into the complete branding of politically unpopular 'subjects'. While these restrictive refugee policies were being carried on in cooperation with other governments, the number of refugees in Switzerland sank from tens of thousands in 1848–9 to several hundreds in mid-1851, and by 1852 there were only 235.

On the European continent there was hardly any place left for political refugees, with the exception of privileged cases. To put it another way, free immigration to England and the United States was all that prevented the critical refugee problem in continental Europe from coming to a head and ending catastrophically for the refugees.

England and the United States

England and the United States were the only countries in the nineteenth century in which the right to political asylum and the right to immigration were closely interconnected. From 1823 to 1905, England did not expel a single refugee. The government had no legal means by which to do so. Here it was precisely the lack of laws that offered refugees a degree of security that was not to be found in any country in continental Europe.[147] From this perspective, England was the most consistent and thus significant asylum-granting country in the nineteenth century on account of its lack of policy towards refugees.

The model country without a constitution offered foreign refugees a right to asylum without any explicit asylum law. However, its government did have options for taking action against 'troublesome foreigners' in 1793–1826 and 1848–50. A legal basis for such action was provided by the Aliens Act of 1793. It certainly did not emerge from a fundamentally anti-immigration or anti-refugee position. On the contrary, Britain took in more refugees prior to the French Revolution than any other European country, from members of the nobility and large segments of the Catholic clergy and royalist military to numerous artisans, entrepreneurs and traders. Migration dates were not recorded, but according to some extant budget details during this time the enormous sum of £2.9 million sterling was spent to support refugees. The Aliens Act aimed rigorously to control all movements of foreigners, prevent 'radicals' from entering the country, open only certain ports and oblige shipowners to keep detailed passenger lists. In the 1790s, on average only 54 people were expelled each year. The options opened up by this 1793 legislation were used only to control the threat posed by the French Revolution, whereas the Aliens Act that was valid from 1848 to 1850 did not result in any rejections or expulsions. The restriction of the right to immigration in the 1905 Aliens Act targeted not 'subversive' political forces but especially Jewish emigrants from eastern Europe.

England's political neutrality with respect to foreign refugees was based on its relationship to state and law, which was fundamentally different from that on the Continent. Looking back to the seventeenth and eighteenth centuries, it is possible to understand the notion behind what in the nineteenth century was Europe's most liberal asylum policy and its connection with the right to immigration: mercantilist population theory and favourable economic experiences with the great immigration wave of the seventeenth century had led to demands for a naturalization policy that supported immigration. At that time, after the Edict of Nantes was repealed in 1685, Huguenot religious refugees brought many artisanal skills to England that were previously unknown there, spurring a lasting innovative economic impulse. An extremely liberal naturalization law was passed in 1709. Foreign Protestants could obtain British citizenship by converting to the Anglican church, taking an oath and paying a fee to the amount of one shilling. The law worked like a magnet. Only months later, around 15,000 impoverished people from the Palatinate arrived in London. The law was therefore repealed after only three years, but it still had a normative impact on nineteenth-century legislation. Modernization of naturalization legislation in accordance with the liberal ideas of the nineteenth century followed with the laws of 1844 and 1870. In a simplified procedure, citizenship could be acquired after three years of residence with a good reputation; rejection was only possible within the discretionary political powers of the interior minister, for example, for foreigners without property or political refugees with undesirable political views, such as Karl Marx.

The granting of asylum in England had nothing to do with active support for refugees, much less with identification with their political goals. Instead, it was a matter of defending the country's liberal political system. These decisive liberal principles included, for one, the principle of territorial rights and equal rights for all, that is, also for foreign nationals, including political refugees. Since the Middle Ages, the territorial principle of *jus soli* applied in England. Whoever was born in the countries of the English crown was considered a natural-born subject with all duties and rights of a citizen, including the right to purchase land, which foreigners were not entitled to do. Furthermore, the legal system protected refugees because some crimes that could be prosecuted on the Continent, such as political conspiracy, political propaganda and even incitement to revolution, were not recognized in the English system as punishable offences. Also, the demands of the democratic and national movements on the Continent (such as freedom of assembly, freedom of the press, introduction of a parliament) did not frighten the English government since these had long since been reality in the United Kingdom. The generous way of dealing with the right to asylum was considered a humanitarian model for its neighbours on the Continent that was worth defending, though as the strongest industrial and commercial power in the world, England did not have to justify any of its actions in any case.

The fact that England became the safest European asylum-granting country in the 1850s was owing less to its own attractive force than to the refugee policies of the host countries in continental Europe. In the 1830s, Italian and Polish emigrants were enthusiastically taken in, in England as in Germany, Switzerland, France and Belgium. All contemporary reports showed a waning of this enthusiasm after the revolutions of 1848–9 in view of the extreme poverty and squalor that the refugees often brought with them. They received no support whatsoever, to some extent because of the radical activities of some of them. Karl Heinzen, a revolutionary from Baden, wrote about the cultural differences from the perspective of a refugee in 1864 in Boston, Massachusetts. From his new country of exile across the Atlantic, he relayed an account of his stay in London in the early 1850s: 'At that time...a Chinese – Ledru-Rollin called the English the Chinese of the occident – was a foreigner not tailored to English fashion and looked to a Londoner like a barbarian; a refugee was like a wild animal. I could not go on the streets back then without having people by the score stop in their tracks to stare at me. Even distinguished ladies stood as if petrified and stared right in my face as if they had never seen a person *generis masculini*.'[148] The inviolability of the right to asylum was never questioned through such behaviour, but no one felt responsible for the refugees either. In any case, as the English government laconically put it in 1853, it was the continental governments that had sent the refugees to England.

After 1851, the leaders of the European opposition movements came together in London, either an unpopular final station marked by poverty on their path of asylum through Europe, or a transit station on their emigration path to the United States. Ever since Louis Napoleon's *coup d'état*, hopes of a rapid return and a political transformation had disappeared. Russian writer and publicist Alexander Ivanovich Herzen later wrote of the ghetto-like political subculture that quickly formed in London exile after 1850: 'Bad luck, idleness and want brought out intolerance, obstinacy and a pathological irritability.... The emigrants disintegrated into small groups, at the centre of which were individual names and a certain hatred, but no principle. Their way of always looking towards the past and their exclusivity of social contact soon started finding expression in their thoughts and speech, in their manners and dress. A new guild – the guild of émigrés – had formed and fossilized alongside other guilds.'[149] Nevertheless, refugees from different countries cooperated in their English exile, beyond all political and intellectual differences. They included Mazzini's European Democratic Central Committee, which had French, Polish, Romanian as well as German representatives. As a political contrast, socialist refugees were in contact with the English Chartists; and the International Association brought together English and foreign socialists.

Since there was no compulsory registration of residents in England, all existing figures on refugees are based on mere estimates. For March 1852, for example, there is a figure of 1,970 refugees; for March 1853, the figure is 4,386. More than half of all refugees in England lived in London. The English government knew only a handful of the leading political figures by name. During this time, most foreign refugees by far came from Germany, followed by France, Hungary, Italy and Belgium. The largest group of German refugees in London were labourers and journeymen in the trades. There was a smaller group of professors, writers, journalists, teachers and artists. In addition, there were a few former officers. Among those in the second-named group were Karl Marx, Friedrich Engels, Wilhelm Liebknecht, Carl Schurz, Gustav Struve and the Baden revolutionaries. They were in contact with politically active refugees from other countries, such as the Italian Giuseppe Mazzini, the French socialists Louis Blanc and Alexandre Ledru-Rollin, the

Hungarian Lajos Kossuth and the Russian Alexander Ivanovich Herzen. The revolutionary leaders tried to keep their supporters together, sometimes to no avail. The disappointment that followed the *coup d'état* in France in 1851, the destitution among refugees and their families in England and the opportunities to emigrate to the United States dispersed the groups. German emigrants also split among the liberal and social democratic camps.

England, which apart from the aforementioned exceptions did not deport refugees, became the preferred destination for Belgium, France and Switzerland to deport their own refugees after 1851. In his report *A Summer in London*, published in 1854, Theodor Fontane wrote about the subsiding enthusiasm of the English in the face of the expanding refugee population: 'In the wake of patriots and men of honour who were thankful to set foot in these places of refuge came all kinds of riff-raff flooding the streets and squares of London, and in place of a warm welcome came immediate rejection and contempt. Hundredfold abuse of the right to asylum justified the coldness and isolation only too much.'[150] The uneasiness in England about the growing numbers and isolated radical behaviour of refugees led only to an attempt to reduce the numbers by discreetly promoting emigration. Since refugees in England could generally never reckon on any financial assistance – the time of the French Revolution was merely an exception that proved the rule – this opportunity was frequently taken. By January 1858, the English government secretly financed the emigration of 960 men, 305 women and 233 children. To prevent fraud in applications for the voyage, leaders of the refugee groups sometimes issued certificates to confirm the applicant's refugee status. However, the English action can be viewed only to some degree as a substitute for expulsion. This became apparent when France announced its willingness to assume the costs of transportation to the United States for French-Italian refugees and submitted to the English government a preferred list for deportation. London made it known that no one would be sent to America against his or her will.

The political significance of the European refugees in the United States diminished as they began to disappear among the mass of immigrants. The number of German revolutionary refugees who went to the United States after 1848–9 alone is estimated at 3,000–4,000.[151] Most stayed permanently and went into a sort of internal emigration in the United States, or else committed themselves to their new homeland all the more. Quite a few left more indelible historical traces there than in Europe. Two such men were the most important political representatives of German-American 'hyphenated' culture of the nineteenth century: Carl Schurz and Friedrich Kapp. Schurz was a captured revolutionary fighter of the democratic movement who had escaped from Rastatt fortress in

1849. He subsequently went into exile in France and England and emigrated to the United States in 1852. There he was a senator from Missouri from 1869 to 1875, and from 1877 to 1881 he was US secretary of the interior. One of the few revolutionary refugees who later returned to Europe in order to continue his political activities, at times in a clearly different direction, was the initially radical early socialist Kapp. He spent most of 1848–9 in exile, living in Brussels, Paris and Geneva, and then emigrated to the United States in 1850. He became an affluent lawyer in New York, also working as a journalist and historian of the German-Americans, almost all of whom joined the new Republican Party virtually *en masse* under the leadership of Kapp and Schurz. Kapp served as New York commissioner of immigration from 1866 to 1870 before returning to Germany in 1870. He was a representative in the Reichstag from 1872 to 1877 for the national liberals (NLP), and then from 1881 to 1884 for the left-wing liberals (Liberale Vereinigung).[152] Playing a similar role as Carl Schurz and Friedrich Kapp in German-American hyphenated culture was, for example, the Baden revolutionary Karl von Koseritz in Brazil. He arrived in Brazil in 1851 aboard the *Heinrich*, a transport ship of the German legion, which fought with Brazil against Argentina and was comprised predominantly of revolutionaries from 1848–9. In Brazil, von Koseritz became a teacher, lawyer, publisher of various newspapers and one of the most significant representatives of German-Brazilian culture of the nineteenth century.[153]

The exile experience in nineteenth-century continental Europe was, aside from the early 1830s, marked by political disappointment and disillusionment for most European refugees. In addition, once nation-states were founded in Germany and Italy, most national revolutionary programmes had become history, except for calls for a Polish nation-state, which disappeared for a long time from the European agenda after the bloody suppression of the Polish uprising of 1863. Struggles for the nation and a constitution were replaced by struggles and in-fighting by the nationally and internally organized labour movement. Fear of the spectre of revolution therefore always remained a political constant in nineteenth-century Europe, but revolution never returned and politically motivated flight and refugee migrations decreased in the second half of the century, with the exception of the refugees after the Paris Commune uprising in 1871 and those fewer in number who left Germany within the scope of the anti-socialist law (1878–90).

Political refugees in the nineteenth century as a whole remained negligible as compared with a new type of refugee that emerged along with the nation-states: the formation of nation-states created minorities, and with them in many cases the basic configuration for flight and forced migrations that were to earn the twentieth century its designation as the 'century of refugees'. Persecution of national, liberal and democratic movements had created a type of refugee who was persecuted for something he or she had done. At the close of the nineteenth century and in the early twentieth, the age of the nation-states would create a type of refugee who was persecuted for something the persecutor viewed him or her as being.[154]

Citizenship and international migration

Many national revolutionaries fought for the idea of the nation-state and became political refugees as a result. With the late state formations in Italy in 1861 and Germany in 1871, the nation-state had finally become the definitive political structure in Europe as a whole. The idea of the nation, which had once encompassed the dream of unity and freedom in a peaceful international community, was amplified in the world views and ideologies of the decades of high imperialism before the First World War into aggressive nationalistic patterns of ideas and judgement that had a dual function: on the one hand, domestic pacification and the stabilization of prevailing social structures by referring to latent or acute external threats to the 'nation'; and, on the other hand, legitimization of the *sacro egoismo* when representing 'national interests' in the power politics of foreign policy.

Imperial Darwinism moved international relations into the context of a 'national' struggle for existence or survival. The concert of the powers sounded cacophonous and shrill. At the same time, nationalistic patterns in images of 'self' and 'other' became ethnically charged into aggressive ethnonationalistic perceptions. These in turn were obscured by ethnocultural concepts as economic, social and political contrasts of interests, and rivalries were given a 'cultural' appearance and disguise. Aggressive nationalistic ideas were conveyed and consolidated through the military, schools and the press and reinforced through the associations of an organized nationalism. They were inwardly integrative and outwardly segregating, though sometimes even internally, minorities were excluded when 'negative integration' served to strengthen the majority. In such cases, these minorities were put under increased pressure to assimilate or suffer segregation and repression.

In the more highly industrialized European nation-states of central and western Europe, the interrelationship of state, economy and society was recast on the way towards organized capitalism by the new structure of the modern interventionist state. It developed after the shift from liberalism to protectionism in the 1870s and 1880s. On the one hand were economic interventions, including state-levied 'protective duties' on national domestic markets in order to – as it was expressed in Germany – 'protect national labour' from cheap foreign products; such duties had already been introduced in the 1870s in, among other countries, Austria-Hungary, Italy, Russia and France. This also included safeguarding overseas markets and resources through state protection in the second and final phase of Euro-colonial expansion, starting with the 'scramble for Africa' in the early 1880s. Then came different kinds of intervention on the labour market, the first steps towards protecting domestic labour forces from foreign competition. On the other hand, there were also social interventions, the most significant of which was the establishment of a national state welfare agency, later called the social welfare state. This path not only led to an increased separation of claims by 'own' and 'foreign' 'nationalities'. It was even based essentially on this ability to separate claims and on controls on immigration and naturalization or citizenship.[155] The flip side of intensified segregation of citizens and foreigners within national borders was growing state protection functions with regard to a country's citizens abroad, which could lead to international negotiations and conflicts.

In becoming an intervening nation-state, the state assumed new economic and social areas of responsibility in which 'national' protection functions often led to protection of one's 'own' labourers at the expense of 'foreigners'. Bilateral legal agreements in these areas were steps on the way to modern international law, which broadly evolved after the First World War but whose subjects were, and still are, not 'peoples' but 'states'. In addition to problems regarding legal and trade policies, migration and labour market policy issues increasingly became the subjects of international and, in the early twentieth century for the first time, supranational negotiations.

The further development of national identities in the late nineteenth century was described by Noiriel based on France as the path from 'untraceable "nationals"' to the 'social construction of national identities'.[156] Far into the nineteenth century, taking in refugees and granting asylum and assistance was based on secure information about the respective foreigners, and not yet on their 'national' affiliation. It was a matter of personal identification, although a national consciousness in political philosophy or parliamentary debate was already very pronounced in early nineteenth-century France. In the national census of 1866, in which only about 35,000 of the estimated 80,000–150,000 'German' residents of Paris were officially registered, a German observer noted 'that the census officials working in the field did not heed the prescribed regulations always to inquire as to nationality'.[157]

The special laws in France pertaining to foreigners that had been introduced in the 1830s at the time of the heavy flow of refugees were repealed in 1853. The *passeport* that, according to an 1839 ordinance, determined arriving groups of refugees' travel routes within French borders, thus serving as a control mechanism, was now intended only to protect the traveller. Moreover, it had nothing to do with 'national' identity, as it could be issued either by the country of origin or the host country. The Anglo-French Cobden-Chevalier treaty of 1860 and the subsequent free trade agreement with Prussia, which included the German Customs Union, guaranteed completely free movement of goods and people within a free trade zone covering vast parts of western and central Europe. For foreigners from the major western European countries, France ultimately abolished the passport requirement for entry and domestic travel in 1874. After the minimum residency requirement for naturalization had been lowered to three years in 1867, the remaining distinction between limited and unlimited naturalization was then abolished in 1874.

Still, for most foreigners in France, whose numbers climbed beyond the 1 million mark in the late 1880s, a permanent residence was more important than citizenship, which was seldom sought since it was expensive and brought the regrettable side-effect of compulsory military service. Many immigrant families therefore preferred to remain foreign nationals, although they were long considered 'French' even without legal confirmation. As such they sometimes even held civil service positions and had seats in district councils and parliamentary assemblies. According to the territorial right established in the *ancien régime* that assigned citizenship based on birth in the country, foreigners were entitled to French citizenship, as of 1851 starting with the third generation in the country, and as of 1880, the second. Children born to resident aliens in France often took advantage of their right to reject citizenship upon reaching legal age. Nevertheless, they were considered 'French' in the sense of an assimilatory understanding of state, yet *de jure* they remained aliens, and thus not eligible for conscription. This 'humiliating privilege' that allowed young foreigners to continue their vocational training and occupations while the French spent three years in the barracks became all the more despised when, for that very reason, some employers started showing a preference for young foreigners in their hiring practices.

Remaining a foreigner was not a material disadvantage in France, even in cases of need. The 1851 law regulating assistance for the needy, for example, specifically impressed upon hospitals their obligation to take in the poor and sick regardless of their origins. In cases of conflict with their native countries, foreigners in France also remained expressly protected by decree under the regime of Napoleon III. This applied to Russians during the Crimean War in 1854, Austrians in the war against the

Habsburgs in 1859, and, during the Franco-Prussian War, Napoleon III explicitly refused to expel the estimated 100,000 Germans in the country in July 1870. As noted above, this situation was soon to change. After the French were defeated at the battle of Sedan in September 1870, an expulsion decree by the new French government required all German men to leave Paris within three days. Some later returned, but in the mid-1880s the situation was again exacerbated for many migrants when the share of foreigners in Paris's municipal service was limited to 5 per cent. This regulation also applied to Marseilles and Toulouse until 1895.

These changes in the 1880s also affected the citizenship law. A seven-year debate began in 1882 with a motion to rectify the shortcomings complained of in the citizenship law. It ended with the mixed form of *jus soli* (territorial principle, or right by birth) and *jus sanguinis* (inheritance or descent principle) that remained determinative for later developments in France. The 1889 law was less a triumph of republican tradition and the idea of human rights than it was a kind of national social compromise. Advocates of *jus soli* included representatives from working-class districts, employers from big industry and the military. Labourers' representatives wanted to lift the disadvantages that French labourers faced with regard to foreign workers; employers thought of their labour force; the military, of their soldiers – certainly not only because of a shortage of recruits owing to the much-lamented low birth rates. The fact that immigrants without French citizenship were deferred from military conscription was criticized also because the army, like the schools, was considered a republican agency for assimilation that was to participate in the further consolidation of 'different nations within the French nation'.[158] Residence and work in France appeared not to be sufficient in guaranteeing this.

In the 1880s, the long tradition of an assimilatory understanding of the state was therefore juxtaposed with the republican notion of consciously creating national identity. The *jus sanguinis* position found greater support among aristocratic groups. In part it was also simply an expression of voting against a purely *jus soli* solution, which would grant citizenship to anyone born in the country. At first it showed only initial signs of an ethnocultural basis. Ethnicity did not gradually work its way into the French concept of nation until around the time of the Dreyfus affair in the 1890s. The compromise of 1889 consisted of a limited *jus soli* conception with a concession to the *jus sanguinis* position by excluding newly naturalized citizens from voting rights for ten years.

The limited *jus soli* tradition that was legally anchored in France in 1889 has been retained despite some modifications ever since. At the other end of the spectrum was Germany's citizenship law (*Reichs- und Staatsangehörigkeitsgesetz*) of 1913, which laid down the descent principle, the core of which remained valid until 1999. This replaced the concept of 'citizenry as a territorial community' with one of 'citizenry as a community of descent', which is unrelated to residence. The German states had laid down the general validity of the principle of descent in the mid-nineteenth century, superseding the territorial principle that had applied up to then in citizenship law. Ethnonational intentions grew gradually, as Rogers Brubaker has shown, and were increasingly interpreted into this principle as ethnic nationalism developed in the nineteenth century.[159] Direct 'German' citizenship did not in any case exist in national law until 1913 in the delayed nation, nor did 'national descent'. People were citizens of, for example, the kingdom of Prussia, the kingdom of Bavaria or the Grand Duchy of Baden, and thus only on the basis of this state affiliation were they citizens of the German nation-state. This did not change until 1913, although even then individual state citizenships continued to exist. In the Weimar Republic, people were still Prussians or Bavarians. A unified Reich citizenship was not introduced until 1934.

The citizenship law of 1913 codified the ethnic principle of descent. It made it possible for Germans abroad and emigrants 'of German descent' to receive, pass down and reacquire German citizenship, provided they had not voluntarily taken on the citizenship of another country – through another country's *jus soli* principle – and were willing to perform military service, for which the regulations were relatively flexible. Conversely, it limited the acquisition of German citizenship for foreigners not 'of German descent' to exceptional cases.

The 1913 law came from the era of Wilhelmine high imperialism before the First World War. It was also an expression of the basic ideas of *völkisch* (nationalist) ideology for the 'preservation of Germandom abroad', and of the equally ethnonationalistic bulwark mentality that feared a 'flood from the east'. This was based on old fears of new 'migrations of nations' driven by massive population pressure from the east, which formed a lasting ideological stereotype that continues to exist into the early twenty-first century. The contemporary background to this had been two parallel east–west migrations over the Prussian-German eastern borders. The transit migration of millions, mostly Jews (about 2 million) and Poles from the multi-ethnic Russian state, passed through German ports on their way to the United States. Despite strict 'transit controls' from 1880 to 1914, about 78,000 foreign, eastern European Jews (*Ostjuden*) remained in Germany, who on the eve of the Great War made up about 12 per cent (in 1925 about 19 per cent) of the Jewish population in Germany. The eastern European Jewish migrant group was conspicuous, aside from what was often considered their culturally foreign appearance and lifestyle, in their high level of mobility and fluctuation. It was usually not recognized that for most of these eastern European Jews, Germany was more or less a short stop on the way to the New World.[160] The idea of a general east–west migration of Jews was reinforced by the internal Jewish migration from the Prussian eastern provinces to the west, especially the cities. The second major east–west movement was the annual seasonal fluctuation of hundreds of thousands of mostly Polish 'foreign labour migrants' crossing Germany's eastern borders, as will be discussed in greater detail shortly.

At the core of these nightmares of undesired immigrants from eastern Europe were anti-Semitic and anti-Polish sentiments. This is what led to the motion to refuse foreign Jews entry to Germany. It was introduced in the Reichstag by the conservatives as early as 1895, but rejected by a large majority. Visions of the threat they posed were also behind the Reichstag discussion of 1912–13 on the citizenship law. This was particularly evident in objections to a 'massive naturalization of Galician pedlars [*Hausierer*]' and 'destitute agricultural workers' as examples of the danger of 'the naturalization of morally and economically questionable [*bedenklich*] elements'. From this perspective, the German citizenship law of 1913 was truly an ethnonationalistic anti-immigration law, specifically targeting the immigration of Jews ('Galician pedlars') and Poles ('destitute agricultural workers').[161]

In England, one of the main asylum-granting countries of western Europe, the territorial principle traditionally predominated. In the eighteenth century, censuses and immigration controls did not yet exist, and immigrants and refugees could enter the country without restrictions. The first law to control immigration, the 1793 Aliens Act, was introduced under the influence of the French Revolution and its aftermath. It did not target immigrants or persecute asylum seekers, as has been discussed, but only people suspected of being 'troublemakers'. Second-generation immigrants had no problems acquiring citizenship (tied to the irrevocable pledge of allegiance to the crown), since they had been born in the country. For the immigrant generation born abroad, however, the acquisition of citizenship through denizenation or naturalization was difficult and expensive, and was linked with political restrictions. Many immigrants thus retained their foreigner status, although this brought considerable economic hindrances, such as the ban on acquiring land. The situation remained unchanged until the age of liberalism, when citizenship law was modernized through the laws of 1844 and 1870. These simplified naturalization procedures and made it possible to be released from lifelong ties to the crown (1844). They finally recognized the same political rights for naturalized foreigners as for native-born British citizens and granted foreigners the right to own land (1870); consequently, future naturalizations were less economically than politically motivated.[162]

In England as well, demands were expressed in parliamentary debates of the 1880s for the protection of the interests of British citizens as opposed to foreign immigrants and especially Jewish refugees from Russia, whose numbers had reached about 51,000 by 1875 and, owing to the heavy migration of Poles, including many Jews, from Russia, rose to about 83,000 by 1901, and roughly 95,000 by 1911. Still, liberal British 'open-door' immigration policies from 1826 to 1848 and again after 1850 had no immigration or entry restrictions for foreigners. Only in the revolutionary year of 1848 were immigration controls and the expulsion of unwanted migrants decreed, though they were never enforced. More than 1,000 refugees from the Paris Commune uprising lived in England from 1871 until they received political amnesty in 1879–80.[163]

The end of liberal immigration policies and the commencement of immigration quotas was marked by the Aliens Act of 1905, which was passed in an atmosphere of xenophobic agitation and violence against Russian Jews. However, it targeted above all the migration of 'Gypsies' from the Continent and contained required penalties for shipping companies and deportation measures for these unwanted refugees. The 1905 Aliens Act is considered not only 'the watershed for aliens' entry' (Vaughan Bevan) and the 'first nail in the coffin of free entry to Britain' (Panikos Panayi); it is also regarded as the beginning of the 'unstoppable decline of liberal England' (David Feldman) and the rise of a national interventionist state, 'from which increasingly coercive measures and encroachments issue forth, which constantly introduces new measures to regulate, control, restrict and expel the foreign population'.[164] Based on the Aliens Restriction Act that came barely a decade later, at the start of the First World War, the control regulations and the rejection and expulsion stipulations of the 1905 legislation might seem relatively limited since it targeted such a restricted circle. But the symbolic significance of this demonstrative break in continuity and its impact as a deterrent were not to be underestimated, and evidently had far-reaching consequences in the history of migration itself: the number of migrations from the Continent to England dropped considerably from 1905 until the First World War. This was not especially significant for the situation on the labour market, since Irish migration offered an absolutely inexhaustible labour pool.

The changes that took place in France, Germany and England with respect to citizenship law demonstrated a trend that could be observed throughout Europe in the age of nationalism: distinguishing between a country's own citizens and foreigners or immigrants. A parliamentary commission was set up in 1888 in France to review the numerous bills for 'protection of the national labour market'. Its report on the corresponding legislation in other European countries came to the 'piquant' conclusion 'that of all peoples, it is those who feel most bound to the ideas of progress, liberalism and democracy who have first seen to it that laws for protection against immigration were passed'. Distinguishing between 'own' and 'other' led not only to stricter distinctions in citizenship law but to national stereotypes and imagery of self, other and the enemy, sometimes with serious consequences for interactions between native majorities and immigrant minorities.[165]

Ethnoculturally charged national stereotypes and increasing xenophobic aggression, propensity to violence and actual violence towards certain groups of foreign labourers and immigrants did not exist only in England. They can be observed in a comparative look at France and Germany, the two most important destination countries for migration on the Continent prior to the First World War. On the French labour market, the Belgians in the textile industry and the coal and steel industry in northern France were the largest groups of foreign labourers, followed by Italians working in the south-east and in the Greater Paris area primarily in structural and civil engineering jobs as well as in agriculture in the south. In Germany, the largest group of foreign labour migrants were from Russian Poland and Italy. They also worked largely in agriculture, construction and the coal and steel industry.

In France it became much easier to become naturalized as of 1889, especially owing to the *jus soli* principle for the second immigrant generation. However, the distinction between citizens and immigrants was made sharper and explicitly emphasized in many democratic laws. French social legislation of the 1890s usually limited benefits to citizens, in contrast to German social legislation which did not make any such distinctions before the First World War, although foreigners were in practice disadvantaged, especially after leaving Germany. French trade union legislation, however, had excluded foreign employees from leadership positions as early as 1884. The lay judge law even prohibited them from participating in the election of worker delegates for the labour court. Legal restrictions on employment for foreigners in 1880s France in municipal service, for public bids in construction and for the railroad have already been discussed. They not only affected Italian construction workers but, for example, also forced a large segment of the German subproletariat in Paris who had migrated there during the Bourbon Restoration period to return to Germany. As previously noted, in Germany, too, there were demands to give special consideration to nationals as opposed to foreigners when awarding public contracts in which the state was the employer, but, to the outrage of the trade unions, they had no impact.

State interventions on the labour market at the expense of foreigners were kept somewhat in check in France by means of intervention by the home country to protect its citizens, as well as because of the growing dependence of various areas of the French economy on foreign labour. Plans for a special tax for foreign labourers were introduced repeatedly from the 1880s within the context of laws restricting foreign labour and were supported by various ministries. The foreign ministry rejected it, however, fearing a possible countermove that would impose restrictions on French workers abroad. Conversely, for the same reason concessions for foreign labourers were also made regarding labour and social legislation originally limited to French workers.

Categorization and classification according to national, nationalistic and ethnocultural criteria increased in the last three decades of the nineteenth century. 'Flemings' became 'Belgians' and 'Piedmontians' became 'Italians'. Xenophobic defensiveness towards foreign labour migrants grew. This was less the case with respect to the 'Belgians' but applied all the more to the second-largest group, the 'Italians', who were accused not only of rate-cutting and demonstrative isolation but also of pushy and 'culturally foreign' lifestyles and manners. External sparks could lead to the violent release of pent-up aggression. When Italians were chased through the streets for days on end in Marseilles in 1881, for example, the incident had been triggered by the French–Italian conflicts over Tunis that dominated the press at the time.[166]

In the wake of the bloody pursuit of Italian labourers through the saltworks of Aigues-Mortes near Montpellier in 1893, state intervention was increased to control and limit foreign labour. As of 1893, prospective foreign workers newly arrived in the country had to report to the local authorities, who were obliged to inform their superior offices about any changes in the foreign workers' residence and so on. Compulsory registration for foreign labourers was at the same time intended as a protectionist measure favouring native workers, since a registration fee also had to be paid. Quotas for the maximum share of foreigners on public works were introduced in 1899. Aside from the areas of employment under state or local municipal direction, which had restricted foreign labour since the 1880s, some entire professions managed to exclude foreign competition completely, among them lawyers and physicians.[167] Having taken these measures, France established, ahead of its time, a partial primacy of native workers on the labour market. The path to the 1926 'law to protect the national labour market' was still a long way off, but the protectionist course had already been set in the 1890s.

In the German Empire, ethnonationalism increasingly began to surface in the late nineteenth and early twentieth centuries in conflicts between nationals and foreign labourers. Aggressive, disparaging stereotypes ranged from the 'cheeky', pace-setting, strike-breaking and, when in doubt, knife-stabbing Italians, to the 'bootlicking Poles' as 'wage-cutters', to the supposedly simple-minded Ruthenians as 'born navvies', to more general talk of 'Slavic' workers (Max Weber) whose 'undemanding nature' owing to their low 'level of culture' led to an existential threat to German labourers in the struggle for decent wage and working conditions.[168] There were also serious, often violent, conflicts between native and foreign workers that had to be broken up by police, especially when foreign brigades were used as strike-breakers, which could frequently be observed among Italian construction brigades. The unions' image of the enemy included Italian construction workers on a par with East Elbian Junkers and the 'smokestack' barons of the coal and steel industry. In contrast to France, Germany did not introduce any protectionist restrictions on foreign labour to favour nationals prior to the First World War, not even for public contracts. The residential and labour restrictions for foreign Poles in Prussia and in the German states that adopted the Prussian model represented an exceptional case, not only in Germany but in Europe as a whole. These measures and the related controls on foreigners had an influence that was much more far-reaching than British and French legislation.

Foreign labour, reasons of state and security policies: The special case of Prussia

About 1.2 million foreign labourers were involved in continental migration in the German Empire in 1914, according to official estimates, whereby about 70–80 per cent of those 'going to Germany' (*Deutschland-gänger*) were actually 'going to Prussia' (*Preußengänger*). Security considerations underpinning anti-Polish 'Prussian defence policies'[169] were determined by fears concerning the inextinguishable dream of Prussian, Russian and Austro-Hungarian Poles of resurrecting a Polish national state. This was the background to the 1885 mass expulsion of foreign Poles from the Prussian border provinces, followed by a ban on their migration to Prussia. The catastrophic labour shortage in agriculture forced the eastern Prussian provinces from the late 1880s to seek a solution that would satisfy their economic interests without jeopardizing security policy considerations. It was a matter of not allowing the flow of labourers from eastern countries to turn into an immigration situation, but instead to keep it within the scope of transnational seasonal migration.

The result was a system of controls developed in the early 1890s in Prussia to monitor and regulate foreign Polish labourers and maintain their transnational fluctuation. It ended in 1907 when its functions were transferred to the semi-state-run Prussian Farm Workers' Agency (Preußische Feldarbeiterzentrale), which was later called the German Foreign

Workers' Agency (Deutsche Arbeiterzentrale). This agency held the identification and registration monopoly (*Legitimationsmonopol*) for Prussia
and found jobs for foreign labourers in other German states as well.
The Prussian system targeted only foreign Polish workers. For reasons
of statistical control, but without the associated restrictions, it was gradually expanded until the First World War to all foreign labourers in
Prussia.

The Prussian system entered the annals of the history of labour market
policies and alien law in Prussian Germany under the headings of 'mandatory registration' and 'compulsory return' during the winter 'waiting
period'. Mandatory registration meant intensified control of foreigners
through residence and work permits, which were limited and had to be
reapplied for every year. Compulsory return was valid only for foreign
Polish workers; it meant they were required to return to their home
regions each year during the restricted period (the so-called 'waiting
period') in winter from 20 December to 1 February. They could avoid
this requirement only by working illegally or going to another German
state during this time. Berlin tried, with limited success, to get other
states to adopt the Prussian system, virtually forcing it on them in an
effort to cut off opportunities to circumvent the restrictions.

Compulsory return was imposed not only on the basis of citizenship
(Russian) and nationality (Polish) but also on social, occupational criteria. It applied generally to the lowest levels of qualifications, that is,
agricultural labourers and semi- or unskilled workers outside of agriculture. It pertained neither to 'intellectual workers' and foremen with fixed
salaries nor to various groups of highly specialized workers and specific
groups of servants with duty rosters.

Mandatory registration and compulsory rotation meant, at the same
time, both mobility and immobility for foreign Polish labourers. They
were kept mobile through compulsory return each year, but were also
immobilized on the labour market in Prussia through registration. Registration cards, the only valid domestic identification foreign workers
possessed, had two names on them, the labourer's and the German
employer's, to whom the worker was required to remain tied on pain
of expulsion for the duration of the residence and work permit.
According to their contracts, labour migrants could not give notice to
leave a job. Foreign Poles were allowed entry only as individual labourers, never as families. Children were required to stay beyond the eastern
border of the eastern Prussian provinces. Men and women were separated in labour brigades. Pregnancy was grounds for expulsion, and return
transport took place at the woman's expense. In addition to time restrictions on their sojourns were the geographical and field-specific employment limitations noted earlier (see section 1).

The outcome of linking forced registration and compulsory return was a picture resembling a temperature curve of annual labour migration across the eastern Prussian border, with a steep rise in the spring, a peak in the summer season and a steep drop at the beginning of the restricted winter period. Despite political scepticism, foreign Polish labourers were welcome each spring for economic reasons, but in winter they became 'troublesome foreigners' in the eyes of alien legislation and risked police expulsion if they did not voluntarily return to their home regions.

Once mandatory registration was introduced and the Prussian Farm Workers' Agency was given greater powers to recruit and find work for foreign labourers, foreign recruiting and domestic brokerage took on a clearer outline in Prussia. As reported by the agency, it compiled assessments on 'anticipated conditions on the foreign labour market' that were brought in by its travelling labour market observers and foreign contract agents from the eastern regions of origin, which, in the jargon of the brokerage business, were known as 'recruitment areas'. It then coordinated these assessments with the results of consultations with agricultural chambers, employers and employers' associations concerning the anticipated domestic demand. From this basis, the agency compiled its annual general 'terms of employment' of foreign labourers for the spring. These terms were sent along with the corresponding 'order slip' to the various distribution offices for domestic brokerage or directly to the respective employers. Returned order slips were submitted to the foreign contract agents, who set the foreign recruitment process in motion via their network of sub-agents and middlemen, recruiters, human smugglers, foremen and brigade leaders. In Galicia the agency also worked with the public employment exchange, the Ruthenian welfare league and the clergy working alongside the Ruthenian national committee.

Direct cooperation with foreign agents (in 1910 with 16 different Galician agencies) and employment exchanges (in Galicia as of 1904) and the arrangement of inexpensive mass transportation made it possible to cut drastically the costs of recruitment and broking per person. Foreign labourers either arrived at the border on their own or were brought there 'free frontier' (no charge up to the border), from where they were taken to their destinations and, when their work and residence permits expired, back to the border. A worker from Russia 'cost' only three marks in 1910; one from Galicia, four marks; and one from Hungary, five marks. Major agricultural producers with high numbers of workers received an additional advantage since surcharges were demanded only for very small, technically difficult orders for up to six people (one mark) or three people (two marks). Of course, small and medium-sized producers could avoid these surcharges by making a 'joint order'.

By 1913 the agency had set up 39 border offices with large camps that could take in and process up to 10,000 people per day. Most of these offices were along the eastern border. In them workers were put through a cursory epidemic control and were then contractually 'hired' by signing an 'obligation certificate' (*Verpflichtungsschein*). In cases of labour migration without fixed contracts or migration destinations, this is also where labour contracts were negotiated. It was a rate-cutting ordeal for the often impoverished job-seekers, since there were charges for room and board in the camp and costs were taken out of wage advances from the employer.

Many areas of industry in Germany, and especially agriculture in Prussia, became increasingly dependent on foreign labour prior to the First World War. There were no restrictions at all, except for those on foreign Poles in non-agricultural fields of employment in Prussia. Despite the anti-Polish regulations within the state borders, county administrative offices and the gendarmerie in Prussia were under strict instructions not to hinder the migration of desperately needed labourers. Anti-Polish measures on the labour market were instead supposed to be implemented in such a way that the authorities in the Russian part of Congress Poland and Austrian Galicia would have no reason to restrict migration.

This is why anti-Polish 'defence policies' were a double balancing act – between conflicting economic and political interests in Prussia and towards eastern 'recruitment areas'. Apart from those who reported on their own (*Selbststeller*), for a long time there were four competing forms of recruitment: (1) private labourer recruitment for personal use; (2) commercial recruitment and brokerage; (3) activities by employment exchanges set up by agricultural chambers; and (4) recruitment, brokerage and registration of foreign labourers through the semi-state-run Prussian Farm Workers' Agency, which received the registration monopoly in Prussia in 1907.

Around the turn of the century, the competitive battle spread to the 'recruitment areas' across the border to the east. Privately commissioned Prussian employers, commercial agents and agents from the chamber exchanges and the Farm Workers' Agency tried to steal each other's workers and contracts. Moreover, German and foreign recruitment agents competed not only with each other abroad, but also with emigration agents from the major transatlantic shipping lines. Growing protests by government offices in the 'recruitment areas' against foreign intervention in the labour market spurred Prussian government efforts to create transparent structures in the recruitment and placement of foreign labour migrants, nearly half of whom in agriculture, as already noted, were women. When the registration monopoly was transferred to the Prussian

Farm Workers' Agency in 1907, these transparent structures were finally achieved. The 'agent problem' was criticized by both sides since their activities were often fraudulent, but restrictions were introduced only in the interests of Prussian-German employers, not those of foreign workers. Foreign employment agencies and government offices became increasingly concerned about middlemen and contract agents working for the agency and about their methods of recruitment that involved stealing workers and contracts. For the Germans, this shifted the conflict over foreign recruitment to the background, but the same issue was brought even more to the fore in the international dispute.

In Galicia, the home region of Polish and Ruthenian labour migrants, there was no legal ban on broking prior to the First World War. The agricultural labour market was therefore a free hunting ground for domestic and foreign brokerage, landowner representatives, recruiters and human smugglers, in spite of various attempts to impose restrictions. Most significant were the commercial agents. They knew how to hold on to their monopoly position even after the gradual introduction of the Galician state labour exchange in 1904, which remained uncompetitive for a long time, especially since the local administration in rural Galicia was stigmatized by corruption. There Prussian, Austrian and other foreign agencies cooperated with domestic agencies, which in turn had their own networks of middlemen, recruiters and human smugglers. They could also often work hand in hand with village mayors and community clerks at the expense of destitute agricultural labourers and land-poor peasants driven by hunger at times of crop failure. Every time a workman's pass was issued, the district council collected between 2 and 4 crowns, which had to be paid by the aspiring labour migrant.

Agents profited more than once from the broking business. They collected brokerage fees, not only from the employers but often also from the labour migrants, who were kept dependent because of wage advances they received. Those who also worked as brigade leaders had additional earnings from 'wage administration', frequently of a number of labour brigades, and on occasion they retained up to half the workers' wages. Before the First World War the migration of people with firm migratory traditions who reported on their own also gained momentum in Galicia. Ruthenian and Polish workers moved along routes that had become familiar through middlemen, human smugglers and agents, with the intention of avoiding the exploitation of commercial 'bloodsuckers', at least as far as the border.

In contrast to the situation in Austrian Galicia, Russian Central Poland had prohibited commercial labour broking by law. Foreign agents were officially not allowed to cross the border. For this reason, people who reported on their own were of primary importance from the outset. But even their movements were not left uncontrolled, apart from the border districts with their traditional forms of transnational shuttle migration over short distances. Middlemen handed out flyers that directed them to the border offices or to the agents waiting at the border.

The movements of these independent migrants in the Russian border-lands long had a dynamic of their own that was fairly unpredictable and was viewed by both sides with suspicion. This is why, as the Prussian Farm Workers' Agency reported, 'the entire border is filled with a tight cordon of employers, agents, guards and foremen, who receive every arriving labourer as soon as they cross the border, and try every possible means of persuasion and bribery to try to win them for themselves'.[170] This cordon lurked day and night; unlike the border gendarmerie, it did not miss a single movement. This was the supreme principle of the business, for it was precisely the Russian-Polish labourers who often crossed the border illegally because of the compulsory passport on the Russian side, which was expensive and often dealt with arbitrarily; then they returned after the work and residence permit expired 'along hidden paths and at night'.[171] This in turn meant that the posts had to change their positions constantly. It was known 'that depending on how the Russian officers policed the border, first here and then there, during the day or at night, through the marshes and water, on roads or without any path at all, the workers streamed over the border. Places where thousands passed through the year before were desolate and abandoned now, and instead, where there is no house or pathway for kilometres around, suddenly new groups of workers appear, and no one has the slightest notion how they got across the border'.[172]

Both sides had an interest in a high degree of transparency in trans-national migrations. For the Prussians there were security policy consider-ations, and for the Russians, the transfer of wage earnings. Furthermore, despite the compulsory registration, Russian government offices remained mistrustful that transnational labour migration might merely be prepar-ation for overseas emigration, or that the workers might emigrate overseas directly after crossing the Russian–Prussian border. This could have caused a lasting destabilization of the supply of inexpensive agricultural labourers in central Poland.

For a long time, the labour surplus had kept down wages on the agricultural labour market in central Poland. The wages for male agri-cultural labourers in Germany were on average 40–50 per cent higher than in Poland. In the 1890s, the average wage of a day labourer without any supplements in kind was, according to the Warsaw statistical com-mittee, 35.5 copecks (25 pence) during the peak season, 23 copecks (15 pence) in spring and autumn and only 17 copecks in the winter, always provided that the day labourer found any work at all outside the peak season. The standard of living was correspondingly low. The main food sources were potatoes and cabbage; meat remained reserved for holidays. This standard, which Polish labour migrants initially retained in Prussia, corresponded to the land-poor peasants in the Prussian-Polish border-lands who Max Weber described as 'potato-consuming smallholders'. This was why Weber, as already noted, assumed that competition from foreign Polish labourers with a 'low level of culture' would 'push out' the Prussian but not the Prussian-Polish labourers, with the consequence of a continuing 'Polonization of the east'.

In the 1890s, emigration from central Poland turned into a social mass movement. By 1900 there were 300,000 people who had definitively emigrated; besides emigration to the United States, the rampant 'Brazil-ian fever' of 1892–3 (40,000 Russian Poles) was particularly significant. It was this expansion of overseas emigration and continental labour migration into mass movements which, in the 1890s, caused day wages on the free agricultural labour market in Congress Poland clearly to rise. In the 1890s, rapidly increasing migration losses had threatened the additional seasonal demand for free agricultural labourers in the gouver-nements near the border; in 1904 wages up to 88 copecks (60 pence) were offered during the peak season. However, even seasonal wage increases could no longer slow down transatlantic emigration and con-tinental labour migration, especially since both mass movements had already established migratory traditions with transatlantic networks.[173]

Isolated attempts by the Russian government to restrict and encumber labour migrations to Germany retarded the movement only minimally and temporarily, aside from the crisis of 1907–8. Berlin showed great concern, not only as regards the 'Russian threat' that kept appearing but failed to become acute until directly before the First World War, but also as regards the Russians' dogged quest for that degree of dependence of German and especially Prussian agrarian production on foreign labour. In the Prussian State Economy Council, it was openly stated in 1906 'that obstacles or restrictions to the access of foreign labour migrants would be like pronouncing a death sentence on agriculture'. A special study com-mission confirmed: 'The absence of foreign labour migrants would call the sufficiency of the food supply into question.' Regarding the situation of the coal and steel industry in the eastern Prussian provinces, the government president in Oppeln, Upper Silesia, stated in 1911 'that the Upper Silesian industry can in fact not be maintained without foreign labourers'. Baron von dem Bussche-Kessel, director of the Farm Workers' Agency, summarized the situation in 1910, in the Budapest conference of the Central European Economic Association on the general organization of the labour market: 'for a long time, employers in the labour-importing states will have a burning need for foreign labour'. He then spoke more specifically about his own concerns: 'For us as an importing state, there is an absolute need to receive labourers from abroad. It can be stated simply in those terms, since experience shows it to be a fact'.[174]

The 1910 Budapest conference was, after previous unsuccessful endeavours, a renewed attempt to reach an international agreement between home and host countries on the controversial issues of labour market and labour migration. But even this attempt only at the level of the Central European Economic Associations failed owing to an irreconcilable clash of interests.[175] Not until the interwar period would the new international organizations develop a more practicable – albeit here too only partially productive – basis for international, and soon global, negotiations on international migration processes.

The assessment that the anti-Polish Prussian restrictions on work and residence authorization in the pre-war period were a direct precursor to 'modern' migration policies between the world wars[176] is both false and correct. It is false regarding the conflict-laden connection between promoting employer interests by admitting foreigners and protecting the national labour force from foreign competition. In the two decades leading up to the First World War, the Prussian system included neither restrictions of in-migration at the border nor preference of nationals on the labour market as a means of coping with the labour shortage that employers everywhere criticized. Also, its purely anti-Polish thrust showed a motivation based on security policy but not protectionism or labour market policy. The notion of a Prussian-German forerunner is correct, however, in view of the organizational experience with systems – albeit only semi-state-run – of foreigner control and restrictions on residence and work authorization.

This experience would later become useful in terms of labour market policy. The prerequisites were the continued development from regional employment agency associations, which started to emerge in Prussian Germany in the 1890s, into public employment administrations, which received a definitive thrust towards modernization during the First World War. But it was not until after the war that the traditional system of foreigner controls joined with the new system of modern administration of labour under the primacy of the national labour force; and this marked the completion of the transition to the protectionist labour market and migration policies of the interwar period.

3

The Period of the World Wars: Escape, Expulsion, Forced Labour

From a political history perspective, the period from the start of the First World War in 1914 to the end of the Cold War in the year of European revolutions in 1989 was the 'short twentieth century'; it was definitively marked by the 'new Thirty Years' War' from 1914 to 1945.[1] Almost all countries in Europe were actively involved in the two world wars, the consequences of which impacted even the few neutral countries owing to the fundamental disruption of the international economic network. The First World War caused a structural break in the history of Europe and its position in the global system of power. At the same time it created and intensified problems in the interwar period that decisively contributed to the outbreak of the Second World War. That war, and the subsequent division of Europe and the world into two hostile blocs, laid a new foundation that would determine global developments up to the end of the east–west conflict in 1989. Immense refugee and forced migrations – beyond the mass military movements, which will not be discussed here – accompanied the two world wars and their aftermath. The 'century of world war' was thus also the 'century of refugees'.[2] The century of world war came to an end in 1989 when the Iron Curtain was opened and the division of Europe overcome. The repercussions as regards migrations in especially central, east central and eastern Europe continued into the 1990s, however. An end to the 'century of refugees' was not yet in sight on the eve of the new millennium.[3]

State intervention in cross-border migrations reached an unprecedented range and intensity in the twentieth century. For the development of migrations in Europe and the Atlantic realm, the First World War was simultaneously an epochal break and a pacesetter. It marked the end of the age of liberal migration policies that had allowed the 'proletarian mass migrations' of the nineteenth and early twentieth centuries to develop a momentum and dynamic of their own. It also accelerated the shift to the 'migration economy' (Karl C. Thalheim) that was characterized by state intervention and restrictions. Cross-border migrations became increasingly limited and forced into prescribed routes. Therefore, the history of migration in the age of world war and refugees must be based on state-imposed migratory conditions; this history will be presented in the third, fourth and fifth chapters of this book.

Chapter 3 begins with the deep break that the First World War represented in the history of international migrations and the contact between nationals and 'enemy aliens' within national boundaries. The second section deals with the development of control and regulatory mechanisms of state migration policies in the interwar period; in Europe this was also an era of escape and expulsion. The third section encompasses the most appalling period in the history of migration, the recent migration history that also includes forced resettlement and mass expulsion in the post-war period.

1   THE FIRST WORLD WAR: INTERNATIONALIZATION AND NATIONAL EXCLUSION

Internationalization of war economy labour markets

At least 8 million soldiers and 10 million civilians were directly or indirectly victims of the 'great seminal catastrophe' of the twentieth century (George F. Kennan). The rapid mobilization in August 1914 did not show any consideration for the economy and the labour market. The countries of Europe that were actively involved in the war believed the conflict would be over quickly, and therefore they neglected to adapt production to war conditions. But alone the mobilization of millions for the military threw the economy and labour markets in Europe into crisis. Production collapsed and layoffs led to mass unemployment, which reached an estimated 20 per cent in Germany and probably affected about 40 per cent of the labour force in France. Continued military conscription and the boom in the armaments industry in early 1915 helped European countries to overcome this phase. The end of the crisis in the warring countries accompanied the beginning of bottlenecks in the availability of weapons and munitions in the transition to the 'matériel battles' of established positional warfare.[4]

These supply crises served in early 1915 to accelerate the conversion from a peace to a war economy. Growing disturbances in international commerce caused the warring countries in Europe, and soon also most neutral ones, to institute state rationing of scarce raw materials and food. Controls on munitions production were especially pushed and, with them, attempts to steer labour markets towards the war economy. The continuing recruitment of soldiers also meant a growing shortage especially of qualified labour. A total of 60 million Europeans served in armies and navies from 1914 to 1918. France had mobilized 7.9 million, Britain 6.1 million, Germany over 13 million and Russia, up to the revolution in 1917, a total of 15 million. In Germany, for example, almost all men of military age were drafted, that is, over 80 per cent of adult men, or almost 20 per cent of the total population. Because these men were all fit for work and most had indeed been in employment, the recruitment of labour was and remained one of the main problems of war economy policy in Europe from 1914 to 1918.[5]

The warring countries experienced an increased demand for labour, especially in the munitions industry, mining and agriculture. The individual national war economies shared many problems and possible solutions. Often in conflict between military and economic interests, measures to cover the steeply rising demand for labour aimed to discharge soldiers who had just been mustered or to give them leave to return to their former places of work. Recruitment of women and young men who had not previously been in paid employment was also promoted. Directly connected with this were manifold considerations to standardize and rationalize production in order to make it easier to hire semi-skilled labour. Obstacles to changing place of work and restrictions on freedom of movement limited labour market mobility, which was a basic condition for the development of migratory movements. The measures enjoyed varying degrees of success. In Britain the labour situation could be largely stabilized despite conscription. In France and Germany the results were more limited: too few soldiers were laid off or given leave, and it was all but impossible to recruit the desired number of women and young men for the war economy. The growing lack of workers caused companies and authorities to push recruitment and enlistment from overseas. Consequently, national war economies became internationalized, as to some extent did the armies themselves.

France and Britain took advantage of their colonial possessions to find people to serve in Europe. Euro-colonial migratory cycles were turned around; during the First World War the colonial powers mobilized at least 1 million Africans. Not only were they used for battles on the African continent, as was the situation regarding Germany, but large numbers also served in Europe. At the start of the war, the French army already had 10,000 black Africans serving in special units (*force noire*). By the end of the war, a total of 607,256 soldiers from the colonies had been recruited for the French army in Europe. The vast majority were from North Africa (293,756) and West Africa (170,891); smaller contingents came from Indochina (48,922), Madagascar (41,355), the French Antilles and French Guiana (22,695) and East Africa (17,910). There were also other minor units of non-European origin (11,191). Britain's non-European mobilization took place mostly in India. A total of 1.2 million non-European soldiers from around the world reinforced British troops in Europe, though they served primarily in theatres of war in East Africa and the Near East.[6]

Let us take a closer look at the history of foreign labour participation under conditions of war with respect to France and Germany, where foreign labour had already started gaining in importance in the pre-war decades. Within Europe the number of foreigners in these two countries alone had already exceeded the 1 million mark prior to the war. The roughly 1.2 million foreign labourers in Germany in 1914 were mostly Poles from Russia and Austria-Hungary, Italians and Dutch. There were also nearly 1.2 million foreigners registered in France, coming primarily from Italy, Belgium and Germany, as well as Spain and Switzerland.

France

At the beginning of the war there were initially several return migration movements in France. The number of foreigners who had migrated to France before the war and remained there is uncertain. What is clear is that during the war another approximately 662,000 foreign labourers went to France. The strongest contingent was from Spain (230,000); the second largest was made up of German and Austro-Hungarian prisoners of war who had been brought in to work (102,000), followed by workers from Algeria (78,566), France's South-east Asian colonies (48,955) and China (36,941). Other labourers came from other French colonies (35,506 Moroccans, 18,244 Tunisians and 4,546 Madagascans); there were also Portuguese (22,800), Greeks (24,300), Italians (20,000), Belgian refugees (30,000) and other groups (about 10,000), including Swedes and Serbs.

Since there was also a lot of out-migration for certain groups in the course of the war, the actual numbers of foreign workers at any particular point in time are always below these total figures. It is especially conspicuous that the main group of foreigners, Spanish labourers, showed a great deal of fluctuation. There were probably never more than half the statistical total figure working in France at any one time. Before the war, there had been few Spaniards relative to other national groups, especially Italians and Belgians. But Italy and Belgium were also involved in the war, so migrations from these countries halted entirely or were extremely rare; in the case of Italians, there was even a lot of return migration. As the only neutral neighbouring country besides Switzerland, Spain became an important pool of replacement labour in France's war economy.[7]

Prior to 1914, there were hardly any workers in France from the colonies. Not until the First World War did migration from North Africa and Indochina take hold, ultimately becoming the predominant regions after the Second World War. Recruitment and employment of labour from the North African and South-east Asian colonies had started in 1915; it became military-related in early 1916. Regarding the Chinese, who began to be mobilized in February 1916, this pertained not to their recruitment but to their working and living conditions. The Service d'Organisation des Travailleurs Coloniaux (SOTC) under military direction regulated and controlled all the living and working areas of its labourers. They were usually accommodated in separate housing or in camps to keep them segregated from the local population and were generally given poorly paid jobs that were physically taxing, even dangerous. Their organization into work brigades was intended to make controls by military authorities more efficient and to prevent them from transferring to easier or better-paid jobs.

Working and living under comparable conditions in northern France were the approximately 100,000 Chinese labourers recruited by British military authorities beginning in 1916 for actions behind British lines. Here too the work was generally physically demanding, dispatching freight or doing construction work near the front. On occasion Chinese workers were made available to French farmers in the area behind the front; towards the end of the war they were also used for rescue work in the firing zone. Measures for monitoring and segregating Chinese labourers were so extreme that the local population thought they were prisoners.[8]

In public and political discussion in France, the employment of non-European or colonial labourers during the war was viewed as a failure: the costs were too high, especially when compared with the costs of using prisoners of war, they were rather ineffective, and there was too much room for conflict with the local population. These arguments were used in Euro-colonial discourse as the grounds and legitimization for restrictive immigration policies towards non-European labourers in post-war France. After rapid repatriation at the end of the war, only 6,000 recruited non-European labourers were still in France in 1920.[9]

As opposed to colonial and Chinese workers, European labour migrants still enjoyed full freedom of movement at the beginning of the war. However, to prevent them from transferring to better-paid jobs, especially in Paris, French authorities began to limit their freedom of movement from mid-1916. Registration passes were introduced, which made it easier to control workplace and change of employer and essentially converted even foreign workers from other European countries into serf-like labourers. At the border offices they were assigned to positions to which they were contractually bound and were not allowed to leave without authorization. Despite such limitations, their working and living situations were subject to far fewer restrictions than those of workers from the colonies and China.

Migration to work in French agriculture remained largely free of state intervention during the war. The Office National de la Main-d'œuvre Agricole (ONMA), one of the agricultural organizations established in 1912, set up a total of 16 assignment offices from 1915 at the borders with Spain and Italy. These offices allocated arriving labourers to companies that had applied for foreign workers. ONMA essentially resembled the semi-state-run Farm Workers' Agency in pre-war Germany. During the war, 146,446 labourers from Spain and Portugal, as well as 2,225 from Italy, passed through ONMA's border offices. Shortly before the end of the war, it also recruited another 7,500 labourers from North Africa and 1,000 from Indochina who were supposed to be used in workers' brigades on the large-scale sugar beet farms. The number of foreign replacement labourers in agriculture remained relatively low compared with the mobilization of 3 million agricultural workers for war duty. Because wages and working conditions in agriculture were worse than those in industry, farming became increasingly a temporary halt for foreign labourers on their way to the urban industrial armament firms.

During the war there was less foreigner employment in French industry than in agriculture. Of almost 81,000 foreign industrial workers, 24,274 came from Greece, 22,849 from Portugal, 15,212 from Spain, 5,486 from Italy and another 12,770 from other countries. The French ministry of arms and the labour ministry, which took over responsibility in 1917, initially endeavoured to get permission to recruit Italians. When negotiations failed owing to restrictive Italian labour policies, recruitment options in Greece were explored from mid-1916. Not long afterwards came negotiations with Portugal and, in early 1917, with Spain. As with foreign labourers in agriculture, industrial labourers were also assigned workplaces at the border offices. Border offices near Marseilles assumed this task for Greek migrants, since most migrant transports by sea came into port there. In addition to those from Greece, transports from the colonies and China also docked in Marseilles.

For the 662,000 foreign labourers who went to France for the first time during the war, placement in certain sectors was emphasized and employment hierarchies between European and non-European labourers were deliberately implemented by the policies that related to foreigners.

The majority of industrial positions were filled by European workers; in agriculture, predominantly those European labourers with previous experience who seemed unsuited for industrial work were used. The armaments industry hired mostly Portuguese, Greeks and Spaniards; in agriculture there were mostly Spaniards, Portuguese and Italians. The agrarian sector took in workers from the colonies for unskilled repetitive jobs in work brigades. Military recruits from the colonies and China were used mostly for hard, physically demanding, hazardous work, especially for construction of military facilities and in ports with heavy war-related traffic. This category of non-industrial heavy labourers also included unskilled prisoners of war deemed unsuited for industrial work.

In France, almost 100,000 out of a total of 501,000 prisoners of war (POWs) were put to work. In contrast, POWs played a wholly insignificant role in England, where even a low demand for foreign workers did not arise until late on. The employment of about 25,000 Belgian refugees was completely unrelated to the war economy's recruitment plans. Not until spring 1916 were there considerations to recruit up to 20,000 labourers in Denmark, and only a few hundred responded. Plans to employ prisoners of war emerged around the same time. Up to then, most POWs captured by British troops either remained in camps in France or were transported to the dominions. By September 1916, the number of POWs put to work in the British Isles rose to 5,332, and by autumn 1918 the figure climbed to almost 60,000, the vast majority of whom were used in agriculture.[10] Beyond that, foreign employment was inconsequential in Britain's war economy. In a European comparison, the employment of foreigners in the German war economy was a special case, since Germany's vast war effort and the effective Allied blockade of foreign trade made Germany increasingly dependent on foreign labour in this first 'total war' (Ludendorff) in history. Without the internationalization of the labour pool, the German 'home front' would have collapsed far sooner and Germany would not have been able to continue the war as long as it did.

Germany

Use of foreign labour in Germany's[11] war economy was more than double the already high level of the pre-war period, corresponding to about one in seven of all workers in the final year of the war. There were obvious differences to France with respect to regions of origin and recruitment methods. Despite a continued high number of voluntary foreign labour migrants, use of foreign workers in Germany was marked in particular by forced labour, especially since the vast majority of foreign labourers came from 'enemy countries'. Among the 2.5 to 3 million foreign workers at the end of the war, no fewer than two-thirds were POWs. Non-commissioned and other ranks apart from officers could be forced to work for the capturing state in accordance with article 6 of the annex to the Hague Convention (IV) respecting the Laws and Customs of War on Land of 1907; this was general practice barring few exceptions.

There were about 1 million civilian workers in the foreign labour force of the German war economy. Unlike POWs, they did not receive uniform treatment by German civilian and military authorities, although they were largely 'enemy aliens'. This was especially true of the 500,000–600,000 Polish labourers at the end of the war from the partially occupied territory of Germany's wartime enemy, Russia. Policies towards foreign Poles from Russia, which had already been restrictive prior to the war, were intensified once the war began and were entirely reversed. Instead of the annual compulsory return that applied in Prussia before the war, as 'enemy aliens' Poles were now prohibited throughout Germany from returning at all. Moreover, they were allowed to change neither their place of residence nor their employer. The ban on returning to Poland converted the compulsory return of Polish labourers from Russia prior to the war into forced labour with a non-voluntary permanent stay (see chapter 2, section 4). Russian-Polish labourers thus often assumed a role similar to that of colonial and Chinese labourers in the French war economy. For the approximately 100,000 Dutch labourers, however, who were of utmost importance for agriculture and industry in the western part of Germany, there were no serious restrictions of their freedom of movement during the war as compared with the pre-war period. This was also the case for smaller contingents from neutral countries, such as Switzerland, Denmark, Sweden and Norway.

Treatment of foreign labourers was not only dependent on which war coalition their native country belonged to. The government-regulated living and working conditions of Italian workers in Germany hardly changed even after Italy entered the war as part of the Entente in 1915–16.[12] Their situation was in fact better than that of the Poles from Galicia who had already been closely monitored prior to the war within the scope of the 'Prussian defence policies'. These Poles continued to be subjected to restrictive employment controls although they came from the territory ruled by Austria-Hungary, which was allied with Germany. In contrast to Poles from the Russian 'enemy territory', they were not banned from returning and their numbers declined significantly due to Austro-Hungarian mobilization once the war started. In the interests of German employers and despite bitter protests from Vienna, however, their return initially faced administrative obstacles and delays.[13]

The labour shortage in Germany increased steadily as of 1915 and could not be covered even by forcibly retaining foreign labourers. Plans therefore started to focus on ways to recruit additional labour from abroad. The outbreak of war in eastern and south-eastern Europe had blocked access to 'foreign labour migrants' from the most significant labour regions before the war, not only with respect to Russia as an adversary but also Austria-Hungary as an ally. The dual monarchy limited foreign recruitment as soon as the war started because of labour needs for its own mobilization, for the armaments industry, and soon also to rebuild the areas of Galicia that had been occupied by Russian troops. Italy was also largely eliminated, at the latest when it declared war on the Central Powers in 1915–16. The situation changed dramatically when the Central Powers' offensive led to the occupation of Russian Poland by October 1915. With that the most important pre-war recruitment area came under direct control.

The labour pool in Central Poland and in Belgium once it was occupied in November 1914 became the target of German recruitment policies in 1915–16. As in the pre-war period, labourers in Central Poland were recruited primarily for agriculture; those in Belgium, mostly for the armaments industry. The boundaries became increasingly blurred between voluntary recruitment, coercion to register and forced deportation.[14] Because there were far fewer volunteers than aimed for, labourers were obtained more often through economic pressures and direct coercion. Deliberate worsening of the economic situation was intended to urge the population in the occupied territories to work for the occupying power in their own country or in Germany. These policies achieved their goals earlier in Poland than in Belgium, where international relief organizations kept the economic cutbacks from having drastic consequences similar to those that became characteristic for the situation in Central Poland.

After only around 30,000 Belgian workers could be recruited for work in Germany, deportations began in October 1916, which then brought around 61,000 Belgian labourers to Germany by February 1917.[15] This action proved to be a mistake, both economically and politically. Almost two months after its completion, only about half the deportees had been assigned to permanent workplaces. Others had not yet been assigned at all; some had fled their place of work after only days or had been sent back to the camps because they refused to work. Furthermore, about two-thirds of those deported had to be sent back to Belgium by mid-1917 as a result of vociferous protest from abroad.

Deportations also began in late 1916 from the occupied areas of Central Poland; these were even less successful.[16] The turnaround was forced in 1917–18 by a policy of systematically worsening the economic situation and thus living conditions, combined with incentives to work in

Germany. This caused the number of foreign Polish labourers in Germany in 1918 once again to reach the 1914 level of 500,000–600,000. Using the same methods, the number of Belgians working in Germany was raised to a total of about 100,000 by the end of the war.

Against this background, the employment of POWs became increasingly important in Germany's war economy. In August 1916, there were about 1.6 million POWs, 90 per cent (1.45 million) of whom were put to work; three-quarters (1.1 million) of these worked for the war economy – more than 650,000 in agriculture and about 330,000 in industry. Shortly before the war ended, there were around 1.9 million POWs doing forced labour. In autumn 1917, they comprised probably more than 15 per cent of all those employed in the German war economy.[17]

Prisoners' working and living conditions were directly dependent on official planning, or rather, lack of planning. Since a short campaign was expected, there were no plans to employ prisoners in the early weeks of the war. In view of the mass unemployment prevalent at the time, they were even seen as undesirable competition on the labour market. No plans had even been made for longer-term accommodation of a large number of POWs. The result was catastrophic living conditions for prisoners in the improvised and quickly overcrowded camps of tents and earthen huts that were scattered throughout Germany. Isolated from the local populations, they were set up on military training grounds, firing ranges and in fortifications. Due to the provisional nature of their lodgings and lack of sanitary facilities, physicians and nursing staff, typhus spread in epidemic proportions. In the winter of 1914–15, for example, 7,100 of 9,700 prisoners in the large camp in Brandenburg contracted typhus and other infectious diseases, especially dysentery and typhoid fever.

The prisoners' working conditions were characterized by the same lack of planning. Prisoners worked, if at all, in the first few months of the war only in their provisionally established camps, setting up and expanding their own lodgings and maintaining, repairing or extending the infrastructure of the military training grounds often used for camps. In addition to reducing the costs of accommodation, the main purpose was discipline through work rather than productive deployment in the war economy. Starting in late August to early September 1914, additional jobs and accommodation were organized outside the camp, especially in cultivating bogs and fens, heathland and marshland. As of early 1915, foreign POWs were used increasingly, and soon exclusively, to replace the millions of German workers drafted into the war effort. This required a fundamental reorientation on the part of military officials. Instead of merely reducing the enemy's military potential by interning prisoners, they were now strategically used in the labour force in all areas of the war economy. At the same time, the hitherto catastrophic conditions of accommodation, nutrition and basic medical care were finally improved in many large camps, which served to increase the number of POWs who were fit for work significantly.

The situation of POWs as forced labourers was very varied, depending not only on the dictates of the military authorities but also on their respective living and working conditions. In late 1917, about 15 per cent (roughly 170,000) of prisoners were employed in mining. Work in the mines was feared because of the conditions that prevailed: extremely hard labour and harassment by the German foremen, internment in camps run by the mines and, in spite of supplementary provisions, comparatively poor nutrition. The situation faced by military-forced workers in the mass factories of the armaments industry was also marked by internment in work camps and poor food supply and treatment. Most POWs were employed in agriculture, where living and working conditions were generally better, not only with respect to food provisions but also because three-quarters of these POWs were accommodated individually on family-run farms without being guarded. The situation was similar for those working in the trades, as well as in small and medium-sized industrial operations in which prisoners did not work in large work brigades. According to a rough estimate, the approximately 1.5 million POWs working in agriculture and industry were distributed at the end of the war among roughly 750,000 different places of work. Consequently, POWs were visible at workplaces throughout Germany. By 1915 at the latest, daily contact with prisoners at work and also within families had become part of everyday life for millions of Germans.[18] The Great War thus contributed even within national borders to an unprecedented degree of contact with people of other nationalities.

Exclusion of 'enemy aliens', escape, expulsion and deportation

Beyond the military movements of people across borders and borders across people, 'enemy' minorities were segregated within national boundaries during the First World War in a way that transposed the international conflict configuration to a societal level. Press and political propaganda during the war reflected and aroused nationalistic sentiments on all sides. Parallel to the battles between millions-strong armies, nationalistic and cultural discourses started waging a 'total' war involving peoples and cultures. The countries involved in the war faced internal fronts in which labour migrants and immigrants from 'enemy countries' were transformed into 'enemy aliens' and threats to internal security. On top of this came efforts to escape, expulsions and forced resettlements.

They were triggered by the war and its aftermath, leaving a mark also on the immediate post-war period and sometimes having an impact throughout the entire interwar period.

On the eve of the world war, there were probably about 5 million people in Europe living permanently or as labour migrants in countries in which they had not been born. In pre-war Britain, for example, there were about 60,000 people of German descent living especially in the urban-industrial centres of London, Manchester and Liverpool. The first coercive measures were decreed in an atmosphere of collective hysteria and fear of espionage, and hit these Germans and the descendants of German immigrants in Britain immediately following the outbreak of war. As early as 5 August 1914, the Aliens Restriction Act enacted serious restrictions on freedom of movement for foreigners from enemy countries. They were no longer allowed to change their place of residence or enter certain zones, and clubs and institutions of 'enemy aliens' were forced to disband. Two days later it was resolved that Germans classified as a threat to internal security were to be interned. Initially 4,300 Germans were affected; about a month later the number had already increased to over 10,000. Further internments were halted only because of space limitations in the camps. In October 1914 there was heavy anti-German rioting. The situation later calmed down somewhat and 3,000 internees were released. Subsequent to exchange negotiations with the German government, about 10,000 people of German descent left the country by January 1916.

After the passenger ship *Lusitania* was sunk by a German submarine in May 1915, British internment and repatriation policies towards 'enemy aliens' from Germany were again tightened and anti-German rioting flared up once more. The riots began in Liverpool on 8 May, the day after the sinking of the *Lusitania*. Storefronts were shattered, shops demolished, storeowners of German descent beaten up. In the days that followed, the riots escalated and by 10 May 1915 about 2,000 people were involved. They gained momentum and unleashed xenophobic aggression against anyone 'foreign', including Scandinavians, Italians and Chinese. Local police were helpless and demanded military support, which was then called back as the situation calmed down. In October 1915, more than 32,000 'enemy aliens' of primarily German and Austro-Hungarian descent had already been interned; from May 1915 to June 1916, about 10,000 of their number were repatriated. There were scarcely any more internments in the last two years of the war and repatriations served to reduce the number of internees, but there were nevertheless more than 24,000 still in camps on Armistice Day in November 1918.[19]

Internment, repatriation and xenophobic violence were not limited to Britain. A total of at least 400,000 'enemy aliens' were interned in all of the warring countries in Europe. In France, for example, as early as 2 August 1914 it was proclaimed that all 'enemy aliens' had to leave the country by the end of the mobilization period. Authorities arrested not only people of German and Austro-Hungarian descent, but also Turks, Bulgarians, Czechs, Greeks, Poles, Armenians and Alsace-Lorrainers. Even naturalized French men and women were not spared the anti-foreigner measures. These xenophobic, ethnonationalistic tendencies collided with republican tradition. In April 1915 almost all French citizens who had been born in an 'enemy state' had their citizenship revoked.

In Germany, on the other hand, foreigners from 'enemy states' faced hardly any restrictions in the first four months of the war. German authorities initially did not view 'enemy aliens' as a security risk. For one thing, there were far fewer British and French living in Germany (about 15,000) than Germans in these two 'enemy states'. In addition, German troops had taken the offensive and felt certain of victory, fearing no 'fifth column'. All this changed with the beginning of positional warfare. The internment of male British citizens of military age beginning in November 1914 was initially meant as a retaliatory measure, but trends to segregate and intern 'enemy aliens' then took hold there as well. In June 1915, a total of 48,000 civilians of various nationalities were interned in Germany; by the end of the war, the number had risen to 110,000 people in 18 different camps.

The most prominent internment camp in Germany was at the former horseracing track in Ruhleben, a suburb of Berlin-Spandau, because of the large number of scholars, writers and students among the 4,400 British men interned there. The camp became famous through the literary works published by the internees; more than 50 books and extended treatises reported on life in the camp. Most of the inmates survived the generally four-year period of internment without serious health problems only because food supplies had been sent from their homeland, which alleviated the problem of poor nutrition in the camp. The exhausting years behind barbed wire in an overcrowded camp were made more bearable through the active cultural life that also could not have existed without materials and support sent from Britain. A camp library of about 5,000 books was built up over the course of the war through donations. Two hundred teachers and 1,400 students participated in 297 different courses at the Ruhleben Camp School, ranging from mathematics to marine biology. Eighty musicians played in the camp's symphony orchestra, having received their instruments through the Red Cross. There was also a Ruhleben Dramatic Society; and the *Ruhleben Camp Magazine* was published from March 1916. Other publications were the *In Ruhleben Camp* magazine and the *Ruhleben Daily News*, which offered half a page of news each day.[20] Among the internees in Ruhleben was the later famous British sociologist Thomas H. Marshall, whose citizenship model will be discussed later (see chapter 4, section 3). He had been interned while taking a German course in Weimar in 1914 to prepare for diplomatic service. Looking back six decades later, he wrote: 'If only I had been a sociologist then, what an opportunity this would have given me to study, by participant observation and any other survey method not requiring a computer, the emergence of a structured society from a miscellaneous collection of individuals (all male) flung together by chance in a confined space (a race course and its stables), and its subsequent fortunes.... Ruhleben breached the defences of the secluded world of the bourgeois intelligentsia in which I had been brought up!'[21]

Warlike images of the enemy underpinned by ethnonationalist and culturalist sentiments did not only lead during the war to the segregation of immigrant minorities, xenophobic aggression and the acceptance of violence, internment and repatriation; it also encouraged mass efforts to flee that had begun during the Balkan Wars, a prelude to the First World War. In the First Balkan War in 1912 alone, 100,000 Muslims fled the areas of Macedonia and western Thrace (Thraki) that had been annexed by the victor states of Greece, Montenegro, Bulgaria and Serbia. An estimated 400,000 Muslims fled from the Balkans to Turkey during and after the Balkan Wars. The end of the Second Balkan War in 1913 marked the beginning of the long series of resettlements of the first half of the twentieth century, based on bilateral treaties which aimed at 'ethnic unmixing' through the exchange of populations. A wide strip of land extending 15 kilometres on either side of the Turkish–Bulgarian border was established in 1913 for the exchange of respective minorities. The regulation affected almost 100,000 people. On the outbreak of the First World War, other exchange agreements, primarily between Greece and Turkey, were already in preparation that were to affect around 1 million people. In general terms, the Balkan Wars, which significantly altered relations among nationalities in the Balkans, resulted in the escape and resettlement of about 900,000 people in 1912–14.[22] This pogrom-like 'ethnic unmixing', which was partly planned and partly spontaneous, did not reduce the potential for conflict, it enhanced it, as the fate of many minorities in the Balkans and the Eurasian border zone of the Caucasus (massacre of Armenians) during and after the First World War would later show.

In central and western Europe, the First World War overshadowed the extent of the preceding refugee migration in the Balkans. Fearing horrific battles and atrocities against the civilian population, about 1.4 million Belgians – one-fifth of the total population of 7 million in 1914 – fled to the Netherlands, France or Britain in the first three months after the German invasion. The flight of the Belgians turned into a mass movement in particular because of the heavy fighting, but also because of German war crimes against the civilian population. The murder of 672 civilians when the town of Dinant was destroyed, for example, became a symbol of the cruelty of German warfare used in war propaganda.

The Netherlands became by far the most important receiving country, taking in a little over 1 million Belgian refugees. In October 1914 alone, when the Germans attacked Antwerp, about 500,000 people fled to the Netherlands in panic within only a few days. Among the refugees were many who had already moved within Belgium to the north-westernmost part of the country to escape the advancing German troops. The sudden swelling of the stream of refugees created huge supply problems. Aid from local authorities and charitable organizations quickly reached their limits. Consequently, in mid-August 1914 the Dutch government intervened with direct support payments and by erecting refugee camps. The intention was not only to supply the masses of refugees and relieve the desperate economic situation, but also to ward off the danger of a growth in anti-German sentiments because of the refugee movements, which could have endangered the country's neutrality.

Statistics relating to communities near the Belgian border, the Dutch provinces of Seeland, Limburg and North Brabant, demonstrate how significantly individual communities were affected by the influx of refugees. Maastricht, with a population of almost 37,000, took in about 14,000 refugees in August 1914. Vlissingen had 21,000 residents and 8,160 refugees. Other communities experienced much more difficult situations with considerable conflict potential; in Rosendaal, for example, 50,000 refugees came to a community of 17,000. Bergen op Zoom, with a population of almost 15,000, was faced with just as many refugees.[23]

After appeals in the daily newspapers and instructions to local mayors from the Dutch minister of the interior to exert 'gentle pressure' in urging the refugees to return, refugee figures started to decline, at first slowly and, as of late October 1914, with increasing rapidity. The Belgian refugee population in the Netherlands had amounted to about 1 million people. In December 1914 there were still about 200,000–300,000, and in December 1915 the figure had dropped to about 50,000–100,000, remaining generally around that mark until the end of the war. Refugee figures in the Netherlands did not continue to decrease after 1915 despite the intensification of German policies in occupied Belgium, but neither did they rise. This was especially because of measures enacted by the German occupying forces to shut off access. In 1915, the entire length of the 180–kilometre border between occupied Belgium and the Netherlands was closed by means of a high-voltage electric fence, bringing border traffic to a virtual standstill. About 3,000 people are estimated to have died trying to get across.[24]

Not as many Belgian refugees went to France and Britain once the war started as went to the Netherlands, but the number remained more stable owing to the unbridgeable front line to the Belgian state territory that was largely occupied by German troops. There were 325,000 Belgian refugees in France during the war, and 240,000 in Britain. While the Netherlands became increasingly reluctant to accept masses of refugees from its southern neighbour and the authorities urged their speedy return, Belgian refugees were welcomed in Britain. They not only became a symbol of the necessity and legitimacy of Britain's entrance into the war, but, in view of the economic consequences of war mobilization, they were also welcomed as an additional workforce.[25]

Hundreds of thousands of people in northern and north-eastern France also fled German troops in the first two months of the war. When the fronts were established according to the tactics of positional warfare, there were vast stretches of land on either side of the front in which soldiers fought and died, but in which no local residents continued to live. In the areas occupied by German troops until the armistice and in the battle zones in northern and eastern France, the population had been around 4.7 million before 1914. In 1919, the first year of peace, the population initially climbed back up to about 2 million.[26] Twice in the course of the war there were also refugee movements from the French capital: at the beginning of the war, when German troops advanced to Paris, and in March–April 1918, when the bombardment of the metropolis by the extremely long-range German heavy artillery began from Crépy-en-Laonnois. Half a million people are estimated to have fled Paris within only a few weeks.[27]

Even greater than the refugee movements in the west were the refugee and forced migrations from 1914 to 1918 in the theatres of war in eastern Europe. They began in East Prussia, which had been largely overrun by Russian troops in the first weeks of August 1914. Half a million refugees streamed westward. Others hid in apparently inaccessible marshes and forests. Moreover, the first deportations in the history of the world war took place in East Prussia. Russian troops were quickly forced back and, as they retreated, they took a total of 13,600 East Prussian civilians and sent them to Siberia. After the war, 8,274 are estimated to have returned. In Austro-Hungarian Galicia, the Russian offensive led to refugee misery and panic-stricken evacuations that involved about 300,000–400,000 people.[28] The eastward advance of German and Austro-Hungarian troops in autumn 1914 in turn uprooted millions of people in the border and battle zones of the Russian western region through escape, expulsion, evacuation and forced relocation. Russian authorities reported 2.7 million refugees and evacuees in the non-occupied Russian territory in December 1915; by May 1916 the number had grown to more than 3.1 million, though in fact the total was probably nearer 5 million.

In addition to evacuation in the face of impending danger, in many cases minorities were also deported. This applied especially to the Jewish population in the war regions. Jews also suffered through pogroms by Russian troops and by the civilian population, with official sanction. They were considered internal enemies and were collectively suspected of collaboration with German and Austro-Hungarian troops. When, after devastating defeats, the Russian troops had to clear Galicia, Bukovina, Lithuania and Courland, scapegoats were sought among the minority populations. Russian authorities deported up to 1 million Jews to the interior from the Baltic Provinces, the environs of Vilnius and Volhynia. Conditions were catastrophic and countless lives were lost. Their alleged crime was espionage, which supposedly enabled the enemy advance in the first place. About 200,000 Russian Germans who were considered a 'fifth column' behind their own frontlines were also held responsible for Russian defeats and were deported eastward, in particular from Volhynia. Of those who survived, many returned after the revolution or emigrated to Germany or overseas via Germany, especially to the United States and Canada. Other Jews and Russian Germans left the Russian areas, fleeing the coercive measures, rioting and deportations across the frontlines. This also included the 200,000 Jews from Galicia and Bukovina who fled westward in panic after the pogroms of late 1914.[29]

Armistice and peace treaties did not mean an end to flight and expulsion. Instead, the Russian civil war and state-formation processes in eastern, east central and south-eastern Europe triggered massive new forced and refugee migrations. The interwar period was also characterized by those seeking political refuge from the newly established dictatorships of Europe.

2   THE INTERWAR PERIOD: PROTECTIONIST MIGRATION POLICIES AND MASS MOVEMENTS OF REFUGEES

The aftermath of the war, protectionism and state intervention

The peace treaties that officially ended the First World War led to far-reaching structural changes in Europe's political order. The three European empires had ended, 14 new states were formed and 11,000 kilometres of new exterior borders were added to Europe. Minorities became majorities, and vice versa. Mass refugee movements and 'resettlements' assumed proportions that had been unheard of even during the First World War. Changes in political cartography transformed the nature of migrations, especially in central and east central Europe. Many earlier internal migrations became international cross-border movements, such as the seasonal migrations from Bohemia to the Austrian heartlands. Old migration traditions and traditional migratory systems dwindled to circular trickles or dried up totally, having been choked off or blocked by border closures, international conflicts or protectionist state intervention. Elsewhere, transnational movements had changed into internal migrations, for example in the re-established Polish state, a quarter of whose pre-war population had been dependent on income from transnational labour migration.[30]

The First World War and the interwar period fundamentally changed the relationship between state and migration. Protectionism and autarkic efforts became characteristic of the world economy, and the interventionist state became the norm in Europe. Against this background, controls and regulation became largely tools of migration and labour market policies aimed at national isolation and exclusion. This had profound consequences for migration processes in Europe.

Economic and labour market developments in most countries that had been involved in the war faced a difficult adjustment period soon after it ended. Human demobilization of millions of soldiers, about 5 million in France and about 8 million in Germany, coincided with economic demobilization from wartime to peacetime economies, combined with the dismissal in the medium term of a large portion of employees from the armaments industries. War destruction, border closures and inadequate transport capabilities delayed efforts to cope with the crisis. Domestic markets had to be rebuilt; post-war inflation made it necessary to undercut international competition through price wars in order to open up export opportunities, though this ruined the national currency.

Inflationary money devaluation affected currency developments in almost all countries that had been involved in the war, since the war had usually been partly financed by increasing the amount of money in circulation. Germany was hardest hit and its currency exploded in the hyperinflation of 1923. But the successor states of the Austro-Hungarian monarchy and the Russian empire also went through serious currency crises, with grave economic and social problems as a result. Even the victorious western countries could stabilize their currencies only after an economically depressing phase of deflation; the United States succeeded in 1921, Britain in 1925 and France in 1927. Inflation in the United States remained relatively insignificant, with price increases of 20–30 per cent as compared to the pre-war period. Britain had an inflation rate of 157 per cent, while in Italy and France it was over 200 per cent. Beyond inflation, deflation and the repercussions in the domestic economies of the respective European countries, the costs of war and its aftermath brought about the collapse of the worldwide currency system.

The First World War marked the end of Europe's global political supremacy through the emergence of new superpowers across the Atlantic and in eastern Europe. Moreover, it also ended the global economic dominance of the Old World. The aftermath of the war led to a shift in the global economic structure that had been oriented towards Europe prior to 1914. Its asymmetrical exchange relations had brought raw materials and food to Europe and accelerated growth of the secondary sector through the export of finished products. The war-related demand for goods reinforced the need for products from the periphery of Europe in 1914–18. The sharp decline in exports from Europe forced and enabled many countries, such as in Latin America and Asia, to develop their own industries in a non-competitive environment. This change could not be undone after the war ended. The exchange of goods between non-European countries made up only 25 per cent of world trade in 1913. In 1925–38 it comprised 40 per cent, which is a clear indication of the economic trend away from the major cities of Europe. Europe felt the increasing effect of the growth of non-European competition on the world market, especially from the United States but also from Japan.

Sinking European export options and growing competition on European markets led largely to overcapacity and an excessively high base of structural unemployment. In the crisis-prone post-war economies, unemployment as a result of job losses due to economic factors became chronic, culminating in the world economic crisis of the early 1930s. There were an estimated 15 million unemployed in late 1932 in Europe, with large discrepancies from country to country: unemployment was disproportionately high in Germany. Though unemployment figures declined after the end of hyperinflation in 1923, they remained at a high plateau that never went below the 1 million mark from the crisis in the mid-1920s – in 1925–6 there were about 2.2 million unemployed, or over 10 per cent – until the end of the Weimar Republic in 1933. The number shot up during the Great Depression, reaching more than 6 million in early 1932, or almost one in three not counting the self-employed.

At that time in the United States there were more than 12 million unemployed, or about one in four; Britain's 3 million unemployed amounted to about one in five. Belgium and Sweden were also hard hit, with unemployment rates of about 24 per cent each, as was the Netherlands, with about 17 per cent. Unemployment was far lower in France. On the one hand, this had to do with the course of industrialization in France described earlier. On the other hand, unemployment was less visible since France had no state unemployment benefits and, consequently, no nationwide statistics on unemployment. Until far into the 1930s, unemployment was not considered a major social problem in France. Even in 1935, at the height of the Depression, among France's total dependent workforce of 12.5 million, only about 500,000 (4 per cent) were unemployed.

Economic policy strategies of the interwar period ranged from protectionist separation of national economic spheres to visions of national autarky that were discussed during the world economic crisis. Protectionist trends had already appeared in Europe during the decades prior to the war, but it was not until the interwar period that free trade came to a definitive end. Even Britain's classic free trade metropolises retained the import duties that had been introduced under war conditions.

In addition to economic crises and protectionist crisis-resolution strategies, the path to the modern interventionist state, which was accelerated by the war, was also marked by economic and social developments in the interwar period. National labour markets in the war economies had become preferred objects for state controls and intervention, and this practice continued after the war. Within the context of intensified welfare state structures and functions in Europe, the trend towards a kind of 'overall state responsibility for the labour market' was the 'most important development of the interwar period'.[31] The modernization thrust that came with the war encompassed especially the expansion of labour administration, regulation of labour relations, job creation schemes and unemployment benefits.

Recruitment of labour beyond the national labour markets had become an essential area of policy during the war, playing a prominent role especially in Germany and France. In the interwar period, the regulation and control of foreign employment remained central to state intervention, now in the sense of a protectionist method of restricting access to the labour markets. Hungarian economist Imre Ferenczi, commissioned by the International Labour Office in Geneva to document and analyse migration movements and migration policies in interwar Europe, clearly distinguished the phase of unfettered 'proletarian mass migrations' prior to the First World War from the post-1918 phase, which he saw as migrations characterized by 'socio-political regulations and interstate organization'.[32] Around the same time, German economist Karl C. Thalheim summarized this development: 'The migration economy of the world is today on the way from liberalism to planned state economy.'[33]

Overseas emigration and restrictive migration policies

Because almost all major emigration countries in Europe were involved in the war, emigration rates declined steeply after 1914–15. After an average annual emigration of 1.4 million Europeans in the period from 1906 to 1910, the next five years from 1911 to 1915 were not yet heavily affected in a statistical sense by the world war, showing only a slight decrease to 1.35 million emigrants per year. From 1916 to 1920, however, the annual average dropped to only 431,000, one-third the previous level. European emigration from 1921 to 1930 (6.9 million) amounted to an annual average of almost 700,000, which was far higher than in 1916–20, but only half the annual average for the statistical pre-war decade from 1906 to 1915. The Great Depression affected the regions of both origin and destination of European emigration and caused a noticeable decline in the figures. In 1931–40, a total of only 1.2 million emigrants were registered for the whole of Europe, which was only 20 per cent of the figure from the 1920s. With an annual average of only 120,000, European emigration had reached its lowest level in the preceding hundred years.[34]

In the pre- and early war period from 1911 to 1915, there were 6.7 million emigrants. Considerably more than one in four came from the British Isles (1.9 million) and almost that many from Italy (1.66 million). Far further down the line came Spain with 830,000 emigrants, Austria-Hungary with 730,000 and Russia with 550,000. In the five years marked most by the war and the immediate post-war period (1916–20), the number of emigrants from the British Isles and Italy each went down to about 40 per cent of the respective 1911–15 figure; the number for Spain, which had not been involved in the war, amounted to 60 per cent of the pre- and early war figure. In Austria-Hungary and Russia, on the other hand, emigration dwindled to a negligible minimum. The same was true for Germany, which reached only one-seventh of the already low pre-war level. In the post-war decade from 1921 to 1930, the British Isles (2.2. million) and Italy (1.4 million) remained the main emigration regions in Europe. Portugal ranked third with 1 million emigrants, ahead of Poland (634,000) and Germany (564,000). Spain had 560,000 emigrants in this period, sliding into the sixth position just behind Germany. The apparently high number of emigrants from Poland remained hidden up to the First World War owing to the partition of Poland and the division of emigrants into separate figures for Austria-Hungary, Germany and Russia. The USSR had such restrictive emigration policies that one of the primary European emigration regions of the pre-war period disappeared almost entirely after the war. Emigration from the Soviet Union sank in the 1921–30 period to 80,000, about one-eleventh of the figure for the decade from 1901 to 1910.

Emigration statistics for Germany in the 1921–30 period were double those of the pre-war decade from 1901 to 1910, moving Germany up to fifth position among European emigration countries. This signalled a temporary interruption in the European trend. A total of 603,000 Germans emigrated overseas in 1919–32. In view of the economic, social and political crisis directly following the First World War, an initial emigration wave of about 1 million, reminiscent of the magnitude of the mass movements of the nineteenth century, had been expected. However, after breaking down war-related obstacles to emigration, German emigration increased slowly at first in 1921 (24,000) and 1922 (37,000), and surged suddenly and for one final time in the inflation year of 1923 to a year's total of 115,431, which had last been recorded during the great German emigration wave from 1880 to 1893.

This was the combined result of several different determining factors: (1) the carrying through of decisions to emigrate that had been made earlier but were delayed owing to the emigration bottleneck during the war and immediate post-war period; (2) the emigration of those uprooted and displaced by war, the decline of the German Empire, revolution and discontent with the new republic; (3) the emigration of those wishing to emigrate at some future time but whose decision was brought forward in an effort to save from inflation the capital put aside to start a new life overseas; and finally (4) the further migration of some people from ceded parts of Germany, German settlement areas in eastern, east central and south-eastern Europe or from the former German colonies who could not, or did not wish to, settle in Germany. Once the post-war crisis and hyperinflation ended in 1923, German emigration also fell back into the downward European trend. Starting with the currency stabilization of late 1923, as well as under the pressure of US immigration restrictions in 1924, emigration figures by the end of the 1920s declined to about half of what they had been in 1923; during the Depression of the early 1930s, they continued to drop back to 10,000–15,000 per year.[35]

The decline in European emigration in the interwar period was caused in part by restrictive migration policies on both sides of the Atlantic. Some emigration countries in Europe used diverse protectionist migration policy measures in an attempt to limit or prevent emigration. This can be seen in a comparison of the policies in the Soviet Union, Italy and Germany.

In the Soviet Union there was no official ban on emigration, but bureaucratic obstacles made it virtually impossible. Special documents that were difficult to obtain had to be presented and high fees were charged. Restrictive emigration policy was part of the massive Soviet industrialization programme that appeared feasible only by tying down and controlling the labour force as far as possible.[36]

There were different motives behind Italy's[37] protectionist migration policies. The fascist rulers who had been in power since 1922 viewed emigration and cross-border labour migration as a national disgrace. Both migratory forms were seen as denouncing Italy for economic underdevelopment and serving to intensify the very economic problems that caused them through the outflow of needed labour. However, choking off migration turned out to be a very difficult undertaking. Italian colonial policy was seen as a way to redirect the migration flow towards settlement colonies. This was reminiscent of British successes and German illusions in this area (see chapter 2, section 3). The corresponding Italian colonial experience was more eventful than the short German one, but in the end it too failed. Up to 1930, only 50,000–60,000 Italians had been settled in the colonial regions, concentrated essentially in the North African cities of Tripoli and Benghazi. In the 1930s colonial migration rose to a total of roughly 400,000 people, but this was less definitive emigration than a Euro-colonial migratory cycle, since the return migration rate was very high. By the late 1930s, there were no more than 85,000 Italians in Libya, and far fewer in the East African colonies, amounting to only 60,000.[38]

In the 1920s alone, however, despite similarly high return migration rates, Italy registered about 2 million emigrants and labour migrants working abroad. Starting in 1927, Italy's state migration policies became progressively restrictive. They initiated strict controls aimed at choking off emigration, forcing return migration and at the same time stemming recruitment of Italian labour migrants by foreign countries or companies. Passports were generously distributed only to highly qualified workers who either wanted to complete their training abroad or who authorities reckoned would either return or send large remittances back home. Aside from combating emigration and other out-migration, the Mussolini regime was interested in reinforcing the fascist movement among Italians abroad and strengthening their ties to the homeland.

In Germany too state efforts could be observed that aimed at influencing the extent and direction of emigration, though this was done neither as openly nor as directly as in the Soviet Union and Italy. Evidence of this increasing state interest in migration issues was the establishment of an office for German return migration and emigration (Reichswanderungsstelle) in May 1918. Its status was enhanced in the following year to the Migration Office responsible for immigration, return migration and emigration (Reichswanderungsamt). In early 1924, however, it was again downgraded to an office for emigration (Reichsstelle für das Auswanderungswesen). This change was due to discrepancies between expected and actual migratory developments in the post-war period. At the end of the First World War, German territorial changes led to massive streams of return migrants from areas that Germany had ceded, of immigrants of German descent and also of emigrants, but only in the final phase of the war and the first post-war months was the task of the new migration authorities in fact determined by the organizing of immigration of Germans or foreigners of German descent. After this point the focus moved completely to emigration issues.

The Migration Office (Reichswanderungsamt) was officially supposed only to advise would-be emigrants to protect them from bad planning and fraud, but the agency saw itself as an 'official organization to direct and influence German migratory movements'. This definition of its purpose had to be ostensibly played down in favour of its advisory role because the constitution of the Weimar Republic guaranteed freedom to emigrate. A wide network of branch offices offered emigrant counselling – which was mandatory until 1924 – in collaboration with the labour offices. Their main purpose was to prevent qualified labourers from emigrating by referring them to appropriate job offers. If the labour office determined that a particular emigration was tenable, it was to be directed overseas to German settlement districts if possible, especially those in South America. This was based on the idea of 'preserving Germandom abroad' that had existed since the expansionist and colonial press of the 1880s, and on an overseas export campaign through concentrated settlement of foreigners beyond the attractive pull of the United States. Such attempts to steer migratory movements through advice proved to be relatively unsuccessful, as is apparent by the fact that in public discussion the Migration Office was given the derisive nicknames 'Prevention Office' (Reichsverhinderungsamt) and 'Office of Lost Words'. During the Weimar Republic there was indeed a rise in South American immigration destinations as compared with the United States. While this was partly due to the advice and counselling activities of the Migration Office, however, at least as responsible was the growing attraction of South American countries of immigration compared with the United States, whose immigration policies were becoming increasingly restrictive and deterrent and served to choke off emigration from Europe in general.[39]

The restrictive immigration policies of the country that, until the First World War, had been by far the most significant destination country for European emigrants[40] existed not so much for economic reasons; as a true economic victor of the war, the United States in the 1920s was in a phase of prosperity. Instead, the strict quotas arose out of a new nativist fundamentalism combined with racism that had been fanned by xenophobic rabble-rousing during the war which targeted everything 'un-American'. This included a revival of the Ku Klux Klan. The 1921 Quota Act introduced quotas based on country of origin. Apart from rejecting non-European immigration especially from Asia and Africa, it was directed with respect to European migration primarily against the new immigration from eastern, east central, south-eastern and southern Europe, which had become predominant from the late nineteenth century. The legislation declared that a contingent of only up to 3 per cent of the total population of the respective nationality in the United States in

1910 was allowed to immigrate. Consequently, annual immigration figures plummeted to around 300,000, half of what they had been.

The National Origins Act of 1924 intensified the quotas further and limited immigration to 164,000 yearly. In 1927 the annual quota was lowered to 150,000 and the system of national quotas became stricter yet for certain nationalities. The highest quotas were assigned to Britain, Ireland and Germany, while Italy, for example, received an extremely low quota of 6,000. The make-up of European immigration to the United States thus shifted with respect to country of origin. In 1910–15, 'new' immigration had still been three times the size of 'old' immigration from western, central and northern Europe. In the 1920s the new immigration countries still dominated, but only just, with a share of 54 per cent of all European emigration. In the 1930s the proportion of new immigration increased slightly to 60 per cent, but it never again achieved the degree of predominance it had had in the two pre-war decades.

The bureaucratization that accompanied these quota regulations, along with their offputting implementation requirements, also contributed to the failure to fill even the greatly reduced yearly quotas. The combined US quota for Britain and Ireland in the 1930s was 835,740, but only 110,094 immigrants entered the country. In this case the competing appeal of the dominions also had some impact.[41] In addition to a decrease in total volume of immigration, there was also a clear change in direction of European emigration flows away from the United States and towards the Latin American countries, Canada, Australia and New Zealand. Among the four main immigration countries in the world – United States, Canada, Argentina and Brazil – about 77 per cent of all immigrants in the period 1901–5 went to the United States; in 1906–10 the figure was 67 per cent. In the years from the first (1921) to the second (1924) Quota Act, only 59 per cent of all European emigrants went to the United States, and after the Quota Act of 1924 the share of US immigrants went down to 32 per cent in the second half of the 1920s. The Depression greatly reduced the magnetic pull of the United States (as well as Canada and Australia), and as the total volume of immigration was repeatedly reduced, the share of US immigrants continued to fall. In this period Argentina and Brazil registered more immigrants (in absolute figures) than the United States for the first time.[42]

Immigration restrictions and bans in the United States during the Depression changed not only the volume and breakdown by country, but also the occupation and gender structures of immigration from Europe, as illustrated by the structure of German immigration to the United States. Admission restrictions for farmers and agricultural labourers reduced the share of all those working in agriculture among the total number of working German emigrants from 23.1 per cent in 1930 to

11.3 per cent in 1931. German emigration in the 1920s showed a large increase in single working women, but the noticeable dwindling of the share of men from 53.5 per cent in 1929–30 to only 44.6 per cent in 1931 was an expression of the bias in issuing immigration permits that gave preferential treatment for women joining family members who had already emigrated.[43]

The boundaries between permanent emigration and temporary trans-atlantic labour migration had become increasingly blurred in late nine-teenth-century Europe. As previously noted, temporary transatlantic migration in the early twentieth century was greatest from southern Europe, especially Italy and Spain, to South America. With a clear preference for destinations in South America over those in North Amer-ica, transatlantic labour and temporary migration in the interwar period in Italy and Spain continued to expand. At least 40 per cent of Italian overseas emigrants from 1921 to 1935 returned; among Spaniards the figure for the same period even reached 65 per cent.[44]

Research sources on transatlantic migration systems have concentrated on the era up to the First World War; beyond that many gaps exist. There is no evidence, however, that there were far fewer *golondrinas* in South America in the 1920s than there had been prior to the First World War. Argentinian statistics show high return migration rates in general. From 1901 to 1910, a total of 1,746,104 people immigrated to Argentina, the highest volume up to that time for any country within one decade. In the same period, 643,881 people migrated out of Argentina, that is, only 63.1 per cent remained. From 1911 to 1920, the return migration rate was much higher due to the war. A total of 1,204,919 immigrated but only 269,094 (or 22.3 per cent) remained. Immigration increased some-what in the decade 1921–30 to 1,397,415 and the return migration rate retreated to the level of the pre-war decade; 62.8 per cent, or 877,970, of the immigrants remained in Argentina.[45] For the same period, Italian sources on emigration to Argentina and return migration to Italy report 670,000 emigrations and 270,000 return migrants (return migration rate of 40 per cent) from 1902 to 1910. In the period 1911–20, there were 310,000 emigrants and 291,000 returnees (94 per cent), and from 1921 to 1930, 500,000 emigrated and 170,000 returned (32 per cent). The figures regarding Italian migrants correspond essentially to the total figures for Argentina. Before and after the First World War, the return migration rate was at least one-third of the emigration rate, and during the war return migration was particularly high.[46]

The Depression reinforced return migration trends. Britain, for example, which for over a century, with few exceptions, had always had the most emigrants annually in comparison with the rest of Europe, showed an immigration surplus for the first time in 1930 due to rapidly falling emigration and steeply increasing return migration. By the beginning of the Second World War this surplus had reached more than 500,000. Declining emigration rates and increasing return migration also caused positive migration balances from 1930 to 1935 in other countries that had long experienced more overseas or continental emigration than migration in the reverse direction, including Belgium, Austria, Hungary, Yugoslavia and Romania. In the decade from the beginning of the Depression in 1929 to the outbreak of the Second World War in 1939, for the first time since the early nineteenth century emigration did not play a significant role in population developments in Europe.

Labour market regulation and immigration restrictions

Protectionist intervention in inner-European migration in the interwar period was far more prevalent regarding immigration policies than emigration policies. Increased state influence could be seen in a number of measures aimed at administering, controlling and regulating in-migration. They ranged from stricter immigration controls to shielding labour markets or individual areas of employment in favour of local workers. By comparing the situations in Germany and France, the two greatest European destination countries prior to 1914, it is possible to identify different, sometimes opposing, intentions and dimensions of protectionist change in immigration and labour market policies in the interwar period.

Germany

In Germany after the First World War, industrial production grew in fits and starts and experienced several interruptions before finally reattaining (without significantly surpassing) its 1913 pre-war level in 1927–9, that is, just before the world economic crisis. The labour market situation was marked by a surplus of labour and the aforementioned high base of structural unemployment in a number of fields, with a definite shortage of qualified workers, especially skilled craftsmen. Against this background there were two sides to the notion of 'protecting national labour', since Germany was a country of both immigration and emigration. For one thing, measures were taken to prevent the emigration of skilled craftsmen. Priority was also given to German over foreign labourers. Before the war this had been the labour movement's unheeded demand, just like the demand to hire foreigners at the same working and wage conditions as nationals in order to prevent their being used deliberately as wage-cutters, pacesetters and scabs. These goals could be achieved in view of the new power of trade unions and labour parties in the Weimar

Republic, as could the proposal to admit foreigners through joint labour–management committees. After a period of transition marked by economic and human demobilization, employment of foreigners was regulated from 1920 according to these guidelines by means of increasingly sophisticated instruments.

Prussian Germany had already developed an extensive and solid system of controlling the foreign labour force prior to the First World War, but 'Prussian defence policies' had been instituted for security and ethnopolitical reasons. They were not intended for labour market policy reasons, and certainly not for protectionism. The compulsory annual return and employment restrictions targeted only foreign Polish workers. Foreign Poles were still officially subject to a compulsory annual return in the Weimar Republic, but because of problems in recruiting foreign agricultural workers this remained virtually unenforced up to 1925–6 for large segments of that group. Regulating the admission of foreigners and limiting them to replacement or buffer functions came to the fore in the Weimar Republic, not only in terms of number but in a qualitatively different way. The migratory patterns of continental migration to Prussian Germany were no longer determined by the strategy of 'defence policies' but by the rationale of labour market policies.[47]

The foreign employment curve took a dive in 1919, essentially due to the fact that a large portion of foreign Polish (and former Prussian Polish) labourers returned to the new Polish state or migrated further to France. As compared with the pre-war period, the annual fluctuation of foreign labour was far lower as a result of restrictive quotas in geographically shrunken and economically depressed post-war Germany. This was true also for the agricultural reserve army from across the border to the east, which – after Prussia's eastern border had been shifted to the west – continued to satisfy its replacement function albeit to a lesser degree, despite high urban unemployment, until the world economic crisis. The new agencies of the labour administration headed by the Office for Employment and Unemployment Insurance in Berlin were established through the employment exchange law of 1922 and expanded up to 1927. Through their preferential treatment of German workers and the required annual registration, they created a legal framework for keeping foreign employment within the limits of replacement and additional demand. Foreign labourers could now receive a work visa only if the employment exchanges confirmed that corresponding local labourers were not available. Companies that hired foreign labour without 'employment authorization' were committing a punishable offence.

In order to keep the employment of foreigners as flexible as possible and enable quick reactions to fluctuations in labour needs as a result of changing economic conditions, work and residence permits were issued for only one year at a time, in agriculture for even shorter periods of time. Exceptions were 'exemption certificates' for foreigners who were either of German descent or who had been living in Germany for a long time, allowing them to receive unlimited residence and work permits. In particular the German–Polish 'treaty on Polish migrant farm labourers' of November 1927 served to extend German control of employment of foreign Polish labour migrants, both male and female, down to determining the conditions of recruitment. The treaty guaranteed that recruitment as well as expulsion of Polish labourers would be carried out according to German conditions. By centralizing the decision-making authorities in the labour administration, foreign employment in the Weimar Republic developed into a purely state-run domain in contrast to the only partially state-run agencies of the pre-war period.

The intensive meshing of labour market and migration policies and the expansion of the labour administration throughout Germany made it possible to establish a sophisticated control instrument in the form of protectionist migration policies. For this reason, the curve of foreign employment in industry and agriculture in the Weimar Republic resembled a kind of crisis barometer of developments in the tension between supply and demand on the labour market. There were only 109,000 foreigners employed in the Depression year 1932 (1925: 263,000). In 1932 about one-third of foreign labour in agriculture and almost all foreign labour in industry were of German descent and had been living in Germany for a long time; most of them therefore had the coveted exemption certificate releasing them from having to obtain annual authorization to work and granting them equal status with German labourers.[48]

France

Before the First World War France was the second most important immigration country after Germany, and the most important in interwar Europe. It therefore had special significance in the development of European migration conditions.[49] Economic and labour market developments in France were in some ways the mirror-image of those in Germany. After victory in the war and after coping with the subsequent transitional crisis, France's economy was a relatively prospering one. The labour demand then started to increase and quickly exceeded the limits of the local labour supply. This was due in part to the consequences of the traditionally low fertility rate, especially since the birth rate and natural population growth remained low even in the post-war period. This was compounded by high population losses during the war. About 1,350,000 soldiers had died or were reported missing, more than 10 per cent of the total male population. Against this background, support for immigration was seen as a way out of the dilemma. France developed into the main destination for economically motivated transnational migration in post-war Europe. French policy had already included initial, albeit only isolated, protectionist measures in the area of public works as early as the late nineteenth century. Now it also took the step of initiating state intervention in transnational migratory events. Regulatory mechanisms were refined and bilateral agreements with the countries of origin (Poland, Italy, Czechoslovakia) facilitated and thus increased immigration controls and regulation.

France opened its borders wide in the 1920s for foreign workers and immigrants. Almost 2 million came in this decade, many for extended sojourns or permanently. For Europeans, France thus became the second most important receiving country worldwide, after the United States.[50] Immigration comprised no less than three-quarters of the total permanent population growth in France in the 1920s. In 1931, two years after the onset of the Great Depression, there were about 2.7 million foreigners in France. The largest groups were Italians (*c*.800,000), Poles (*c*.500,000), Spaniards (*c*.350,000) and Belgians (*c*.250,000).

Shortly after the First World War had ended in 1918, there was broad consensus across France in favour of immigration. The military victory was to be converted into economic expansion in an effort to replace wartime enemy Germany as the leading economic power on the Continent. After the experiences of the pre- and post-war periods, however, immigration and employment of foreigners were seen as needing state controls and regulation, similar to the situation in Germany. Consequently, foreign labourers were recruited directly for employment areas for which there were insufficient or no French labourers available. Prerequisite for an entry permit was a work contract. In addition, recruitment policies excluded certain groups as unsuitable from the outset. This exclusion was directed against labour from France's African and South-east Asian colonies and China (see section 1) which had been recruited during the First World War, thereby reversing Euro-colonial migratory cycles.

Fearing high unemployment through the impending demobilization of about 5 million soldiers and the transition from a war to a peace economy, France had closed its borders to in-migration in November 1918. The labour recruited during the war from the French colonies and China was hastily sent back. But demobilization progressed more smoothly than had been expected and in early 1919 there were already signs of renewed labour shortages in some areas of employment. Demand was especially high directly after the war to rebuild the destroyed war zone in northern and eastern France. For this reason, recruitment of foreigners as dockworkers, construction and quarry workers as well as in mining and glassworks was initially permitted. In order to secure recruitment, France concluded bilateral agreements with Poland, Italy and Czechoslovakia from September 1919 to March 1920, whereby these countries retained control of number, regional origin and qualifications of their labour migrants. They had no say in matters concerning working and living conditions and wages within France, however. France nevertheless granted the countries of origin greater say in these treaties than Germany had done for Poland in their 1927 treaty. In the German–Polish agreement, for example, Polish authorities were not allowed any influence in the regional configuration and qualifications of their labour migrants.

Clearing away the destruction caused by the war was a long-term endeavour that allowed the French building and construction industry to flourish for a decade. It was difficult to find French workers willing to do the earthwork, fill trenches and reconstruct buildings, industrial facilities and infrastructure, because this was very heavy labour and accommodation was in barracks in the largely devastated zone. From 1919 to 1924, a total of about 400,000 workers were hired. In 1920, for example, French authorities recruited 200,000 Belgian labourers alone for clearing-up operations in the reconstruction zone. In September 1922, there were 135,000 foreigners working on reconstruction, 44 per cent of all workers in this area.

When construction work superseded the purely clearance work, there was a shift in the breakdown according to nationality and qualifications of foreign workers. In particular Italians, Portuguese and Spaniards moved ahead of the Belgians, who had previously dominated. The share of skilled craftsmen – many of whom were Italian – had risen to 57 per cent of the 135,000 foreign workers in September 1922. A total of over 1 million foreign labourers were brought to France in the phase of mainly reconstruction work from late 1919 to 1924. There were 1.4 million registered in 1926, almost half of whom worked in industry. The second most important area of employment was clearly agriculture, at almost 15 per cent, followed by mining and trade at 11 per cent each. At this time, one-third of all foreign labourers came from Italy, followed by those from Belgium (14 per cent), Spain (13 per cent) and Poland (12 per cent). Poles were hired mostly in agriculture and mining in northern and north-eastern France. A considerable portion of them came from the Ruhr valley, where the Ruhr Poles who had migrated there before the First World War from the eastern Prussian provinces had formed a large minority.

The Depression of the early 1930s did not hit France nearly as hard as it affected Germany or the United States; nevertheless, the French government, too, choked off immigration in the early 1930s after it had already intervened directly in migration events by closing borders in the critical years of 1921 and 1927. Over 220,000 new immigrants were registered in France in 1930. In 1931 only 102,000 were allowed to enter the country. The government closed the borders completely in 1932 and in subsequent years continued to allow the in-migration of foreign workers only in exceptional cases and in accordance with strict quotas. The French state intervened in the development of transnational labour migration and employment of foreigners in the interwar years with more than just recruitment agreements and immigration controls and regulation; it also intervened directly in employment situations. Like the situation in Prussia prior to the First World War, police and prefects searched for anyone violating their contracts and under certain circumstances returned them to the companies. As in Germany, it was a punishable offence in France for employers to make offers, such as higher wages, that prompted foreign labourers to breach their contracts. Additional measures aimed at limiting legal albeit unwanted workplace fluctuation by foreign labourers and preventing them from working in certain fields of employment or regions.

In general, foreign employment in the interwar period was thus characterized in both France and Germany by protectionist controls and regulation, despite the fact that economic and labour market developments in the two countries varied greatly. Bilateral agreements on recruitment and employment of foreign labourers ostensibly secured national control and regulatory systems. However, multilateral agreements on emigration, immigration and transnational labour migration demanded by various parties, and especially by international organizations formed after the First World War, proved worthless since they tried to accomplish the impossible feat of reconciling antagonistic interests. 'Since the Great War most countries recklessly regulate as they see fit the right of citizens to emigrate and the immigration of foreigners', criticized Imre Ferenczi with regard to the biased regulations to protect labour markets in the interwar period, 'whereby their demands *vis-à-vis* other states are perhaps even more contradictory to their own actions than was the case in the area of customs policy.'[51]

These contradictions were greater in Germany than in France because Germany was simultaneously both a country of origin for overseas emigration and a destination of continental labour migration. This hybrid situation led to a unique ambivalence in Germany's position in the 'global migration economy' (Karl C. Thalheim): as a country of emigration Germany was opposed to the drastic immigration restrictions in the United States, the main overseas immigration country. However, as a 'labour-importing country' (Imre Ferenczi) it had to defend a restrictive system of imposing quotas for continental immigration, which in many respects was on a par with the protectionist intentions of the new US immigration policies. This ambivalence also determined Germany's stance towards multilateral efforts to regulate emigration and immigration, which failed because of the diverse contradictions between the countries of origin and destination of emigration, immigration and labour migration.

Bilateral agreements with the home countries of foreign labour migrants were sought in Germany, as well as in France, in line with the recommendation of the International Labour Conference in 1919 in Washington, DC. The German position remained mixed regarding multilateral negotiations on regulating international migration, however, depending on whether the issues under discussion affected Germany as an emigration country or as a 'labour-importing country'. This was true for government representatives and representatives of organized labour interests alike. The ambivalence could already be observed at the Central European Economic Conference in Budapest in 1910. Apart from a meeting of delegates from countries of emigration in 1921 in Rome in which Germany did not participate, this ambivalence continued throughout the First International Conference on Emigration and Immigration in 1924 in Rome, the World Migration Congress convened in 1926 in London by the International Federation of Trade Unions and the Labour and Socialist International, and the Second International Conference on Emigration and Immigration in 1928 in Havana, to which Germany sent only an observer without speaking or voting rights.

After the promising first conference in Rome in 1924, the only lasting outcome of the disappointing second conference in Havana in 1928 was the impression shared by participants that negotiations on issues of emigration and immigration could be better resolved by the International Labour Office in Geneva than at conferences of the countries of emigration and immigration, with their often opposing interests. The International Emigration Commission established in 1920 by the International Labour Organization (ILO) was consequently not spared having to deal with the virtually unbridgeable differences in interests between emigration and immigration countries, nor was the Standing Committee on Emigration set up in 1925 in Geneva, with equal representation by both sides.

Flight and expulsion

Forced and refugee migration that opened the 'century of refugees' during the First World War continued to expand in the immediate post-war period. The driving force behind this migration was, in addition to the Russian civil war, especially the state-formation processes in eastern, east central and south-eastern Europe. The signatory powers of the Entente drew new borders in east central Europe and the Balkans. Taking up Wilson's idea of the right to self-determination of peoples, they supported the founding of new nation-states, within which ethnocultural and religious groups became minorities once and for all, because they were denied the character of the nation. The principle of self-determination was generally dealt with rather arbitrarily, granted to some peoples and groups and denied others. Regulations to protect minorities were ineffectual – with the sole exception of the autonomy regulations in the interests of the Swedish minority in Finland – because enforcement mechanisms were lacking. Hopes linked to the notion of self-determination were not fulfilled. None the less, the Moravian settlement (*Mährischer Ausgleich*) in 1867 and the Bukovina deal in 1910 were implemented historical experiments that offered personal autonomy in ethnically mixed regions, but they disappeared along with the multi-ethnic Austro-Hungarian Empire. As when the Ottoman Empire disintegrated, in place of the destroyed multi-ethnic state came smaller states which considered themselves nation-states but which were *de facto* also multi-ethnic states that used the principle of the nation-state to justify the exclusion of minorities.[52]

Behind this were ideas of national 'homogenization' or 'unmixing' of nation-states in order to avoid international conflicts. These were expressed comprehensively under the influence of the First World War in 1915 for the first time by Swiss anthropologist and ethnologist George Montandon. He suggested 'purifying' national states established in 'natural boundaries' through massive transplantation of 'non-members of the nation'. Such ideas centre around the classical idea expressed by Fridtjof Nansen, high commissioner for refugees of the League of Nations, that 'to unmix the populations of the Near East will tend to secure the true pacification of the Near East'. British foreign secretary Lord Curzon ('Curzon line'), who presided over negotiations at the Conference of Lausanne in 1922–3, referred to this with respect to the forced Greek–Turkish population exchange that was decided there. He was not mistaken in his gloomy warning that the decision that had been viewed as inevitable was in fact 'a thoroughly bad and vicious solution, for which the world will pay a heavy penalty for a hundred years to come'.[53]

All of the many shifts in borders after the First World War led to refugee migrations and 'resettlements'. Even the political changes that stemmed from the peace treaties themselves prompted, obliged or coerced probably about 5 million people to cross borders against their will. The first to go were usually administrative officials, police, teachers and other professional groups who had been directly connected with the previously ruling state. They were often followed by industrialists and businesspeople who saw their businesses threatened by new customs borders, currencies or legislation. If the new government enforced restrictive minority policies, then out-migration could quickly grow into a mass movement.

After losing the war, the Central Powers were forced to take in at least 2 million people from their former territories. This migration reached major proportions in Austria, which experienced considerable territorial changes. In the late 1920s, a total of 764,000 people, or more than 10 per cent of the total Austrian population, had been born outside the new borders on the territory of another successor state to the Habsburg Empire. Of these, 440,000 came from Bohemia and Moravia alone, the new core area of the Czechoslovakian state founded in 1918. The situation was similar in Hungary, with about 200,000 people from Czechoslovakia, just as many from Romania and about 100,000 from Yugoslavia.[54]

This kind of 'unmixing' motivated by 'nationality-based policies' was also practised elsewhere in south-eastern Europe.[55] The aforementioned treaty of Lausanne of 1923, which brought an end to the Greek–Turkish war (1920–2), served to revitalize the resettlement measures of the pre-war period in the Balkans. Here it was mandated that all Greeks except those in Istanbul leave Turkish territory and all Muslims leave Greek regions. A total of about 1,350,000 Greeks and about 430,000 Turks were subsequently resettled. After that, one-sixth of the Greek population had been born outside Greece. Greek provinces that had previously been settled almost exclusively by Muslims, such as Kavála, Drama or Néstos, became almost 'purely' Greek, whereas the percentage of Greeks in Macedonia increased from 42.6 in 1912 to 88.8 in 1928.[56] The often forced 'return migration' of Muslims from other Balkan states to Turkey, which had started in 1912 with the First Balkan War, resumed in the interwar period. This involved around 1 million people by the end of the 1920s; besides Greece, they came mostly from Yugoslavia, Romania and Bulgaria. They were often settled in areas of Turkey that Greeks had been forced to abandon.

Heavy refugee and resettlement movements also headed towards the German Empire, which had shrunk after the Versailles treaty. The census of 1925 recorded about 1.35 million Germans (2 per cent of the population), who in 1914 had lived outside the new German borders. About 150,000 came from Alsace-Lorraine and about 16,000 from the former German colonies. Migration from the eastern provinces that had been ceded to Poland in accordance with the treaty of Versailles was even greater. The German statistics office registered about 850,000 Germans who had left the western Polish territories by mid-1925. Many of them were initially accommodated in refugee camps spread throughout Germany ('homecoming camps'). The 26 refugee camps set up from 1920 to 1925 reached their highest occupancy between late 1922 and early 1923 with about 40,000 people at one time.[57] In the turmoil of the Russian civil war, another 120,000 Russian Germans left their settlement areas in 1918–21 bound for Germany. When the civil war ended and Soviet rule was firmly established, out-migration from the Russian-German settlement areas decreased substantially. As noted above, the Soviet government attempted to prevent emigration by increasing bureaucratic hurdles.[58]

The total number of refugees and those forced to resettle in Europe in the mid-1920s was probably no less than 9.5 million; this figure includes more than 1 million Germans from the ceded territories, roughly 1.5 million Greeks and Turks affected by the resettlement agreements, and refugees from the civil war and revolution in Russia. Most refugee movements started in eastern, east central and south-eastern Europe. The largest group of about 2 million refugees were those escaping the Russian revolution and civil war; behind the frontlines between Bolsheviks, Tsarists and Nationalists there were also renewed bloody pogroms against the Jewish population. In the Ukraine alone, about 60,000 people were killed in 1,326 pogroms, while about 300,000 Jews from Russia were able to flee to Lithuania, Latvia, Poland and Romania.[59] Here, most of those who remained would later fall victim to the genocide organized by the German occupiers in the Second World War (see section 3). In the revolution year of 1917, only a few people had left Russia, many of whom were members of the high nobility and industrialists who were often able to save large portions of their assets. At the time of the civil war, the flight swelled into a mass movement. Especially after the defeat of the White Army in 1920–1, the number of refugees rose abruptly. The devastating famine of 1921, in which about 22 million people suffered starvation and about 3 million died, drove the number of refugees yet higher. Moreover, there were several expulsions from the Soviet Union, the peak of which was reached in 1922.[60]

The Russian diaspora was spread out literally around the world, and there were even large refugee colonies in the Chinese cities of Harbin and Shanghai. Most Russian refugees first collected in the Balkans, Germany and France, however. Receiving refugees caused severe social problems in the post-war situation that presented a difficult challenge for the destination countries. This essentially led to an innovation in international law initiated by the League of Nations that marked the beginning of the history of international refugee aid organizations. The League of Nations' High Commission for Russian Refugees was soon followed by other independent refugee organizations of the League of Nations, such as that responsible for settling Greek refugees in 1923–30 and about 250,000 Bulgarian refugees in 1926–9. League of Nations' activities to aid refugees were consolidated from 1930 to 1938 in the International

Nansen Office for Refugees, named after Fridtjof Nansen (1861–1930), 1922 Nobel Peace Prize laureate and first high commissioner for refugees of the League of Nations. The so-called Nansen passport for stateless refugees, especially Russians, created a certain international legal security for refugees.

Immediately after the war, Germany initially became the most important host country for Russian refugees. According to figures from the Russian Delegation for Prisoners of War and Return Migration in Germany, there were a total of about 100,000 refugees in Germany in 1919. The American Red Cross even reported in 1920 a total of 560,000 Russians in Germany. According to the statistics of the League of Nations and the German Foreign Office, there were about 600,000 Russian refugees in Germany in 1922 and 1923, more than half of whom (about 360,000) lived in the capital Berlin. The shortage of housing in particular escalated the acceptance of refugees into a serious social problem. Numerous collective accommodation centres were set up, often in former POW camps. Large 'Russian camps' sometimes served as makeshift accommodation for refugees for many years.

Housing shortages and employment difficulties decreased Germany's attractiveness as a country of exile. After 1923 the number of Russian refugees steadily declined, especially since there was a high rate of further migration. The Refugee Inspectorate of the International Labour Office in Geneva registered 150,000 Russian refugees still in Germany in 1925, the same number in 1928, and still around 100,000 in 1933. 'Russian Berlin', with its important cultural, social and political functions, was initially the European centre of the Russian diaspora. After many refugees had left Germany, 'Russian Paris' assumed this role in the mid-1920s, until German troops invaded in 1940. France, or more precisely Paris and its adjacent *départements*, became the main destination for Russian emigrants partly because the French government supported immigration and the French economy sought labour. But the emphasis on exile and definitive emigration shifted, accelerating from 1940 to further migration beyond the continental realm across the Atlantic. North America increasingly became the final destination of the Russian emigrants in their stepwise geographical separation from the Russian homeland. The Second World War brought the final shift in the heart of the Russian diaspora to the United States with its cultural, social and political focus in New York.

Related processes of flight, further migration and temporary formation of diasporas were apparent in escape from Nazi Germany. For many it ended in definitive emigration. Those who left were referred to now as 'émigrés', whereas in earlier and later periods the term 'refugee' was more prevalent. It was used for outspoken opponents of the regime and those the regime declared to be opponents, especially those of Jewish descent in the broadest sense. The Nazis' racist ideology made them foreigners in their own country – humiliated, stripped of their rights and ultimately murdered, except for those who could flee in time or managed somehow to survive, in isolated cases in hiding, aided by courageous helpers. In addition to racist, religious, ideological and political reasons, bans imposed on critical journalists, writers, scholars and artists barring them from practising their profession prompted a considerable portion of Germany's cultural elite to leave the country. For many, especially the Jewish emigrés, escaping to other European countries and overseas meant being saved from a deadly threat.[61]

Emigration occurred in several waves,[62] with different configurations depending on the targets and severity of the respective regime measures, which developed with criminal energy: Hitler's seizure of power in 1933 along with the first measures of political persecution and anti-Semitic legislation triggered the first emigration wave. A second wave followed after the Nuremberg Laws of 1935. The last major emigration wave started after the Nazi regime staged 'spontaneous' excesses of violence against Jews in the nationwide pogrom of November 1938; it ended when the Second World War began in 1939, which largely eliminated options for emigration, until emigration was finally banned completely in 1941 and the path of systematic genocide of German and European Jewry began.

The exact number of emigrants from Germany is not known. Many were forced to cross borders either illegally or disguised as 'travellers', after which their traces were lost. By far the largest group of emigrants were those of Jewish descent, about 280,000–330,000 of whom left Germany. Including Jewish emigration from Austria after its 'annexation' to Germany in 1938 (about 150,000) and those from Czechoslovakia after the Munich agreement in the same year (about 33,000), the number of people of Jewish descent alone who emigrated from areas of central Europe under German control was at least 450,000–600,000. Throughout the world, a total of more than 80 countries took in refugees escaping the Nazi regime.

Many emigrants held fast to the hope that their exile would be only temporary. They escaped to neighbouring European countries to evade the Nazis and remained there, 'still oriented towards Germany' (Otto Wels). When the threat of German military expansion grew, many of them fled these 'transit countries' farther overseas, especially to the United States as the main final receiving country, where refuge and exile turned into permanent emigration for most. In the United States, the number of emigrants from Germany and 'annexed' Austria in 1941 exceeded 100,000. More than 80 per cent were Jews, about half of whom had arrived in 1938 or later. Argentina was the second largest receiving country in 1941, with about 55,000, ahead of Britain with about 40,000 emigrants from 'Greater Germany'. In the course of the Second World War, the main destination of the German diaspora of refugees and persecutees of the Nazi regime shifted across the Atlantic, with the United States ultimately taking in more than half of all emigrants, to the extent that they were able to reach the New World at all. The laborious struggle for emigration and immigration papers and transit visas forced many to remain helplessly behind, where they were interned, deported back to Germany or where they committed suicide to escape that fate. Novels such as *Transit* by Anna Seghers (1944, German and English) and *Die Nacht von Lissabon* by Erich Maria Remarque (1963; *The Night in Lisbon*, 1964) recount these stories.

Compared with the large number of Jewish emigrants from central Europe, the number of non-Jewish political refugees from Germany, Austria and the German-speaking regions of Czechoslovakia was far lower after 1938, amounting to about 25,000–30,000 people up to 1939, primarily social democrats and communists. France, Spain, Britain and the Soviet Union, as well as Scandinavia, Czechoslovakia, Switzerland and the Saar region, were initially the main centres of German political exiles. A comparison with fascist Italy is informative here: because the Mussolini regime did not establish a system of anti-Semitic oppression and persecution up to the Second World War despite German pressure, emigration from Italy remained limited almost exclusively to political refugees. From the time Mussolini took power in October 1922 until 1937, probably about 60,000 people left the country for political reasons, about 10,000 of whom went to France.[63] As regards Italian political exiles, like those from Germany, most opponents of the regime tried to remain in Europe as long as possible in order to be able to continue their political work from abroad.

The last major refugee movement in Europe in the interwar period took place in 1939, the year the Second World War began. In the aftermath the refugee issue in Europe would assume unanticipated proportions. The Spanish civil war led to the flight of millions. The number of refugees increased as Franco's troops advanced northward. Most refugees remained within the country, however, and Madrid and Barcelona in particular recorded large refugee populations. In August 1938, there were about 2 million refugees in the remaining part of republican Spain; by the end of that year the number had increased to 3 million. After the Spanish civil war ended, probably more than 500,000 republicans fled across the border to France, about half of whom were civilians. The French authorities were unprepared for such a massive influx of refugees and the country's camps could accommodate only 6,000–7,000 people. Living conditions in the refugee camps hastily erected at the beginning of the wave of refugees were thus miserable. The two huge camps at Saint Cyprien and Argelès directly on the beaches of the Mediterranean had to accommodate 100,000 and 80,000 people, respectively, until new camps could be set up in the interior in March–April 1939.

More than 300,000 Spanish refugees left France by the end of 1939, mostly with the assistance of aid organizations. A large portion migrated further to Latin America, especially Mexico, and about 150,000 returned to Spain. Spanish refugees who had to remain in France got caught up in the whirl of events of the Second World War. Some were extradited to the Franco regime after the French defeat in 1940 by the German occupying forces or by the Vichy government; others fought in the French Resistance or were murdered in German concentration camps.[64]

3   THE SECOND WORLD WAR AND THE POST-WAR DECADE

Escape, expulsion and deportation during the war

The Second World War, far more so than the First, involved mass military movements over immense geographical distances that go beyond the scope of this book. But also with regard to European population developments, the repercussions of the Second World War were far greater than those of the First. In contrast to the First World War, there were many more civilian than military casualties in the Second World War. This was due especially to Germany's war of extermination in eastern Europe and the air raids on civilian populations. Even five years after the war ended, in 1950, Europe's total population was 531 million, about 6 million less than in 1940 despite the high fertility rate that followed the Second World War (as was also the case after the First).[65]

Beyond and overlapping with the military dimension, the face of the Second World War and the period immediately following was marked by escape and expulsion, deportations and forced labour. The huge increase in forced relocations in the 1940s formed the peak of the 'new Thirty Years' War' in Europe from 1914 to 1945. Eugen Kulischer estimated the number of refugees, expellees and deportees in the phase of German military expansion of 1939–43 alone at 30 million throughout Europe, that is, at least 5 per cent of the European population.[66] After the bloody expansion, in 1943 began the equally bloody contraction of the 'Greater German Reich' and its satellite states that had hitherto been ravenously accumulated. Adding the massive forced relocations of 1943–5 to Kulischer's approximation yields a total of 50–60 million refugees, expellees and deportees, or more than 10 per cent of Europe's total population including the European part of Russia.[67] After the war ended, forced relocations in the scale of millions continued.

Allowing for diverse overlap, four main groups of forced migrants can be defined for the Second World War and the immediate post-war period:[68] (1) refugees from the war zones and those evacuated or fleeing advancing troops; (2) those deported or interned during the war, including forced labourers, especially for the Nazi war economy, POWs, 'resettled' or deported parts of local or foreign populations; (3) displaced persons in the period immediately following the war, who largely overlapped with the 'foreign workers' in the Nazi war economy; (4) expellees at the end of the war and immediately afterwards from the former eastern provinces of Germany and the German settlements in eastern, east central and south-eastern Europe.

As of 1939, all kinds of refugee movements had developed to escape advancing German troops. There were perhaps 300,000 refugees in Poland, 50,000–100,000 of whom crossed borders to the south and east. About 35,000 Poles found refuge up to mid-1940 in Britain, where a Polish exile government was established. Due to the German advance on western Europe, Britain soon counted more than 100,000 refugees from the Continent. Thousands each came from the Netherlands and Belgium, France, Denmark and Norway. A far larger number fled the advancing German troops in early 1940 by going first to France, and then moving on from there. About 5 million refugees from the Netherlands, Belgium and northern France used every conceivable means of transport or went on foot to save themselves by reaching central and southern France. This included a large portion of emigrants from Germany and German-occupied areas who had left Germany between the time the Nazis seized power and the start of the war, initially fleeing to neighbouring countries. The stream of refugees served to collapse the entire transport system and helped make French resistance to the German invasion increasingly futile.[69]

'But the great exodus began after the Germans had overrun Belgium', wrote Erich Maria Remarque, an emigrant himself, in his novel *The Night in Lisbon*. 'First came automobiles piled high with household goods and bedding, later vehicles of every kind, horse carts, handcarts, baby carriages, and, as time went on, endless streams of people on foot, all headed south in the lovely summer weather, pursued by dive bombers. . . . Members of separated families took to writing names and messages in coal, chalk, paint, or anything that was handy on walls, house fronts, road markers. It got to be something like a roadside gazette.'[70]

The attack on south-eastern Europe, after autumn 1940 by Italy and starting in spring 1941 by the Germans, marked the beginning of the plight of hundreds of thousands of refugees. This was far outstripped once the Nazis started their war of extermination against the USSR. An estimated 12 million people in the western part of the Soviet Union either fled German troops or were evacuated or forced to resettle. This included those whom Soviet authorities deported to the east: more than 1.5 million Poles, Ukrainians and White Russians from the eastern territories of Poland that were occupied by the Red Army according to the Hitler–Stalin pact of 1939, as well as about 200,000 people from the Baltic states, which came under Russian control in accordance with the pact. After the Germans attacked the Soviet Union in 1941, Stalin also ordered the deportation of about 400,000 Volga Germans to Siberia, charging them collectively with 'collaboration' with the German invaders. Also suspected of collaboration were the 640,000 Kalmucks, Chechnyans and Ingrians deported in 1943 and the 250,000 Crimean Tatars deported in 1945. They had all lived under German occupation and were charged with having provided the German occupiers with 'auxiliary troops'.[71]

Labour as spoils of war: Forced labour in the Nazi war economy

Nazi Germany was able to wage war for almost six years only because it was planned and carried out from the outset as a war of conquest. The countries allied with Germany and those countries and regions 'acquired', in other words, conquered starting in 1938–9, had the task of putting their populations, production and raw materials at the disposal of the German war economy. In the course of the war, the importance of these 'stolen' human resources and goods for the war effort grew immensely. In October 1944 there were almost 8 million foreign forced labourers in Germany, including almost 6 million civilians and 2 million POWs. They came from a total of 26 different countries. No exact figures for the subsequent months are available, but it is probable that the number of foreign labourers working for the German war effort continued to rise until the end of the war. In autumn 1944, the largest contingent of forced labourers were 2.8 million from the Soviet Union, or more than one-third, followed by 1.7 million from Poland and 1.2 million from France. Several hundred thousand workers each came from Italy, the Netherlands, Belgium, Czechoslovakia and Yugoslavia.[72]

The enormous economic significance of the mostly forced 'foreign labourers' working for Germany is apparent by their proportion of the total labour force. In September 1944, foreign labourers made up about one-third of all non-self-employed workers. They worked in all business fields, all sizes of companies, throughout the entire Reich. They played a particularly large role in certain areas of employment and business, such as agriculture, in which 46 per cent of all workers in 1944 were foreign forced labourers, and mining (36 per cent). In companies with low qualification demands, up to 80 per cent of all workers came from abroad. There were also some extremely specialized fields with a very high level of foreign workers. In the aviation industry, the level of foreign workers reached 80–90 per cent, although aircraft construction was among the highest-security military areas. The average age of foreign workers was between 20 and 24 years and one in three was female, a large proportion of whom were under 20 years old.

Compulsory recruitment of foreign labour began within Germany right after the start of the war. The first major group were 300,000 Polish POWs who were put to work in German agriculture in 1939. Owing to recruitment of the civilian population in occupied Poland, the number of Polish labourers in Germany went up within six months after the start of the war to about 1 million. This resulted from a change of tactics from what the occupying authorities felt was insufficiently productive recruitment for volunteers; they now went on raids and downright hunts for labour. The German labour administration in Poland followed on the heels of the advancing German troops and had set up 115 labour offices within six weeks of the German invasion. These were intended primarily to collect workers for German agriculture. The counties and districts of Poland had to put up certain contingents 'voluntarily'. From September 1939 to May 1940 alone, about 560,000 Polish farmworkers had already been 'recruited'. The labour administration, police, SS and Gestapo worked together to muster workers. As a result of their efforts, a total of 1.8–2 million forced labourers from Poland were ultimately deported to work for the German war effort. Yet even this was not sufficient to cover the demand for labour by the expanding German war economy, which drafted increasingly greater numbers of workers into the army. One million French POWs supplemented this amount in spring and summer 1940; recruitment activities and deportations followed in the countries conquered in 1940, from Norway in the north to France in the south.

At the beginning of the next German offensive in spring 1941 in south-eastern and eastern Europe, the number of foreign workers, most of whom were recruited by force, had reached 3 million; the predominant area of employment remained agriculture. Around this time the number of foreign workers in Germany had already exceeded the peak volume from the First World War. When Germany invaded the USSR on 22 June 1941, the demand for labour skyrocketed with the mobilization of reserve troops and the intensification of arms production. Nevertheless, the Nazi leadership initially prohibited putting Soviet POWs or recruited civilians to work in the German war economy, since these 'racially inferior' and 'Bolshevik' 'sub-humans' were considered a risk for racist and political

reasons. The Nazis assumed that their expected speedy victory over the
USSR would lead in short time to a decline in the demand for labour in
the German war effort. More than half of the 3.3 million Soviet POWs in
1941 died within a year. In the camps or on the way there, they were shot
or they starved or froze to death. A total of 5.7 million Soviets were taken
as POWs by the Germans from 1941 to 1945; 3.5 million did not survive
captivity.

Because the victory against the Soviet Union never came despite high
losses at the fronts and despite a continuous rise in arms production, the
labour shortage in Germany continued to worsen. However, there were
hardly any able-bodied Soviet POWs still available, so recruitment of
civilian workers was pushed all the more in the conquered regions of the
Soviet Union. Between spring 1942 and September 1944, when the Red
Army reconquered the German-occupied Soviet territories up to the
Polish border, 2.5 million forced civilian workers from the Soviet
Union were deported to Germany for 'deployment'; this corresponded
to more than 20,000 people each week.

The 'topography of terror' (Reinhard Rürup) created a new German
map with a comprehensive system of 'foreigner camps' for forced labourers, with numerous sub- and satellite camps; there were an estimated
20,000 or more camps in all. Foreign labourers were everywhere and
visible in everyday life for many Germans, in cities as in the countryside,
in craft workshops and major factories, on small farms and large agricultural operations. 'Foreign labourers' were treated differently by German
authorities in accordance with Nazi racial ideology. Forced workers from
'enemy states' were divided into two main groups, those from the west
(French, Belgians, Dutch) and deported forced labourers from the east,
especially Poland and the Soviet Union. The 'western workers', members
of the 'master races' according to Nazi ideology, were thus treated far
better in the early years of the war and faced fewer restrictions on their
civil rights and liberties than workers from the east, who were totally
deprived of their rights, limited to the absolute minimum for survival and
largely concentrated in 'helot tasks in natural areas of work' (agriculture,
stone quarries, construction).[73] They were usually not allowed to leave
the work camps and had to wear special cloth markings, like the yellow
star for the Jews. Forced labourers from Poland had a 'P' marking and
those from the Soviet Union had '*Ost*' for '*Ostarbeiter*', or workers from
the east. The *Ostarbeiter* from the USSR were forced to endure the
harshest working and living conditions.

The concentration camp prisoners who worked as forced labourers in
arms production formed a special group. For some of them, being
assigned to concentration camp arms production meant being saved
from certain death in the camps; for others it was simply a delayed

death in industry. This was especially the case for those areas of arms production in which the SS reckoned they would 'use up' the human labour – including torturous death within only a few months or even weeks – and thus 'arranged' to keep a steady supply coming. The concentration camp system grew rampantly until ultimately there were about 1,000 main, sub- and satellite camps spread throughout the Reich. Hundreds of thousands of concentration camp prisoners worked in catastrophic and often fatal conditions, especially where the work was extremely hard and often life-threatening, such as clearing bombs or working on the ruthlessly expanded underground armaments factories.[74] The exploitative German economy became increasingly dependent on foreign labour over the course of the Second World War, much more so than during the First. As early as 1941 it was impossible to satisfy the target output in arms production without foreign labour; in agriculture this point had already been reached in late 1940.[75]

The labour-hungry Nazi economy did not only take advantage of POWs and deportees from the conquered territories as labour in Germany; for one thing, economy and labour were put at the disposal of the German war machine up to 1942–3 in the constantly expanding area of German occupation, in which about 154 million people lived at the time. Furthermore, Germany recruited ever greater numbers of people from the occupied territories and the countries with which it was allied to serve as soldiers in the divisions that had suffered the heaviest losses. Between 1943 and the end of the war, the Wehrmacht and SS mobilized no fewer than 21 formal, independent military units from a total of almost 30 countries. Many soldiers throughout Europe who were incorporated into German units had enlisted voluntarily, though most had been forcibly recruited. There were Spanish, French and other units in the German Wehrmacht and, finally, two divisions of the 'Wlassow Army' made up of Soviet POWs. The Waffen-SS was comprised of almost 1 million soldiers in December 1944; about 300,000 came from the German Reich, but the rest were from the occupied territories and countries allied with Germany. In view of the state of war, larger numbers of 'non-Germanic' troops had to be mustered even though this completely contradicted Nazi ideology. The 'Germanic' 'volunteer division' of the SS included Norwegians, Danes, Dutch, Flemish Belgians and 'ethnic Germans', mostly from south-eastern Europe. The 'Waffen divisions' of the SS accepted 'non-Germanic' troops – from the 33rd SS-Waffen grenadier division 'Charlemagne', made up of French soldiers, to Latvian, Estonian and Galician divisions, to the Muslim 'East Turkish Corps' and the 30,000 soldiers of the Cossack Corps.[76]

It can be assumed that in addition to the 2.8 million who were deported to Germany to work, another 20 million workers in the occupied territories of the USSR were used there directly for the occupying forces, especially in agriculture.[77] In the occupied western countries, too, a large segment of the workers in some branches of industry actually worked for the German war economy, in France for example in all locomotive production, almost all machine tool construction and in the aviation and automobile industries.[78] But the final aim of the German forces in the occupied territories, especially in eastern and east central Europe, had not yet been achieved with the ruthless economic exploitation of people and economy.

'Resettlement' and mass murder: Deportations of local populations, settlement of 'ethnic Germans' and murder of the Jews

Nazi policies in occupied Europe aimed to secure permanent rule and the establishment of a racist 'German order' with a barbaric hierarchy of population groups and nationalities. The implementation of this racist world order brought devastating consequences, especially in eastern and east central Europe.[79] Its essential elements were expulsions disguised as 'resettlements' and deportations of entire populations. The goal was to open up new settlement and supply spheres for a 'people without space' (*Volk ohne Raum*), even though the demographers involved in the ideological legitimization of this expansion had been lamenting a 'people without a youth' in the early 1930s because of the declining birth rate.[80] About 9 million people were affected by these measures. From 1939 to 1944, about 1 million people of German descent were brought 'home to the Reich' from their settlement areas outside German borders, especially in south-eastern, east central and eastern Europe. They were to be resettled in the conquered parts of Poland and Czechoslovakia that had been incorporated into the German Reich.

The resettlement of 'ethnic Germans' had already begun in 1939, when about 100,000 people from South Tyrol, which had belonged to Italy since 1918, were settled in the Austrian (up to 1938; later 'Greater German') states of Tyrol and Carinthia. In 1940–1, about 130,000 'ethnic Germans' from Estonia and Latvia as well as about 100,000 Bessarabian Germans were settled in the areas of Poland that had been incorporated into the Reich ('Danzig-West Prussia Reichsgau', 'Posen Reichsgau'/'Warthegau'). The last group of about 250,000 'ethnic Germans' came from Volhynia, Galicia and Transylvania in 1944.[81]

The prerequisite for the settlement of these 'ethnic Germans' was the prior expulsion or deportation – referred to as 'resettlement' – of the resident Polish, Czech and Jewish populations. This was initiated on a large scale in 1939–40 and ended in genocide. In the interest of relocating 'ethnic Germans', for example, about 1.2 million Poles, including 500,000–550,000 Jews, were expelled in 1940–1 from the former Polish provinces that were now incorporated into the Reich as the 'Danzig-West Prussia' and 'Wartheland' 'Reichsgaus'. In the master plan for this region, however, this was only the beginning. Of the more than 10 million people living there, only 1.7 million were considered 'capable of being Germanized'; 7.8 million Poles and 700,000 Jews from these regions were to be expelled. The direct organizational connection between the settlement of 'ethnic Germans', the expulsion of Poles and the deportation and murder of the Jews was illustrated by Götz Aly based on the example of camps in and around Lodz. The German occupiers set up a ghetto with a Jewish population of 160,000 people herded together from the surrounding areas; in the direct vicinity of the ghetto, a camp was established with 30,000 Poles who had been driven from their property, as well as a transit camp for 30,000 'ethnic Germans' who were to acquire the property of the expelled Poles and Jews.[82]

In the end, the SS who 'implemented' the 'Germanization policies' in Poland were responsible for these resettlement and expulsion policies. The 'General Plan for the East' set out in 1942 by the SS aimed to expand to eastern Europe as far as the Ural mountains the policy of millions of brutal 'resettlements' that had already been partly carried out for Poland. Ultimately, the 'resettlement' of 45 million people was planned. The only ones to remain were those who still appeared useful to work as slaves for the German 'master race'.

According to the racial hierarchy of Nazi ideology, Jews and people the Nazis declared to be Jews had no justification to exist nor any entitlement to '*Lebensraum*' (living space). Before finally banning Jewish emigration in October 1941, the Nazi authorities had expelled or forced the flight of about 455,000 people considered Jews according to the racist Nuremberg Laws of 1935. They were from the German Reich and the areas annexed by the start of the war (Saar region, Austria and parts of Czechoslovakia).[83] About 160,000 Jews were still living in Germany at the time emigration was banned and deportations were begun to Poland, that is, to death in the extermination camps erected there. In Poland itself, there were almost 3 million Jews in 1941. They were incorporated into the 'resettlement' and 'space planning' that meant deportation and ultimately death. A total of 2.7 million Polish Jews, including a large portion of the Polish elite designated for 'liquidation', were victims of the murderous Nazi policies that culminated in industrial mass murder in the extermination camps.

The Jewish populations of almost all European countries within Germany's sphere of power shared the fate of Polish and German Jewry. In eastern Europe, about 140,000 Czechoslovakian Jews were murdered, about 200,000 Romanian, about 550,000 Hungarian and about 2.2

million from the USSR. In south-eastern Europe, about 60,000 each were murdered in Yugoslavia and Greece. In the occupied western countries, the willingness of the respective populations and authorities to participate in collaboration and denunciation affected the numbers of victims there. About 28,000 victims were counted in Belgium, about 76,000 in France and about 100,000 in the Netherlands, where the willingness to denounce Jews – not only those from abroad – was apparently relatively high. The name Anne Frank long shrouded the fact that while the famous Jewish girl was indeed hidden by Dutch neighbours, she was also ultimately betrayed for a few guilders.[84]

Even before the fighting ended in Poland in 1939, the SS had already started herding the Jewish population together. The Polish state was destroyed on the basis of the German–Soviet agreements in the Hitler–Stalin pact. A major part was ceded to Germany and incorporated into the German Reich; the eastern territory was annexed by the USSR; and in between was the German-occupied Generalgouvernement (General Government). Countless ghettos were established for local Jews and those deported from Polish areas that had been annexed by Germany, such as in Warsaw, Lodz, Krakow, Lublin and Radom. Starting in February 1940, there were isolated and, as of October 1941, massive deportations from German territory. In October–November 1941, for example, about 20,000 Jews from major German cities were transported to the Lodz ghetto. In the following four months, after the invasion of the Soviet Union, ghettos were set up in Riga, Minsk and Kovno (Kaunus) for another 40,000 Jews.

Deportations of Jews in the occupied areas of western Europe started in spring 1942. In France, until German troops finally occupied the whole country in autumn 1942, the Vichy government in the initially non-occupied southern part of France had already passed far-reaching anti-Jewish regulations and prepared the deportation of Jews by registering and partly interning them. About 75,000 of a total of 300,000 Jews living in France in 1940 were deported eastward; one-third were French and two-thirds were foreign Jews who were easier to identify and more likely to be denounced. Only a fraction of the deportees survived the death camps in eastern Europe. This applied also to the 140,000 Jews in the Netherlands, 112,000 of whom had been deported. Only in Norway and Denmark, and to a lesser extent in Italy, could the Jewish populations be largely saved from deportation, either in hiding or by fleeing the country.

Deportations were carried out by the SS, usually using cattle trucks, with high death rates due to hunger, epidemics, cold and harsh treatment by brutal guards. Later transports no longer went to the ghettos but ended directly in the extermination camps. In autumn 1941 began the clearing of the ghettos and the transport of Jews to camps erected specifically for the purpose of systematic mass murder. The last-remaining ghetto was ultimately cleared in spring 1943, after an uprising of 70,000 Jewish inhabitants of the Warsaw ghetto was suppressed.

Behind the German front in the USSR, no large, long-term ghettos were set up as they had been in Poland. The four *Einsatzgruppen* (special units) of the Security Police (SP) and the Security and Intelligence Service (SD) rampaged here once the Soviet Union had been invaded; their task was to murder the Jewish population and functionaries of the Soviet communist party on the spot. In the first year of their operation, millions of Soviet Jews were murdered by the *Einsatzgruppen* through mass shootings.[85]

In the Generalgouvernement, industrialized mass murder in the Belzec and Sobibor camps in the district of Lublin and in the Treblinka camp near Warsaw took the lives of at least 1.7 million people. The camps at Auschwitz (erected in summer 1941) and Majdanek (summer 1942) served a somewhat different purpose from summer 1942. These were extermination camps attached to huge work camps and large industrial complexes. The affiliated companies paid wages to the SS for the labour of the camp prisoners who were not murdered immediately. About 200,000 people died in Majdanek; at least 1 million, perhaps 1.5 million, in Auschwitz.

The advance of the Red Army and the capture of the Polish territories meant salvation only for a few from mid-1944; but for many it was the beginning of the 'death marches' westward. This was no longer a matter of migration to death; it was death by migration, ranging from those who starved to death or were shot or beaten at the roadside to those put on ships that were sunk in the Baltic Sea or those prisoners who were deliberately put in the line of fire of Allied bombers. Some of these ships washed up somewhere with dead, fatally ill or almost starved prisoners, such as the death ship with a few survivors from the Stutthoff concentration camp near Danzig (Gdansk) in winter 1945 that ran aground by the port of Klintholm on the Danish island of Møn.

Flight and expulsion of the Germans at the end of the war and in the post-war period

The last resettlements in 1944 to bring approximately 250,000 'ethnic Germans' from Volhynia, Galicia and Transylvania 'home to the Reich' already had the character of fleeing the Red Army, which finally reached the German border in East Prussia in August 1944 and crossed it in October of that year. There were about 18 million German citizens and 'ethnic Germans' in the parts of Germany east of the Oder and Neisse rivers and in eastern, east central and south-eastern Europe in 1939.

About 14 million of them fled westward in the final phase of the war, or were expelled in that direction after the war or deported to the east. The balance of the millions who fled or were driven out or deported is illustrated in the census data for western and eastern Germany from 1950. These figures show that in the Allied occupation zones and the two German states that emerged, a total of almost 12.5 million refugees and expellees had managed to come from the former eastern provinces of the Reich that were ceded after the war to Poland, Czechoslovakia or the Soviet Union and from the settlement regions of the 'ethnic Germans'. Another 500,000 refugees and expellees lived in Austria and other countries.[86] The expellees and their interest groups long played an important political role in the Federal Republic of Germany. In East Germany, they were euphemistically referred to as 'resettlers' out of consideration for the neighbouring countries whence they came. Their 'integration' was implemented according to a strict concept of the East German state party (SED); it was declared 'completed' in the early 1950s and was absent from public discussion from that point on.

Nearly 2 million people of German nationality or descent did not survive the flight, expulsion or deportations. About 1 million had been deported to the Soviet Union. Of the 12.5 million refugees and expellees in East and West Germany in 1950, the largest group of 7 million were from the former eastern German provinces beyond the Oder and Neisse rivers. After 1945 these areas were part of Poland, except for the northern half of East Prussia, which had been ceded to the USSR. The next largest groups were almost 3 million refugees and expellees from Czechoslovakia, about 1.4 million from Poland according to its pre-war borders, about 300,000 from the 'Free State' of Danzig, which had been under the administration of the League of Nations until 1939, almost 300,000 from Yugoslavia, about 200,000 from Hungary and about 130,000 from Romania.

The German population in the eastern territories of the Reich that had been taken by Soviet and Polish troops was still over 4 million in April 1945. Within three months more than 1 million refugees returned to these areas, some voluntarily in the hope of protection and a chance to survive in the communities from which they came, others because they were overtaken on their trek by the Red Army and thus could not go any farther. Two months after the war ended, in late July–early August, the Oder and Neisse were blocked, breaking off the voluntary return migration movement eastward. In summer 1945, there were unofficial expulsions, in which Germans still living in the new areas of western Poland and in Czechoslovakia were driven out, often violently. This affected up to 800,000 Sudeten Germans in Czechoslovakia and up to 300,000 Germans along Poland's western border at the Oder and Neisse rivers.

The unofficial expulsions in summer 1945, however, were not isolated political actions by Czechoslovakia and Poland. At the conferences in Teheran in 1943 and Yalta in early 1945, the Allied forces had already resolved to transfer large parts of the population in eastern Germany, though the transfers were to take place in as regulated and humane a manner as possible. Minority conflicts and Germany's political exploitation of German minorities, as had been the case in the interwar period, were to be avoided in the future in Poland and Czechoslovakia. At the Potsdam Conference (17 July–2 August 1945), Britain, the USSR and the United States as the victors of the war again set out the goal of an 'orderly transfer of German populations'. But even the 'organized' expulsions were not very 'orderly'. Mass transports in catastrophic supply conditions, brutal guards and constant plundering led once again to countless victims. In 1946, another approximately 2 million people, and in 1947 another 500,000, from the areas east of the Oder and the Neisse were driven out to the four Allied occupation zones of Germany. On top of these came about 1.2 million people from Czechoslovakia and about 170,000 from Hungary in 1946.

All in all, post-war Germany was a turntable of immense transnational and internal migrations: in addition to the almost 10 million refugees and expellees in late 1946 and 12.5 million in 1950, the second largest group of forced migrants were the roughly 11 million displaced persons, most of whom had been forced labourers in Germany's war economy. Their repatriation or further migration took months or even years. The Soviet Union focused on forced repatriation, which many tried to avoid by escape or suicide, since for most it meant being sent to a 're-education centre' as a 'collaborator'; for several it also meant death, as was the case regarding soldiers and especially officers who returned to the Soviet Union after having been POWs in Germany.[87]

In the four Allied occupation zones after the war, there were also 10 million people who had fled the bombardment of the cities or had been evacuated. Some could not return to their hometowns for years. They lived like the refugees and expellees, provisionally and largely in overcrowded rural regions. Within a year after the war's end, about 5 million of a total of 9 million German POWs were released by the Allied forces. They had been spread out around the world; 20 different countries had German POWs in their custody, especially the United States (3.7 million), Britain (2.3 million) and the Soviet Union (1.8 million). Many of them were involved in reconstruction work. For this purpose, for example, the US and British military authorities passed on 1 million German POWs to France, and others to the Netherlands and Belgium.

Flight and expulsion of Germans from east central and south-eastern Europe led in turn to millions of subsequent migrations into the areas of expulsion. Within a short period of time, for example, 1.8 million Czechs and Slovaks settled in Czechoslovakia in the Sudetenland, after the German populations there had been expelled. In Poland, too, the confiscated land of Germans who had fled or were expelled was quickly redistributed and settled. The population in the new Polish areas had already exceeded 5 million in August 1947. Three million had come from central Poland, another million from the eastern Polish provinces that had been ceded to the USSR; 1 million Poles had already lived there before 1945.[88] These and other migrations to the former German settlement regions in eastern, east central and south-eastern Europe led in turn to subsequent migrations in ever-expanding chain reactions. After the immense shifts of populations during the Second World War and owing to the flight and expulsion of the German population, these migrations contributed to a further restructuring of the map of nationalities in eastern Europe during the Cold War.

4

Migration and Migration Policies in the Cold War

The final phase in Europe's historic transition from a continent of emigration to one of immigration encompassed the period from the end of the post-war mass migrations to the migratory movements triggered or facilitated by the end of the Cold War. In the history of refugee movements within and to Europe, however, the Second World War represented a twofold break. As previously discussed, it spurred the most immense forced and refugee migrations in European history. Moreover, the war also accelerated the disintegration of the European colonial empires, which sent millions of colonial and post-colonial immigrants and return migrants off to Europe.

Overseas emigration from Europe recovered from the Second World War and regained its momentum. It took up old migration traditions whose networks could be used in the Cold War even for purposes of mass political manipulation. Half a century after the peak of Italian-American mass immigration, the CIA launched a huge campaign in the run-up to the 1948 Italian elections that made use of these still existent or at least revivable transatlantic networks. Americans of Italian descent were called upon to write letters to their relatives in Italy warning them not to vote for the Communists. The result was a flood of an estimated 10 million messages of this kind. They had an extraordinary influence on the elections of 18 April 1948; the Christian Democrats obtained an overwhelming majority, while contrary to expectations the Communists lost almost half their vote.

Until far into the 1960s, the number of European overseas emigrations was still appreciably higher than migrations to Europe from non-European regions. Consequently, Europe had a net loss of 2.7 million inhabitants from 1950 to 1959. Not until the decade of the 1960s did the balance of European migration register slightly in the black (+ 250,000).

The shift to a continent of immigration then came in the 1970s. Since 1970 there have been significant immigration gains throughout Europe. In 1970–9, the increase was 1.9 million; in 1980–9, it was 1.6 million; and from 1990 to 1995, it was 2.1 million. Gains and losses stood out less in net European migration figures than they did in individual national figures, since transnational migration within Europe outstripped the volume of migration to Europe by far, especially at the time of the major migrant labour movements.[1] However, the most expansive migratory movements of all time that emerged in the second half of the twentieth century took place in non-European spheres, especially the 'Third World', only about 5 per cent of which even touched Europe.

Statistics on foreigners in the European realm, which at the end of the twentieth century included 15 European Union (EU) countries plus Norway, Switzerland and Liechtenstein, showed a rise from about 4 million foreigners in 1950 to almost three times that amount (roughly 11 million) in 1970–1. By 1982, the number had increased almost fourfold (about 15 million) and by 1994–5, finally, it reached five times that amount (about 20 million). In the late 1990s, one-third of foreign nationals were from other countries of central, western and northern Europe. At that time they made up about 5 per cent of the total population of the region. This should not be confused with the much larger in-migration population that had been naturalized, to varying degrees depending on the country, since the 1950s and whose children were born in the receiving countries. The country with the largest foreign national population in the 1950s in absolute figures was France (1.8 million), followed by a distant West Germany with about 570,000, Belgium with about 370,000 and Austria with about 320,000. There are no reliable figures for Britain for this period. The picture had clearly changed in 1970. At the peak was now West Germany (*c*.3 million), followed by France (*c*.2.6 million), Britain (*c*.2 million), Switzerland (*c*.1.1 million), Belgium (*c*.700,000), Sweden (*c*.410,000) and the Netherlands (*c*.260,000). West Germany still held pride of place in 1982 (*c*.4.7 million), ahead of France (*c*.3.7 million), Britain (*c*.2.1 million), Switzerland (*c*.926,000), Belgium (*c*.886,000) and the Netherlands (547,000). If the relative size of the total population of the respective countries is taken into consideration, a very different order results. For 1982, far ahead of the rest (apart from the exceptional case of Liechtenstein, with 34.1 per cent) was Luxembourg with a foreign population of 26.3 per cent including many employees of international organizations and supranational institutions, followed by Switzerland (14.4 per cent) and Belgium (9 per cent). Then, finally, came West Germany (7.6 per cent), France (6.7 per cent), Britain and the Netherlands (3.8 per cent each).

On the whole, this picture is also skewed by the very different naturalization regulations in individual European countries. Most of those who
migrated permanently to France and Britain were naturalized and thus
quickly disappeared from statistics on foreigners, so the number of
naturalized immigrants for these countries was considerably higher
than the number of foreigners. Until its citizenship law reform of 1 January 2000, the opposite was true in Germany, where in-migrants generally
remained foreign nationals even if they stayed in Germany permanently;
and their foreigner status was even passed on to their children in the
second generation. Figures for the foreign population were thus often
dramatized and made to appear scandalous, though the problem was at
least in part a home-made statistical one.

Migratory movements that arrived in Europe after the end of the post-
war mass migrations proceeded in partly overlapping waves from different home regions to different destinations. In the colonial countries
involved in the decolonization process, European return migration and
non-European immigration to Europe from released or liberated overseas
territories were initially predominant. Parallel to and following these
movements, largely inner-European labour migrations developed from
the mid-1950s in countries that had no colonial or post-colonial migration, and sometimes also in former colonial countries. This labour
migration was stopped or limited in the early 1970s by restrictive intervention in the main receiving countries. Families were still allowed to
join family members who had already immigrated, however, and this
soon assumed the size and contours of an independent major migration
movement, though it developed differently depending on the respective
migrant group. Family reunification hardly played a role for Greeks who
emigrated early on, but it was all the more pronounced for Turks who
migrated later and was stabilized through migration networks centred
around kinship relations.

Into the 1980s, labour migrations divided Europe into a northern
in-migration region and a southern out-migration region. The in-migration
of refugees and asylum seekers in northern Europe moved into the foreground of public discussion from the late 1970s, although it played a far
less significant role up to the late 1980s than did family reunification that
followed labour migrations. In southern Europe in the 1980s, intercontinental south–north movements instead predominated, which long had
largely the character of regular migration to irregular employment. In
the Euro-Mediterranean zone, they gradually transformed the former
regions of origin of inner-European south–north labour migration into
south–north in-migration destinations.

The three main European receiving countries based on absolute
numbers in the Cold War era were France, West Germany and Britain.

The related migratory patterns and routes were determined partly by 'privileged' migration conditions that maintained established migratory traditions or built upon cultural and historical connections, and partly by dominant, newly emerged migratory relations that quickly became established through transnational networks with chain migrations and family reunification. In the case of France, this applied to migrations from North Africa and from overseas territories that were still under French administration, and to labour migrations from Italy and later Spain, as well as especially Portugal. In West Germany, this applied to labour migrations from at first Italy and Greece, later Spain and Portugal, and finally especially from Yugoslavia and Turkey, as well as migration from east central and eastern Europe. European migration to Britain was mainly from Ireland; Britain's most significant non-European in-migration were Anglo-Caribbeans and Indians (from India and East Africa), as well as Pakistanis and Bangladeshis.

The weighting of the home regions of migration within and to Europe shifted over time. Not counting refugee migration from East to West Germany up to 1961, the main region of origin in Europe in the 1950s and 1960s was Italy, followed in the 1960s by Spain and Portugal, Greece and Yugoslavia. The main non-European regions of origin in the 1950s and 1960s were Algeria, India, Pakistan and the Caribbean; and in the 1970s, Turkey, Morocco and Tunisia. In the 1980s, migration increased from the Near East, North Africa and sub-Saharan Africa to France in the west and to Greece, Italy, Spain and Portugal in the south.

Boundaries distinguishing the different immigrant groups and immigration forms were often fluid and overlapping. Colonial and post-colonial bridges also brought labourers, refugees and asylum seekers to Europe. Recruited labour migrants often became *de facto* or *de jure* immigrants who were later joined by their families. After the end of recruitment and authorization of labour migrations in central, western and northern Europe in the early to mid-1970s, the same routes then served chain migrations from non-European regions – such as Turkey or Algeria. They sometimes assumed the form of asylum migrations since conditions in the countries of origin had worsened dramatically or because there were scarcely any other ways to enter Europe, except for family reunification. The group of refugees and asylum seekers itself included not only individuals who were politically persecuted in the ever-narrowing sense of European asylum law definitions, but also war and civil war refugees as well as immigrants from the world's economic and environmental crisis regions. In-migration of eastern European minorities who had suffered long-term oppression or were subjected to renewed hardship was made possible by state agreements during the Cold War; subsequently, it increased considerably, based on overlapping personal motivations and self-defined identities, especially as regards the immigration of binational families. In all of these areas there was always also irregular or illegal in-migration and extended stays, the number of which can only be estimated though it clearly rose as Europe increasingly closed itself off to in-migration.

Overlapping migration forms, motivations and migrant identities are not evidence of the plausibility of possible doubt regarding the 'correct' identity of 'true' refugees, labour migrants or immigrants. They simply reveal the superficiality of common notions that claim it is possible to distinguish clearly between different migrant identities, even apart from any statistical and data-collection difficulties. Among the unintended consequences of migration policy anchored in law is that migrants are defined using attributes which, while being consistent with the law, often do not reflect actual life experience yet force migrants none the less to fit into certain categories. Migration networks and home region communities[2] help make it possible to cope with the everyday legal and social limitations that arise from this kind of categorization and definition of self and other. All of this must be borne in mind when reading the overview of the main groups given below, the smallest common denominator of which is not personal identities but assigned characteristics of legal status.

The overview of migration within and to Europe up to the end of the Cold War is concentrated on three main areas: Euro-colonial, colonial and post-colonial migration (see section 1), labour migration (sections 2 and 3) and refugee and asylum migrations (section 4). The migrations of eastern European minorities described as 'ethnic migrations' began during the Cold War within the scope of international treaties, but they developed to a much greater extent only after the Cold War ended. They will be reviewed in the next chapter on migratory events of the 1990s (see chapter 5, section 2).

1 DECOLONIZATION, COLONIAL AND POST-COLONIAL MIGRATION

There had been discussion worldwide about breaking down the conditions of colonial rule since the end of the First World War. Moritz J. Bonn, German emigrant and economist in London, coined the term 'decolonization' in the 1930s to describe the process.[3] The actual end of the European colonial age, however, did not come until after the Second World War. The war shattered colonial rule once and for all and accelerated the emancipation process that was then pushed further by the Cold War's competition of systems. European colonial empires collapsed around the world, first in Asia and then in Africa, as a result of either peaceful negotiations or bloody battles for liberation. Among the outcomes of decolonization were two large migration movements to Europe that converged and overlapped. First came European settlers and members of colonial administrations and militaries. Parallel to or following them came auxiliary colonial troops or pro-colonial ethnic groups and other groups of non-European descent who had remained in the service of the colonial powers to the end and then had to reckon with discrimination or persecution as 'collaborators'.[4]

There were about 7 million Euro-colonial immigrants, or people of European descent, who arrived in Europe from the colonies between 1940 and 1975. Precise statistics are lacking on the immigration of ethnic minorities or 'collaborators' of non-European descent, especially considering the great mixing of European and non-European populations, for example in the Dutch colonial empire. All that is certain is that Euro-colonial immigrants predominated by far.[5] Many had not left Europe until the first half of the twentieth century, when emigration to the colonies was particularly heavy. Other families had already spent generations living in the colonies, whose European populations usually remained tied to those in the 'mother countries' through continual migration cycles. The largest contingents of Euro-colonial immigration to Britain came from Kenya, India and Malaysia; in France and Italy they came from North Africa; in Belgium, from the Congo; in the Netherlands, from Indonesia; and in Portugal, from Angola and Mozambique.

The regions of origin, directions and sizes of these Euro-colonial, colonial and post-colonial migrations were determined by the imperial decline that progressed in stages as the respective countries ended their colonial status. Estimates of the volume of return migration and immigration from Europe's colonial regions triggered by the process of decolonization range from 5.5 million to 8.5 million. As of the late 1940s, Britain, Belgium and Italy were affected the most. Between 1953 and mid-1962 (Commonwealth Immigrants Act), an estimated 391,000 migrants left the New Commonwealth for Britain (plus another approximately 60,000 Irish per year). The stock of foreigners in Belgium grew from 368,000 in 1947 to 453,000 in 1962, and about 40,000 migrants came from the Congo in 1960 alone. Between 1940 and 1960, at least 550,000 migrants returned to Italy from the colonies and the rest of Africa, though estimates go as high as 850,000. Immigration to the Netherlands came from Indonesia and, in 1951–2, from the Moluccas (Spice Islands); in the 1970s, immigrants came mostly from Surinam and the former Dutch Antilles. On 1 January 1990, more than 800,000 of the total population of about 15 million in the Netherlands had come from the former Dutch colonial regions. After the Evian accords (1962) between France and the Algerian National Liberation Front (FLN) came the resettlement of more than 1 million Algerian-French ('*pieds noirs*') (who had originally come mostly from Italy, Spain and Malta), Algerians who fought for the French (*harkis*) and Algerian Jews.[6]

While post-colonial chain migrations were already underway bound for England, France and the Netherlands, Euro-colonial immigration to Portugal had just got started in the 1970s from the embattled African colonies. Once it got going, however, it was very strong. Within 18 months in 1975–6, about 800,000 *retornados* arrived in Portugal, especially from the disputed African colonies of Angola and Mozambique, as well as from Guinea-Bissau, the Cape Verde Islands and São Tomé and Principe. The economically underdeveloped 'mother country', which was also receiving its demobilized troops after the end of the colonial wars, experienced a population growth of 10 per cent within a very short period of time, serving to aggravate the problem of unemployment.[7]

Long after European rule ended, post-colonial conflicts in the former colonial regions continued to provide impetus for Euro-colonial emigration and return migration, and especially for refugee migrations of ethnic minorities (see chapter 5, section 4). On top of that, foreign 'scapegoats' were sometimes sought for post-colonial mismanagement, such as in 1997–8 in Zimbabwe. Post-colonial migration, whose course was set by traditional contacts with the former colonial metropolises, was given a push not only by conflicts and economic and social crises in the regions of origin. It was also accelerated by the interests of former 'mother countries' for cheap labour to perform semi- and unskilled tasks at wage and working conditions that were no longer tolerated by local labourers. Migration from the earlier colonial regions developed its own, self-propelling momentum through chain migrations with family members following later on, intercontinental migration networks, and a focus on ethnocultural and ethnosocial settlement. The mythos behind the foundation of post-colonial chain migrations included, in Britain for example, the sensational landing of the *Empire Windrush* in Tilbury docks in 1948 with 492 passengers from Kingston, Jamaica aboard. These were by no means the first immigrants to Britain from the Caribbean, but their arrival represented a symbolic anchoring of migration chains that resulted in the Anglo-Caribbean population in Britain growing to about 265,000 people by 1971.[8]

Euro-colonial immigration and parallel and subsequent colonial migrations were facilitated through citizenship and linguistic-cultural bridges as well as through return migration and integration programmes for Europeans and colonial immigrants, who to some extent ultimately received equal rights. Guaranteed rights and reintegration programmes could not prevent some people from reacting defensively towards even

Euro-colonial return migrants, such as the Algerian-French on Corsica. Indeed, sometimes the reaction was precisely because of the integration aid. But the state-supported integration of Euro-colonial immigrants was usually met with understanding and benevolence, and generally progressed without any major social problems.

The situation was different regarding immigrants from colonial auxiliary troops or pro-colonial ethnic groups and other colonial 'collaborators' who left the country along with or after the colonial power. Mental structures of subordination, racist thinking and latent or even open discrimination that had characterized colonial rule sometimes survived in Europe beyond the end of colonialism overseas. Many non-European immigrants from colonies that had obtained independence long remained economically and socially disadvantaged, such as the Moluccans in the Netherlands, former members of the Dutch East Indies elite troops who drew attention to their precarious situation through the notorious train hijacking of 1973. A similar situation existed in England for the Indians who had settled in East Africa under British colonial rule, and in France for the Algerian *harkis* and generally the Arabs and members of the second generation of North Africans, referred to using the defamatory slang term *beurs*. About 150,000 *harkis* were abandoned after the Algerian War, in which they fought for France, and persecuted as 'traitors' and 'collaborators'; some were even killed. Those able to flee to France were put up in 'transit camps' under miserable conditions; some were still living there in the 1990s. Though they were finally granted French citizenship, roughly 70 per cent were unemployed.[9]

Post-colonial immigration pressure prompted the European colonial powers, especially Britain and France, to seek ever-tighter immigration restrictions for non-European immigrants, which was difficult to justify in view of their colonial past. This led to increasing signs of Euro-racism,[10] with exclusive self-images and racist notions of foreigners. Since his notorious 'Rivers of Blood' speech of April 1968, Enoch Powell had been agitating in Britain, warning against the imminent displacement of the native population by the excessive growth of the black immigrant population, and against the loss of 'national character' and 'cultural identity' ('Englishness'), thus laying the cornerstone for a racist construction of social and political contexts. In the 1970s, also under the influence of Powellism, the anti-immigration National Front in particular was in the headlines. In France, where the political leadership had still sworn indissoluble ties to Algeria in 1962, debate on North Africans was dominated in the early 1990s by the catchwords 'ghetto' and 'Islam'. In 1989, about 800,000 entry visas were still being issued for North Africans, but in 1993 this figure was only around 100,000. Non-European immigrants from former colonies became targets of racist agitation by rightwing extremist currents and parties. Anti-immigration sentiments were directed against 'Arabs', '*beurs*' and the 'blacks', whose parents were from sub-Saharan Africa and the Antilles. North Africans became a particular target of aggression of the radical rightwing Front National under the leadership of Jean-Marie Le Pen, who achieved a spectacular breakthrough in the 1983 local elections from what had hitherto been a marginal position. Front National agitation gave particular weight to the demagogic distinction between what it considered 'integrable' (Catholic) migrants from the overseas territories of Guadeloupe and Martinique, who received citizenship and free access to the metropolis, and the demonized (Muslim) migrants from the Maghreb. Even where legislation strove to ensure equal economic and social opportunities, disadvantages remained egregious. In the Netherlands, for example, despite virtually exemplary legislation guaranteeing equal rights and equal opportunity, in the early 1990s there was mass unemployment of about 40 per cent among young people of Surinamese descent.[11]

More difficult sometimes was the situation of those with guaranteed admission or passports issued by the former colonial powers who remained in the now independent states of the earlier colonies. Later, when many tried to escape discrimination or persecution by resettling in Europe, they found themselves confronted with unexpected obstacles to entry in the former 'mother countries'. Non-European immigrations were countered with a series of defensive measures that has been described as the 'racialization' of European migration policies in the sense of the concept developed by Frantz Fanon and operationalized by Robert Miles.[12] This applied to the Indians of East Africa, for example, who despite their British passports were the targets of a racist anti-immigration campaign in the late 1960s and early 1970s in England because they came, or wanted to come, at a time when defence mechanisms were increasingly being sought to fight post-colonial chain migrations along established migration routes. 'Immigration' became a topic of political confrontation after the racial unrest in 1958 in the London district of Notting Hill and in Nottingham in the English Midlands, as well as in the subsequent discussion on immigration restrictions. It often carried clearly racist undertones and was equated with the influx of migrants of colour from the Commonwealth. Interest groups and task forces started emerging after 1960, such as the Birmingham Immigration Control Association and Southall Residents' Association (1960), and the aforementioned National Front (1966), which took part in the 1970s elections on an anti-immigration platform. There was also the 'Halt Immigration Now' campaign and the British Campaign to Stop Immigration (1972). The racist election platform of Conservative Peter Griffiths for the 1964 general election and Powell's notorious 'Rivers of Blood' speech in 1968 have to be seen within the same context.[13]

Official British policy as of 1960 supported the maxim that stable ethnic relations could only be guaranteed by means of strict immigration controls. After the Commonwealth Immigrants Act was passed in 1962, legislation concentrated on limiting 'non-white' immigration. This also included continued restrictions on demands by Commonwealth citizens for full British citizenship. In 1968 the Second Commonwealth Immigrants Act was hastily passed, aiming to prevent the immigration of British citizens of Indian descent from East Africa who had escaped to Kenya and wanted to flee renewed persecution. The Immigration Act of 1971 served the same purpose, and in 1972 Uganda's Asian population was forced out, leading to the flight of about 27,000 Asians to Britain. That gave new fuel to the anti-immigration campaign, especially when Margaret Thatcher made populist concessions in early 1978 that legitimized fears in the British population of being 'swamped by people with a different culture'. Culturalist and racist arguments helped keep the immigration issue on the political agenda into the 1980s. In 1981 a new law was passed that restricted acquisition of British citizenship; in 1988 another law, the Immigration (Carriers' Liability) Act, also opposed immigration of asylum seekers and fined airlines £1,000 for every passenger without valid entry documents. Britain had entered the 'Dark Age of obsessive control' (Panikos Panayi) in the early 1970s, and by the end of the 1980s it had more immigration controls than any other European Community country. At the same time, graffiti such as 'Blacks go home' or 'Send them back' could be seen in the streets and there was brutal rioting against immigrants (so-called 'Paki bashing').[14]

The British colonial empire had once spanned the globe, and in the early 1980s it still united more than 900 million people in the Commonwealth. Starting with the 1981 British Nationality Act, British passports and thus unrestricted opportunities for immigration were available only in two old-style colonies, Gibraltar and the Falkland Islands, which had two notable characteristics in common: white populations and strategic or economic significance. The largely non-European inhabitants of the other 12 British Dependent Territories spread around the world no longer had full British passports since the 1981 law introduced three classes of citizenship, which were to serve above all to tighten immigration controls. In contrast to British citizens as bearers of all rights, citizens of the British Dependent Territories and British overseas citizens are no longer released from immigration controls and are subject to the same conditions as those that apply to citizens of the New Commonwealth. The British Dependent Territories are not seeking independence, however, because except for Bermuda they are all dependent on financial subsidies from the disgruntled 'mother country', from Anguilla in the Caribbean to the South Sandwich Islands in the South Atlantic to the 55 residents of the Pitcairn Islands in the Pacific, including the descendants of Fletcher Christian, who led the mutiny on the *Bounty* in 1789.

The history of Euro-colonial migration ended in the late twentieth century with severe anti-immigration policies to restrict and ultimately cut off post-colonial chain migration. Its overall balance, and that of colonial history in general, was decidedly marked by one-sided European profits, notwithstanding the many tragic and often fatal individual fates of Europeans in the colonies. Even in the process of decolonization, Europe profited from the reversal of Euro-colonial migratory directions, again excepting the individual fates of Euro-colonial emigrants and return migrants. Economic growth in the prospering (except for Portugal) former 'mother countries', which facilitated the integration of Euro-colonial return migrants who were more qualified, went hand in hand with a great additional need for cheap semi- or unskilled labour that could be covered in the former colonial powers through colonial and post-colonial immigrants.[15]

2 LABOUR MIGRATION: 'GUESTWORKERS', IMMIGRANTS, 'ILLEGALS'

Receiving countries in central, western and northern Europe

Transnational labour migration in the industrial countries of central, western and northern Europe since the 1950s comprised largely inner-European movements; in the early 1970s it had achieved a migration balance of almost 15 million.[16] The most important regions of origin – apart from England (Ireland/Commonwealth) and Sweden (Finland) – were in the Euro-Mediterranean zone (Portugal, Spain, Italy, Yugoslavia, Greece) and in Turkey. In the Afro-Mediterranean zone, aside from other former colonies and their migrations to the respective 'mother country', was the Maghreb (especially Algeria), whose migrations were initially directed mostly towards France. The largest migration contingent was initially from Italy, followed by Spain, Greece and Portugal. From the late 1960s, Yugoslavia and Turkey came more to the fore. The sequence corresponded largely to that for bilateral recruitment agreements, some of which initiated labour migration and some of which supported existing migration; especially in France and to some extent in Germany, they were soon superseded by transnational migration networks, chain migrations and family reunification.

Migrations were determined especially by the status tension[17] rooted in the economic gap between highly developed industrial destination areas and often still agrarian, pre-industrial regions of origin. In all countries of origin in southern Europe, labour migrants in the 1960s and 1970s generally came from poor rural, often mountainous regions with insufficient employment opportunities, including northern Portugal, western Spain, southern Italy and northern Greece.[18] They sought ways out of structural unemployment or underemployment, or a chance to earn a lot in a short period of time, thus improving or expanding their economic subsistence base at home. However, labour migration often threw these economically underdeveloped regions back even further, such as the small farming regions in the out-migration areas of Calabria and Apulia in southern Italy, because labourers of prime age either migrated to the industrial centres of northern Italy or emigrated abroad. Those who remained were not in a position to keep the low-yielding small subsistence farms operating that still practised extensive production. In the receiving countries there was interest in inexpensive semi- or un-skilled labour, notwithstanding France's population policy consider-ations. This corresponded in the countries of origin to an interest in the controllable export of semi- or unskilled unemployed labour and a foreign exchange offset by means of wage remittances.[19] In addition to the interests of employers and their associations in the receiving coun-tries, as well as those of the employees in the 'sending' or 'recruitment countries', political interests in European integration and state economic aid also played a role on both sides. Regulated transfer relations were supposed to support Europe's economic approach.[20]

At the beginning of what would soon become millions of labour migrants, there was thus mutual interest in importing or exporting labour forces. It continued with gradual economic growth, interrupted only temporarily in the recession of 1966–7, into the early 1970s and was implemented differently in the immigration and integration policies of the respective receiving countries. Labour migration was choked off in the early 1970s in a one-sided action by the in-migration regions. The worldwide 'oil price shock' in 1973 shook people's faith in boundless growth. For the main European receiving countries it was cause enough to stop recruitment and migration, a step that had already been demanded, considered and partially implemented. With economic growth slowed down and unemployment increasing, albeit at different rates, in-migration limitations in the 1980s were usually maintained or even tightened.

Foreign labour migrants in Europe's welfare-state industrial develop-ment centres, and also non-European immigrants in the former colonial states, again assumed important replacement, expansion and buffer functions. They greatly resembled the European labour migrants during the period of economic growth from the mid-1890s to the eve of the First World War. This was true despite far-reaching changes in basic condi-

tions, especially as regards economic structures, operational organization, production technology and the complex systems that have since
been developed for modern labour and social administration, incorporating foreign labourers into welfare-state protection and benefit schemes
in a way that varied from country to country.[21]

At the beginning of European labour migration in the mid-1950s, there
had been no acute labour shortage with respect to the economy as a
whole in the prosperous destination countries. To some extent, in fact,
there was even a relatively high level of unemployment: in West Germany, which concluded its first recruitment agreement in late 1955 with
Italy, the average annual rate of unemployment was still around 5.1 per
cent. Only in the summer months, at 2.7 per cent, had it actually already
sunk to the level of full employment; outside the peak season it still
reached almost 7 per cent, and in some rural regions it even exceeded
10 per cent. Nevertheless, the first demands for recruitment of foreign
labour came from the Baden-Württemberg farmers' association.[22] At
first it was less an issue of labour shortage than of replacement demand
on the labour market.

Most important were replacement functions in occupational areas in
which native labourers found neither the wages nor especially the
working conditions attractive. Foreign labour migrants still did, though,
compared with conditions in their country of origin; and especially in
view of their main interest in the highest possible wage remittance, they
neglected labour conditions decisive for permanent employment.

On the one hand, moderate wages that could be increased considerably
through overtime or piecework dominated here in areas in which capital-
intensive modernization forced by a shortage of labour would have led to
a 'purging crisis'. The result would have been the demise of many
marginal businesses that were short on capital or which in any case
could not, or not entirely, be modernized through labour-saving means
and machinery. This was true, for example, for the fish and meat processing industry and, until the general 'death of textiles' in Europe in the
1960s and early 1970s, for semi- and unskilled work in companies in
the textile industry that were at the break-even subsistence level. It also
remained the case in construction and cleaning services, as well as the
catering trade and to a lesser extent also for some seasonal agricultural
jobs that could not be automated, such as the grape and asparagus
harvests. In such fields of work, and not regarding the economy as a
whole, foreign employment could temporarily slow down the increase in
wages. This wage pressure specific to certain fields or groups also
affected native workers in these jobs, which gave nationalistic currents
renewed occasion to agitate against foreigners 'pushing out' the local
workers.

On the other hand, foreign labour migrants did collect around jobs which paid agreed rates but which were especially difficult or dangerous or which posed a health hazard, such as the asbestos industry, or in highly modern but nerve-wracking areas of work such as on the assembly line. Foreign labourers suffered under such working conditions no less than local workers, and after a certain time they frequently stopped working because of the same occupational health problems. This was hardly noticeable because many victims of occupational illness took their health problems back with them to their home countries. None the less, the legitimizing legend again circulated in many receiving countries – like that of the 'eager and cheap' foreign labour migrants in pre-First World War Germany – that foreign workers were better able to cope with such working conditions and were generally more resilient than the 'weakling' nationals.

When the European labour migrations of the 1960s swelled into mass movements, in addition to the general reduction in working hours in most immigration countries, different degrees of upward social mobility among native labourers had started, underpinned by increasing, often company-fostered career qualification. Upward mobility and qualifications were both clearly facilitated through foreign employment: while in West Germany, for example, the number of local workers declined by 2.3 million from 1960 to 1972, the share of foreigners in the total labour force increased from 1.3 per cent in 1960 to a peak of 11.9 per cent in 1973. The influx of 2 million foreign labourers in the 1960s only caused the total number of workers to increase from 26.3 million to 26.7 million. It thus largely closed up labour gaps, increasing the total number of workers only minimally. The possibilities for professional and social advancement were usually not open to foreign labour migrants, though they supported them indirectly by the development of a sub-stratum below local labour in the divided labour market that was characterized by a highly internationalized lower stratum. The slipstream caused by professional and social advancement, as could be observed in many areas of work, served to increase the labour shortage in other areas that were not linked to these developments. This could be balanced with the help of foreign labour; the social climb of local labour could thus be eased operationally and economically by the emergence of a sub-stratum of foreign labour.[23]

In cases of high economic growth and generally increasing labour shortages, the foreign reserve army fulfilled both replacement and expansion functions in central areas of production, especially mining and heavy industry. Foreign labour also served as an economic buffer, or 'shock absorber', as was apparent for the first time in the economic recession of 1966–7, when it dropped abruptly (by about 30 per cent in Germany) in areas largely dependent on economic factors. Many foreign nationals then exported their unemployment through return migration, which drew the home regions into the buffer function for the benefit of the destination countries. International disturbances in economic growth also had an impact on the home regions of labour migrants, whose economies were then further burdened by reimporting unemployed workers in addition to the problems of reintegration.[24]

In contrast to the chiefly permanent immigration from the former colonies, labour migrants recruited through bilateral agreements usually came for either a limited or open-ended period of time. Although fluctuation was still high in the late 1960s, a change typical of the transition from circular migration flows to chain migrations could already be identified. For instance, permanent stays increased and a shift in the main living base to the destination regions was clearly discernible especially through family reunification, which accelerated greatly from the mid-1970s. Unintentional consequences of immigration restrictions of the early 1970s reinforced this impact.

The 'oil price shock' of 1973 was less a trigger than a final chance to stop recruitment and immigration. Switzerland had led the way as early as 1970 and Sweden in 1972, followed by Germany in 1973 and France and the Benelux countries in 1974. Among the reasons were not only acknowledgement that resources were limited, fears of the end of economic growth and general crisis perspectives, but also scepticism about the shift from work stays to permanent stays, that is, actual immigration situations and the attendant social problems. Also, defensive stances were growing with respect to certain immigrant groups, reinforced by a xenophobic, culturalist discourse. In France it was mostly directed towards North Africans, in West Germany towards the Turks; both were Muslim minorities. Receiving countries tried to break the chain migrations that were increasing via firmly established migration networks and routes by imposing restrictions, which were also directed against migration from the former colonies. Whereas migration and integration policies went their separate ways, the diversity of these restrictive measures protesting immigration formed a consensus of defence, marking the beginning of the historical path that would end in 'Fortress Europe' after the end of the Cold War.

The recruitment and immigration ban of the early 1970s usually had only a short-term effect, and in the long term sometimes even worked against its objectives. There were various reasons for this. Foreign labourers were abruptly faced with the alternative to 'stay or go', since taking leave from the labour contract to return for an extended period of time could mean leaving for ever. In many cases this would have meant disqualification, because the new qualifications acquired in the receiving countries were difficult or impossible to apply in the home countries. Moreover, returning would have meant giving up what had become a clearly different standard of living. Many therefore decided to stay, which accelerated the decrease in transnational fluctuation, increased the base of permanent residence and shifted the main living bases to the destination countries by having the rest of the family join the migrant. Family reunification was guaranteed by European regulations for the protection of the family (Article 19, Section 6 of the European Social Charter), despite all national attempts to impose restrictions, especially relating to adult children who had been born and raised abroad and other family members following their family.[25]

Special social benefits, such as child benefits in West Germany, led to increased immigration of children and adolescents to join parents. Consequently, from 1973 to 1975, more than 31 per cent of all new immigration was attributed to family reunification,[26] which in other countries, too, quickly developed into one of the largest immigration movements or even – as in the United States – the largest. In the wake of the Commonwealth Immigrants Acts of 1962 and 1968, Britain tried to limit the immigration of Commonwealth citizens by restricting work permits. The ordinances were wholly ineffectual regarding family reunification: from July 1962 to December 1968, only 77,966 male workers entered Britain, as opposed to 257,220 dependants. In 1969–77, 58,875 workers came and 259,646 dependants.[27]

For countries of the European Community (EC), labour force transfer in Europe, as previously noted, also had to do with issues of European integration from the outset. The goals were not only to dismantle customs barriers but also to ensure freedom of movement on the labour market, which left the recruitment ban for member states largely ineffective. This was the case for Italy as a founding member of the European Economic Community (EEC), for Greece starting in 1981, and Spain and Portugal as of 1986. In West Germany, for example, the number of foreign nationals decreased for a short time after 1973 (3.97 million), but as of 1978 it had already climbed back up (3.98 million), exceeding that level in the year of the recruitment ban and continuing to rise. Behind the dysfunctionality of the immigration restrictions was the 'liberal paradox' (James Hollifield) that does not allow liberal states operating under the rule of law completely to cut off migration processes that are underway, without violating basic humanitarian obligations or principles of human rights.[28]

The migration restrictions hit Turkish immigrants the hardest. As the last to grow into a mass movement, Turkish immigration was broken off by the recruitment ban in the midst of a phase of massive expansion. Further growth of the Turkish population in the European countries of immigration resulted largely from natural population growth, family reunification and, to a minor extent, from migration for reasons of asylum (especially Kurds). In virtually all central, western and northern European host countries, there was a clear shift in weight from European to non-European foreigner populations from the late 1970s to the late 1980s; in France in particular, this was partly influenced by naturalization. While the number of Portuguese, Spaniards, Italians, Greeks and Yugoslavs decreased in the period 1978–89 (except in Switzerland, where the number of Portuguese and Yugoslavs increased), there was a great increase in the number of Turks and North Africans. In some countries, in fact, the number doubled (Moroccans in the Netherlands; Turks in France).[29]

The shift from work stays to immigration situations was accompanied by changes – accelerated by recruitment bans and immigration restrictions – in the demographic structures of immigrant populations and their status on the labour market: the employment rate, usually high with respect to temporary labour migration, went down as a result of family reunification, since there was a rise in non-working family members. Instead of exporting unemployment in times of crisis by means of return migration to the home countries, an internal buffer function set in, in the form of unemployment that was far above the average among resident foreign populations in the receiving countries. The replacement function generally remained, whereas the function of filling the lower stratum as local workers advanced socially and professionally was often passed on to more recently immigrated groups in a kind of 'change of shifts in the substructure'.[30] In the long term, there was often limited professional and social advancement from the level of semi- and unskilled labourer to that of skilled craftsman, apart from greater upward social mobility of isolated groups also in the area of self-employment, especially in ethnic business. However, a lower stratum clearly marked by ethnosocial characteristics usually remained intact.[31]

In West Germany, for example, the social security systems of the welfare state, in which foreigners with firm residence status also participated, did prevent structural marginalization, in the sense of an ethnosocial subproletariat, of the foreign minority that evolved from the 'guestworker population'.[32] But they did not break down the inequality of professional and social opportunities, from the blatant overrepresentation of foreign nationals in unemployment to their no less conspicuous underrepresentation, albeit with clear group-specific differences, in school, vocational training and higher education. In unified Germany, where youth unemployment grew dramatically in the 1990s, one in eight young Germans (including immigrated ethnic Germans from eastern Europe) had not completed any vocational training in 1999 and was thus without a decisive qualification for the labour market; among young foreign nationals in Germany, the ratio was one in three.[33]

In the late 1970s to early 1980s, all receiving countries in central, western and northern Europe had become immigration countries at least in a quantitative sense, to the extent that permanent immigrations outnumbered emigrations. The British Isles remained an exception in this regard, where the Republic of Ireland was still an emigration and out-migration region with a negative migration balance, and Great Britain (including Northern Ireland) also noted continued overseas emigration, retaining a negative migration balance until 1985–9. In the rest of Europe, only Belgium had a negative balance in 1980–9, owing to high emigration and low immigration. In all cases, the immigrated popula-tions helped to balance out the declining population growth of the receiving countries.[34] Section 3 will use selected examples to discuss the different forms of integration policies in the receiving countries of cen-tral, western and northern Europe.

Southern Europe: From 'sending countries' to 'receiving countries'

In concluding this discussion of the history of inner-European south–north labour migration, let us look at the home regions of labour migra-tion in the Euro-Mediterranean zone that also changed from being sending regions to receiving regions in the 1980s.[35] A common historical trend in migratory developments in the Euro-Mediterranean zone since the late nineteenth century was the progression from abandoning over-seas and European emigration and labour migration to the increased emergence of European south–north migrations to the commencement of intercontinental south–north migration. Inner-European south–north migration from the more traditional regions of origin of 'guestworker migrations' was characterized from the mid-1970s – in contrast, for example, to the historically more recent labour migration from Turkey – by minor but consistent chain migrations of family members and (strongest among the Greeks) remigrations to the regions of origin. The economic development gap diminished as compared with northern Europe, while at the same time the head start of southern European regions of origin over those in the 'Third World' turned into a bigger lead. In the mid-1970s, labourers from there began to flow to the north-ern Mediterranean realm, especially from the Euro-African zone with its disproportionately high population growth: the total population in that area grew between 1950 and 1990 from 69.5 million to 189 million. Up to 1980 the average population growth was 2.6 per cent as compared with 0.7 per cent north of the Mediterranean; up to 1990 the ratio was

2.6 per cent to 0.4 per cent. Ageing and rejuvenation of populations coincided: in the early 1990s the share of the population over 64 years in the countries of North Africa was about 4 per cent; in the EC it was 14 per cent. The share of those under 15 years in North Africa was about 50 per cent, while the figure for the EC was about 18 per cent.[36]

In addition to this tension of demographic economic developments, other factors also helped to determine the course of migration. Northern Europe remained largely closed, starting with the recruitment ban and immigration restrictions of the early to mid-1970s and continuing through the increasingly restrictive and efficient controls in the 1980s against unwanted immigration, especially from the 'Third World'. Apart from family reunification, special authorization and desired or contractually arranged immigration, access to Europe essentially opened up only through petitions for political asylum, which have increased substantially since the late 1970s (see section 4). They were frequently used as a substitute for absent regular options for immigration and were therefore treated all the more restrictively by the European side.

Options for immigration to southern Europe worked almost the opposite way around. There, political asylum played an insignificant role up to the late 1980s as a means of gaining access to Europe, while border-crossing and irregular employment in the shadow economy were comparatively simple. Though these countries had had administrative experience with emigration and labour migration abroad, they had scarcely dealt with the admission of foreign labourers, much less immigrants. In Italy, where intercontinental south–north migration to the Euro-Mediterranean region emerged earliest and strongest, immigration controls were deliberately treated liberally, unbureaucratically and for a long time generally without a visa stamp, because the overwhelming majority of foreigners were tourists.

Furthermore, the Euro-Mediterranean region traditionally had a strong informal sector with a broad spectrum of semi- and unskilled jobs, especially in agriculture, the service sector (e.g. restaurants), travelling sales, construction, fishing and fish processing. Because of poor wage and working conditions, few local workers could be enticed to take these jobs. Those seeking work or better income under more tolerable conditions decided instead on labour migration in central, western and northern Europe. After returning, they were even less interested in these positions. The resulting replacement demand was filled increasingly by foreign labour from regions with incomparably worse job opportunities. The jobs taken on by foreign labourers also included some that native labour migrants themselves had also performed in countries to the north, though for better pay, such as positions in the catering trade, municipal cleaning services and in construction. Moreover, expansion demand existed in areas of economic growth, such as in northern Italy. In-migration and/or professional and social advancement of native workers in these areas of work in turn left replacement demand in other, less attractive areas.

Though there was a labour surplus in the regions of origin of European south–north labour migration with respect to the economy as a whole, as previously noted this was certainly not the case for all economic areas. Similar to the situation prior to the First World War in the Austro-Hungarian out-migration region of Galicia, foreign labour from areas with high population growth that were economically less developed were then incorporated into the labour markets in an effort to balance out the labour shortage in certain sectors. For foreign labour, apart from the high proportion of irregular foreign employment, all of this led to a context of employment and function – from replacement and expansion functions to economic buffer functions – that is well known from the history of labour migration and also related to the earlier recruitment period in northern Europe.

It was very difficult for labour migrants from non-EC countries to gain entry to northern Europe, while southern Europe had relatively open borders and a wide range of jobs, including a large degree of irregularly accessible work. Thus migration from the 'Third World' to the Euro-Mediterranean zone rose substantially as migration distances also continued to increase. Into the 1980s, irregular employment of foreigners without residence and/or work permits generally did not have the character of unlawful, secret border-crossing, despite their common description as 'illegal immigrants'. Instead, it largely involved legal entry by 'tourists' who then overstayed their – in Italy usually three-month – visas and started working illegally. The receiving countries, as in France, usually tried to legalize the work arrangements through amnesty and *régularisation* offers. This situation did not change until other European countries, in preparation for the elimination of border controls in the European single market, expressed concern about irregular overstayers and illegal immigrants migrating further northward and were prompted to exert political and ultimately also public pressure. Protests against this form of immigration and employment also grew in Italy itself. Against this background, for example, Italy introduced compulsory visas in September 1990 for a number of major home countries of irregular workers and asylum seekers, including the Maghreb states, Gambia and Senegal, as well as Turkey. Not until these measures were enacted did 'illegal immigration' in a narrower sense, especially by sea, also start to unfold in southern Europe.

Irregular employment and ethnic stratification were significantly interrelated, which allowed distinctive areas of ethnic sub-stratification and concentration to develop in the informal sector of the Euro-Mediterranean zone. Foreigners in irregular work situations are especially dependent on migratory networks, which are generally structured through communities based on their place of origin. These in turn contribute to 'ethnicizing' irregular areas of work, particularly when the networks of the home community are highly organized. Some examples of this are the women in Italy from the Philippines and eastern Europe who work largely as domestic servants or in the hotel or cleaning trades; Tunisians who work especially in fisheries in Sardinia; or in northern Europe, for example, Turks working in the declining textile and clothing industry in Amsterdam, or the ethnic milieu of the dockworkers working irregularly in Rotterdam.[37]

The largest group of irregularly employed foreigners in Italy, which involved an estimated 500,000–1,000,000 in the late 1980s, were immigrants from the Maghreb countries (especially Morocco and Tunisia). Some also came from the former Italian colonies in Africa (Somalia, Eritrea) and other African countries; the destinations of the African migrants were predominantly in southern Italy. There were also groups from diverse corners of the world, from Latin America (especially Brazil) to Asia. In the 1982 law on foreign labour, severe penalties were established for smuggling illegal immigrants into the country and exploiting their labour, but this entirely missed the point regarding irregular foreign employment in the Italian shadow economy. An initial legalization programme had limited success, as only about 119,000 reports were made from 1986 to 1988. A second programme introduced in February 1990 and considered to have had considerable success registered about 217,000 reports by June 1990. It must be kept in mind, however, that legalization is only possible in agreement with the employer and generally does not register precisely the most problematic work situations.

On 31 December 1992, Italy registered 778,458 foreigners from non-EC countries with regular residence permits, including only 7,450 who were entitled to political asylum. Most were employed (311,003) or registered with employment agencies as seeking work (145,762), and 102,876 were dependent family members. The largest groups were Moroccans (95,791) and Tunisians (50,405), followed by citizens of the Philippines (44,155), ex-Yugoslavians (39,020) and Albanians (28,628). There were a total of 226,472 people from Africa (Morocco, Tunisia, Egypt, Ghana, Senegal, Somalia), or 29.1 per cent of the non-EC foreigners with regular residence permits. According to estimates by the Istituto Italiano de Statistica, 30–35 per cent of all foreigners from non-EC countries were 'illegal immigrants' in 1989, although the percentages are much higher with respect to certain areas and seasons, for example in the Mezzogiorno (southern Italy) and especially during seasonal agricultural work, which is not regulated in Italy.

In contrast to the industrial countries in northern Europe with high foreign national or immigrant populations, Italy's foreign labour (and especially the irregular workers among them) is employed less in the highly developed regions of the north and more in the less industrialized, economically underdeveloped regions of the south that have high unemployment. This hindered or even blocked many plans for developing and modernizing the Mezzogiorno. It also further favoured the traditional shadow economy, which even began absorbing legal economic areas, and generally strengthened the anti-immigration movement. Public opinion in the former 'sending country' Italy took an increasingly anti-immigration stance in the late 1980s. In surveys, almost 50 per cent of those questioned in 1987, and almost 75 per cent in 1991, argued against 'further immigration', and 61 per cent of those were convinced that immigration brought only or at least mostly disadvantages.[38]

In the early 1980s, Spain also changed into an immigration country and accordingly adapted its legislation and institutions to accommodate this reversal in migratory direction. In 1985, the year Spain joined the EC, Spain passed an alien law (*Ley de Extranjeria*), bowing to pressure from the European Community. After the closure of the Dirección General de Migraciones, which was responsible for Spanish labour migrants abroad, the Instituto Español de Emigración, despite the fact that its name recalls Spain's emigration history, was primarily involved with issuing work permits for migrants from the 'Third World' or legalizing their work stays. A compulsory visa was introduced in Spain in 1991, partly in response to internal xenophobic and racist currents to control the immigration of annually about 1 million North African seasonal workers. Spain, too, attempted to lower the number of 'illegal' labourers through legalization programmes; as a result, the number of legal workers increased from 198,000 in 1981 to 361,000 in 1991 (the last offer of legalization was in 1999). The major groups involved in irregular employment of foreigners, which was estimated in the late 1980s at about 250,000, came from Morocco and Latin America (Peru, Argentina); the number of Moroccans especially rose sharply. The highly flexible shadow economy of the industrial centres of Barcelona and Madrid in particular is strongly dependent on irregular foreign labour. The situation is similar for agriculture, the construction industry and not least for domestic service: domestic servants in the late 1980s to early 1990s came from the Philippines, the Dominican Republic and Peru, as well as Portugal and even Poland.[39]

In Portugal most foreign nationals employed in irregular (150,000, according to official estimates) and regular positions came not from the

Afro-Mediterranean zone but from the former colonies with Portuguese as the national language (PALOP countries), that is, Guinea-Bissau, Angola, Mozambique, São Tomé and Principe, as well as the Cape Verde Islands. When a legalization programme was offered here in 1992–3, only 55,000 reports were filed.

The situation in Greece developed very differently with respect to migratory events and migration policies. After experiencing heavy repatriation, it was the last to change from an emigration to an immigration country. Up to 1973, about 1 million Greeks had worked abroad. Half of them returned from the early 1970s. In 1967–77, 68 per cent of the 240,500 repatriates came from western Europe, more than half of those (57 per cent) from West Germany. In 1978–81, about 9,000 of 25,300 Greek labour migrants registered as seeking work in West Germany returned to Greece. Return migration from Germany exceeded the volume of family reunification to Germany as of 1981. In the early 1990s in Greece, on the other hand, there was an immigrant population of a total of about 603,000, about 340,000 of whom were regular immigrants, about 260,000 'illegal immigrants' according to a 1993 estimate of the ministry of the interior, and only about 3,000 refugees recognized as entitled to asylum from 1980 to 1992. Among the regular immigrants, the group of Greek 'repatriates' dominated by far, especially the Pontic Greeks who immigrated in 1980–92 from the former Soviet Union. Only about 17,000 people came from African countries beyond the Afro-Mediterranean zone. The largest group of 'illegals' were from Albania (*c.*150,000), far ahead of Poland (30,000), followed by countries of the 'Third World', led by Egypt (*c.*25,000) and the Philippines (*c.*15,000). In Greece's comparatively restrictive migration policies there was no legalization programme for foreigners working in irregular positions; instead there were mass deportations of Albanians (see chapter 5, section 3).[40]

In the Euro-Mediterranean zone, especially Italy and Spain, high growth in the North African segment of the foreign population could be observed up to the late 1980s. However, it was not the 'migrations of nations' from North Africa extending through the northern Mediterranean region bound for 'the heart of Europe', as was gloomily prophesied in northern Europe and used as a political argument in debates on the asylum issue. Irrespective of this, the share of irregular immigrations from North Africa was still higher in France than in Italy. Altogether, the number of 'illegal immigrants' or irregularly employed foreign nationals in the countries of the EU in 1991 was about 2.6 million, or 14 per cent of the total foreign population, according to estimates by the International Labour Organization (ILO). Italy, with at least 600,000 (1–1.5 million according to other estimates) took pride of place, followed by Germany with about 350,000 (although another approximately

300,000 refugees without legal residence status have been estimated). Since then the numbers have risen sharply according to a reasonable assumption, estimated at about 4 to 5 million for 1993.[41] This was partly due to the shielding of Europe against refugees and asylum seekers from the 'Third World', and soon also from eastern Europe, which prompted a growing number of migrants to make their way to Europe by irregular or, in a narrower sense, illegal means.

3   NATIONAL WELFARE STATES AND TRANSNATIONAL LABOUR MIGRATION

Transnational migration and social participation

Knowledge of the transition from labour migrations to true immigration processes has been more or less openly accepted, sometimes also repressed or, against one's better judgement, politically 'denied'. In any case it led to substantial conflict on immigration and integration issues in the receiving countries of central, western and northern Europe. This was due to differences in citizenship law and in collective notions of national and cultural identity. Complicating matters were the different relationships of the highly regulated national welfare states to the attendant social circumstances and subsequent problems of transnational migration. They were based on the common experience that citizenship was gradually losing its selectivity in distinguishing between demands for social participation by nationals and by 'foreign' citizens. An increasing number of migrants have acquired greater civil and social rights and have grown into the status of denizens, notwithstanding differing interpretations of the latter term.[42] On the other hand, the tendency of citizens to question the legitimacy of rights granted to migrants often grew with the benefit problems the welfare states were facing.

In positioning national welfare states with respect to the problems of transnational labour migration, there are a number of classification and interpretation options,[43] two of which will be mentioned here. Thomas Faist's model originally developed for a transatlantic comparison takes up Gosta Esping-Andersen's distinctions among liberal, conservative-corporatist and social-democratic types of welfare states. From this foundation by way of some transitions and intermediate forms, two means of including migrants tend to be distinguished: a more 'market-oriented' means, that is, imparted particularly via economic mechanisms on the labour market, and a more 'policy-regulated' means, imparted via welfare-state programmes. Based on this perspective, it is possible to analyse the connection between so-called migration and welfare regimes.[44]

Another approach to systematizing immigration and integration policies in European receiving countries is offered by Stephen Castles and Mark J. Miller, taking up the ideas of Thomas H. Marshall and recent discussion on the 'citizenship' issue: a structural model[45] developed for global orientation with three types. These apply globally to many receiving countries though only to a few European countries, so this model too must be used with caution:

1   An 'exclusive model' applies in countries that accept immigrants and their children as citizens only in exceptional cases, because the citizenship law is based on the principle of descent or inheritance (*jus sanguinis*), with an ethnonational orientation. An example of this outside Europe is Japan; within Europe, Germany in particular, which relaxed its naturalization law in 1990–1, however, and expanded its citizenship law in 1999–2000 to include elements of the territorial principle, or right by birth (*jus soli*).

2   An 'assimilatory model' characterizes countries that view acquisition of citizenship as a motivating factor in identifying with the culture and value system of the host country, thereby deliberately, and in part programmatically, excluding room for multicultural or polyethnic development. In Europe this could apply, again not in a strict sense, to France with its hybrid system of citizenship rights including aspects of both inheritance and territorial principles. France, like the UK, attempted to limit immigration even from the former colonies by creating obstacles to acquiring citizenship. Even today internal political discussion is concerned with legitimate access to citizenship and the question of how much cultural pluralism the republican nation can or must allow.[46]

3   The third, 'multicultural model', which, outside Europe, applies to Australia, Canada and to some extent the United States, also binds acquisition of citizenship to acceptance of the political culture and the related democratic core structures of the host country and the value system upholding them. However, it also deliberately and programmatically opens up broad social scopes of action and sociopolitical options for developing multicultural and polyethnic structures. In Europe, for example, in the 1980s this would still apply to Sweden and to some extent the Netherlands, although since the mid- to late 1980s here, too, considerable tension has arisen between a typological categorization and empirical stocktaking.[47]

Some central aspects of this complex issue are revealed by a comparative view of the two German states as receiving countries without a colonial tradition, on the one hand, and the post-colonial receiving countries

France and Britain, on the other; the discussion will concentrate, however, on West Germany and France.

West Germany

In West Germany[48] the 'economic miracle' on the labour market was supported by three major immigration thrusts. After the Second World War about 12 million German refugees and expellees streamed into the three western occupation zones. From the foundation of the two German states in 1949 to the building of the Berlin Wall in 1961, about 3.1 million Germans emigrated from East to West Germany (as well as about 400,000 in the other direction). In the mid-1950s, only ten years after the end of Nazi forced labour, a new form of foreign employment began on a large scale. The new labour migrants from abroad, generally recruited through bilateral treaties, were referred to in public discussion – but not officially – in West Germany as 'guestworkers' (*Gastarbeiter*) to dissociate them from the 'foreign migrant labourers' (*ausländische Wanderarbeiter*) of the German Empire and especially from the 'foreign workers' (*Fremdarbeiter*) of Nazi Germany. Germany concluded recruitment agreements with Italy in 1955, Spain and Greece in 1960, Turkey in 1961, Portugal in 1964, and finally Yugoslavia in 1968. Treaties that had relatively minor impact were also concluded with Morocco (1963/1966) and Tunisia (1965).

The share of Turks in the total foreign population in West Germany doubled from 1968 to 1973 from 10.7 per cent to around 23 per cent. The same was true for the growth of the Yugoslav population, from 8.8 per cent (1968) to 17.7 per cent (1973). As of 1971, Turks represented the largest nationality group from the recruitment countries. Their numbers rose from about 8,700 in late 1961 to more than 1 million in 1974. Turks worked mostly in central areas of industrial production as well as in mining in the Ruhr valley, where a transition took place over time from 'Ruhr Poles' to 'Ruhr Turks'.

As with other foreign immigrant populations, among Turks there was also a large share of women working in industry early on. After 1967, one-third of Turkish migrants were women, some of whom came as pioneer migrants, later joined by friends and relatives. Family reunification in labour migration predominantly, but by no means exclusively, involved families joining male labourers who had immigrated first. This was notable among Turkish immigrants to the extent that migration was connected with emancipation processes and the attendant tension within families.

Because Turkey was not a member of the EC, the working Turkish population was disadvantaged in many areas until a supplement was added in 1980 to the 1963 EEC association treaty with Turkey. This was the case also for the Yugoslavs and the small population of North Africans in West Germany. Conditions were initially aggravated by the large socio-cultural distance between the societies of the sending and receiving countries as well as barriers to integration associated with Islam characterized by defensiveness of the host society. Turks were perceived in West Germany as the 'most foreign' group, similar to the North Africans (also a Muslim minority) in France and the Afro-Caribbeans or Pakistanis and East African Indians in Britain. Almost half of all Turkish youths between 16 and 20 years old in 1980 went neither to school nor to an apprenticeship or regular job. Two-thirds of those aged 15 to 19 had no vocational training at all. Language difficulties ('a generation of bilingual illiterates') and incomplete schooling and vocational training continued to hinder social integration, even in the second generation, so that with good reason the situation of Turks in Germany has often been compared to that of North Africans in France.

In the recruitment period 1955–73, German 'recruitment commissions', with the participation of the national labour administration, carried out the selection and medical examination of applicants in the 'recruitment countries'. At first limited contracts and a rotation system were considered, but rotation was never compulsory and limited contracts could be easily extended. The rotation clause in the German–Turkish recruitment treaty of 1961 is an exception. Until it was rescinded in September 1964, it limited work periods to two years, thus initially also barring family reunification. Because of the recurrent costs of training new workers, German employers spoke out strongly against the idea of compulsory rotation of foreign labour. Many circumvented the recruitment commissions by directly recruiting foreign workers abroad, often through arrangements with labourers already working in the company. A bottleneck on the labour market developed in 1961 when the flow of labour from East Germany – which West Germany unilaterally declared to be politically motivated escape from the eastern bloc – was cut off by the building of the Berlin Wall. As economic growth continued, the number of foreign labourers quickly exceeded the 1 million mark. Without this massive expansion of the labour pool through foreign employment, the bottleneck of the early 1960s on the West German labour market could probably only have been managed through far-reaching and substantial structural changes.

What had begun in West Germany in the 1950s as officially organized temporary labour migration went through various smooth transitions that finally led to a genuine immigration situation starting in the mid-1970s. This development was supported by the unintended impact of the recruitment ban of November 1973, which, as has been shown (see section 2), boomeranged with respect to policies relating to foreigners. While it allowed stays to become longer and longer, which prompted family reunification, the different lengths of stay referred to in the residence legislation offered foreign labour migrants with permanent residence status increasing security against the imponderables of the 'guestworker existence'. The unpopular 'stabilization' of the residence status of foreign workers from 'guestworker' to *de facto* immigrant was thus a home-made consequence of alien policies and alien law. According to a survey conducted in 1989 for the German ministry of the interior, only 11 per cent of foreigners questioned had concrete plans to return to their home country.

Policies in West Germany long seemed to produce a contradictory impact as regards this development. The lowest common denominator was repeated by every German government from the late 1970s to the early 1990s, denying that Germany was an immigration country: '*Die Bundesrepublik ist kein Einwanderungsland.*' Migration and integration policies in a 'non-immigration country' were, on the one hand, characterized by the extension of residence permits and the resulting increased security in residence status; and, on the other hand, by the development of concepts to 'encourage willingness for return migration' or for 'temporary social integration' that would keep this 'desire to return home' alive. This was especially clear when in 1979–80 – as in the Netherlands – there was discussion in politics and the media on the legal recognition of the immigration situation in the form of local voting rights for foreign residents, eased conditions for naturalization and long-term concepts for integration ('Kühn Report', 1979).

Against the background of the second 'oil price shock' of 1980, the discussion became submerged in the heat of emotionalized fear, protest and fundamental party-political debates that mostly targeted the integration of the Turkish population in Germany and led to a wave of anti-Turkish sentiment accompanied by acts of violence. A politics of separation, including monetary 'repatriation incentives', was intensified; it superseded the short debate on integration in the early 1980s, especially after the change from the social–liberal (SPD-FDP) to the conservative–liberal (CDU/CSU-FDP) coalition in 1982. To some extent, the change in government was brought about by the politicization of the 'foreigner discussion' in the election campaign. This development was diametrically opposed to the outcome of the same discussion in the Netherlands, which led to a basic national consensus on residence security, local voting rights and ease of naturalization for foreigners.

Nevertheless, in practice West Germany was moving along the unacknowledged yet unmistakable path from 'discontinuous' to 'continuous' integration policies. Foreigners participating legally on the labour market and 'muddling through' the welfare state were in the long term granted virtually all basic economic and social rights on the basis of residential, labour and social legislation. Foreign nationals of another EU country additionally had transnational freedom of movement on the labour market and local voting rights within the European Union. To this extent, welfare-state Germany offered a model of integration that was 'policy-oriented' and determined by the regulatory structures of the welfare regime. In terms of political programmes, however, it was unacknowledged or even not understood; it favoured EU (or EC) citizens and disadvantaged other foreigners, including its largest minority, the Turks, which evolved out of labour migrations.

A counterpoint to this 'policy-oriented' integration was a one-sided, anti-immigration citizenship law oriented along the principle of descent or inheritance. The 1990–1 measures to ease naturalization did little to change the fact that children and even grandchildren of 'guestworkers' who had immigrated to Germany decades earlier remained 'foreigners'. This disadvantaged especially foreigners from 'third countries' who were only partly included in the welfare-state model of integration. Naturalization was more significant for these foreigners than it was for EU (or EC) citizens, for whom citizenship brought additionally only the right to vote in national and state elections.[49]

For this reason Germany was not only an ambivalent *de facto* immigration country with integrative welfare practices and exclusive citizenship rights. The foreign population, too, that developed from the former 'guestworkers' entered the immigration situation unexpectedly and without any corresponding offer by the stubborn immigration country. This made it more difficult for many immigrants to decide to renounce their former citizenship as the necessary prerequisite for naturalization in Germany. In particular, the foreign populations from 'third countries' who had been in Germany for a long time, even for generations, developed partly dual loyalties, partly transnational or transcultural identities in this ambivalent immigration situation that was artificially held open through political defensiveness.[50] Related configurations of social and political issues could possibly have been offset for the pioneer generation and their descendants born in the country through acquisition of dual citizenship, which, however, remained restricted to exceptional hardship cases. Legal acknowledgement of the immigration situation through a limited reform of citizenship rights by implanting some elements of the territorial principle (*jus soli*) was obstructed until 1999 by ethnonational traditions of thinking that go far back into German ideational and legal history.

East Germany

Foreign employment also existed in East Germany (German Democratic Republic, GDR), at first in conjunction with support for vocational training. Recruitment of foreign labour beyond contracts for training was triggered by an acute labour shortage caused especially by the large outflow to West Germany until the Berlin Wall was built in 1961 and, to a lesser extent, indirectly even afterwards. There was far less foreign labour in East Germany than in West Germany, but the GDR, where foreigners made up about 1 per cent of its working population, still held pride of place among the countries of the Council for Mutual Economic Assistance (CMEA or Comecon). Of the roughly 190,000 foreigners that were still in East Germany in 1989, the largest contingent were employed by state-owned companies, including about 59,000 Vietnamese and about 15,000 Mozambicans on the eve of German unification in 1989. There was no family reunification in this strictly rotational system of foreign labour. Foreign workers in the GDR generally came as individual labour migrants. International agreements referred mostly to young, unmarried workers. Direct anti-family regulations also existed, such as the choice between abortion and deportation in the case of pregnancy, which was dubiously reminiscent of similar stipulations in work contracts for Polish labourers on East Elbian agricultural estates prior to the First World War.

Immigration problems associated with foreign labour arose in East Germany only in the rare cases of marriage between foreign workers ('*ausländische Werktätige*') and citizens of the GDR. Foreign labourers entered the country for a limited period of time and were bound by bilateral agreements to return to their home country after the end of the work contract; a portion of the wages earned was also transferred to the governments of those countries. The GDR offered its foreign workers administratively managed, authoritarian 'supervision', but generally less social integration and more officially prescribed social segregation in a kind of state-run aliens' administration. Foreign labourers were often quartered in separate group accommodation and thus also socially kept at a distance. Closer contact had to be authorized and reported on. East Germany experienced the emergence of its 'own form of apartheid' (Wolfgang Thierse) or 'xenophobia behind closed doors' (Cornelia Schmalz-Jacobsen). Latent xenophobic tensions would later be released openly with the end of the prescribed social discipline that accompanied the collapse of the East German regime.[51]

France

When comparing France with West Germany, the confrontation between citizenship and alien legislation and policies relating to aliens, on the one hand, and the mass migrations during the Cold War, on the other, reveal aspects of a tension-filled convergence: West Germany remained a reluctant *de facto* immigration country with integrative welfare practices but an exclusive, one-sided citizenship law based on the descent or inheritance principle. After naturalization procedures were relaxed in 1990–1, it took until 1999 for elements of the territorial principle to be implemented, thus adapting the law more to the immigration situation that had already existed for decades. France, on the other hand, was the classic European immigration country and was not outstripped by West Germany in terms of numbers of immigrants until the 1960s, even though immigration was not part of the mythos of the nation's founding in the French collective memory, in particular since mass immigration did not become part of France's history until a century after the French Revolution. Into the 1990s, the problems of transnational migration in a welfare state played only a secondary role in public debate on immigration and integration. The 1993 legal reform curtailed the traditional territorial principle regarding citizenship rights.[52]

The balance between inheritance and territorial principles in France's citizenship law was a kind of historic compromise: the territorial principle that had been valid until the Revolution of 1789 was replaced in Napoleon's *Code civil* of 1804 by the inheritance principle. In a prolonged historical process, however, citizenship was gradually opened back up to the territorial principle. Fear of military and economic weakness due to 'depopulation'[53] contributed considerably to expanding rights and opening up access to citizenship for immigrants through a number of reforms. Nevertheless, the leitmotif of the emerging French-style welfare state remained the idea that assuming the national 'identity' was a prerequisite to participation in state welfare. The last legal reform along this traditional line came in 1973, shortly before France stopped immigration in 1974. Two decades later this line was broken through the restrictive change in immigration, residency and naturalization regulations by the *loi Pasqua* of July 1993, based on a constitutional reform that adapted French legislation to the Schengen agreement. This break in tradition was not only a matter of supranational adaptation requirements along the road to 'Fortress Europe' (see chapter 5, section 1); instead, it was also about a crisis of naturalization, integration and participation issues and their political implementation, which allowed immigration and naturalization to become subjects for political conflict, especially since the 1980s.

Following long migratory traditions, Italian labourers in particular immigrated to France in the late 1940s and early 1950s. From 1946 to 1962, their numbers increased from 450,000 to 630,000, though the 1931 maximum (810,000) was never reattained. The National Immigration Office (Office National d'Immigration, ONI), established in 1945, was planned to be responsible for recruiting and assigning foreign labourers and, at the same time, for taking measures to promote integration. At first, mostly temporary labour migration was considered, which included the recruitment of about 150,000 Spanish seasonal workers for agriculture. However, French immigration policies remained determined not only by considerations of labour market policies but also by those of population policy.[54] The overlapping of measures that aimed to promote temporary labour migration as well as permanent settlement with change of citizenship gave the impression that France's migration policies were sometimes inconsistent, selective or even racist.

France's immigration preferences were depicted in the hierarchy of nationality groups, the proportions of which were supposed to be in the ratio of 50:30:20 according to a 1945 plan that was never implemented. The first group included the Benelux countries, Switzerland, Scandinavia, Ireland, Britain, Germany and Canada. The second group were the countries of the northern Mediterranean, and the third group included Poles, Czechs, Slovaks and Yugoslavs. Greeks, Armenians and migrants from the Near East were undesirable, as were Jews from eastern Europe, who were considered difficult to assimilate.[55] The desired ratio remained illusory, since the preferred origins could not cover the demand. Moreover, Italian labourers, who predominated at first, increasingly went to Switzerland and Germany from the 1950s, owing to more attractive wage conditions there. Recruitment for labour from southern and south-eastern Europe and North Africa was therefore intensified in the 1960s by means of bilateral agreements (among others, with Spain, Portugal, Yugoslavia, Turkey and the former colonies of Morocco and Tunisia).

In the early 1960s, Spaniards became the main immigrant group in France, reaching a historic peak of 616,000 in 1968. They were soon outstripped by the rapidly growing number of Portuguese labour migrants in the mid-1960s and early 1970s, of whom 883,000 were registered in 1976. The number of Algerians, who had been guaranteed freedom of movement in the Evian accords (1962), climbed considerably despite restrictions from both sides in the late 1960s and early 1970s, finally just surpassing the number of Portuguese. The number rose from 350,000 in late 1961 to 884,000 in late 1975. The share of foreign labourers among the entire working population in France increased from about 6 per cent in 1960 to about 11 per cent in 1973. In some occupational areas it was far higher; in building and construction, for example, which was affected first by the economic upswing, the rate was already 11.7 per cent in 1954, rising above 15.2 per cent in 1962 and up to 35.6 per cent in 1975.

Spanish and Portuguese migrants usually entered France with a tourist visa, intending to 'legalize' their stay after having already begun work. Both countries of origin were dictatorships and very few people in Portugal were in possession of passports. Although there had been a French–Portuguese recruitment agreement since 1963, the Salazar (d. 1970) regime even banned women from emigrating and tried to sign up all young men to military service in an effort to avoid losing its colonies in a bloody colonial war. None the less, the Portuguese, who quickly became socially integrated, formed the largest European foreign population in France in the early 1980s.

Among immigrants from Portugal up to the end of the colonial wars or until the Carnation Revolution (1974) were not only men of military age but also a relatively high percentage of women. The ratio of women to men in the still young Portuguese migrant population in the mid-1970s was about one to five, thus corresponding to the historically older, and more established, Italian and Spanish immigrant populations. It was far higher than the corresponding ratios for Algerians (1:12), Tunisians and Moroccans (1:30), Poles (1:20) and Yugoslavs (1:40). The rate of employment among Portuguese women was more than 50 per cent, which was extraordinarily high especially as compared with Algerian women (18 per cent), who were limited in many ways owing to religious, cultural and family restrictions. Unmarried Portuguese women worked largely as maids, married women as cleaning ladies or *concièrges* (porters), thus in integration-promoting personal contact with families of the receiving society. This too distinguished them considerably from Algerian women, who – similar to Turkish women in Germany – worked primarily as semi- and unskilled industrial labourers.

The number of officially registered foreigners (not including Algerians) in France grew in 1955–65 from 1.6 million to 2.3 million; in the same time period, 305,000 people were naturalized and thus disappeared from the statistics on foreigners. In the boom years, immigration was beyond control: although the ONI had a monopoly on issuing immigration permits, migrants came more and more frequently without advance notice or had been requested through private means. Consequently, the practice of 'legalizing' irregular stays and work contracts after the fact, which was still under 50 per cent up to 1956, applied to 82 per cent (90 per cent among the Portuguese) of all labour migration in 1968. In order for the government to regain control of immigration and assignment of foreign labour, France considered the rotational model that was also discussed yet never implemented in Germany in connection with the recruitment of 'guestworkers'. At the same time, it was a matter of reducing dependence on the Spanish, Portuguese and Algerian labour pools and focusing on individual immigration of younger, unmarried workers instead of chain migrations with family reunification. This was the background to the recruitment agreements with Morocco and Tunisia (1963) and with Turkey and Yugoslavia (1965), as a result of which the number of Moroccans in France increased from 171,000 in 1970 to 493,000 in 1992, thus becoming the third-largest foreign population, ahead of Italians.

The loss of control of immigration and employment in the late 1960s and early 1970s and the increase in irregular employment situations ('*sans-papiers*') served to further limit the possibility of linking job services and working and living conditions to minimum social standards. This led to the expansion of *bidonvilles*, the scrap-metal-and-plank shantytown slums at the outskirts of major cities in the late 1960s and early 1970s. In Marseilles or Paris, for example, there were about 25,000 *bidonville* residents in 1970. The *bidonvilles* were destroyed in the early 1980s in the course of redevelopment measures, sometimes with the use of force, but the heavy regional and local concentration of immigrants or foreigners remained: in the mid-1980s, 60 per cent of all foreigners registered in France lived in the conurbations of Paris, Lyons and Marseilles. This concentration formed the core of the '*banlieue* problem', often depicted in dismal colours as the 'French variant of the ghetto problem' (Manfrass), in the suburban areas traditionally neglected in municipal politics. Irregular employment and extremely high unemployment intensified the tensions between nationals and especially North African immigrants, and also between different ethnocultural immigrant environments. Moreover, there was a large degree of deviant behaviour in lawless areas sometimes avoided by police. At the close of the century, the emergence of parallel social structures characterized some of these districts, in which open rioting and street fighting with police have occasionally occurred since the early 1980s.

The 1974 recruitment ban, preceded by the wave of violent anti-Algerian riots from summer 1973 until the end of the year, meant a move towards a change in policy, similar to the situation in Germany. On the one hand were the goals of limiting immigration and encouraging return. On the other were attempts to socially integrate foreigners living permanently in France. Because these were practical and not programmatic objectives, they faded entirely from public discussion, in contrast with restrictive measures. The ban on recruitment did not end immigration to France; it merely changed its nature. Henceforth, here too it was primarily marked by family reunification; but similar to immigration of refugees and asylum seekers, immigrants came increasingly from non-European regions: from 1978 to 1989, among the entire foreign population, only the number of Portuguese remained high with low naturalization rates; Italians and Spaniards dwindled in numbers, in part due to naturalization, in part due to repatriation, while figures for Turks and North Africans increased all the more.

Increasingly, 'migration' was understood 'as a threat to welfare'.[56] Growing demonization of the subject of migration led to tightened entry regulations, border controls and their dramatization in public and political discussion, stricter review of family reunifications (as of 1983), a visa requirement for most non-Europeans (as of 1986), and tightened sanctions against employers of illegal workers (1989). Instead of 'legalizing' irregular residences and jobs after the workers arrived, efforts were made in 1981–2 to resolve the situation through legislation by offering to legalize all foreigners who entered the country prior to 1981 with irregular work situations, but only about 130,000 took advantage of the offer.

The controversial issue of 'illegality' strained the immigration discussion all the more, as it was intensified by the pointed failure of President Giscard d'Estaing's efforts to encourage 35,000 Algerians each year to be repatriated through the 1979 return agreement with Algeria. Against this background, public discussion of immigration issues came increasingly under pressure and influence from the right wing; Patrick Weil has even described the Front National phenomenon as the defining element of French domestic policy of the 1980s.[57] In the increasingly Euro-racist public discussion of immigration issues, ever more clear-cut distinctions were made between supposedly 'good' (European) and 'bad' or 'problematic' (North African) immigrants. With increasing frequency from the early 1980s they became victims of racist attacks, which were being opposed by anti-racist organizations such as SOS Racisme and France Plus. In France too, however, the 'liberal paradox' (James Hollifield) condemned many restrictions to virtual ineffectiveness. In a residential population of 53.1 million in 1990, French statistics registered the population of *immigrés* (born abroad) holding French (1.3 million) or foreign citizenship at a total of 4.1 million people. In the mid-1990s, about 18 million in a total French population of 55 million had at least one foreign parent or grandparent.[58]

Statistics on foreigners remained relatively stable despite the fact that naturalizations constantly brought 'new French', since there was also a high number of 'new foreigners' owing to the continued heavy flow of family reunification (annually about 100,000). Citizenship was relatively easy to obtain, but it lost strength as a means of inclusion in the welfare state. Far more significant than the distinction between French and foreigners was the dividing line between citizens who were socially included and those who were not. This affected especially the Maghreb immigrant population, within which 'localism' became more important as a collective identification pattern than national identification, which offered no help in confronting unemployment and social discrimination. This development collided with the guiding principle of national identification, that is, naturalization as a means of access to inclusion and participation in the welfare state. Since the mid-1980s, therefore, demands have been made with growing pressure from the right wing to link acquisition of citizenship not only to length of stay or birth in the country but to social and intellectual achievements, especially 'earned affiliation' and a noticeable 'will to peaceful coexistence'.

Thus began the path to limiting the territorial principle and decomposing the republican elements in the citizenship law that led to the legal reform of July 1993. At the core of this reform, which was partly toned down after the change in government of 1997, was the elimination of automatic acquisition of citizenship by children born in the country whose parents were foreigners or immigrants born in the former colonies (with respect to Algeria, those who immigrated in 1963 or later). Instead of automatically being granted citizenship, these second-generation immigrants could opt for citizenship at age 16–20, though certain preconditions had to be satisfied, such as not having been imprisoned for more than six months. Corresponding somewhat to the regulations in Germany (until the limited territorial principle was introduced in 1999), obtaining citizenship in France was then seen more as a result of a completed process of integration and no longer primarily as an aid towards integration, as had been the case since the legislation of 1889.[59]

The migration issues in Germany and in France were comparable in terms of their conflict configurations, wherein the inclusion of migrants and the legitimacy of their structurally incorporated opportunities to participate in the welfare state were vociferously challenged. In Germany, migrants had almost no access to citizenship until naturalization was eased in 1990–1; there the political conflict centred around the scandal whipped up over foreigners' claims to welfare-state benefits, especially with respect to asylum seekers and other refugees denounced as 'economic refugees'. In contrast, naturalization rights were incorporated tacitly and beyond the political discourse on migration, until discussion on introducing the territorial principle and acceptance of dual citizenship began in 1999. In France as an old immigration country with a long tradition of naturalization, attention was drawn especially to the increased border controls and limits on options for obtaining citizenship, because, in contrast to Germany, immigration in France leads towards naturalization, which to that extent is the – *de facto* unequal – portal to participation in the welfare state. In Germany, on the other hand, it is the stepwise incorporation into the welfare system that ultimately opens the door to citizenship. Debates on citizenship in France therefore brought up in particular fears of economic competition threatening prosperity because of migration, in addition to annoyance at discovering the state's limited autonomy in granting citizenship and the related devaluation in the political understanding of the community as the '*Grande Nation*'.

Britain

The example of Britain fits only partially into the picture of the major labour migrations starting in the 1950s. Britain's economy covered its replacement and expansion labour needs especially through long-term migration traditions from the Republic of Ireland, for which immigration rights were guaranteed despite restrictions when it was separated from Great Britain in 1923. In 1945–59, about 350,000 Irish immigrated to Britain. In 1971, there were almost 1 million (957,873) Irish-born people in Britain, which at 2 per cent of the total population was the largest immigrant group. The second large pool of immigrant labour came from the Commonwealth, primarily those of Afro-Caribbean and Asian descent. In 1971, there were about 265,000 immigrants from the Caribbean, about 128,000 from Pakistan and about 241,000 from India/East Africa, when labour was only directly recruited in exceptional cases (such as London Transport in Barbados). A special group among post-colonial immigrants were those from the former colony of Cyprus (Greeks and Turks), whose numbers rose from about 10,000 in 1951 to about 73,000 in 1971. Except for the Irish, for a long time there were only far smaller immigrations from the rest of Europe. The next largest European immigrant group in 1971 were those of Italian descent (about 104,000), whose numbers remained relatively constant up to 1991, showing only a slight decrease (roughly 98,000).

Against this background, British migration policies were concerned primarily with either fostering or limiting not labour migration but immigration from the former colonies and the Commonwealth, which, as has been shown, were subject to ever tighter restrictions from the 1970s (see section 1). The mechanism used was to introduce a national citizenship that replaced Commonwealth membership, thereby acting, as in the other European countries, exclusively against all non-natives. This did not affect the free immigration from EC member states (nor did Britain's preferential treatment of nationals on the labour market), among which Germans became the second largest European immigrant group (about 216,000) by 1991, after the Irish.[60]

Despite differences in migratory patterns and legal, political and cultural positions, migration developments and policies in receiving countries in western Europe gradually became harmonized in the period from the immigration restrictions of the early 1970s to the late 1980s: immigration situations had developed everywhere; they became further stabilized through migratory networks, chain migrations and, after being restricted, through unstoppable family reunifications. This sometimes led to serious political confrontation around issues of acceptance and how to proceed. At the centre was the question of whether, and to what extent, host countries were domestically able to meet the social challenges in legal, social and cultural policy terms that were connected with their actual evolution into immigration countries, or whether they sought to oppose these development trends.

Differences in migration and integration policies evolved from countries' respective attitudes towards the tension between integrative and defensive trends. On the one hand were immigration restrictions (no longer valid within the sphere of EC freedom of movement) for foreign labourers, sometimes combined with efforts to encourage voluntary return and accompanied by tightened asylum regulations, which will be discussed below (see section 4). On the other hand were, in conjunction with continued family reunification, attempts to support integration of immigrant populations that had already become permanently settled. Endeavours both to limit immigration and to promote integration at a national level converged with efforts at the European level for supranational regulatory systems to guarantee social security for cross-border migrations within Europe and to limit and control undesirable immigration to Europe (see chapter 5, section 1). With that, the link between external defence and internal integration became more and more evident in the 1980s and, initially with a clear priority for external defence, would be decisive for the migration policies of 'Fortress Europe' in the 1990s.

Formal and informal immigration countries

Based on the type and extent of political and legal acceptance of the immigration processes actually underway, formal and informal immigration countries[61] can be distinguished that have gradually developed in Europe since the 1970s. Formal immigration countries can be viewed as those countries characterized as such through their self-definition, legislation, institutional structures and political practices. Informal immigration countries could be those which see themselves as receiving countries only for certain immigrant groups, such as foreign labourers and their families. However, they also tolerate a great deal of permanent residencies bordering on immigration situations, either in the form of relaxed naturalization procedures or special opportunities for participation, such as local voting rights for foreign denizens. Common ground and fluid boundaries, differences and contrasts can be illustrated using the examples of Sweden, the Netherlands and Switzerland.

Sweden

Sweden was the first to move in the direction of becoming a formal immigration country and had also progressed the furthest up to the mid-1980s. Immigration figures fluctuated considerably depending on employment opportunities, long remaining relatively low. In 1946–60, there was an annual average of about 10,000 immigrants; a peak was reached in 1969–70 with about 40,000 each year; the number then dropped to about 15,000 in 1971 (with about 18,000 return migrations). Immigration continued even after it was banned for foreign labour migrants in 1972, since the measure targeted only labour migrants from third countries outside of the Nordic labour market that was created in 1954 and granted freedom of movement for labour migrants of the member states (Denmark, Finland, Iceland, Norway, Sweden). The 1972 measure also failed to affect the immigration of refugees and asylum seekers, which was soon to increase rapidly.

The multicultural immigration and integration policies developed in Sweden were aimed at an immigrant population within which cultural differences covered just as broad a spectrum but were clearly less pronounced than in other European receiving countries. Up to the 1980s, immigration to Sweden came predominantly from Finland, initially 20 per cent of which in fact was from the Swedish-speaking north-eastern and southern minority regions, and only a small portion came from other countries, mostly from southern Europe. Labour migration from Finland was largely agricultural into the 1970s and served approximately the same function that labour migration from southern Europe, Turkey and Morocco did in countries of the EC. Generally, these migrants returned to Finland as the country became industrialized. Finnish labour migration to Sweden from 1946 to 1986 showed a remarkable gender ratio in immigration and repatriation: the share of women among all immigrants dominated substantially at the beginning and end of the period, and was consistently over 50 per cent. The female return migration rate, however, was clearly lower than the male, due to marriages and partnerships started in Sweden. Finnish labour migration was primarily 'betterment migration'; about 75 per cent of the migrants left their jobs in Finland for better opportunities in Sweden. Their migration took place between two economic spheres whose different developments had determined migratory movements but which were becoming increasingly similar in the 1980s.

Foreign labourers in Sweden were treated as immigrants (*invandrare*). Sweden's self-image as a multicultural country of immigration was based on the Immigration Act of 1975. Its guiding principles, established in 1969, were social equality of immigrants in the welfare state, 'partnership' with the Swedish majority population, promoted by the state as well as supported by immigrant associations, and the right to cultural self-determination. This involved an amendment to the Swedish constitution in 1976, which raised the protection and fostering of the cultural identity of ethnic, linguistic and religious minorities to a constitutional right. Correspondingly, the right of parents to request supplementary instruction in their mother tongue for their children was laid down in the 'home language' law of 1977, as a result of which more than 50 languages were taught in some schools in the Stockholm area in the early 1990s. Aids to integration, local voting rights for foreigners after three years and the option to be naturalized after five, active immigration and naturalization policies with corresponding institutions: all this led to the highest naturalization rate in western Europe (annually 5 per cent of the total foreign population).

The sensational Swedish model, which had been practised for a decade without major problems, was put under pressure from the mid-1980s as a result of rising immigration, especially by refugees and asylum seekers, under worsening economic conditions, including growing unemployment from the late 1980s in particular. From 1950 (*c.*200,000) to 1995 (*c.*936,000), Sweden's foreign-born population increased almost fivefold. The convergence of increasing immigration, economic recession and unemployment led here as well to internal political conflicts – accompanied by anti-immigrant rioting – which clearly reduced the consensus on issues of immigration policy. Demands to limit immigration as a prerequisite for integration became louder. Despite the modifications that were pushed through as a result, Sweden remained a multicultural immigration country with respect to its immigration and integration policies. One of two government reports commissioned in 1995 on refugee and immigration policies confirmed Sweden as having become a 'multicultural society' whose basic principles should continue to be social equality, cultural freedom of choice and partnership with the majority society.[62]

The Netherlands

Aspects of a multicultural type of informal immigration country were apparent early on in the Netherlands. Because of heavy colonial and post-colonial immigration, foreign labourers had not been recruited until the 1960s. For this reason, very few came from the regions of origin in southern Europe, originating instead largely from Turkey and Morocco. The share of Turks in the entire foreign population – including the resident foreign population from Europe and overseas – grew from 21.8 per cent in 1976 to 28.3 per cent in 1986; that of Moroccans grew from 12 per cent to 21.1 per cent. Family reunification increased after recruitment had been banned, thus hitting a period of economic recession and rising unemployment. Still, after a decade of improvising alien policies, the Netherlands was already beginning to show distinct features of an informal immigration country in the late 1970s. Contrary to ideas of introducing repatriation measures that had briefly been discussed, the government followed the assessments and recommendations of the Netherlands Scientific Council for Government Policy, which had confirmed in its 1979 report (Rinus Penninx, *Ethnic Minorities*) that the Netherlands had become a polyethnic and multicultural society as a result of irreversible immigration processes.

The report's recommendations were implemented pragmatically: immigrants were granted equality in terms of social law, and measures were taken to promote their political participation such as through local voting rights for foreigners, anti-discrimination policies, eased naturalization procedures, and national and local promotion of organized group interests. The white book (*Minderhedennota*) submitted in 1983 also encompassed minority policies (*Minderhedenbeleid*) intentionally oriented towards not only foreign labourers and their families but ethnic minorities in general. The traditionally pluralistic social system was underpinned by – highly denominational – 'pillars' with a high level of autonomy regarding schools, hospitals, media and political parties; minorities were incorporated as additional 'pillars'. Care services previously performed by welfare associations were transferred to the municipalities. Acceptance of the multicultural immigration situation was also apparent through symbolic actions such as leading politicians visiting religious and cultural immigrant centres.

All of this could not prevent the ethnosocially disproportionate distribution of job insecurity from becoming extreme. In 1987, 13 per cent of autochthonous Dutch were unemployed, 27 per cent of Surinamese, as much as 42 per cent of Moroccans, and 44 per cent of Turks. The implementation of minority policies under these circumstances became largely a list of measures opposing social discrimination of minorities at work, in school and in training; consequently, multicultural components became secondary to combating the firm establishment of a polyethnic subproletariat. Dutch political and social analysts argued that the flip side of accepting multicultural diversity with limited autonomy of organized group interests meant accepting the permanent 'minoritization' of immigrant groups in less privileged social situations. A fundamental improvement of integration options was finally offered by the Integration of Newcomers Act (WIN) of September 1998: proposals that had been developed in preceding years were made mandatory and greatly expanded. The law obliges all Dutch municipalities to offer state-subsidized integration programmes responding to the individual needs of the new immigrants as determined by an 'integration inquiry'; 'newcomers' have to participate in these programmes or risk having their social benefits cut or even being fined.[63]

Switzerland

A counter-image to the formal or informal acceptance of the immigration situation in Sweden and the Netherlands is offered by Switzerland. After an initially segregative and later integrative concept, Switzerland finally bowed to the pressure of xenophobic protests and tried to slow down the immigration trend that was emerging there too and push migration back into the framework of temporary and seasonal labour migration. The 'non-immigration immigration country' had received its labour migration up to 1960 from four main sources, primarily Italy, with which a recruitment agreement had already been signed in 1948, and to a lesser extent from Germany, Austria and France. After the Second World War, Switzerland went through the most massive economic growth in its history; this continued for almost 30 years and employment of foreigners rose steeply as a result. The share of foreigners, which once before – in 1914 – had grown to 15.4 per cent of the total population and triggered public discussion about 'overforeignization' (*Überfremdung*), reached a new historic peak of 16.7 per cent (1.1 million) in 1974. At the same time, the breakdown according to nationality shifted somewhat due to the emigration and return migration of a large part of the main immigrant group, the Italians. The proportion of Yugoslavs increased in 1975–91 from 3.4 per cent (34,300) to 14.5 per cent (172,700), that of Turks from 2.6 per cent (26,100) to 5.9 per cent (70,500). The proportion of Portuguese, which was only 1.2 per cent (10,900) in 1980, climbed to 8.5 per cent (101,600) by 1991.

   In discussions on the concepts of migration in 1948, 1963 and 1970, Switzerland was a much greater pioneer than most other receiving countries: its 1948 recruitment agreement with Italy marked the beginning of the Swiss rotation model with limited but renewable labour contracts for 'seasoneers' and 'year-stayers'. It included, in the interest of the national labour force, equal wage and working conditions but lacked any social components such as unemployment insurance and old-age and surviving dependants' pensions, as well as entitlement to changing place of work or even family reunification. Criticism came especially from Swiss employers because of the high operational costs of the strict rotation model and from the Italian government, whose foreign minister protested in 1961 in Switzerland against the miserable working and living conditions of Italian labourers, even calling upon them to resist.

This criticism, as well as the out-migration of Italian migrants in particular to other European countries, led Switzerland to open up and expand the rotation model in 1963 with options for integration that even included permanent residence status. After working for 18 months, migrants were offered the right to family reunification; after five years, they were offered free choice of workplace with yearly renewable work and residence permits; after an additional five years, permanent residence was permitted with complete equal status. Only political rights remained excluded, since they were tied to national or cantonal citizenship, which was traditionally difficult to obtain. The flip side of opportunities for integration was to be immigration restrictions and limitations on foreign employment within a company ('company ceilings').[64]

Massive protests began against foreign labourers' receiving equal rights in labour and social legislation as laid down in the second Italian agreement of 1963. Protests escalated into xenophobic movements and 'anti-overforeignization parties'. Instruments of direct democracy pressured the government; as early as 1964 there was a shower of bills demanding everything from a stricter reduction of immigration to forced expulsion of those immigrants who were already permanently settled. Whereas all related referenda had hitherto gone against the initiators, a new 'overforeignization initiative' threatened to pass in a referendum of 1970, which might have forced the government to take measures violating human and international rights. Alarmingly, the 'National Action against the Overforeignization of the People and the Fatherland' failed by only a whisker. Under this pressure a 'limitation decree' emerged in 1970; it remained the main instrument of control in migration policies in Switzerland into the 1990s. Among the subsequent innovations were general preferential treatment for nationals on the labour market and annual quotas for first-time residence authorization and all new immigrants, with strict authorization requirements. A central registry for foreigners was set up in 1972 to implement and control these measures.

Proposals for integration were explicitly mentioned in the limitation decree and even expanded in the area of national insurance legislation in 1972, 1976 and 1982, but the focus of public discussion remained limitation rather than integration. The number of foreigners declined under the influence of the migration policy control mechanisms that had been created even before the onset of the crisis in the mid-1970s.

While there was continued family reunification of resident foreigners and growing immigration of asylum seekers, protest movements died down and did not reappear until the late 1980s. In Switzerland, as elsewhere, there was consequently a long-term shift to pragmatic acceptance of the immigration situation. However, politics and public discussion in the 1970s and 1980s were dominated by a defensive stance, that is, to limit foreign employment – in demonstrative self-interest – to replacement, expansion and buffer functions.

Other European countries

The positions of the other receiving countries in Europe on issues of immigration and integration[65] can be charted among the concepts of Sweden, the Netherlands and Switzerland. In general practice, on the one hand, the proximity to informal immigration countries grew with strict efforts for restrictive immigration controls. On the other hand, populist concessions to xenophobic discourses and movements covered up the practice of integration, with 'foreigner' and 'alien' policies symbolizing a readiness to take defensive action, and paralysed the development of comprehensive and integral immigration and integration concepts. Finally, in the European context, Austria broke new ground in immigration legislation with its residence law of 1992, which was not oriented towards ethnonational criteria, as is the case with German law. Instead, based on US and Canadian models, it set upper limits of gross immigration, incorporating the demographic, economic development of the receiving country and the number of recognized refugees. After more than five years' residency, prospects for permanent residence status open up.[66]

Behind the controversies over acceptance of and ways of structuring the immigration situation, there were also basic questions of traditional national, social and cultural identity.[67] Discourse on foreignness ranged from multicultural to assimilationist to Euro-racist positions. Ideas on the coming together of majority and immigrant minorities spanned from charitable social 'care and supervision' to civil partnership.

Since the early 1970s, British policies relating to minorities, with their group-oriented integrative concepts, increasingly took on the characteristics of a 'race relations industry'. Although 'ethnic' and 'race relations' were indeed understood as social and socio-political descriptive and structural concepts, the policies' racist connotations targeted only the non-white immigrant society from the New Commonwealth.[68] In France, the *république une et indivisible*, on the other hand, the dominant view was 'integration' of individuals by rejecting group rights and group organizations. Foreigners were even barred from forming associ-

ations, even in the period of leftwing-oriented immigration and integration policies in 1981–93. Within the concept of 'integration', minority
claims to a 'cultural identity', especially in school instruction, were
recognized, albeit only within the limits of republican laicism. This is
why the battle over headscarves worn by Muslim schoolgirls in 1989
took on the dimensions of an episodic crisis of cultures.[69]

In West Germany there was extraparliamentary discussion in the
1980s on the acceptance of the immigration situation, especially among
trade unions, charitable associations, churches, officials for foreigner and
refugee interests (*Ausländerbeauftragte*) and concerned scholars. The
conservative Christian-liberal federal government demonstratively pre-
tended not to hear. In the ethnonational political semantics of official
government declarations in the immigration country against its will,
what dominated instead was talk of top-down 'social integration' for
'foreign co-citizens' (*ausländische Mitbürger*) who in reality remained
politically uninvolved non-citizens, regarding local voting rights for
example, and who were not viewed as permanent immigrants. Charitable
associations, beyond national and local agencies, were responsible for
them, as well as relatively uninfluential advisory councils for foreigners
(*Ausländerbeiräte*) and (German) officials for foreigner and refugee interests. However, residential, labour and social law as well as administrative
practices managed and pragmatically carried out the everyday routine of
what was constantly denied in political semantics: a genuine immigration
process.[70]

In the receiving countries of labour migrations in northern Europe
west of the Iron Curtain, the normative power of genuine evolution
into immigration countries in the Cold War era therefore asserted itself,
not only in the practices of the welfare state but also in its political
acceptance. The total picture was characterized by different developments, both forward-looking and, in contrast, apparently delayed. Progressive structural concepts in countries such as Sweden, the Netherlands
and Switzerland (1963), on the one hand, had to be limited to some
extent or their defensive components tightened under the pressure of
domestic policy controversies that played on popular prejudice concerning the migration issue. In countries such as West Germany, on the other
hand, the pragmatic constitutional welfare-state administration of
the immigration situation, with the stubborn rhetoric of the 'non-
immigration country' taboo, was well in advance of its socio-political
acceptance or even conceptual form. For the receiving countries in north-
western Europe, the 1980s was a decade of dichotomous, antinomic
concept formation to describe social transitions that were not, or only
reluctantly, accepted domestically, from 'labour-importing countries'
(Imre Ferenczi) to immigration countries. This was true for Germany,

for example, as regards talk of a 'non-declared immigration country' (Dietrich Thränhardt), or of 'immigration in the non-immigration country' (Hedwig Rudolph), or of the 'immigration country against its will' with 'native foreigners' (*einheimische Ausländer*) or 'Germans with a foreign passport' (Klaus J. Bade), or of 'foreign natives' (*ausländische Inländer*, Daniel Cohn-Bendit and Thomas Schmid), and as regards Switzerland for its aforementioned classification as a 'non-immigration immigration country' (Hans-Joachim Hoffmann-Nowotny).[71] Related discussions on immigration and integration issues, apart from the public outrage whipped up over the issue of 'illegal immigration', did not develop in the Euro-Mediterranean zone until the 1990s.

All in all, state migration and integration policies in the countries of the European Union have been put under increasing pressure since the late 1980s as regards the functions and scope of action of nation-states, externally, from above, from below and internally: externally through the process of globalization; from above through the delegation of national functions to the supranational European level (see chapter 5, section 1); from below through processes of regionalization and even 'localism'; and internally in two ways; first, through the above-noted diminishing selectivity of citizenship with respect to claims for social participation, and second, through the formation of transnational and transcultural identities. This development was certainly promoted as interest in changing citizenship declined because, as has been shown, most basic economic and social rights are achievable even without a new passport after residing in the country a sufficiently long period of time and acquiring the corresponding permanent residential status. But this development also seems to ensue from the fact that national welfare states have forfeited some of their political power to regulate and, for immigrants, they thus lose their central status as a reference point and orienting framework.[72]

4　Asylum and Refugee Migrations

After the major labour migrations were cut off by the recruitment bans and immigration restrictions of the early to mid-1970s, there were basically three types of transnational migration to and within Europe – apart from elite, training and betterment migrations and labour migration between EC countries, which are not affected by restrictions. The first included movements of family reunification and return migration, which tended to be in opposite directions. Family reunification from countries that entered the major movement of labour migration relatively late, such as Turkey, was greater and lasted longer than that from southern Europe, where it was outweighed in the long term by return migration, especially in Greece. A second form included regular in-migrations ('tourists') largely by people of non-European descent who entered into irregular employment, especially in southern Europe but to some extent also in France, with a rising percentage from the Afro-Mediterranean zone. A third form of migration was that of asylum seekers from the 'Third World' and later, in increasing numbers, from eastern Europe. Their destinations were mostly in central, western and northern Europe, especially Germany, with its right to asylum that was long the most liberal in Europe. As Europe shielded itself off more and more, applying for asylum was used by many as apparently the only immigration option still open, sometimes standing in contrast to the many applications motivated by true political persecution, even in the sense of the ever-tighter stipulations of European asylum law, but often also overlapping with such motivations.

In public and political discussion on migration in the 1980s, preoccupation with the immigrant population that emerged from labour migrations in central, western and northern Europe receded behind the subject of 'asylum'. At the same time, the subject of 'illegality' moved to the fore in the Euro-Mediterranean zone, whereas it did not become a focus of discussion in central, western and northern Europe until the 1990s. In southern Europe, migration for purposes of asylum played only a minor role up to the late 1980s. Here the regular immigration for irregular employment noted in section 2 above was predominant. The following overview therefore centres on immigration by asylum seekers and other refugees in central, western and northern Europe with special consideration given to Germany, which was most affected; in closing we shall also look at developments in the area of asylum in southern Europe.

The divide between the north and south also applied to asylum issues for the two different immigration axes in both major regions. Until the end of the Cold War, northern Europe was at first affected primarily by continental east–west migrations and later increasingly by intercontinental south–north migrations of asylum seekers. The south was mostly affected by intercontinental south–north migrations until after the end of the Cold War, when continental east–south–north and intercontinental south–east–north migrations also became significant (see chapter 5, section 4). In France, Britain, Belgium and the Netherlands, immigration of African and Asian asylum seekers came to the fore, following the path of established migratory traditions. East–west migrations dominated at first in (West) Germany, Austria and Switzerland for geographical reasons. Germany, which in absolute numbers was the most significant immigration country for asylum seekers, was the destination of most African and Asian asylum seekers.[73]

Several factors were responsible for the different immigration profiles of asylum and refugee migrations in central, western and northern Europe: (1) geographical proximity between home and destination regions, relativized through global networks of transportation systems, apart from the separating impact of the Iron Curtain; (2) economic, political and cultural connections and linguistic bridges from colonial history; (3) migratory traditions created through chain migrations and networks that emerged in the destination regions, stemming from colonial, post-colonial, 'ethnic' migrations and labour migrations, which continued to have an impact through family reunification even after chain migrations were restricted.

A fourth factor was the different economic and social attractive forces of individual host countries. These were often overestimated as an independent determining factor, however, which led to dubious attempts to reduce the supposed attractiveness of admission conditions through deterrent measures, at the expense of the asylum seekers and refugees taken in. In reality, the effectiveness of these attractive forces was essentially dependent on the transfer of information through migratory networks and was consistently obstructed by a fifth factor, the asylum policies and legal practices of the host countries. These had varied degrees of trenchancy, were often changing and sometimes set up deliberately as a deterrent, that is, to break down 'pull' factors. This produced the situation that the economic and social conditions of a destination country that might have attracted asylum seekers were made accessible to them only partially, temporarily or even not at all, such as in Germany, owing to restrictions on freedom of movement, bans on employment, accommodation in mass lodgings with communal meals, and so on. Such information also made its way back to the home regions through migratory networks and could lead to a change in the direction of asylum migration, which was described in the disparaging jargon of European political asylum authorities as 'asylum tourism' or 'asylum shopping'. This is why migratory networks as well as asylum chain migrations must be viewed as important determinant forces in migratory events.

From the late 1970s the annual number of asylum seekers in Europe rose substantially, passing the 100,000 mark for the first time in 1980 and exceeding 150,000 by the end of that year. Looking back from 1992 (more than 690,000 petitions for asylum), this might not seem very dramatic; however, at the time it was indeed spectacular, less so in Europe in general than in West Germany, where more than 100,000 asylum seekers arrived in 1980 alone. The figures for 1980 were politically emotionalized and made to seem scandalous against the background of the previous years. In the 1970s, the annual number of petitions for asylum in Europe was initially rather low. It quickly rose to about

77,000 in 1979 and then abruptly to almost double that figure in 1980. This was largely due to the crisis in Poland and the military seizure of power in Turkey, whereby Polish and Turkish asylum seekers were in part already living in the west at the time and filed their petitions from there. By 1983 (73,700), the number of petitions declined to around the 1979 level, but then quickly rose again in the second half of the decade, reaching almost 430,000 by the decade's end, a level that had not been reached since the end of the post-war migrations. Most refugees and asylum seekers in Europe to the mid-1970s came from eastern Europe; up to the second half of the 1980s, more came from the 'Third World'; and since the end of the Cold War most came again from eastern and south-eastern Europe.

The 1951 Geneva Convention signed by all countries of western Europe was concerned primarily with the protection of refugees from eastern Europe who could not or did not wish to return to their home countries following the Second World War. The supplementary Protocol of 1967 removed the geographical and time restrictions of the 1951 document. Since then a refugee is defined as a person who 'owing to well-founded fears of being persecuted for reasons of race, religion, nationality, membership of a particular social group or political opinion, is outside the country of his nationality and is unable, or owing to such fear, is unwilling to avail himself of the protection of that country or who, not having a nationality and being outside the country of his former habitual residence as a result of such events, is unable or, owing to such fear, is unwilling to return to it'.[74]

In practice little remains of this precept of humanitarian protection. In place of long-standing, almost unlimited acceptance came distanced reserve in the 1980s, including towards refugees from the 'eastern bloc', and extremely limited willingness to admit refugees from the 'Third World'. This unwillingness was quickly transformed into national strategies, which initially varied from country to country, of specific defensiveness towards refugees. Behind such strategies was the public and political demonization of the asylum issue, growing to different extents throughout Europe. This had less to do with the reasons for people to seek refuge having changed since the Geneva Convention than with collectively suspected abuse by asylum seekers. The main, if not sole, reason for this change in sentiment was the substantial rise in immigration since the late 1970s. In contrast to the relatively smooth integration of the predominantly well-qualified refugees from the 'eastern bloc' who had come in the preceding long period of economic growth, these asylum seekers came at a time when unemployment was high and on the rise, putting pressure on the social budget and making refugees appear as nothing more than extra boarders. The costs associated with admitting asylum seekers, which in 1989–90 amounted to about 4,000 million DM annually in West Germany, played a central role in the populist anti-asylum campaign that developed especially during election campaigns. Unemployed nationals, employed foreigners and foreign asylum seekers requiring assistance were set against each other in flawed equations, in which the subject of 'asylum' pushed farther and farther ahead of the subject of 'foreigners'. The appeal of this populist and demagogic rationale consequently seemed irresistible to moderate parties as well, because unemployed voters appeared more important politically than asylum-seeking refugees.

Material burdens connected with admitting large numbers of refugees and asylum seekers had long been politically and ideologically relativized. Even in the years following the Second World War, huge numbers of refugees had been reckoned with, especially since mass refugee movements were part of everyday experience at that time. The same applied for the discussion on the soon-famous right to asylum in West Germany's Basic Law of 1949, which comprised only four words in German: '*Politisch Verfolgte genießen Asylrecht*', 'Persons persecuted on political grounds shall have the right of asylum'. It did not say that the state had the right to grant asylum, as in other countries' constitutions. On the contrary, it guaranteed those who were politically persecuted legal entitlement to asylum, that is, to be secured refuge until a review of their petition was completed. This was the response of West German post-war policies to the experience regarding the admission – or non-admission – of victims of Nazi persecution who sought asylum abroad from 1933 to 1945. In the constitutional debate on the wording of this basic right to asylum, some members of the parliamentary council warned in 1948–9 of mass refugee movements. In this context, 'economic refugees' (then Germans from the Soviet occupation zone) were mentioned for the first time. Nevertheless, any and all restrictions on the German right to asylum were deliberately excluded.[75]

But these were European refugees during the Cold War. After the suppression of the Hungarian revolt in 1956, around 194,000 people were able to leave their country, mostly across the Hungarian–Austrian border until it was again closed by the Kádár regime, with the help of Soviet troops. After the Prague Spring was crushed beneath the tanks of the 'fraternal assistance' of the Warsaw Pact, about 170,000 Czechs and Slovaks fled to western Europe in 1968–9.[76] Both refugee movements were welcomed with respect for their political heroism and with sympathy that was reminiscent of the acceptance of Polish revolutionaries in the German Confederation and in nineteenth-century France.

Until the construction of the Berlin Wall in 1961, mass emigrations millions strong from East to West Germany were received with an equally warm welcome. Theirs was viewed as politically motivated 'flight from the Communist sphere of control', although in this case particularly there was a great deal of overlap in political, economic and social motives: here too there were many victims of political persecution. But economic and social disadvantages also played a role in decisions to emigrate, for example because of insufficient willingness to adapt politically or even because of the 'wrong' social background or 'class situation'. Furthermore, the attraction of the 'economic miracle' in the west was just as strong a motivating factor. In such cases, despite any possible political background, the configuration of motives for leaving would never have led to their recognition as politically persecuted persons according to the practices of asylum law as applied to refugees who were not from the 'eastern bloc' or even from the 'Third World'. But the axiomatic Cold War configuration functioned well: refugees from East Germany, the People's Republic of Poland, the Soviet Union and Hungary, and even North Vietnam and Tibet annexed by China were welcomed with open arms in the west, especially in West Germany, Switzerland, France and Sweden.[77]

The situation changed after the 1970s. The 250,000 or so Poles who had fled to the west in the early 1980s to escape the threat of Soviet intervention (Brezhnev doctrine), martial law (December 1981–December 1982) and political oppression were no longer viewed across the board as political refugees, nor were they warmly received as such. Germany retained its visa requirement for Poles; Austria even reinstituted it in 1981. The scepticism that grew along with the numbers of refugees and asylum seekers consolidated into an aggressive mistrust when the number of asylum seekers from the 'Third World' rose significantly from 1980 and then increased even more steeply starting in 1985,[78] because this development collided with the Eurocentric concept of refugees that had been marked by one-dimensional east–west notions and the European background of the Cold War. In contrast to the east–west refugees, 'Third World' refugees arriving in large numbers were immediately placed in the harsh light of prohibitive doubt as to whether they were 'genuine' refugees, that is, politically persecuted refugees rather than 'simply' 'economic refugees'.

The costs connected with granting asylum to large numbers of people were soon generally made the subject of biased agitation – initially with the exception of very few countries, such as Sweden – and new provisions emerged, sometimes disguised as cultural, sometimes openly Euro-racist. Racist defensive arguments surfaced that were fomented by ethnic visibility in countries without a colonial history, or whose colonial history had ended long ago. These scarcely differed from those in the former colonial countries, except that these discursive patterns had emerged much earlier there. Moreover, nightmare visions gained momentum through ethnonational and extreme rightwing currents and were used successfully in election campaigns[79] against social democratic governments by populist conservative parties in Britain as well as in France and Germany. They were greedily taken up by the yellow press and were obviously accepted in broad circles. Chief among them was the warning of Europe's decline in the 'floods' of new 'migrations of nations'.[80] This warning was doubly absurd, since refugee migrations increased worldwide yet barely touched Europe; moreover, the historical 'migrations of nations' was a long, polymorphous migratory process and not a human storm tide. Of special importance in this context is the equally unrealistic idea of a mass invasion of 'poverty refugees' from the misery of the 'Third World' and eastern Europe.[81]

In the late 1970s and especially in the 1980s, largely uncoordinated trends towards defensive 'asylum policies' grew all the more in the European countries affected most by the immigration of asylum-seeking refugees. They took the form of restrictive changes in legislation, regulations and procedures. After Europe had been closed off at national levels three times – against post-colonial chain migrants, against European and non-European labour migrants and against asylum-seeking refugees from the 'Third World' – access to Europe consequently shifted increasingly from the 'main gates' to the 'side gates' and 'back doors', often with fluid transitions. Would-be immigrants who had no chance of admission within the scope of family reunification tried to find a way as an asylum seeker (such as Kurds from Turkey). Others entered as tourists or to visit family, overstayed their entry permits and started irregular employment in the informal sector of the labour market, protected to some extent in their everyday routine through networks of family, acquaintances and compatriots.

Slowly at first in the 1980s, and then at a faster pace with the systematic closing off of 'Fortress Europe' at a supranational level in the 1990s, there came the group of illegal immigrants in the strict sense, under the direction of what soon became internationally organized human smuggling. The irregular employment of overstayers and 'sans-papiers' in the 1980s, as has been shown, did not generally have the character of an illegal attempt to circumvent immigration barriers; also, it was very much a 'market-oriented' response to changes in the supply and demand situation at the lower levels of the informal labour market of European receiving countries. By the late 1980s, however, parallel to asylum-seeking 'economic refugees', 'illegal immigrants' appeared as a new 'enemy'.

In an overview of the distribution of a total of about 1.7 million asylum seekers in certain countries of Europe from 1983 to 1990, in absolute figures Germany clearly held pride of place (703,318), followed by France (277,474), Sweden (141,864) and Austria (100,330). All other countries remained decidedly below the 100,000 threshold: Britain (86,972), the Netherlands (72,161), Belgium (51,250), Denmark (40,371), Italy (37,510), Norway (27,661) and Spain (26,840). Britain was well under the EC average for petitions for asylum, while Germany was always above the average. If absolute numbers for 1985 are compared, Germany had almost nine times and France almost five times as many asylum seekers as the United Kingdom.[82] Since these statistics are very complex, only limited comparisons can be drawn. A very different picture emerges if the absolute figures are compared to the population of the host countries. Sweden and Switzerland took in the highest percentage of asylum seekers relative to their total population. In 1985, there was one asylum seeker to 567 residents in Sweden (296 in 1995); in Switzerland the ratio was 1:666 (188 in 1990). In 1985 Germany was next with a ratio of 1:827 (413 in 1990) and Austria with 1:1,128 (342 in 1990). In such a comparison of asylum seekers to total population for 1985 and 1990, France (1,916 and 1,016 residents per asylum seeker, respectively), Belgium (1,860/768) and the Netherlands (2,550/708) held an intermediate position. Some European countries took in very few asylum seekers relative to their population, such as Italy (10,481/ 12,073), Spain (16,732/4,520) and Portugal (100,143/131,639). Britain (9,222/1,489) and Greece (7,107/1,632) moved from a very low position in a European comparison for 1985 to an intermediate one for 1990.[83]

The findings are again very different if the number of recognized petitions are compared. In 1988 there was an acceptance rate of 8.6 per cent of all petitions for asylum in West Germany; in Britain the rate was 23 per cent, France 35 per cent, Belgium 21 per cent; and in the Netherlands only 7 per cent of all asylum seekers were granted asylum. In 1989 and 1990, the figures dropped in Germany to 6 per cent and 5 per cent, respectively; in Belgium, to 14 per cent and 6 per cent. In Britain (32 per cent and 22 per cent, respectively), however, the rates did not dive until 1991 (9 per cent); in 1992 the rate dropped to only 3 per cent. In every country that granted asylum, there were considerable fluctuations in acceptance rates depending on country of origin.[84]

The following overview is based on developments in West Germany, since that is where by far the largest number of asylum seekers arrived, starting in the late 1970s. Furthermore, the transition from acceptance of refugees to rejection of asylum seekers was particularly pronounced in the country on the frontline of the Cold War.

West Germany

In West Germany[85] the number of petitions for asylum in the 1950s and 1960s was relatively low, apart from the refugee movements after the suppression of the uprisings in Hungary and Poland in 1956 and the Prague Spring in 1968. Until the early 1970s, most asylum seekers were refugees from the 'eastern bloc'. Their acceptance was considered a humanitarian mission and also served the political and ideological legitimizing function noted above. East–west refugees were welcome 'deserters' who voted with their feet in the contest between systems. The flip side of the axiomatic acceptance of east–west refugees in the Cold War was the exclusion of socialist refugees persecuted in the west. This became obvious in West Germany in 1973, the year of the recruitment ban, which was also the year of the military coup against socialism in Chile. Considerations by the social democrat–liberal coalition of the federal government to take in socialist refugees from Chile gave rise to a campaign led by the conservative CDU/CSU opposition against the Chileans, whom they denounced as Communist terrorists. About 2,000 were taken in by East Germany where they received special integration support, like refugees from the Spanish and Greek civil wars before them.[86]

Ever since this campaign against Chilean refugees, political suspicion of refugees became part and parcel of all West German discourse on asylum. On top of this, especially regarding refugees from the 'Third World', there was a growing presumption that refuge was sought under false pretences and that the true reasons were in fact not political but economic and social. Refugees and asylum seekers were systematically disparaged politically and polemically through the pejorative and defamatory German term *Asylanten*. The coining and systematic use of this term, also picked up by the media, turned it into a xenophobic leitmotif running through the political debate. At the same time, rising unemployment aggravated social fears. Labour market competition phobias against refugees were unfounded, since asylum seekers were prohibited from working – as of 1987 for five years, that is, generally encompassing the entire asylum proceedings. Even after the ban was lifted in 1991, nationals still received definite preferential treatment on the labour market. Yet fears and xenophobic aggression continued to increase. They were kept alive, or awakened, through political campaigns against 'bogus asylum seekers' (*Scheinasylanten*), 'asylum spongers' (*Asylschmarotzer*) and 'economic refugees', especially from the 'Third World'. These would flare up again and again, fanned especially during election campaigns and supported by segments of the media.

In the 1970s, a decisive turning point occurred in developments in Germany's right to asylum. Defensive and restrictive, the change eroded the constitutional principle that 'Persons persecuted on political grounds shall have the right of asylum'. The central concept of 'political persecution' was progressively narrowed down through 'anti-asylum jurisprudence' (Reinhard Marx); in 1977 it was shifted from the reasons the person was seeking refuge, that is, the experienced or feared persecution, to the reasons the persecuting country committed the persecution. For example, torture as punishment for non-violently claiming banned basic democratic rights in a country that routinely used torture as a punishment or interrogation technique was no longer recognized as 'political' persecution and thus no longer sufficient grounds for asylum in the Federal Republic of Germany.[87]

In 1973, when recruitment was stopped, only 4,792 petitions for asylum for 5,595 people had been filed. The number of petitions doubled the following year, but then remained relatively constant until 1976 (8,854 petitions for 11,125 people). From the late 1970s, the statistical curve of asylum seekers in West Germany climbed steeply from 28,223 petitions for 33,136 people in 1978 and 41,953 petitions for 51,493 people in 1979 to the peak of 92,918 petitions for 107,818 people in the election year of 1980. That corresponded to almost two-thirds of all asylum petitions filed in Europe that year (roughly 150,000). West Germany furthermore continued to be the country where by far the most asylum petitions were filed in Europe.[88]

The influx of refugees in the late 1970s no longer came predominantly from the 'eastern bloc' countries but from the 'Third World' and fluctuated according to changes in the crisis situations there. This was evidence of the fact that immigration of refugees to Germany was not one-sided, induced only by the attractive economic force of the main European destination country, but that the impetus came largely from problems in the country of origin. For this reason, the battle that would soon ignite in West Germany to fight 'economic refugees' by lowering the 'flight incentives' was questionable from the outset in its biased approach. Moreover, worsening the living conditions for asylum seekers as a supposed deterrent usually hit the wrong people, namely, the 'genuine' refugees. Genuinely fraudulent asylum seekers, human traffickers and smugglers, on the other hand, could scarcely be discouraged by such manoeuvres.

The scandalous accusations of 'asylum abuse' and demands to 'speed up asylum proceedings' or for 'consistent deportation' of rejected asylum seekers became central election campaign topics against a background of economic recession, rising unemployment, discovery of the actual immigration situation behind the 'guestworker' issue and the annual increase in asylum petitions beyond the magic threshold of 100,000 in 1980. Once this atmosphere was created, it continued, and arguments became frozen into stereotypes. Even when the number of petitions for asylum dropped dramatically in the early 1980s, politicians continued to talk of the 'continuing flood of bogus asylum seekers and economic refugees'.[89]

The number of asylum petitions dropped off in the early 1980s (to 16,335 petitions for 19,737 people in 1983), to a large extent because of the defensive measures against 'poverty refugees' from the 'Third World' that were passed by the federal government in June 1980. These were intensified by the introduction of special controls for a number of major countries of origin. 'Asylum policies' became more and more an expression of efforts to hinder entry to Germany by people who were 'suspected' of wanting to file petitions for asylum. After politics discovered the power of chain migrations and migratory networks in promoting migration, there were increased attempts in the 1980s to slow down the transition from refugee migrations to chain migrations from certain countries through tightened restrictions in a manner reminiscent of epidemic control. Instead of the noble and heroic, albeit fictional, political refugee, the stereotype emerged of the 'bogus asylum seeker' and 'asylum defrauder', viewed on all sides with suspicion. However, because asylum proceedings were geared towards the ideal of the political refugee, refugees were in fact forced to tell white lies in order to fit the prescribed image of the individual victim of political persecution by the state.

In the mid-1980s, the number of asylum seekers in West Germany started rising again rapidly and in 1986 there were 67,429 petitions filed for 99,669 people. The background to this steep rise in 1986 was the persecution of the Tamil minority in Sri Lanka and the general increase in crises and civil war-like conditions in many 'Third World' countries. In addition, human smugglers were becoming increasingly active through the gateway of Schönefeld airport in East Berlin and there were more Turkish asylum seekers hoping to circumvent the guidelines for family reunification. In a game of cat and mouse against asylum migration, the curve of asylum petitions was pushed back down in 1987 by defensive control measures. These ranged from blocking entry via East Germany and East Berlin through the introduction of a visa in October 1986 to an amendment to the asylum law in January 1987 that brought, among other measures, restrictive visa requirements for travellers from nine major African and Asian countries of origin of asylum seekers.

After immigration by asylum seekers was cut off through various measures of differing effectiveness in the course of the 1980s, it temporarily slipped out of control in the late 1980s. The curve of asylum seekers again passed the 100,000 mark in 1988, climbing in 1989, the year of European revolutions, to about 120,000 and then to 190,000 in 1990. The number continued to skyrocket; in 1991 it reached almost 260,000, and in 1992, almost 440,000. This post-Cold War line of development was to lead to devastating domestic policy conflicts and xenophobic excesses, culminating in the 1993 constitutional amendment ('the asylum compromise') that marked the end of the liberal form of German asylum law that had been laid down in 1949 (see chapter 5, section 1).

Other European countries

Other countries of immigration in central, western and northern Europe were also affected, albeit to a far lesser degree, by the increase in asylum migration since the immigration restrictions of the early to mid-1970s.[90] Sweden ranked third after West Germany and France among European receiving countries: while the number of petitions increased almost six-fold from 1982 (2,500) to 1985 (14,450) and then doubled again by 1989 (30,350), most asylum seekers came from the 'Third World', parallel to a sharply rising number of chain migrations. Hence, the number of Chileans in Sweden almost doubled from 1982 (8,400) to 1989 (19,100); that of Iranians increased almost tenfold, from 3,600 to 35,100. Refugees also came from Lebanon and Turkey.

All major European countries that admitted asylum seekers attempted in the 1980s to stem the growing immigration, and in particular the noticeably rising chain migrations, of refugees and asylum seekers by tightening the stipulations of asylum law and occasionally through deterring measures. As noted earlier, the attractive pull of the destination countries was viewed one-sidedly as the determining criterion for migration. The subject of asylum had been increasingly politicized since the late 1970s, especially for election campaign purposes, which led to a narrowing down of political options under the pressure of an agitated public, sometimes mobilized through demagogic means. The demonization of asylum issues in politics and the press, the criminalization of asylum seekers ('asylum defrauders', 'drug dealers') and the denunciation of opponents of restrictive asylum concepts, on the one hand, interacted with the rise in currents opposing asylum, foreigners and ultimately anything unfamiliar, on the other, which exerted their own pressure for political action or were used as a means to that end.

The restrictions and defence mechanisms prompted by such a background were oriented towards the nation-state. They remained uncoordinated and were largely characterized by a redistribution of burdens at the expense of neighbouring countries which, in turn, introduced their own defence mechanisms to redirect or pass on these burdens. This set in motion a spiral of chain reactions and mutual coercion. Restrictions in Germany, the main receiving country, had serious consequences for neighbouring countries, pushing up the number of asylum seekers in France and Switzerland in the 1980s, and in the Netherlands and Belgium in the early 1990s.

However, some opposite effects also emerged. Behind the sharp drop in the high asylum-seeker statistics in Switzerland from 1991 (41,600) to

1992 (18,000) was the safe-country doctrine. Switzerland was the first country in Europe to pronounce such a doctrine. In October 1990, the Swiss council of ministers had simply declared a number of main countries of origin of asylum seekers to be 'safe countries': Hungary, the Soviet Union, Poland and, a short time later, Bulgaria, Algeria and India. In November 1991, Angola and Romania (affecting Roma asylum seekers) were added to the list. Citizens of these countries no longer had any chance of being granted asylum in Switzerland. The aftermath of this declaration significantly affected Germany, where a total of 73,800 Romanian citizens, mostly members of the Roma minority, applied for asylum in 1993 (in contrast to only 200 in Switzerland). Parallel developments in Austria brought similar consequences for Germany, where a partly hysterical and partly demagogic discourse on asylum had paralysed the political ability to act. A new asylum law was introduced in Austria in 1991 centred on the 'first country of asylum' clause, which was used to exclude petitioners from eastern Europe. In 1993, only 300 asylum seekers from Romania went to Austria (73,800 to Germany) and only 100 from Bulgaria (22,600 to Germany), while the total number of petitions filed in 1991–3 in Austria went down from 27,300 to 4,700 (whereas in Germany it rose from 166,514 petitions for 256,112 people to 231,889 petitions for 322,599 people). Bernhard Santel aptly described this way of resolving problems through redirection as the 'logic of a negatively competing policy' according to 'Saint Florian's principle' (i.e., 'Spare my house, burn another').[91] However, before Germany's 1993 asylum law reform, the same applied even within the main European receiving country, where different implementations of restrictive regulations in the individual federal states could lead to internal 'asylum flight' from, for example, Bavaria to North Rhine-Westphalia.[92]

The 'first country of asylum' clause, which was increasingly included in European asylum law regulations in the 1980s, could turn asylum seekers into 'refugees in orbit' if they were sent back to a first country of asylum which then refused to readmit them. This *sacro egoismo* in nation-state asylum policies reached its hitherto greatest expansion – and limitation, with respect to the 'refugees in orbit' – in European guise in the EC-wide concept of the first country of asylum as laid down in the Schengen agreement (Schengen II) and in the Dublin Convention of 1990. This concept was soon extended to central and eastern European countries through corresponding bilateral treaties. It was intended to prevent multiple petitioning; without having had their petitions dealt with, asylum seekers could be sent back to countries in which they had already filed, or might have filed, a petition. This was actually the geopolitical logic – absurd in a Europe that is growing together – of each country having to bear the responsibility of dealing with migratory events arising due to its geographical location.[93]

Asylum migration in the Euro-Mediterranean zone, in contrast to northern Europe, long remained a secondary problem. This was largely owing to the fact that the alternative of regular, irregular or even illegal migration for irregular employment was easier to achieve, even in the 1980s. In Portugal there was a total of a mere 3,200 asylum seekers from 1983 to 1989; in Spain there were 18,200; in Greece, 30,450; and in Italy, 43,300.[94] Until the end of the Cold War, the number in Italy was relatively high compared with other countries in southern Europe, but with respect to all of Europe it was low. This was partly because Italy granted asylum only to refugees from Europe, which was possible because of the passage about 'geographical reservations' in the Geneva Convention on refugees. Immigrants from non-European countries – including Turkey – had no chance of asylum in Italy until the end of the 1980s; consequently, virtually all asylum seekers there were from eastern Europe. Non-Europeans had the choice only between staying in Italy with irregular status or migrating further northwards to file a petition for asylum there. This spurred outrage over a kind of Italian asylum selection at the expense of other countries. The situation changed when the 1989 asylum law reform lifted geographical restrictions and Italy's asylum law was modified to correspond to the basic regulations valid in the rest of Europe west of the Iron Curtain.

The Iron Curtain was opened in 1989, releasing a wave of migration that seemed to confirm all the worst fears about floods. By that time, the struggle to determine the 'genuine' refugee had long since become a battle against asylum seekers who were more or less fundamentally suspected of deception. The definitive thrust towards inter- and supranational 'harmonization' of nation-state asylum egos in the common interest of security of the receiving (or defensive) countries was finally supplied by the opening of the European single market. Consequently, with no controls at inner-European borders, insecurity mounted with respect to transnational migration processes, or 'migratory vulnerability' in the jargon of security policy.[95]

5

Europe: A Continent of Immigration at the End of the Twentieth Century

The end of the Cold War represented a major break for migration and migration politics in Europe. This was not only because of the migratory movements themselves. The descriptions of migration that were circulating in public and political discourse played an equally if not more important role, as did the visions associated with these social constructions of a Europe under suddenly growing 'migration pressure' no longer merely from the south, but now also from the east. Observations, projections and visions of migration in the late twentieth century determined migration policies in a European Union (EU) whose integration and openness with the internally border-free single market went hand in hand with the isolation of 'Fortress Europe' against undesirable in-migration from outside its borders.

1   CULTURAL DIVERSITY, 'MIGRATION PRESSURE' AND 'FORTRESS EUROPE'

Europe west of the Iron Curtain had generally transformed itself by the late 1980s into a continent of immigration; immigration had become a central political issue in all European countries affected by it. From 1950 to 1990, the total foreign resident populations in the present EU countries and Switzerland, Norway and Liechtenstein grew more than fourfold, from 3.7 million (1.3 per cent of the total population) in 1950 to over 10.7 million (3.2 per cent) in 1970 and to 16 million (4.5 per cent) in 1990. The highest absolute figures in 1995 were in Germany with 7.7 million (8.8 per cent), France with 3.6 million (6.3 per cent) and Britain with 2 million

(3.4 per cent). The highest ratios of foreign nationals to the total population in 1995 were in Liechtenstein (38.1 per cent), Luxembourg (33.4 per cent) and Switzerland (18.9 per cent). Other countries in Europe with a high proportion of foreign nationals were Belgium (9 per cent), Sweden (5.2 per cent) and the Netherlands (5 per cent).

Figures on numbers of foreigners and ratios to total resident populations in an international comparison say little about actual immigration processes on account of the already noted differences in naturalization practices and acquisition of citizenship based on the *jus soli* principle, for which there are no separate statistics in most cases. From 1986 to 1994, for example, the number of naturalizations in Britain was 537,000; in France, 486,000; and in the Federal Republic of Germany, 253,000. In the Netherlands there were 247,000 and in Sweden, 228,000. However, the naturalization rate in 1986–94 relative to the total foreign population in 1985 was highest in Sweden (58.7 per cent) and the Netherlands (44.7 per cent), and lowest in West Germany (5 per cent), not counting the naturalization of 'ethnic Germans' (*Aussiedler*) from eastern Europe and the Soviet Union. Migrants lived almost exclusively in urban environments, concentrated in certain urban districts and in suburbs of conurbations.

In the former colonial countries, the share of immigrant populations from overseas had grown substantially. In the Netherlands there were a total of 728,400 foreign nationals (5 per cent) registered in 1995 in a population of 15.5 million. A total of 1.4 million people had been born overseas, however, of which 57 per cent possessed Dutch citizenship. The largest groups of foreign-born were Turks (182,000), Surinamese (181,000), Indonesians (180,000), Moroccans (159,000) and Germans (131,000). More than 40 per cent of the entire immigrant population, but only 11.5 per cent of native-born Dutch, lived in the four largest cities in the Netherlands: Amsterdam (20 per cent of the Surinamese), Rotterdam, The Hague and Utrecht.

In 1951, only 74,000 people from the New Commonwealth had been living in Britain. Their numbers climbed from 336,000 in 1961 to 2.2 million in 1981. The 1991 census, the first to request data regarding ethnic descent, registered about 3 million (5.5 per cent) members of these 'ethnic minorities', 46.8 per cent of whom were British-born. More than half were of Asian descent and one in five, Caribbean. Most of those of foreign descent lived in the Greater London area, in the West Midlands with its centre in Birmingham, in West Yorkshire with its centre in Bradford ('Little Pakistan') or in Greater Manchester.

According to the census of 1990, there were about 1.3 million naturalized immigrants and about 500,000 French citizens from the overseas *départements* living in France. There were also 3.6 million foreign nationals, who comprised 6.3 per cent of the population. Ten million French have at least one foreign parent or grandparent. North and sub-Saharan Africans have been the largest immigrant group for decades (45 per cent in 1990). They make up the major portion of foreign schoolchildren (63 per cent) and a high proportion of all school-age children (8 per cent). The major share of residents of foreign descent live in Greater Paris (Île de France, 38.3 per cent), Rhône-Alpes with its centre in Lyons (12 per cent) and in the Provence-Alpes-Côte d'Azur region (between Marseilles and Nice, 8.4 per cent).

The number of immigrants in Sweden also increased sharply, as noted earlier, where the number of residents of foreign descent grew from 1950 to 1995 from almost 200,000 to 936,000. This brought considerable changes in the composition of the diversifying resident population, more than 10 per cent of which was foreign-born, i.e., aside from southern Europe, ex-Yugoslavia, Turkey and Morocco, especially Chile, Ethiopia, Iran, Iraq, Lebanon and Somalia. Around 532,000 or 5.2 per cent of the total population were foreign nationals.

In Switzerland in 1990, most of the 1.1 million foreigners, who comprised 16 per cent of the total population, lived in the cantons of Geneva (119,000; 31 per cent), Ticino (68,600; 24.3 per cent), Basel-City (41,600; 20.9 per cent) and six other cantons in which the proportion of foreign nationals was over the national average of 16 per cent. The proportion of foreigners from the neighbouring countries of Germany, Austria and Italy dropped from 87 per cent in 1960 to 40 per cent in 1993.

Austria's population grew from around 6.5 million at the end of the Second World War to more than 8 million in 1995. In this period, 3.8 million people migrated to Austria, roughly 1.2 million of whom remained in the country. Most came from the territory of the former Austro-Hungarian monarchy, especially ex-Yugoslavia.

Of the 7.7 million foreigners living in Germany in 1995 (20 per cent of whom were born in the country), 28.1 per cent were of Turkish descent, 18.3 per cent ex-Yugoslavian and 8.2 per cent Italian. In absolute figures, the largest foreign populations were in Berlin, Hamburg, Munich, Frankfurt am Main, Cologne and Stuttgart; relative to the total population in the respective cities, however, the major populations (over 20 per cent) were in Offenbach, Frankfurt am Main, Munich and Stuttgart. With the end of the division of Europe, east–west migration clearly shifted the structure of the immigrant population in Germany: the number of immigrants of German descent from eastern Europe and the former Soviet Union (*Aussiedler*) is on its way to outstripping the foreign minority population that evolved from the former 'guestworkers'.[1]

The late 1970s and early 1980s, as has been shown, remained marked by a clearly different weighting of trends of liberalization and restriction in European immigration countries. In the course of the 1980s, restrictive forces became stronger and a xenophobic defensive stance came to predominate. The subject of 'immigration' was frequently dramatized and demonized in party politics and by extraparliamentary protest movements. This situation was often triggered by political ineptness in coping with the unexpected social repercussions of migratory processes as well as by political presentations of corresponding 'discoveries' by national conservative parties and ethnonational and racist currents, fostering both fears and aggression. In Germany, for example, as of 1979–80 the matter in hand was the shift from work stays to immigration situations; in Britain from 1979 it was about the emergence of ethnic minority populations from colonial and post-colonial in-migration; and in France from 1984, both of these developments occurred at the same time.

At the centre of these debates was the concentration of immigrant groups in ethnic or regional communities based on place of origin or in mixed immigrant districts. It is a well-known phenomenon in migration history that these concentrations formed as a result of chain migrations. The formation of polyethnic structures prompted many locals, encouraged by political agitation and support by the media, to set in motion processes of negative integration and defensive crowding together at the expense of 'strangers'. The migration discussion was politicized and emotionalized in the 1980s, pushed by the rapidly rising immigration of refugees and asylum seekers from the 'Third World'. Public discussion soon began to focus on their perception, which simultaneously influenced attitudes towards minority populations that evolved from colonial migration and non-European labour migration.[2]

Three main changes were common to the discourse on immigration issues in politics and the media:

1   In the 1980s, the idea was reinforced that limitations on in-migration were a prerequisite for integration of migrants and their acceptance by the receiving societies. While European integration through freedom of movement on the labour market gradually eliminated the inner-European impact of the recruitment ban, its exclusionary functions were moved to the external frontiers of the emerging EU. After labour migration was limited, the next issue was restricting asylum migration, which in the 1980s came increasingly from outside Europe and already showed some aspects of chain migrations. In addition to needing refuge from the tragedy of expulsion, persecution and flight, some asylum seekers also aspired to immigrate. This point was one-sidedly pushed to the fore in anti-asylum agitation, although

immigration was virtually impossible in any other way as Europe was becoming gradually closed off. Limited admission to asylum proceedings and deterrence measures coincided with increasing frequency with the tightening of entry controls at Europe's exterior borders agreed upon throughout Europe. Thus the past history of European migration policies relating to non-European in-migration began as security policies agreed by the ministries of the interior of European countries, largely bypassing the European Parliament. The notion that integration and exclusion were interdependent and growing defensive attitudes towards non-European in-migration initially came together in the European process of integration as a convergence of basic national migration policy positions. By increasing the permeability of internal European borders and ultimately opening them in the single market, the focus at international and supranational levels was first and foremost protection against non-European in-migration. Concrete conditions for European migration and refugee policies, on the other hand, did not assume any fixed form until the Amsterdam treaty entered into force shortly before the turn of the millennium.

2 With respect to immigrant groups, an outward shift could also be observed from intra-European to extra-European cultural definitions and characterizations of foreignness and ideas of exclusion, sometimes with clear Euro-racist connotations: while labour migrants from southern Europe were still described as 'foreign' in the 1960s in central, northern and western Europe – disregarding in any case colonial and post-colonial immigrants – in the 1970s this was less the case for southern Europeans but more so, for example, for Turks. In the 1980s, in turn, aversion to the growing immigration of refugees and asylum seekers from the 'Third World' became evident. As the European Community was growing into the European Union and preparing a limited eastward expansion, isolation and defensiveness within 'Fortress Europe' also moved outward, in terms not only of migration policies but of collective mentalities as well.

3 Populist alarmism and dramatization and demonization of the migration issue in discourses of politics and the media were occasionally worlds apart from the pragmatic administration of immigration and integration processes. On the one hand, the conflict over defensive measures against mass immigration, which was supposedly already underway or at least imminent, dominated political and media discussions of a 'Fortress Europe' with bulwarks at the border against the threat of migration. On the other hand, these borders remained passable for a large number of immigrants owing to the economic or social interests of the host countries (labour and minority migrations)

or their immigrant communities (family reunification), and to a limited extent for humanitarian reasons (refugees, asylum seekers) – apart from a broad spectrum of migrations that were controlled but not considered relevant to security issues, such as, for example, elite or betterment migrations or education and training migrations.[3]

Discourses of politics and the media generally exhibited conspicuous differences between reality and the descriptions that determined their perceptions. The immigrant populations that evolved from colonial and post-colonial migration as well as from European labour migration were still the largest in the 1990s; they usually increased through natural growth and transnational family reunification. Asylum migration, with a much smaller total volume, nevertheless dominated migration discourse in many receiving countries, as did fears of 'new migrations of nations' from the 'Third World' that were concrete only in 'migration scenarios' or gloomy forebodings. Fear of mass migrations from eastern Europe had not yet become a major issue in the divided world of the Cold War. Defensive attitudes targeting non-European mass migration and especially asylum migration, on the other hand, had already become widely manifest when the end of the Cold War opened up the subject of east–west migration as the second large dimension of fear.

The end of the Cold War began in 1989 with the opening of the Iron Curtain. Migration played more than just a symbolic role in the external course of events: on 2 May 1989, Hungarian soldiers cut through the barbed wire on the border to Austria, opening the way to the west for would-be emigrants from East Germany (GDR) who had made their way to Hungary. A short time later, locked trains filled with East German citizens who had sought refuge on the grounds of the West German embassy in Prague rolled from Czechoslovakia through their own country – that was an East German condition – to the Federal Republic of Germany. The collapse of the East German regime under the pressure of the peaceful revolution by its citizens and the opening of the GDR to the west without intervention by the USSR signalled the end of the Cold War and accelerated at the same time the process, in many ways with a momentum of its own, that would end with the demise of the 'eastern bloc'.

In the late nineteenth and early twentieth centuries, east–west migration had led millions of emigrants across the Atlantic and hundreds of thousands of labour migrants annually to central and western Europe. On top of this came a large portion of the over 20 million people who were forced to resettle after borders were shifted or who were victims of expulsions from the end of the First World War until the late 1940s. The Cold War served to cut off east–west migration for decades and also allowed old fears of such mass migration to recede in the west. The Iron Curtain was condemned in the west as an ideologically motivated bulwark of the 'evil empire' (Ronald Reagan) against the pull of freedom.

When the fortified border of the Cold War was broken down in 1989, it became apparent that it had also been a barrier against east–west migration. Border openings, crisis and collapse of the Soviet Union, revolutionary changes, tension and conflict in and between its former member states, from 1991–2 in particular the bloody explosion of the multi-ethnic Yugoslavian republic in wars and civil wars – all of this caused, from 1989 to 1992, the most massive migrations in and from eastern Europe since the refugee and forced migrations of the Second World War. After the end of the permanent state of emergency and of the ideological, political, economic as well as 'migratory division of Europe', a kind of fear of normality returned in Europe with an eye towards east–west migrations.[4]

'Migration pressure' on Europe increased sharply from the late 1980s. It appeared to be the common outcome derived from the much-described, varied complexity of factors leading to migration from potential regions of origin of south–north and later east–west migrations. The apocalyptic inevitability of the feared 'flooding' of Europe by 'new migrations of nations' existed more in the imaginations of Europeans, however, than in the actual migratory events in the east and south. Massive migratory movements did take place. They were not bound for Europe, however, but occurred in the eastern and especially southern parts of the world where it was often the poorest neighbouring countries that took in 'floods' of refugees, in addition to large numbers of 'internally displaced persons (IDPs)' within the country's borders and immense rural–urban migrations (see section 4).

In discussions of 'migration pressure' on Europe, opinions diverged as to the question of whether, and to what extent, the lack of mass migrations from the east and south in the late twentieth century was also a result of the massive shielding of 'Fortress Europe' against movements from both these directions, and especially of the deliberate stemming or breaking off of new chain migrations. A closely related question was how such isolation could be justified without migration-oriented developmental policies or development-oriented migration policies.[5] Undisputed, on the other hand, was the fact that certain countries of Europe were affected by the increase in east–west as well as south–north migrations far more severely than others. This applied especially to Italy with respect to south–north migrations in the Euro-Mediterranean zone starting in the 1980s (see chapter 4, section 2). With respect to the new east–west migrations from the late 1980s, in the north it applied above all to Germany, far ahead (in absolute figures) of Switzerland and Austria.

After the fall of the Iron Curtain, Germany, like Austria, regained its historical position owing to migratory geographical factors as a transit country or an east–west bridge or the central European turntable in transnational migratory events.

Directly after the Iron Curtain collapsed, European, especially German, fears of a 'flood' from the east returned, in which new and old aspects were sometimes intermingled. These projections were supported by partly rash 'migration scenarios' of a scholarly or popular scientific nature, whose image of humanity appeared to be that of a homeless *Homo oeconomicus* or (human) *animal rationale migrans* acting on economic speculations who was drawn as if by a magnet to the comparative wealth of Europe. Underlying this image were not only fearful visions in the west, however, but also the political, demographic way of dealing with migration prospects in the east, as a threat when demanding economic aid.

French demographer Jean-Claude Chesnais estimated that from 1992 to 1995 a total of 4–5 million people would migrate to the west from the territories of the toppling Soviet Union. Yuri Reshetov of the Soviet foreign ministry, on the other hand, estimated about 4–6 million annually for the same period. Diplomat and deputy chairman of Novosti Russian Information Agency Vladimir Milyutenko reckoned on as many as 7–8 million per year or 25–30 million by 1995. Boris Khorev of Lomonossov University predicted an east–west migration of 40 million by 1995 and Anatoli Vishnevski of the Scientific Council for Social Development in the USSR council of ministers even estimated 48 million, or one-sixth of the population, by 1995.[6] With increasing frequency, the potential countries of origin more or less strategically mentioned the feared 'new migrations of nations' as a kind of migratory threat in discussions on debt relief, economic aid and questions of global economy. The Polish prime minister was reluctant to rule out the possibility that insufficient economic aid could set millions of unemployed Poles on a westward course and intimated that, if necessary, he would even open his borders to the east and west, 'so that refugees from Russia could migrate further to Germany'. From the Russian side, in turn, it was publicly speculated that the size of westward migration from eastern Europe after freedom to travel had been introduced could depend solely on the capacity of the passport printing office. Threatening prophecies from the east joined open threats from the south, such as that by Senegalese president Abdou Diouf in an interview with the French newspaper *Le Figaro*, in which he expressed an extremely imaginative medieval image: Europe must offer Africa far more massive economic aid than it had hitherto, 'otherwise you will be overrun by hordes as in the Middle Ages'.[7]

Most short- to medium-term predictions and calculations on migration to Europe would turn out to be wrong, oversimplified or grossly exaggerated. The existence of massive migration potential in the east and elsewhere was undisputed, but mass migrations remained limited to the east. East–west movements soon assumed a more manageable volume; by the end of the 1990s, temporary and shuttle migrations increased as permanent emigration declined.[8] The different fears and threats of xenophobic 'ghosthunting'[9] and the equally different impacts of actual migrations all served to increase the phenomenon in European receiving countries that migration policies were generally understood as security policies.

Violent attacks on foreigners and general xenophobic excesses in Germany in the early 1990s became best known. Germany was by far the most strongly affected by migration in the first few years after the end of the Cold War in Europe.[10] This involved, first, asylum seekers from the 'Third World' and eastern Europe, the geographical weighting of which had completely reversed since the mid-1980s. In 1986, 74.8 per cent of all asylum seekers in West Germany came from the 'Third World'. In 1993, 72.1 per cent were from Europe, primarily eastern Europe. This was not only because of the collapse of the Iron Curtain and the crises that developed in eastern Europe. Additionally, even before the end of the Cold War, defensive measures against 'poverty refugees' from the 'Third World' had started to take effect. Second, it involved minorities from eastern Europe (ethnic Germans, Jews, Roma), some of which (Roma) also applied for asylum. Third, it involved refugees and expellees from ex-Yugoslavia, of which Germany took in more in the early 1990s than all other EU countries combined (see section 3). Fourth, there were additional burdens arising from the unification process that at the time triggered a massive east–west (since unification in October 1990, inner-German) migration. From 1989 to March 1992, more than 800,000 people, that is, more than 5 per cent of the population of the former East Germany, went west.

On top of this, the aforementioned migration scenarios or migration threats about east–west migration usually referred to Germany as a kind of central catchment or overflow basin for the 'flow from the east'. The Basel research institute Prognos estimated in 1992 that because of labour market developments in western Germany, not only would there be continued in-migration of about 1.4 million eastern Germans by the end of the 1990s, but that 'even with restrictive asylum policies' there would be in-migration and transit migration up to 2010 involving about 17 million people from eastern Europe, two-thirds of whom would, however, later leave Germany again.

Switzerland and Austria had already closed their borders to asylum seekers from eastern Europe in 1990–1; Switzerland did so also for a number of main countries of origin in the 'Third World' (see chapter 4, section 4). In Germany, on the other hand, where partisan disputes paralysed the government's ability to act and further heated the already highly emotionalized the government's debate, immigration figures rose quickly: from 1989 to 1992, there were around 1 million (1,008,684) asylum seekers in Germany. The convergence of different, rapidly growing migration flows in Germany, and the fears fostered by migration scenarios and threats that it would continue to develop, caused the visions of 'floods' from the east to seem like concrete predictions in Germany. Officials for foreigner and refugee interests, people giving practical support on behalf of foreigners, and critical scholars participated in the debate, indicating in vain that many asylum seekers, refugees and other foreigners left Germany each year. Demographic arguments accomplished less and less against everyday experiences of *de facto* increasing encounters with greater numbers of new 'strangers' who many perceived as threatening. Meanwhile, the government coalition and the opposition accused each other of blocking the resolution of a migration situation that mayday messages had demonized into a catastrophe ('The boat is full!'). Anti-asylum arguments often went around in circles: generally only about 5 per cent of all applicants for asylum were recognized as 'politically persecuted' in the strict sense and were thus entitled to asylum. Politicians and the media spread demagogic ideas that the remaining 95 per cent who had been rejected were 'economic refugees'. They regularly made themselves ridiculous in view of the fact that, despite rejection, a considerable portion of applicants and their dependants nevertheless had to be granted either protection from deportation for various reasons or refugee status based on a higher law, which in turn was interpreted as the state's failure to carry out 'strict deportation'.

This was the backdrop to the anti-foreigner and xenophobic rioting driven by growing fear and aggression in unified Germany of the early 1990s. Yet prior to this crisis there had already been long-standing, unresolved immigration and integration issues in the 'immigration country against its will'. As a national welfare state, Germany pragmatically organized the social integration of immigrants, but in its appeals it stubbornly and demonstrably refused to face facts, insisting that it was 'not an immigration country' and would not become one. It ultimately became clear that the helplessly escapist attempt simply to 'denounce' the reality of the long and unmistakable actual immigration situation was merely the flip side of the lack of a socio-political concept for immigration issues. Social fears grew, as did annoyance and frustration with the absence of policies for the immigration situation, which was nothing short of uncanny, since it was experienced in everyday life yet was politically declared not to exist. Frustration flared into aggression against 'strangers' and those thought or declared to be such. 'Below' there was fear of the other; 'above' was fear of citizens as voters. Convergence of fears from 'below' and helplessness from 'above' contributed substantially to the first political legitimization crisis in unified Germany. It threatened for a short time to become a crisis of the democratic parliamentary system; consequently, Chancellor Helmut Kohl spoke of a 'state emergency' in autumn 1992 and of bypassing parliament in changing the asylum law, which even fanned a short but heated debate on 'plans for a coup' by the conservative-liberal federal government.

Fears of foreigners and xenophobia were not a specifically 'German' problem. They existed in other EU countries, even those affected clearly less or, as with Britain, hardly at all by the abrupt climb in immigration in the late 1980s and early 1990s. The excesses in Germany caused a worldwide sensation, to some extent because news reporting was on the lookout for signs of a revival of Nazism in a new form. But the xenophobic movement did not come from rightwing radical splinter groups, which is what made it particularly dangerous, but from the centre of the population, and was stemmed not by politics or the police but by the civil pressure of the majority, which was outraged by the rioting. Countless initiatives opposing xenophobia, violence and tolerance for violence as well as nationwide counter-demonstrations with the famous 'candlelit marches' isolated the perpetrators and destroyed the image they tried to create of acting on behalf of a silent majority. All this prompted the observation of one critical observer that one could get the impression that Germany 'was comprised entirely of pyromaniacs: some throw Molotov cocktails and the others hold candles'.[11]

The outcome of factional disputes on migration policies was the 'asylum compromise' of December 1992, which became law in 1993. It was improvised under considerable pressure by the conservative–liberal government coalition of CDU/CSU and FDP with the oppositional Social Democrats (SPD) – against resistance by the Greens (Bündnis 90/Die Grünen) and the East German successor party for democratic socialism, PDS. In reality, the 'asylum compromise' went far beyond the scope of asylum issues; it was a comprehensive, restrictive 'migration compromise' that also included limitations on immigration by ethnic Germans from eastern Europe and the former Soviet Union (Act to correct the laws dealing with late consequences of the Second World War, *Kriegsfolgen-bereinigungsgesetz*) (see section 2). The legal reform also introduced into Germany's basic right to asylum the 'first country of asylum' clause as well as the 'safe-country' doctrine,[12] which was much more effective as a defensive strategy and had at times already been previously applied. From then on virtually no one who came from 'persecution-free' countries or who entered Germany via 'safe third countries', which, based on unilateral German declarations, surround Germany on all sides, stood a chance of being granted asylum in Germany. Consequently, since then it is generally no longer possible for asylum-seeking refugees to enter Germany legally – that is, with an entry visa – by land. In other words, Germany is accessible by land only through irregular or illegal means. This further profited the already booming international human smuggling organizations (see section 4). Entry by air was used to a very minor degree (5 per cent); due to the costs it clearly served a social selection function (see chapter 4, section 4). This form of entry also generally no longer leads directly to regular asylum proceedings but to summary proceedings in the extraterritorial transit area, especially at Frankfurt am Main airport, to decide whether the refugee is to be deported or allowed to enter into regular proceedings.[13]

Up to 1992–3, Germany had the most liberal asylum law in Europe and the most restrictive asylum law practice to limit the law's application. The restrictive reform of 1993 adapted the immigration-friendly asylum law to the anti-immigration practice, lowering it at the same time to European standards. The German restrictions went even above and beyond those, forcing other European countries to make restrictive modifications in order to limit the number of asylum seekers switching to their country as an alternative. These and other legislative, judicial and administrative chain reactions served a negative coalition of defence in a Europe that is growing together. However, alone they would hardly have led to supranational concepts of defence beyond bilateral or international security policy agreements. The final definitive thrust was the constraint on action linked to the development of the border-free single market within the tension between integration and isolation. Against the background of steeply increasing migration to Europe in the late 1980s and early 1990s and the progressive elimination of internal borders in the process of integration, the isolation of 'Fortress Europe' against unwanted immigrants from outside its borders has been accelerated since the end of the Cold War.[14]

Legal developments in the 1990s were rooted in the history of the EEC, which began with the treaties of Rome in 1957. Its final aim as the European Union was outlined in the Single European Act of 1986: to create a European single market by 31 December 1992. This marked what began in 1986 as the politically meshed process of integration of EC/EU states internally and their closing off externally. Legal developments within these two processes, however, for the most part proceeded separately. The creation of the single market took place within the scope of the EC/EU, while external closing off was negotiated at bi- and multilateral levels between the ministries of the interior and of justice of EC/EU countries. The treaties of Maastricht (1992) and Amsterdam

(1997) then finally transferred visa policies (Maastricht) and asylum policies (Amsterdam) from the competence of the respective countries to the EC/EU level. This represented the decisive step to 'communitization', that is, EC/EU-wide application of asylum law.[15]

The basic trends of this dual-track development were the steadily increasing freedom of movement with social security within the single market for EC/EU citizens and the simultaneously decreasing freedom of in-migration for citizens of 'third states' not belonging to the EC/EU. Internally, the objective was to adapt the social standards either 'up' or 'down' to achieve international agreement. Externally, it was a matter of deciding which cross-border in-migrations should be treated as desired, tolerated or irrelevant for security issues and which were deemed unwanted and treated accordingly. Of course, the above-noted 'liberal paradox' (James Hollifield) prevented Europe from shielding itself off completely due to its humanitarian obligations in international law (such as the Geneva Convention on Refugees and the European Convention for the Protection of Human Rights and Fundamental Freedoms). We shall review this dual-track development of integration and isolation more closely in order to try to identify the conditions thereby determined for in-migration to Europe in the 1990s.

In accordance with the treaty of Rome (1957), freedom of movement in matters of residence and employment was guaranteed as of 1968 on the basis of citizenship in the initially six member states of the EEC. This is why, for example, the recruitment bans and immigration restrictions in the early to mid-1970s had increasingly less long-term influence, and ultimately none at all, on the Euro-Mediterranean region of origin that was gradually entering the EC. Their powers of exclusion were then enforced only against third-country nationals. The aim of the Single European Act of 1986, which entered into force in 1987, was, in addition to promoting the integration process and economic growth by eliminating Europe's internal borders, to implement the 'four freedoms' of movement of persons, services, goods and capital. The establishment of the single market brought with it far-reaching equal treatment of EC nationals, which meant not only free movement in choosing a place of residence and work, but also protective regulations for these labour migrants. However, this did not create general regulations valid for all EC citizens, that is, including students or dependants of employees. Complete freedom of movement for persons was not guaranteed until the Amsterdam treaty was implemented in 1999, finally eliminating all controls at internal European borders.[16]

Freedom of services was achieved in late 1992, which allowed services to be offered EC-wide. This also meant, however, that a British building contractor could send workers to construction sites in Berlin, or a Portuguese contractor could send work brigades to France to build a TGV (high-speed train) line. Both contractors sold regular services but were engaged indirectly in wage dumping, since they paid their labour according to British or Portuguese law, while German and French law offered workers higher rates and obliged employers to pay higher social security contributions. Rate-cutting resulted and local employers were forced to hire inexpensive foreign labourers, which led to higher unemployment rates for the national labour force. This problem is countered by the 'posted workers directive' that was passed in 1997 and came into force in 1999, which provides for general minimum wages; but it is hardly able to cope with the problem of 'dependent self-employment', in which 'self-exploiters' from the EU appear in the destination country as both employer and employee.[17]

Much more problematic than regulating transnational migration within the EC/EU was the question of access to this region from the outside. Border and entry controls are classic responsibilities of state sovereignty and had led, up to the 1980s, to greatly varying entry regulations among the different countries. Creation of the single market by opening internal borders led to a loss of control, which, according to the respective ministries responsible for internal security, had to be compensated for by intensifying controls at the external borders, viewed as particularly necessary since immigrations from outside the EU had increased considerably since the mid-1980s, above all in the area of asylum. This led to the development of the instruments of the Schengen agreement (Schengen I, 1985), the corresponding implementation treaty (Schengen II, 1990) and the Dublin agreement of 1990. These agreements were the outcome of intergovernmental cooperation by the ministries of the interior and of justice beyond the actual EC/EU integration process.[18]

Compensation measures in the 1985 Schengen agreement to maintain a constant high level of security served as complementary elements for breaking down inner-European border controls. The contracting states (Benelux, France, Germany) committed themselves, among other things, to moving their entry controls to the EC/EU external borders, to aligning their entry conditions and regulations for issuing visas, and to taking measures to combat illegal entry. Not until 1990 were the general objectives of this working programme expanded by the implementation agreement (Schengen II). It entered into force EU-wide in 1993, but was not implemented until 26 March 1995 in Belgium, Germany, France, Luxembourg, the Netherlands, Portugal and Spain. The Dublin agreement of 1990, which was identical to Schengen II as far as asylum law regulations were concerned, was intended primarily to prevent the filing of multiple applications for asylum ('asylum shopping'): every asylum seeker was to be permitted to petition for asylum in only one EC/EU country and rejection from one would apply to all other EC/EU countries. Implementation of the agreement was problematic from the outset, however, because every signatory country had a different asylum law with correspondingly different practices. This could lead to differences in asylum rulings in the ratio of 1 to 100, considering that, for example, in 1990 only 0.7 per cent of all asylum petitions by Tamils were decided positively in Britain as compared with 70 per cent in France.

Political issues also complicated the implementation of the agreement, such as Denmark's and Britain's unwillingness to transfer control over admission of third-country nationals to the EC. In Britain's view, freedom of movement applied only for EC/EU citizens. France, too, insisted on retaining border controls for reasons of internal security until 1996. There were also conflicts over jurisdiction with the EC/EU Commission, which considered itself responsible for migration issues since 1986, while individual countries held to their sovereign decision-making jurisdictions. Institutional diversification, chaos over jurisdiction and different national standpoints all contributed to delaying implementation of the treaty, which entered into force long after it was signed. Schengen II did not enter into force until 1995 and the Dublin agreement in 1997. The EC/EU Commission, European Court of Justice and European Parliament therefore played only a secondary to insignificant role on migration issues until the end of the 1990s.

The Maastricht treaty founded the European Union in 1992 with its three pillars. Supranational decision mechanisms apply for the first pillar encompassing the European Community, European Coal and Steel Community (ECSC) and the European Atomic Energy Community (Euratom). The affairs of the second (Common Foreign and Security Policy, CFSP) and third (Justice and Home Affairs) pillars are decided at inter-governmental level. Regulations relating to migration issues were consequently dealt with by the first and third pillars, which is why, for example, the list of countries for which a visa is compulsory could be issued as an EU decree. At the London summit of the ministers for immigration of the 12 EU member states in November–December 1992, resolutions (WGI 1281–3) were also made concerning 'manifestly unfounded applications' for asylum, a 'harmonized approach' to questions concerning host third countries and countries in which there is generally no serious risk of persecution. These were not treaties under international law, but the treaty of Maastricht opened up the possibility of 'communitizing' areas of national policy, that is, transferring them to EU law, if approved unanimously by a council resolution. It was also possible to set EU-wide standpoints in the area of migration, make agreements and take measures. Subjects that had been treated in the 'ad hoc group on immigration' under ministries of the interior were consequently taken up by the third EU pillar and declared to be matters of common interest. This included asylum policies, border-crossing regulations, immigration policies and policies towards third countries, including combating illegal immigration and stays.

This intermediate step towards 'communitizing' asylum and immigration law was followed by the Amsterdam agreement of 1997, which became effective in May 1999. It transferred to EC/EU law the subjects of the Schengen agreements that had previously been treated outside the EC/EU, and the entire area of visas, asylum and immigration issues was transferred from intergovernmental cooperation (third pillar) to the jurisdiction of the EC (first pillar). The agreement was presented to the political public as a major step forward in the direction of a European 'area of freedom, security and justice'. The flip side was joint isolation against unwanted immigration from outside the EU, whereby decisions on positive and negative lists for visa-free countries or those requiring a visa remained tied to qualified majorities. Until the Amsterdam treaty entered into force, legal developments of the 1990s generally involved a slow adjustment of asylum and immigration regulations of individual member states, connected with extraordinary problems. The focus remained on border controls, combating crime and defence against unwanted immigration. In addition there were problematic regulations such as the concepts of 'safe third countries' and 'manifestly unfounded applications'. Both possibly contradict the regulations of the Geneva Convention on Refugees and the European Convention on Human Rights and could lead to a kind of 'complicity between receiving and persecuting countries' at the expense of refugees.[19]

The path to a common EU asylum and immigration law[20] was still a long way off at the end of the century. But the patterns of migration from third countries into the Europe of the EC/EU had long since been determined by diverse regulations, limitations and prohibitions.

An initial stable and lasting immigration movement, despite some attempts to restrict it, has been created by chain migration in the form of family reunification, with narrow- to wide-ranging interpretations of the concept of family. As has long been the case in the United States, family reunification in Europe is on the verge of becoming one of the most important forms of immigration. It has developed, in cases of limited admissions, increasingly at the expense of other immigrant groups because it includes only those who already have, or wish to start ('marriage migration'), close ties to the destination country, or those who want to create them for their children by their being born in the country ('birth migration'). A second large area of admission includes traditionally privileged migration relations, sometimes still in the form of post-colonial in-migration, though since the opening of the Iron Curtain it is more often mainly in the form of 'ethnic' or minority migrations within the scope of east–west migrations.

A third area includes international and global labour migrations, within which two major dimensions should be distinguished: expert and elite migrations at the 'top' or relatively 'high up'; and the often limited stays of certain employee groups in some occupational fields at the 'bottom' or relatively 'low down'.

At the top of the professional and social pyramid is the mobility of those in elite functions. They generally show high transnational and intercontinental or global mobility and are considered politically safe or irrelevant for migration controls. In the 1990s there was strong growth in this area owing to the market-oriented mobility of technicians, businesspeople and managers of companies operating internationally and multinational firms. In addition to the extra-European mobility of European specialists and managers, there was also an increase in work stays of non-Europeans in the major European economic regions and metropolises. Where immigration restrictions and recruitment bans were in force, this kind of migration was generally made possible through applications by employers with the help of exceptional or special authorization. At the same time, there was an increase in transnational elite mobility within the economic region merging to form the EU. Unlimited mobility, that is, not only transnational but clear openness to global mobility, has become a self-evident prerequisite since the 1980s, and especially the 1990s, for professional and social advancement in leadership positions of multinational firms with the attendant management structures and worldwide internal labour markets spread out via global networks of branch offices.[21]

After the Iron Curtain opened, European corporations made greater and faster strides in the age of globalization of production and sales organization and personnel management. Highly qualified economic and technical specialists and management from 'western Europe' also increasingly took action in eastern Europe, a sign of the end of the separation of systems. Conversely, a growing out-migration of technical experts ('brain drain') to the west could be observed, which soon became problematic for the economic future of the 'reforming countries'. The area of elite migration also includes the transnational mobility of, for example, artists, scholars, migrants for study and/or training purposes and (usually not included in the statistics on the resident population) the staffs of embassies, consulates and international organizations.[22]

At the bottom of the social pyramid, usually employees from third countries cross Europe's external borders, with limited authorization within the framework of bilateral agreements. Their migrations often lead to work and employment areas that can no longer attract nationals, earlier immigrants or citizens of other EU countries. This includes fixed seasonal agricultural work that is sometimes highly paid, but according to piece rates, such as flower, grape, asparagus and hop harvests. It also applies to parts of the building trade. In Germany, admission quotas agreed upon within the scope of east–west migration have special significance in this context for the status group of 'guest employees', 'contract employees' and 'seasonal employees'. Also part of temporary east–west migration are the pronounced movements of cross-border commuters. Especially as regards temporary or seasonal east–west migration, misplacement at lower qualifications on the labour market is often taken for granted because of exorbitantly high wages. Polish surgeons can earn considerably more working on the grape or asparagus harvest in Germany than in their highly specialized profession in Poland.[23]

There is also a new transnational mobility among low-wage labourers within the EC in a number of areas of employment at the lowest levels of the internationalized labour market that have low demand, or none at all, despite extremely high unemployment: the number of Italians in Germany in 1987 had dwindled to about 500,000, while the new immigration country Italy had moved up to being one of the leading economic powers in the world. In the 1990s the number of Italian immigrants (often with family) rose again considerably. Many of them, like the earlier 'guestworkers', come from southern Italy. They are unable or unwilling to live on the wages offered there, leaving the largely agricultural jobs mostly to North African seasonal workers. These Italians seek work in northern Italy and, if unsuccessful there, in Germany, often working for Italians or Germans of Italian descent, especially in the catering trade or in construction. Many are forced to work illicitly or are perhaps paid the same wages as illegal workers from eastern Europe by Italian subcontractors on construction sites. The number of illicit Italian labourers in Germany was estimated in 1997 by Fillea-CGIL, the Italian building and construction union, at 27,000 at least; illegal work contractors (*caporalato*) are most widespread in the new federal states (the area of former East Germany). Beyond the labour market, there is hardly any contact between the socially advanced descendants of the 'guestworker' population and the 'newcomers' starting 'right at the bottom'.

A fourth major form of legal immigration to Europe includes refugees and expellees. Though to a greatly restricted extent, Europe still offers these groups two ways to enter: political asylum and generally limited stays with various different forms of refugee status. Entry as an asylum seeker is still possible, albeit severely limited by the measures described above, or through ways that are often irregular or illegal. There is also event-related, or rather catastrophe-related, admission of quota refugees and larger numbers of refugees from war and civil war. This group comprised almost entirely refugees from Europe; in the 1990s, it included especially those driven from former Yugoslavia. Facultative agreements, as during the 1999 Balkan War (see section 3), displayed substantial discrepancies among individual countries as regards admission declarations as well as between the declared willingness to take in refugees and actual admission. A binding regulation at the European level that covers the crucial financial sphere and thus the long-demanded implementation of 'burden sharing' remained a postulate until the turn of the century.[24]

Where no legal 'main gates' or 'front doors' were open, and even legal 'side doors' appeared hardly accessible despite migrants' willingness to adapt, irregular or illegal 'back doors' are being used more and more: after the recruitment ban and the immigration restrictions of the early to mid-1970s, there was a distinct rise in asylum migrations; and after these in turn were sharply limited in the 1980s and early 1990s, irregular or illegal immigration and employment rose all the more. Closed doors – also for asylum-seeking refugees without any chance of legal immigration – are circumvented in part by means of regular entry to irregular employment and in part by illegal immigration in the strict sense. In Europe, this still affects primarily but no longer exclusively the countries of the Euro-Mediterranean zone (see chapter 4, section 2); since the end of the Cold War, a similar situation exists in 'reform countries' of east central Europe such as Poland, the Czech Republic and Hungary. Together with southern Europe, they have become buffer or bottleneck zones for immigration unwanted in the west and the north.[25]

The flip side of shielding off Europe against unwanted immigration and of the increasingly confusing restrictions on entry, stay and participation is new forms of immigration and residence that have become firmly established in the grey zone between legality, irregularity, illegality and criminality. They range from regular shuttle migration that has a legal appearance ('tourists', 'family visits') in order to engage in illegal employment (such as across the Polish border to work in Greater Berlin) to going 'underground' after being instructed to leave or informed of deportation measures. Fictitious or contract marriages occasionally arranged through 'agencies' or performed abroad are also used to establish legal residency. These can lead to serious, far-reaching dependencies, for example when the foreign national spouse loses his or her residence permit if divorce is filed before a certain length of time has passed.[26]

With some qualification, it is possible to distinguish four main – complex and occasionally overlapping – forms of irregular or illegal migration.[27]

The first area begins with legal entry, for example as a tourist, seasonal worker, business traveller, asylum seeker or refugee. The person's status

turns illegal when they become undocumented, staying beyond the approved length of stay and/or through employment without a work permit
('overstayers', '*sans-papiers*'). This is particularly prevalent in the Euro-
Mediterranean zone, as well as, for example, in France. A second area
includes illegal or secret entry or crossing the border with forged documents, followed by staying in the country and working illegally, not
being registered or being registered with false papers. Sometimes a series
of related violations takes place when working without a work or residence permit or having entered the country illegally, not to mention the
related violations or subsequent offences that can often be unavoidable
when living illegally, such as renting a flat under false pretences.[28]

Both of these forms involve irregular or illegal labour migration
leading to the informal sector, which varies throughout Europe but is
generally expanding. It is primarily in the areas of construction and
related trades, cleaning services and fixed seasonal employment as well
as a wide variety of replacement and additional employment. Based on
sound estimates, about one-third of French motorways were built by
'illegals', and about one-third of all automobile production in France
was and still is done by irregular workers. In Italy, about 20–30 per cent
of the gross national product is earned by irregular labour.[29] 'Immigrant
labour is part of a clandestine workforce which keeps the wheels going
round', commented the *Financial Times* with respect to Britain as early as
1990; 'the construction industry including the Channel Tunnel relies on
it, the fashion industry would collapse without it, domestic service would
evaporate'.[30] In unified Germany it was an open secret that at 'Europe's
largest construction site', Berlin in the 1990s – even apart from the
irregular work arrangements on private construction sites – the margin
on costs set by the federal government would have been difficult to keep,
and the 1999 completion date impossible, without illegal labour. In
nursing and care services, women from eastern Europe are increasingly
employed in Germany in poorly paid irregular or illegal positions. Physicians and clerics occasionally even discreetly refer their patients and
congregation members to them, since they do not know how else to
help those who receive insufficient care because of nursing costs.

The informal sector therefore depends on this irregular or illegal
labour, in which a far higher level of illicit national workers also partici-
pates. Consequently, irregular or illegal arrangements, cunning and difficult to detect, enjoy a high degree of unspoken approval, ostensible social
legitimacy and often also tacit tolerance by authorities. This is so despite
the well-known fact that irregular or illegal work is usually underpaid,
uninsured, untaxed and often connected with extremely hard labour and
health hazards. Symbolic threatening gestures and occasional raids to
deter the employment of 'illegal immigrants' are therefore rather suited

to reinforce xenophobic defensive attitudes in the broad public. This is also true of Germany, where about 3,500 staff members of the labour administration and customs office were assigned to combating illegal employment in the late 1990s; however, the tightened control measures and increased penalties, especially in the building sector, obviously acted only as a minimal deterrent or were relatively easy to evade.[31]

The third form caught in the tension of migration and illegality includes the predominantly international human smuggling organizations, serving a kind of feeder and bridging function for would-be immigrants lacking any other options. Smuggling organizations appear in cities of the 'Third World', often as regular 'travel agencies' specialized in this lucrative business, and are the main profiteers abroad from the closing off of 'Fortress Europe'. This international feeder criminality frequently overlaps with the international organization of fraud, theft and violent crime, and even negligent homicide: fraud and theft as regards the deception and looting of migrants, who are helplessly at the mercy of their smugglers; violence and negligent homicide in cases where, if there is a chance of being discovered at the coasts, the victims of international human smugglers are put out at barely crossable rivers or elsewhere under life-threatening circumstances, or left to their fate aboard dangerous methods of 'transport', for example in sealed containers or on unseaworthy ships. Only the rescued victims and recovered bodies are counted by the European border authorities, the number of which steadily increased in the 1990s.[32]

A fourth form of illegality, sometimes overlapping with the third, is the diverse area of criminal migration in the strict sense, that is, cross-border mobility for criminal purposes or to avoid prosecution for crimes that have been committed.[33] This includes connections – often one-sidedly emphasized in popular notions – between ethnic communities or migratory networks and criminal milieus, especially in the area of Mafia-like organizations. These no longer exist only throughout east central Europe but also in its diaspora, such as among Albanians in Germany. Movements of individual criminals across borders also belong to this category, which can be a minor form of criminal 'labour migration', such as for smuggling and transnational fencing of stolen goods. Also to be mentioned is the deliberate employment of bands of trick thieves and burglars, which are occasionally made up of children and adolescents brought over the border in groups.

These and other forms of transnational mobility for criminal purposes or flight across borders to avoid criminal prosecution will not be discussed here. Relevant overlap between migration and criminality, on the other hand, occurs in the cases of irregular or illegal migration and internationally organized crimes of human smuggling and trafficking.

In the area of irregular or illegal migration, this overlap emerges, for example, regarding forged documents. In south–north migration in particular, visas are needed; in east–west migration, it is primarily verification of minority affiliation in the Commonwealth of Independent States (CIS) that opens up prospects for immigration in the west. The overlap between migration and criminality is most significant, however, in worldwide human smuggling operations. Though there is also much overlap here, a kind of informal service sector can be distinguished from the area of organized serious crime.

Belonging to the first-named area are illegal 'travel agencies' and human smuggling organizations, operating worldwide and with increasingly complex networks. 'Travel agencies' outside Europe offer for sale real albeit unenforceable contracts for people to be taken across the border or referred to work, with a wide range of services offered, from 'smuggle guarantees' to 'children's discounts'. The area of worldwide organized crime includes in particular international trafficking in women, which, often overlapping with related referral businesses (such as fraudulent job placement and marriage referral), has become a serious crime of massive proportions. In Germany, the International Organization for Migration has estimated that about 80 per cent of women criminally trafficked for prostitution purposes are from east central Europe and the CIS.[34]

Since the Iron Curtain has opened, in addition to migration patterns, the routes of intercontinental south–north and east–west migrations have changed. There is increased overlapping, forming south–east–west and east–south–north migrations. The implosion of the eastern bloc, especially the Soviet Union, led to an abrupt rise in migration, not just in and around the region. Migration from the south also increased and affected countries of the former eastern bloc to varying degrees. This was the result of liberalization in the post-Soviet age, deficient administrative structures for managing migration processes and weak border controls, which made it easier to enter and remain in CIS countries. With growing success, western European governments therefore pushed for tightening of the corresponding control regulations, especially the practice of having visa stamps in passports, based on western examples.[35]

Nevertheless, more and more migrants become 'stranded' in transit countries in east central and eastern Europe or fall victim to smuggling organizations there, if their paths to those countries were not determined by smuggling arrangements in the first place. A clear increase in transmigrants from Africa and South-east Asia bound for western Europe and North America could generally be observed in the 1990s in east central and eastern Europe. In Moscow alone, an estimated 250,000 Asians, mostly from China and Sri Lanka, were waiting to be transported further to the west in the mid-1990s, as arranged by the smugglers. The number of illegal migrants from Iraq, Iran and Afghanistan is estimated at 500,000 to 1 million for the whole of Russia. Many of them live in dire circumstances, not just because they are without refugee status or residence permits but because people of colour there especially are looted and blackmailed on all sides, discriminated against, harassed and abused on the streets and by the police.

Even though central Asian countries also report having transit migrants, the western CIS countries – Belarus, Ukraine, Moldova and the Russian Federation – have become the main transmigration destinations. According to government estimates, there were, for example, about 150,000–300,000 illegal residents living in Belarus in the mid-1990s. Only a small portion of them were from other CIS countries, whereas more than 70 per cent came from Asia and Africa, and about 15 per cent from the Near and Middle East. Illegal transmigrants of up to 36 different nationalities were rounded up and arrested in Belarus. The illegal transport of migrants or their pseudo-legal camouflage for the purpose of crossing the border and remaining illegally have become, in addition to drug traffic, big business. Most of those illegal migrants arrested viewed Belarus as a stopover on their planned route to the west, especially to Germany, France and Scandinavia.[36]

Chinese migrants travelled via Hong Kong, Singapore and Bangkok to Moscow in order to move farther on from there to western Europe. Another route led through east central Europe: in 1989–92 there were no visa requirements between China and Hungary, so Chinese migrants could travel to Hungary and obtain a residence permit there, which in turn made it easier to apply for a visa for a western country. Once the visa requirement was reinstated in 1992, some Chinese returned while others had since settled in Hungary, where Chinese communities and migratory networks developed serving an intermediary function for new immigration and further migration. There are considerable differences in estimates on the number of foreign nationals residing illegally in Hungary, ranging from 40,000 to 150,000 in the mid-1990s. These estimates were based on the 10,000–20,000 from more than 100 different countries who are apprehended annually trying to cross the border illegally. With about 250,000–300,000 foreigners living there in the mid-1990s either legally or illegally, Hungary too went through the transition from a country of emigration to one of immigration or transmigration.[37] The Baltic states, Poland and the Czech Republic also became east–west transit countries or 'waiting rooms' for migrants from Asia, Africa and Arab countries of the Near and Middle East as well as the Asian part of the CIS.

A special area, mentioned here only peripherally within the context of migration patterns, includes mass tourism and affluence and retirement migrations from northern and western Europe. These existed as a north–south migration within Europe, at first in the opposite direction to the transnational labour migrations of the 'guestworker' period. In the area of mass tourism it included especially trips to Italy, Greece, Portugal and Spain. It also applied to Yugoslavia in the 1970s and 1980s. Like Turkey, Yugoslavia was increasing significantly as a destination until the multi-ethnic country collapsed in war and civil war, cutting the area off from mass tourism from 1992 apart from a few coastal strips. Parallel to this development, from the late 1960s there was also a north–south affluence migration with shuttle migrations and extended stays, as well as some permanent relocations. This movement was at first strictly limited to the socially privileged from Germany, Britain and Scandinavia who had a second residence or retirement home in southern Europe, such as in the Dordogne, Tuscany, on the Canary Islands, the Costa del Sol and especially on Mallorca. From the 1970s the numbers started to grow and were made up increasingly of the upper middle class. In the 1980s, more and more people in the lower middle class migrated in this direction as temporary retirement migrations. Retirement at discount prices in the off-peak season on the Balearic Islands or Spain's Costa Blanca was not only more relaxing in spring, autumn and winter, it was occasionally even less expensive than retirement in wet and cold central, western and northern Europe. This led to considerable seasonal fluctuations in age structures in some destination areas. On the Spanish 'vacation island' of Mallorca, for example, spring, autumn and winter in the late 1980s belonged to the European elderly; in the summer the vacation population regularly became 'rejuvenated'.

In the 1990s, inner-European north–south migration led to isolated instances of tension between local populations in southern European destinations or in-migration regions. Their protests against the 'selling out of their homeland' expressed fears of cultural 'overforeignization' and that they were being economically and socially cheated. This happened in the late 1990s on Mallorca, where exclusive 'German' and 'English' districts developed parallel infrastructures with residential settlements, stores, medical and other forms of care, while the local population felt the pressure of increased property prices, rents and costs for everyday commodities.[38]

Temporary in-migration for tourists from third countries remained unrestricted in Europe as long as they were not from the 'Third World', in which case they were considered 'suspect' and presumed to want to 'abuse' their tourist visa to file an application for asylum. Conversely, regions outside Europe became dependent on seasonally fluctuating, short-term and wide-ranging mass migrations of tourists, many of whom came from Europe. This applied especially to regions of the 'Third

World' which either did not have sufficient resources of their own or which became dependent on multinational firms because of low producer prices of agricultural monocultures that had partly been implanted in colonial times. These multinationals took the place of earlier colonial companies, while the descendants of their former colonial overlords returned as tourists. Even torturous hells have been discovered for tourism, such as the West African slave trade centres or the penal colony island known as Devil's Island in French Guinea, on which most of the prisoners did not survive to complete their sentences.

Apart from family reunification and elite and affluence migration, which were not subjected to any group-specific rules or restrictions, the tension between attributes assigned as either 'own' or 'other' identities was further reinforced in migration and migration policies at the close of the century, a tension between migrants' images and descriptions of themselves and migrant identities as defined by migration policies. Yet migrants have to attempt to correspond to these assigned identities in order to achieve their goals of crossing the border and obtaining residency permission. Therefore, the boundaries between legal definitions of what comprises 'labour', 'asylum', 'flight' or 'minorities' have become more fluid in the 'multiple identities' of migrants than ever before.[39] This must also be kept in mind when considering the major groups selected as examples for discussion in the following sections.

2   MINORITIES FROM EASTERN AND SOUTH-EASTERN EUROPE: ETHNIC GERMANS, JEWS, ROMA

Very few groups formed major minority migrations from eastern Europe during the Cold War: the largest groups of the 1.2 million people who were able to leave the USSR between 1948 and 1990 were those of Jewish (52 per cent) and German (36 per cent) descent, followed by much smaller groups of Armenians (7 per cent), Greeks (2 per cent) and others (2 per cent). Emigrants of German or Greek descent were bound almost entirely for West Germany and Greece, respectively; Jews went to Israel, the United States and in smaller groups to central and western Europe; Armenians went mostly to the United States (California) and France. Emigration options negotiated by organized interest groups for certain minorities that were referred to in the USSR as 'nationalities' offered bridges to the west. In this context, the agreements of the Commission on Security and Cooperation in Europe (CSCE, 1975) on cooperation in humanitarian areas played an important role. They led to a limited liberalization of exit practices in Poland, Yugoslavia, Hungary, Czechoslovakia and especially the USSR, which hoped they would bring relaxed or beneficial relations with the United States (regarding Jewish emigrants) and West Germany (regarding those of German descent).[40]

The opening of the Iron Curtain and the collapse of the Soviet Union changed the basic conditions entirely. The minority groups thereby mobilized were considered, or regarded themselves, partly as having been liberated, partly as being driven out as expellees or as refugees. Others were viewed or saw themselves as return migrants or homecomers, even if their ancestors had left their homeland generations earlier. Still others, as in the conflict-ridden establishment of new nation-states after the end of the Austro-Hungarian monarchy and the Ottoman Empire, were again victims of the movement of borders over people, without their or their ancestors' ever having crossed borders to emigrate or immigrate. Migrations of minorities in eastern Europe exhibited strongly opposing movement patterns after the end of the Cold War. At an international conference on refugees and persons in refugee-like situations in the CIS, held in May 1996 in Geneva, United Nations Secretary-General Boutros Boutros-Ghali reported that about 9 million people in the CIS were refugees as of 1991. Of those, according to the Office of the UN High Commissioner for Refugees (UNHCR), about 3.6 million were seeking refuge in other CIS republics due to 'open ethnic conflict' (for example in Chechnya, Georgia, Armenia and Azerbaijan). Roughly 3.3 million people had fled back to their 'former homeland' due to 'latent ethnic tension'. There were also refugee movements and resettlements on other grounds, such as environmental catastrophes (see section 4).

In the European part of the CIS, there were a number of migrations in opposite directions across external CIS borders. They were bound, for example, for Finland (from Karelia), Greece (from Macedonia), Poland (from Lithuania, Belarus, Ukraine), the Czech Republic (from Volhynia and Serbia), Slovakia (from Hungary and Carpatho-Ukraine [Zakarpats'ka]) and Hungary (Slovakia, Transylvania, Carpatho-Ukraine). In the other direction, millions of former Soviet citizens, such as Russians and Ukrainians, who became non-dominant minorities in the independent former republics of the Soviet Union, migrated back to the territorial centre of the collapsed empire or to the Ukraine. The only relatively reliable statistics are the migration data collected at the soon to be fortified borders in the west. Data on migration within the eastern and southeastern regions remain unreliable, often based only on estimates: in 1990 and 1991 alone, more than 1 million people each are estimated to have left the Soviet Union and Romania; about 400,000 people left Bulgaria. From 1989 to 1992, a total of more than 4 million people left the territories of the former Soviet Union and other former eastern bloc countries.[41] They were largely members of minorities that had long been oppressed on political, religious or, in a broad sense, cultural grounds.

Within these east–west minority movements, the largest group by far in central Europe were 'ethnic Germans', or *Aussiedler*, people of German descent from the successor states of the USSR and from Poland and Romania, who immigrated to Germany. Though far smaller, the next largest of the eastern European migration groups in central Europe were Jews from the CIS and Roma from Romania, Yugoslavia and Bulgaria. East–west migration of ethnic Germans and Jews shot up after the borders opened; the history leading up to these movements during the Cold War is described in the following overview. The Roma minority in eastern Europe, on the other hand, did not have a powerful lobby in the west and consequently had very little chance to emigrate before the Iron Curtain opened, except for participating in labour migrations that originated in Yugoslavia.

Ethnic Germans

Before the start of the Second World War, there were about 9 million Germans living on German territory east of the Oder and Neisse rivers, in Silesia, East Brandenburg, Pomerania and East Prussia. Beyond the eastern border of Germany, there were another approximately 8 million Germans or people of German descent, predominantly in Czechoslovakia, Poland, Romania, Hungary, Yugoslavia and the Soviet Union, but also in Estonia, Latvia, Lithuania, the Memel region and the Free State of Danzig. After the Russian war deportations eastward and, in the immediate post-war period, the mass refugee and expulsion movements westward, there were still an estimated 4 million people of German descent in eastern Europe and the Eurasian realm (see chapter 3, section 3). Many no longer lived in traditional settlement areas but, like almost all Soviet citizens of German descent from 1941 on, they had been forcibly resettled, scattered throughout foreign environments, isolated, deprived of their rights and discriminated against as 'fascists'.[42]

In-migration from eastern Europe to West Germany continued throughout the stream of refugees and expellees of the post-war period and the strong influx from East Germany until the Berlin Wall was built in 1961. From 1951 to 1988, almost 1.6 million *Aussiedler* of German descent passed through West German border transit camps, but most of them arrived starting in the second half of the 1970s. A minor portion were German citizens who had been deported to the east; most of them, however, were ethnic Germans with foreign citizenship, whose ancestors had left the German-speaking realm generations or even centuries earlier. Acknowledgement of these *Aussiedler* as Germans had to do with the long ethnonational tradition of the one-sided German citizenship law based solely on *jus sanguinis*, as well as the German law dealing with late consequences of the Second World War (*Kriegsfolgenrecht*). Prerequisites for being granted German citizenship were, first of all, proof of German descent and a 'commitment to Germanness' as manifested by one's life history. Helpful in providing evidence of this, in addition to the German language tradition and noticeable maintenance of German customs and traditions in the family, were, for example, being listed as having 'German nationality' on Russian documents and, for a long time, corresponding classification by Nazi agencies at the time of the German occupation and even membership in organizations of the Waffen-SS. Tacitly presupposed, on the other hand, was the experience of consequences of war concomitant with this German descent. Accordingly, these ethnic German emigrants were considered equal to refugees and expellees of the post-war period based on the legal fiction of 'pressure of expulsion' in their places of origin, as well as with respect to generous state aid towards integration. In East Germany, on the other hand, integration of refugees and expellees was declared 'completed' in the early 1950s by a resolution of the East German state party (SED) in consideration of the neighbouring countries whence they came. The issue was therefore absent from public discussion from that point on, and there was only an insignificant number of ethnic German immigrants. On the basis of current research, their volume is estimated to be about 10,000 at most.[43]

Immigration and integration of ethnic Germans from eastern Europe and the Soviet Union in West Germany took place fairly quietly up to the mid- to late 1980s. The issue only occasionally emerged into the spotlight of an outraged public when financial return services were brought up: when the Polish government approved exit visas for 125,000 Polish citizens of German descent within one year, for example, it was connected with a credit of 2.3 thousand million DM to Poland (Schmidt-Gierek agreement of 1975). In Romania, the migration business assumed the character of outright human trafficking worth thousands of millions. The virtually bankrupt regime of the megalomaniac '*Conducator*' Nicolae Ceauşescu, who by the end was obviously also confused before being executed in the Romanian revolution of 1989, took in up to about £35,000 for an exit visa for a single person. On top of that, would-be emigrants were forced to pay huge bribes to the corrupt bureaucracy.

Poland was the main country of origin of ethnic German emigrants in the period 1950–87. Sixty-two per cent of all these *Aussiedler* (848,000) came from there; only 8 per cent (110,000) were from the Soviet Union, with its still restrictive emigration policies. Following Poland, and far ahead of the Soviet Union, was Romania, with 15 per cent (206,000). When the Iron Curtain opened, immigration from the Soviet Union and its successor states rapidly outstripped immigration from Poland and Romania. The tacit approval of the immigration of ethnic Germans also decreased when people were confronted with the social problems of mass immigration, which no one had seriously reckoned with in the shadow of the Cold War.

For decades, the anguishing memory of the apparently unattainable wish to emigrate of the 'brothers and sisters in the east' formed part of the firm repertoire of West German Cold War policies towards the east. The opening of the Iron Curtain fulfilled the dreams of many hundreds of thousands in the east; in the west it brought fears of new 'migrations of nations' from the east, following on the heels of ethnic German immigration, which had abruptly swelled to a mass movement. The annual volume of ethnic German immigration had already started to rise sharply in 1987; in 1988 it just exceeded the 200,000 mark and reached a peak of 377,055 in 1989; in 1990 it increased yet further to almost 400,000. Immigration declined considerably in 1991 to a volume of 221,995, despite a continued high number of applications; it essentially stabilized at this high plateau from 230,565 in 1992 to 217,898 in 1995. The number of immigrants dropped substantially to a level of 177,751 in 1996 and 134,419 in 1997, reaching 103,080 in 1998, corresponding to the low level that had been suddenly broken ten years earlier. The consolidation of immigration figures at a high level and their slow decline were the result of treaties between Germany and the countries of origin to improve the situation in the eastern regions of origin through German financial support as well as indirect German measures taken to influence the immigration of ethnic Germans, especially by limiting the annual number allowed to enter to a maximum of 220,000 as of 1993.[44]

At the same time, an immense shift in regions of origin could be observed: from the late 1980s Poland, which had been far ahead of Romania and had initially taken pride of place as regards ethnic German emigration, dropped behind the successor countries of the former Soviet Union. By 1990, these countries were the origin of 37.3 per cent of *Aussiedler* immigration, the figure then skyrocketing to 66.4 per cent in 1991. Immigration of ethnic Germans from the CIS ultimately comprised 96.8 per cent in 1996, when 172,181 of a total of 177,751 came from the former Soviet Union. The share of ethnic German immigrants from Romania (2.4 per cent in 1996) and Poland (0.6 per cent in 1996) declined accordingly. The shift in regions of origin was not only a result of the exit policies of the CIS countries and their incomparably high migration potential with respect to minorities of German descent. It was also influenced by a change in German admission procedures. Post-war experiences ('expulsion pressure') had to be proven by the applicants in Poland and Romania as of 1993 (Act to correct the laws dealing with late consequences of the Second World War, *Kriegsfolgenbereinigungsgesetz*), while it was still presupposed with respect to applicants from the CIS.

The phrase 'ethnic German immigrants' (*deutsche Aussiedler* or *Spät-aussiedler*) is an ethnonational euphemism, because those who are recognized are simultaneously both Germans and foreigners. They came, and still come, into a genuine immigration situation, not in a legal sense but in a cultural, psychological and social one. This situation was made easier materially by immediate incorporation into all benefit areas of the welfare state. Moreover, ethnic German immigrants long received generous integration support, making them a privileged minority in comparison with immigrated populations of foreign nationals. At the same time, the migration situation also posed psychological problems because trust in the supportive strength of ethnonational bonds caused everyone involved to underestimate the difficulty of this immigration situation in the receiving country.

Ethnic German immigrants from eastern Europe are a very diverse group based on their origins, self-image and religious and cultural connections. Still, their integration was considered exemplary even in an international comparison and was often recommended as a model for other immigrant groups in Germany. However, for different reasons, integration of these ethnic Germans led to several social problems from the 1990s. The rise of immigration into a mass movement coincided with a public budget crisis that forced cutbacks in integration assistance for *Aussiedler*, including measures for vocational qualifications and language courses. Professional qualifications often did not correspond to requirements in the host country, and, in the transition to a mass movement, the language competence of immigrant groups declined considerably as of the early 1990s. Consequently, one-time-only language exams were introduced in 1996 in the regions of origin, which at the same time served as an indirect means of restricting immigration. Unemployment among the *Aussiedler* climbed dramatically, to 32 per cent in 1993 according to a representative survey. Only 46 per cent of men, and a mere 17 per cent of women, had work at the time they were surveyed. Women in particular are often both under- and overqualified simultaneously. They are underqualified, or have the wrong qualifications, for the options for regular employment that are open to them; and they are overqualified for irregular work in the informal sector, in which many of them work as domestic servants in private households.[45]

Ethnic German immigrants, in addition to Jewish immigrants from the CIS, were still clearly a privileged group among all immigrant groups in Germany, even with the cutbacks in integration assistance. Their integration nevertheless revealed ever-clearer signs of an integration crisis starting in the mid-1990s. This was due in part to changes in the ethnic German population emigrating from the CIS countries in the first half of the 1990s: the large numbers of mostly highly motivated pioneer migrants in the late 1980s and early 1990s who, often at great personal cost, had been fighting for years or even decades for their exit visas were replaced by a mass movement that pulled many people along with the current. Insufficient motivation, especially among young people 'brought along' with their parents, quickly turned into disappointment and disorientation in the process of integration.

Decreasing language competence among the new ethnic German immigrants led to an increased concentration of Russian-speaking communities, which were growing as a result of subsequent chain migrations. They had their own press and exhibited some of the colony-forming aspects of a 'Russian minority' that were familiar from the immigration processes of the nineteenth and early twentieth centuries. In the late 1990s, this also included growing tension between young 'Russians' and locals and the no less local German Turks, who were clearly discriminated against relative to ethnic German immigrants. For settlement areas with a high concentration of ethnic German immigrants, studies from 1996–7 have also shown that in areas with a high immigration rate, high unemployment and decreasing integration assistance, crime rates grew significantly among disillusioned young ethnic German immigrants lacking any prospects, as compared with other youths in similar social situations. Social services and state hospitals reported conspicuous social and psychological effects of stress in an integration process that became a high-priority social problem in the late 1990s for many communities.[46]

Jews

Jewish emigration from the USSR/CIS has two things in common with that of ethnic German *Aussiedler* from eastern Europe and the former Soviet Union. For one thing, their emigration was also made possible as a result of pressure by western (in the case of Jews, mainly US) interest groups.[47] Second, a common factor in the east–west migration of both ethnic Germans and Jews from the territory of the former Soviet Union is the fact that they have been fully included as citizens and are privileged in comparison with other immigrants through integration assistance in, respectively, Germany and Israel. Whereas the recognition of ethnic Germans as German citizens is founded on a combination of *jus sanguinis* tradition, ethnonational notions and the law dealing with late consequences of the Second World War (*Kriegsfolgenrecht*), in Israel all Jews have a basic right to *aliyah* ('return') to the Holy Land and, according to the Law of Return of 1952, automatically become Israeli citizens.[48]

Looking back, the situation of the Jews in the Soviet Union improved slightly between the end of the Second World War and the founding of the state of Israel in 1948, which had been supported by the USSR. This was immediately followed by the renewed emergence of anti-Jewish defamation campaigns. In 1952, prominent Jews were secretly murdered, followed by a wave of arrests of Jewish physicians under the pretext of a conspiracy to murder Stalin; before his death, plans for mass deportations of Jews to Siberia and central Asia had become known. Stalin's death in 1953 brought an end to these five years of renewed segregation, persecution and oppression, but even the subsequent détente resulting from the de-Stalinization policies of Khrushchev were not able to inspire the confidence of the Jewish population that there would be a lasting improvement in their situation. Furthermore, after the Israeli–Arab Six Days' War in 1967, a massive 'anti-Zionist' propaganda campaign was initiated that aimed also to have an impact abroad. As a result, requests to Israel and western countries, especially the United States, became even louder to support the emigration wishes of Soviet Jews. After a total of 24,000 Jews had been able to leave the USSR between 1948 and 1970, the numbers clearly increased in the 1970s, reaching peaks in 1973 (34,000) and 1979 (50,000).[49]

At the same time, there was a growing trend away from Israel as an emigration destination. This had to do with fear of conflict after the Yom Kippur War, but also with changes regarding the main intermediate stopover in Vienna. Up to 1973, Jews from the Soviet Union – whether they arrived by aeroplane or, due to limited flight connections, railroad – were accommodated before their flight to Israel in Schönau castle outside Vienna, which was virtually cut off from the surroundings by Israeli guards. Schönau castle was closed in the summer of 1973. In the new transit camp under Austrian control near the Vienna airport in Simmering, Austrian personnel as well as representatives of American-Jewish aid organizations had access to Jewish emigrants. Many of these emigrants were told here for the first time that they were not obligated to continue to Israel and that automatic naturalization upon arrival in Israel coincided with their loss of refugee status, which would greatly facilitate entry into the United States. The repercussions on their migration behaviour were dramatic: the number of those in Vienna (and later also Rome) who opted out of continuing to Israel increased from 0.8 per cent in 1972 to 48.9 per cent in 1976. The zenith of this development was reached in 1988, when only 135 (1.7 per cent) of 7,700 Soviet Jews decided to go to Israel.

September 1988 marked the end of the period of 'free' decision making in Vienna. The backdrop to this was the cooling of US–Israeli relations in the aftermath of Israeli protests against the United States 'wooing away' immigrants, and also because of US outrage over the exposure of J. J. Pollard, an Israeli spy, and increasing annoyance over Israeli policies towards the Palestinians. At the beginning of the US fiscal year for 1990

(1 October 1989), the US immigration quota for the USSR was restricted to a maximum of 50,000 people, including immigrants from the Armenian Soviet republic, who also had a strong lobby in the United States. In fact, however, only 6,500 Jews (and 6,500 Armenians) from the USSR entered the United States in 1990. In addition, the expensive US transition homes in the transit stations in Vienna and Rome were closed, where, in June 1989, around 11,000 Jews from the Soviet Union had still been waiting for their entry visas for the United States. Since then, Soviet citizens wanting to emigrate to the United States had to apply for immigration from the Soviet Union and wait there, sometimes for years, for their visas. Consequently, immigration to Israel began to rise again.

As with ethnic German emigrants, the opening of the Iron Curtain also led to increased, and largely unrestricted, emigration of Jews from the CIS. The reduced US immigration quotas channelled CIS immigration to Israel, but it also reinforced a certain degree of smaller emigrations to Canada, Australia and central Europe (see chapter 4, section 2). Increased immigration to Europe was especially noticeable in Germany. From the opening of the Iron Curtain to the end of 1998, a total of 122,593 Jews from the Soviet Union/CIS received entry guarantees for Germany; between 1991 and 1998, almost 93,000 had immigrated (17,781 in 1998 alone).[50]

Background motivation for Jews from the CIS in their decision to emigrate was fear that history would repeat itself in view of the increase in a mixture of anti-Judaism, anti-Zionism and anti-Semitism with violent rioting against Jews; though it was not 'state-sponsored', it was indeed commonplace and spread by nationalist movements. Repeated rumours of planned pogroms, even with specific dates, did not turn out to be true, but from 1993 to 1999 alone, more than a hundred attacks on synagogues, Jewish cultural centres and cemeteries were counted. Also came fear of civil war-like situations with minorities being made into scapegoats, connected with the experience of political destabilization, economic chaos and the proliferation of Mafia-like structures. In the foreground of decisions to go to Germany were down-to-earth, concrete choices between conflicting concerns, especially regarding political stability, social security, professional options and educational prospects for children. An important but not decisive point was the desire to become involved in religious and cultural Jewish community life. This is only slowly developing again in Germany, especially since a decision for Germany is always also a decision against Israel's firm invitation grounded in religious and cultural life. Based on a survey in which immigrant Jews in Berlin from the Soviet Union and its successor states described themselves, only 22 per cent said they had a strict Jewish identity in which they intensively maintained religious and cultural traditions.[51]

Jewish immigrants from the CIS have been taken in by Germany since 1991 as quota refugees, in accordance with a law passed in 1980 to acknowledge the 'boat people' who arrived in the late 1970s from Southeast Asia. Jewish immigrants would certainly have no chance as regular asylum seekers, despite all the persecution and oppression they had endured and the well-founded fear of repetition, because German asylum law is directed towards acute individual persecution by the state in the absence of any safe way to evade the persecution in the country of origin. The collective status as quota refugees that Jewish immigrants receive in Germany corresponds approximately to refugees deemed to be entitled to asylum with unlimited residence permits and protection from deportation to the country of origin even if they commit a criminal offence. They receive work permits, social security with full entitlement to the welfare system and integration assistance (such as language courses and assistance for training programmes). Socially, they are fully included in the welfare state and have equal status to German citizens in broad areas of legal, social and economic life. Their situtation is not as outstanding as that of ethnic German immigrants from eastern Europe, who receive more comprehensive integration assistance, but incomparably better than the situation of other immigrant groups in Germany. Jews from the CIS receive identity papers in Germany that confirm their refugee and residence status (which is also valid in other EU countries). Like ethnic Germans, they are allowed to reclaim the Russian documents they submitted, consequently retaining or reattaining their original nationality. In contrast to ethnic Germans, however, they are not allowed to return to their country of origin without special authorization if they do not want to risk losing their refugee status.

Beyond documenting the fact that they are members of the Jewish minority, Jewish immigrants from the CIS are not required to satisfy any other preconditions in Germany due to the recognition of their group as quota refugees. The criteria for their admission are thus much milder than those for ethnic Germans, especially since Jews are not required to demonstrate competence in the German language. Classification as part of the Jewish minority was marked in passports of the Soviet Union, since like the German minority it was treated as a 'nationality' there. It is an open secret that many documents have been forged. But even cases of abuse are generally treated with discretion: a person whose Jewish identity is in doubt is obligated to return but only rarely expelled by forcible deportation. Considerate treatment of would-be immigrant Jews from the CIS in the country of the Holocaust is a German response to the darkest chapter of its history. Many immigrants from eastern Europe, however, are facing special problems of integration in Germany, as in Israel: they emigrated as Jews and were taken in and supported as such by Jewish communities, although a large proportion did not have a Jewish identity in a religious or cultural sense in their society of origin and thus often finally rediscover it in the host country.

Altogether, immigration of Jews to Germany from the CIS has remained virtually 'invisible' up to the end of the 1990s. This had to do not only with their relatively small numbers in comparison with other immigrant groups, but also with their high level of willingness to adapt. Furthermore, Jewish emigrants from the CIS generally prefer living in large cities, in contrast to ethnic German immigrants' preference for rural areas and smaller towns. This corresponds to their occupational structures and social situations, which resemble those of the Jewish CIS immigrants in Israel, including the attendant problems in the process of integration. While ethnic German emigrants from the CIS, relative to German social situations, could be classified as lower middle class, Jewish refugees from the CIS are generally from the upper middle and upper classes. According to a representative survey in 1993–4, 71 per cent had a university degree, 35 per cent had been engineers or natural scientists in the Soviet Union, and 21 per cent had been physicians, teachers or artists. This structure of qualifications and occupation often led in Germany in the 1990s to their high unemployment or obtaining employment below their professional qualifications. Social differences between Jews and ethnic German *Aussiedler* from the CIS were often the background in the 1990s for anti-Jewish, anti-Zionist and anti-Semitic sentiments expressed by *Aussiedler* towards Jews from the CIS.[52]

Roma

Immigration of the Roma from Romania, Yugoslavia and Bulgaria to central Europe first became possible through the revolution in Romania in December 1989 and was then pushed by subsequent chain migrations and by the conflict in former Yugoslavia. At first, Roma immigrants went mostly to Germany, to a lesser extent also to Austria; they then spread out to other European countries through further migration.

The Roma were not released from 'Roma slavery' in Romania until 1862. Except for a peasant group and a group that advanced to the lower middle class, they remained a legally unrecognized minority without any social prestige; the nomadic Roma were the most severely ostracized group. Under the Ceauşescu regime, they did not live in friendship with other ethnic groups but were at least 'free' to the extent that no one was concerned with them or felt responsible for them. Not until the end of the Ceauşescu dictatorship, in connection with the regime's disastrous 'reform plans', were state measures again used to intervene in the lives of the Roma and their settlements, though these could hardly be brought to bear any more. After the revolution of 1989, the Roma were again subjected to historical prejudice against their group, which merged with racist nationalism, accusations of having collaborated with the collapsed regime and allegedly having received undue advantages regarding land redistribution. In various regions, acts of violence and attacks against Roma settlements took place, such as in the city of Turu Lung. About 1,000 Romanians with torches forced their way into the Roma district, setting 36 of 41 houses on fire; one child was killed and dozens of Roma were badly beaten. Almost 30 pogroms were registered in 1991–2 in Romania.[53]

Such exclusion and harassment, as well as hopes for economic betterment, were the main reasons for the Roma's migration westward. Up to 1993, Germany's liberal asylum law appeared to offer secure residency, at least temporarily. Contacts also existed dating back to Roma from Yugoslavia who had worked in Germany as seasonal labourers. This was true also for Austria, where Roma were even supported as a recognized minority. However, as with other autochthonous minorities, they were not granted this recognition until the third generation living in the country, a grim consideration in view of the fact that many long-established Roma and Sinti families had been victims of the genocide during the Nazi period. On the other hand, foreign Roma, seasonal labourers for example, had – as compared with Germany – extremely uncertain residency authorization in Austria, where it was dependent on a work contract and could be revoked at any time. If they violated any regulations or missed any deadlines, residency authorization could be ended abruptly, as often happened with the Roma who were inexperienced with and mistrustful of the bureaucracy. Asylum-seeking Roma, even from war-torn Bosnia, did not have any *a priori* chance in Austria based on the asylum law. This is why many preferred living illegally, which meant they could at any time be put on remand pending deportation and then be deported.

Roma from eastern Europe therefore regarded residence in Germany to be safer than in Austria. In the early 1990s, about 50,000 Sinti and about 30,000 Roma with German citizenship lived there permanently. Their families had survived Nazi genocide, some with serious injuries from the medical 'experiments' in concentration camps, forced sterilization, and so on. There were also an estimated 30,000–40,000 Sinti or Roma labour migrants of various citizenships from eastern and south-eastern Europe. Data on Roma from eastern Europe in Germany, most of whom were registered as asylum seekers, are based on estimates because asylum seekers in Germany are recorded according to citizenship and not ethnic affiliation. According to official estimates, from January 1990 until the new asylum law came into force on 1 July 1993, about 250,000 Roma refugees had arrived in Germany; the largest group of them (60 per cent) came from Romania, a group half as large (30 per cent) from Yugoslavia, and a far smaller group (5 per cent) from Bulgaria. After the promotion of 'repatriation' and 'voluntary return migration', after being obligated to leave under threat of deportation, and after regular deportations and further migration to other European countries, there was still an official figure of at most 125,000 Roma refugees in Germany in mid-1993, although Roma organizations assumed there were only about 75,000.

The numbers continued to dwindle in subsequent years against the background of measures that reveal a glaring contrast to the treatment of ethnic German and Jewish immigrants from eastern Europe. As has been shown, their immigration was desired or at least tolerated and was accompanied by state measures under the guiding principle of welfare-state inclusion and social integration. The opposite was true regarding the unwanted immigration of 'Gypsies' from eastern Europe, who experienced exclusion and repatriation. The Roma from eastern Europe comprised a conspicuous group in early 1990s Germany with respect to their lifestyles, manners and social forms. Their social behaviour in everyday life and public discussion was described largely as strange and a nuisance. In 1993, local German administrations came under pressure from outraged citizens complaining of all kinds of everyday pestering or even the mere presence of 'Gypsies'. Threats of physical violence against immigrants from the east were alarming from a security standpoint.

Instead of attempts to gain sympathy or even tactful reserve, as was the case regarding ethnic Germans and Jews from eastern Europe, the Roma were met from the outset with a mixture of scepticism, distance and suspicious reserve, even by the media and politicians, with typical comments that they were 'not refugees' but 'real Gypsies'. Aggressive begging, petty crime and sometimes organized offences against property, which could be traced back to individual Roma families, was attributed to the Roma as a group and their networks ('bands of fences for stolen goods'). This served ostensibly to confirm historical prejudice. Both latent and openly racist characterizations turned the 'Gypsies' into an anti-social opposite to the orderly, bourgeois world. 'Gypsy *Asylanten*' were soon considered the incarnation of asylum abuse *per se*. Indeed, the acceptance rate of Roma in asylum proceedings, if they were even registered, was under 1 per cent as they were hardly in a position to present proof of individual persecution by state institutions, as is necessary for acknowledgement, and 'group persecution by third parties' allegedly did not take place, according to the status reports of the German Foreign Office in the places of origin.[54]

As chain migration increased, authorities in Germany, as in Austria, kept a lookout at the borders to turn Roma back, to make it difficult for those who illegally entered the country to apply for asylum, and to create contractual foundations for them to be deported in cooperation with the countries of origin. This happened although it was known that Roma were excluded, oppressed and attacked as a minority in their countries of origin, even if this was not done systematically and throughout the country. In a comparable context, the conditions that sufficed for the collective recognition of Jews from the CIS as quota refugees in Germany were not to apply for 'Gypsies'. This recognition could not even be forced through with political pressure since the Roma lacked a powerful lobby in the west. There were only interest groups and relief organizations such as the Central Council of German Sinti and Roma, the Rom and Cinti Union, the Society for Endangered Peoples, and a few supporting initiatives and pleasant-sounding explanations at a European level. This context had already become clear when they were neglected 'compensation' or 'reparations' in the sense of German payments, although about 500,000 members of this minority had been killed in the Holocaust, second only to the Jews. The collective memory of violent Nazi crimes also did not serve to make it easier for the 'Gypsies' of south-eastern Europe to be recognized as refugees or asylum seekers in Germany. Moreover, established members of this minority in the west at times showed a certain reserve, sometimes for purposes of self-protection, towards the Roma from south-eastern Europe, which is reminiscent of the scepticism that many assimilated Jews in the United States exhibited towards the large numbers of eastern European Jews who immigrated in the late nineteenth and early twentieth centuries during the new immigration. Friendly defensiveness was apparent in general appeals for improvement in the deplorable circumstances that gave a reason for migration in the regions of origin, but not for protection of the Roma from impending deportation back to precisely those circumstances.[55]

Roma were treated differently in the German federal states, as refugees, asylum seekers or with temporary toleration. They lived in collective accommodation or tent camps, caught between being forced to leave, being threatened with deportation or being granted a stay of deportation. Meanwhile, treaties were frantically negotiated between the German government and eastern European countries of origin and transit countries. 'Repatriation' of the homeless was described by its defenders as 'return agreements' with the countries of origin; many critics and those affected referred to it as 'deportation'. First came the German–Romanian 'return treaty' of November 1992; similar agreements followed with other countries in eastern and south-eastern Europe. Most were associated with millions in subsidies to cover the costs of the deportees' 'return'. These international 'return treaties' were not only about deporting people who crossed the border illegally and in-migrants who were forced to leave the country, including many Roma. It was also a matter of cooperating with the border controls. The German Federal Border Guard and Polish troops in the German–Polish borderlands, for example, engaged in outright 'Roma hunts', which for Roma interest groups conjured up images of the '*Zigeunerstreifen*' of the early modern age, which, unlike these border patrols, sometimes even systematically hunted down 'outlawed Gypsies' with a licence to kill. West–east chain deportations often appeared in place of the east–west chain migration that was interrupted by the defensive measures of 'Fortress Europe'. Roma forced to leave the country who were apprehended in the borderlands were deported in stages back to their country of origin, where they sometimes again became victims at the hands of incensed nationalists. This was true, for example, in Romania; however, because it is considered a 'safe third country' according to the German asylum law of 1993, no applications for asylum can be filed from there. The same also applies to Bulgaria, Poland, the Czech Republic, Slovakia and Hungary.

At a German state level, the 'Roma return programme' is an example of support for 'voluntary' return. After heated political battles over deportation versus a moratorium on deportation, the situation was resolved in September 1990 by the state of North Rhine-Westphalia (NRW) in cooperation with the Catholic charity Caritas and Macedonia, which was then still part of Yugoslavia. This took the form of an emphatic offer to in-migrants from Macedonia who had neither asylum nor any other authorization to remain in the country. After the lifting of a temporary moratorium on deportation, they had to reckon with being forced to return in the foreseeable future in any case. Their destination was the district of Shutka in Skopje, which, with more than 40,000 inhabitants, was the largest Roma settlement in Europe. The state of NRW provided integration assistance and the first year's rental costs in a settlement that it constructed. NRW held the right to fill the settlement housing for at least five years, after which it was transferred to the property of the Republic of Macedonia. The 'reintegration programme' was also connected with a local development programme with loans available to start new businesses and create jobs.

What the state government considered a contribution to 'new refugee policies' geared to reintegration and combating the conditions that led to flight, the Roma National Congress in Europe viewed as an expensive deportation into squalor: 'Macedonia has already been paid roughly 30 million marks to serve as a "garbage heap" for deported "Gypsies". A couple of tidy "little homes" were hypocritically set up at the edge of the Roma ghetto in Skopje (Shutka) for the "homecomers". The new homes are at the edge of one of the most abominable Roma ghettos in Europe, in which over 40,000 Roma are forced to "live" like animals, sometimes in cardboard boxes, where child mortality is over 50 per cent. There is no sewerage system, no running water, no medical care . . . . Entire countries meanwhile profit from the misery of our people.'[56] The only remaining option for Roma from eastern and south-eastern Europe striving for the west was illegal immigration; and this was increasing as 'Fortress Europe' continued to shield itself off, despite border security with modern technology, despite the lengthening arm of the German Border Guard that reached far into the country's interior, and despite the close cooperation on matters of deportation with countries of origin and transit. Roma who managed to enter a western country legally were generally war or civil war refugees from the area of conflict once called Yugoslavia.

3   REFUGEES AND EXPELLEES FROM EASTERN AND SOUTH-EASTERN EUROPE: YUGOSLAVIA, ALBANIA, KOSOVO

The tumbling of old structures in south-eastern Europe after 1990–1 brought great streams of refugees in its wake. The two major regions of origin were Yugoslavia and Albania. The multi-ethnic federal republic of Yugoslavia collapsed into a prolonged economic and political crisis, irreconcilable interests between the federal states and nationalistic posturing. In the case of Albania, disintegration followed the sudden opening of a country that had been hermetically sealed by the Hoxha regime for almost half a century, a country whose mismanagement had turned it into Europe's poorhouse.

Yugoslavia

Millions of people became homeless in war and civil war in former Yugoslavia. The UNHCR reported 3.7 million IDPs in 1995. Hundreds of thousands fled to other countries of Europe, which offered them temporary humanitarian protection on the basis of the regulations of the Geneva Convention on Refugees.[57]

According to the 1981 census, of the 22.4 million people in the multi-ethnic republic of Yugoslavia, there were 8.1 million (36.3 per cent) Serbs, 4.4 million (19.7 per cent) Croats, 1.8 million (8 per cent) Slovenians, 1.3 million (6 per cent) Macedonians and 0.6 million (2.6 per cent) Montenegrins. Among the remaining 11.2 per cent of the population were 1.7 million Albanians and 1.2 million of mixed-ethnic parentage who took advantage of the option of referring to themselves as 'Yugoslavs'. Hungarians, Turks, Slovaks, Romanians, Roma and other ethnic groups also lived there. This ethnocultural patchwork included not only different historical traditions in the Ottoman and Austro-Hungarian multi-ethnic empires, but also bloody divisions based on affiliation to Croatian and Serbian partisan groups (Ustasha and Chetniks) fighting on opposite sides in the Second World War. All this gave rise to tension-filled relations between the various groups. The latent conflicts that existed were partly bridged and partly repressed under Tito.

After Tito's death the federal union collapsed as a result of constitutional deficiencies, strong regional differences in development, distribution disputes and conflicting social and economic interests. Economic problems that had been growing since then damaged the Yugoslavian economy considerably, as did excessive bureaucratization and mismanagement, bad investments and an increasing technological development gap. Members of the Federal Council blocked each other, which prevented domestic and in particular economic policies from functioning. At the same time, nationalist interests and power politics, with varying degrees of international support, mobilized and exploited old ethnic prejudice, exclusive self-images and hostile images of the other.

Tensions within Yugoslavia need not inevitably have led to war. The conflicts were initially triggered by Slovenian and Croatian efforts to achieve autonomy, which were encouraged by the west, and the rise in nationalist emotions in support of a Greater Serbia since 1987–8 and their manipulation in maintaining the power of the Serbian leadership under Milosevič. Slovenia and Croatia declared their sovereignty and independence on 25 June 1991, leading the Yugoslavian People's Army to attack both countries. This marked the beginning of a series of wars: in Slovenia in June–July 1991, in Croatia from June–July 1991 to January 1992 and in May and August 1995, in Bosnia-Herzegovina from April 1992 to November 1995. Discussion of 'ethnic cleansing', which had supposedly long since entered the annals of history, gained frightening new relevance in view of the fact that such cruelty towards civilian populations was no longer considered possible in 'civilized' countries of the western world since the 'breach of civilization' (Dan Diner) by the Nazis and the experience of the Second World War.

In Croatia, whose population in 1990 was 4.7 million, 85 per cent of which was Croatian and only 11.5 per cent Serbian, the Krajina Serbs declared their independence and their own republic and started driving out the Croatian population. By the end of 1991, 500,000 had fled, about 300,000 of these from the Serbian-occupied regions of Croatia. Most of these Croats remained IDPs. Only very few refugees and expellees from Croatia managed to flee to other countries: out of a total of roughly 80,000, for example, about 13,000 fled to Austria, where they were taken in by friends and relatives and received state welfare benefits.

After the situation calmed down in the Croatian conflict, most of them returned.[58]

The hitherto worst devastation and material, physical and psychological aftermath for the civilian population came about during the war over Bosnia-Herzegovina from April 1992 to November 1995, which followed with scarcely a break after the Croatian war. The pre-war population of about 4.5 million in Bosnia-Herzegovina was made up of 44 per cent Bosnians, 17 per cent Croats and 32 per cent Serbs. From April to August 1992, the Bosnian Serbs conquered up to 70 per cent of the entire territory with the aid of the Yugoslavian People's Army; all non-Serbs were forced out. By May 1992, about 700,000 had already fled; by August 1992, the number had risen to 1.7 million. There were more than 2.5 million refugees by the time the Dayton agreement was signed in November 1995. More than 650,000 of the roughly 1.2 million IDPs fled to other republics in the territory of the former Yugoslavia. 'Ethnic cleansing' in both parts of Bosnia continued in 1996. Again, minorities in all territories were robbed of their economic basis for survival, driven from their homes, robbed, threatened, humiliated, raped, killed. Ethnic separation was further reinforced. About 1.3 million people in Bosnia-Herzegovina were directly affected as refugees. In March 1998, there were 550,000 Serbian refugees living in Serbia and Montenegro, 250,000 of whom had come from Bosnia-Herzegovina and 300,000 from Croatia. Outside the region there were, for example, about 350,000 refugees registered in Germany alone.

Of the approximately 500,000 people who were supposed to have returned to their home regions according to the Dayton agreement, by mid-1997 only 300,000 refugees and IDPs had done so because of numerous obstacles preventing their return. About 60 per cent of all homes in Bosnia were damaged or destroyed, and some mined areas were not inhabitable at all. Furthermore, there were serious economic problems. The per capita gross national product had dropped by two-thirds from 1990 to 1995; industrial production in 1995 was only 5–10 per cent of what it had been in 1990; unemployment had climbed to 65–75 per cent. It was especially the authorities' lack of support for return migration, however, that led to the fact that in 1997, for example, of 210,000 returnees to Bosnia, only 34,000 could reclaim their largely destroyed apartments or homes. In their pre-war homeland they now comprised a minority who were often met with hostility, while another 1.8 million were still displaced, half within the country and half abroad. Roughly 350,000 refugees were taken in permanently in other countries in Europe or the United States, Canada and Australia.[59]

Albania

Emigration from Albania began in mid-1990 when about 4,000 people fled to western embassies. The country had been largely cut off from outside contact for more than 45 years, aside from contact with China and the Soviet Union. It planned a rather cautious opening towards the outside world, but in 1991 the long repressed curiosity, the desire to be able to travel and the lure of the outside world that was known through television forged ahead, encouraged by the success of the embassy refugees. Structural poverty, which intensified in 1990–1 due to the constantly worsening economic situation, provided another impetus. The combined effect of these events, social unrest and flight on political grounds were the most important factors leading to two major migration waves, in February–March and August 1991, bound primarily for Italy and Greece. The Adriatic ports of Brindisi and Bari, only 60 kilometres from Albania across the Strait of Otranto, and the surrounding, extremely underdeveloped region of Apulia (Puglia) were hardest hit. In March 1991, about 12,000 Albanians arrived in Italy in chaotic circumstances; in August of the same year another 17,000 came, giving the term 'boat people' a European significance.

Western willingness to take in Albanian refugees was initially part of its episodic acceptance of refugees fleeing the system of a country that had experienced a somewhat delayed awakening from the Cold War. As immigration pressure increased, this acceptance rapidly declined. The first group of migrants was almost entirely permitted to travel further to the west in July 1990; 3,000 went to Germany, about 900 to France. Part of the second group was still granted political asylum in Italy in February–March 1991. In mid-1991, however, the admission policies of Italy and Greece, who were the main receiving countries, began to change to defensive policies and finally to fighting refugees by sea and land. From then on they were generally categorized as undocumented, that is, illegal economic migrants, and were forced to leave as quickly as possible, although their reasons for migrating were far more complex. In Italy as in Greece, where there was in any case steeply rising irregular inmigration and employment of foreigners, this change in policy was driven by domestic policy issues and the desire not to be considered as weak links at the southern edge of 'Fortress Europe' within the gradually unifying EU, and especially within the circle of Schengen countries.

Moreover, the two large migration waves in 1991 had quickly reached and exceeded the capacities of the host countries as regards entry and care. This was still the case to some extent regarding the third wave that brought more than 15,000 Albanians to Italy in March 1997. But the chaos that had ensued in March 1991 when authorities were caught by surprise was not repeated: navy patrols now kept watch for boats with illegal immigrants at the maritime border, which was difficult to control on account of its length. In some coastal areas, an infrastructure had been created that facilitated temporary admission and speedy deportation. Compared with 1991, the structures of illegal immigrants' movements to Italy had also changed entirely. Primarily controlled by international human smuggling organizations, flexible escape routes had been established between Italy and the Albanian ports of Vlorë in the south and Durrës in the north. The migrants were no longer transported in death traps overloaded to the point of being unsailable, as had been the case in 1991. High-powered small speed boats were used instead, or fishing boats with human freight. The result was a steady stream of illegal migration between Albania and Italy, which meant a daily, and mostly nightly, game of cat and mouse between smugglers and migrants on the one hand, and navy patrols and coast guards on the other. At least 50,000 Albanians might have made it across the maritime border to Italy in 1998, when about 200 of the average of 450–600 who landed or approached the coast each day were apprehended by Italian police and navy, which sometimes saved them from drowning.

An Albanian minority has lived in the northern part of Greece since it separated from Albania in 1878. This part of Greece was affected most by in-migration. After 1991, members of the Greek minority in Albania initially fled to Greece, followed some time later by Albanians. The ethnic structure of the area, with minorities on both sides of the common border, noticeably strained and complicated the relationship between Albania and Greece from 1990. In two major operations in mid-1993 and late summer 1994, a total of about 100,000 Albanians were deported from Greece. The deportation from Albania of a priest of Greek descent in June 1993 triggered the deportation of 26,000 Albanians who lived and worked irregularly in northern Greece. Another 70,000 Albanian migrants met the same fate in 1994. From 1991 to 1994, a total of at least 200,000 Albanians are said to have been formally forced to leave, some of them several times; far more were picked up directly at the border and sent back. None the less, between 1991 and 1997 there were apparently up to 300,000 Albanians in Greece at any one time. In a total population in Greece of about 10 million (in 1994), migrant Albanians probably comprised up to about 3.5 per cent. Conversely, more than 10 per cent of the total Albanian population lived outside their country, which became increasingly dependent on wage remittances from abroad. Relations between Albania and Greece did not become relaxed again until 1995–6; a treaty on Albanian seasonal labour in Greece was signed in 1996 but was not put into effect until later due to unrest in 1997.[60]

Kosovo

In 1989–90, Kosovo actually lost its autonomy and experienced a state of emergency in a Serbian police state. Initially the Kosovo Albanians supported peaceful resistance, but the prolonged tension worsened after the Dayton agreement in autumn 1995. The crucial point came when the majority population (90 per cent) of ethnic Albanians demanded autonomy and ultimately independence from Serbia. This was totally unthinkable for the Serbs for historical reasons and on power politics grounds. Of the approximately 2 million inhabitants of Kosovo in 1989, about 1.8 million were ethnic Albanians. The steep rise in the Albanian population in Kosovo, and thus the decline in the proportion of Serbs, was attributable to the high birth rate of the Albanians as well as the out-migration of some Serbs (and Montenegrins) from the poorest region of the republic to other republics within Yugoslavia (later Serbia). Roma and other smaller minorities also lived in Kosovo.

The despotic rule of the Serbian leadership intensified in 1996–8. The background here, too, was the Greater Serbian nationalism of the Milosevič regime which, for example, prohibited use of the Albanian language in schools and universities in Kosovo. In preceding years, Kosovo-Albanian professors and students had been expelled from the university in Priština, capital of the Kosovo region. Similar measures were taken in almost all facilities of the health services and state-controlled concerns. A kind of apartheid system therefore evolved, to which the Kosovo-Albanian majority population responded by gradually establishing parallel structures, from state institutions to educational and health systems. These parallel structures were supported by special taxes, international organizations, remittances from Albanians who had emigrated or were working abroad, and a wide range of self-help initiatives. For a while, these structures were able to compensate for the effects of the exclusion of the majority population by the Milosevič regime and limit violent conflicts. But the guerrilla movement Ushtria Çlirimtare e Kosoves (UÇK), or Kosovo Liberation Army, grew into an underground army and began carrying out attacks in 1996, which were intensified in 1998, when the conflict crossed the threshold to war.[61]

The Serbian attack on the province of Kosovo began in February 1998, so that there too civil war-like circumstances prevailed. Paramilitary police units supported by the Yugoslavian military plundered and destroyed many villages. At least 300,000 people were driven from their homes, becoming internally displaced. At the same time, refugees from Kosovo had pride of place in Europe in 1998 with respect to asylum applications; among others, there were around 32,000 in Germany and about 15,000 in Switzerland. International pressure brought a ceasefire in October 1998, but nothing changed in the area until spring 1999; on the contrary, Serbian massacres of Albanian civilians turned another 20,000 people into refugees in January alone. In the first half of 1999, massacres, looting, destruction, mass flight and refugee misery continued in Kosovo, where a total of 15,000 regular Serbian troops and another 15,000 paramilitary troops were stationed.

Even during the 'peace negotiations' in Rambouillet near Paris, the fighting and expulsion continued undiminished. International efforts to find a peaceful resolution failed and NATO bombing started on 24 March 1999. The resulting mass expulsion of Kosovo Albanians marked the beginning of the most massive and violent 'ethnic cleansing' in Europe since the mass expulsions after the Second World War. Tens of thousands fled to the mountains, but most went to the neighbouring countries of Macedonia and Albania, as well as Montenegro. Others were forced to the borders by the Serbs or, as in Priština for example, forcibly herded into overcrowded trains and thrown out at the border. Everything they left behind was pillaged and sacked in a scorched-earth policy. Nothing was supposed to remain of the Kosovo Albanians, which is why passports were burned after they crossed the border; even car number plates were removed and destroyed, and schools, libraries and archives in their towns were burned.

Refugee numbers skyrocketed. At the border crossings at Blace and Kukës, around Easter 1999 there were up to 50,000 people at times waiting to be allowed to enter Macedonia and Albania. Some estimates spoke of up to 4,000 refugees an hour passing through these border crossings. The west was unprepared for such a mass exodus. The relief operations that were immediately approved were delayed and faced many obstacles. Admission conditions in the beginning were therefore catastrophic; to some extent, no preparations had been made at all. At the same time, the media of the Milosević regime broadcast demagogic appeals according to which the federal government in Belgrade had called upon Albanians to stay in Kosovo; public opinion in Belgrade ignored the fact that the expulsions had ever taken place.

In May 1999, the US Department of State issued a report entitled 'Erasing History: Ethnic Cleansing in Kosovo'; it reported that Yugoslav army units and affiliated band-like militias 'are conducting a campaign of forced population movement on a scale not seen in Europe since the Second World War'.[62] As a result of flight, expulsion and systematic deportations, between April and June 1999 about 900,000 people crossed the borders out of Kosovo; many others hid in forests. At least 500,000 fled to Albania, a large portion of whom were at first taken in privately by families, although northern Albania in particular is destitute.

Macedonia thought it would be able to accommodate at most 20,000 refugees, but according to UN figures, at least 125,000 Kosovars had already arrived in the first week of April. At the peak of refugee movements in May–June 1999, the figure reached 220,000. At the same time, more than 30,000 tried to flee over the snow-covered mountain path to Montenegro, where up to 70,000 refugees were taken in. Only when Macedonia threatened to turn away all further refugees if they were not allowed to migrate on to the west did western countries start issuing admission statements. According to these, 100,000 refugees were to be distributed among the NATO countries; Germany was to take in the most (40,000), and the United States and Turkey 20,000 each. Far fewer people were in fact flown out; only about 15,000 entered Germany, for example. This is again evidence of the 'protection loophole' in the asylum law: those expelled from Kosovo were without a doubt in need of protection, yet in Germany, for example, they had to be content with insecure status granting them temporary protection against deportation, tolerated 'as quasi-illegals'.[63]

As soon as the fighting ended in June 1999, Kosovars began to return, sometimes following directly on the heels of the United Nations KFOR troops. By late July 1999, 737,000 of about 900,000 refugees had already returned to Kosovo. This took place despite the destruction – in Peć, for example, 80 per cent of all homes and shops were destroyed – and despite urgent warnings by the KFOR troops and relief organizations regarding Serbian landmines, booby traps and scattered explosives from the bombs used in the NATO attacks.

When Serbian units retreated and Albanians started returning, the refugee movements within Kosovo reversed; the Serbs now fled or were driven out, as were often Roma, who were considered pro-Serb. Based on data from the UNHCR, more than 172,000 people had already fled to escape revenge by the Kosovo Albanians by early June to late July 1999, headed for Serbia and Montenegro. Roma attempted to cross the Strait of Otranto on smuggler boats as the Albanians had done before them; they were chased out of Kosovo and unwanted in Italy. An illegal crossing in a high-powered open boat costs more than £300 per person. They race across the Adriatic Sea at night without lights and often lose passengers on the way, or, if threatened with being caught, smugglers simply throw passengers overboard in order to turn those chasing them into rescue squads, enabling them to escape all the faster. In Kosovo itself, some returning Albanians looted homes of the new refugees that the KFOR troops could not manage to protect everywhere, and sometimes even attacked Roma and Serbs. The establishment of an International Protectorate, in which the 'international community' aims to rebuild society, turned into a 'test case for post-Cold War liberal internationalism'[64] from the outset.

The outcome of Milosevič's Greater Serbian power politics was not only the suffering of civilian populations in the areas of conflict; for the third time the Serbs were expelled from the respective region – after Croatia (200,000 from the Krajina) and Bosnia (50,000 from the suburbs of Sarajevo alone), this time from a space that was even considered 'the cradle of Serb culture and civilization' in Greater Serbian national mythology, and which was to be 'ethnically cleansed' of Albanians. Whether the territory of ex-Yugoslavia ceases to be a centre of conflict after the end of the Kosovo War depends not only on the effectiveness of programmes for international development and, if necessary, pacification to fight the causes for these refugee movements. It depends on how seriously Europe takes the economic and social, political and humanitarian challenges that are in the background connecting past and present. The new Balkan War at the end of the twentieth century was a 'symptom of a profound European crisis' (Eric Hobsbawm), a 'key event in recent European history' (Dan Diner). It reminds us that Europeans have not been able to secure peaceful coexistence of different ethnic groups in stable, liberal and democratic states since the decline of the authoritarian multi-ethnic empires at the end of the First World War. This is why Mark Mazower called his history of twentieth-century Europe *Dark Continent*.[65]

4 INTERCONTINENTAL SOUTH–NORTH MIGRATION: MIGRATIONS FROM THE 'THIRD WORLD'

In late twentieth-century Europe, the 'Third World' continued to be a formidable opponent of the first order in terms of migration. As such it was the subject of defensive security policy strategies at national and European levels, although two-thirds of all migrants in western Europe had come from eastern Europe and only one-third from the south, and although south–north migration to Europe increased by only about 1–2 per cent in the 1990s, whereas east–west migration rose 21 per cent.[66] Ideas about the course and future of south–north migration reflected, on the one hand, a warning sign of Africans on the 'march' to Europe that was reminiscent of the earlier nightmare visions of Enoch Powell in his 1968 'Rivers of Blood' speech or of Jean Raspail in his 1972 novel about the fictional landing on the Côte d'Azur of an invading fleet of starving immigrants from Calcutta. On the other hand were prevailing images of a kind of successive migratory infiltration, in which asylum seekers (in central and northern Europe) and irregular labourers (in southern Europe) were pioneer migrants who would open up immigration routes for family reunification and irregular or illegal chain migrations.[67]

However, by far the major part of the global migration movements that involved an estimated 120 million people in the late 1990s continued to take place within the 'Third World', about one-third in Africa alone. Most of the refugees in the sense of the Geneva Convention on Refugees who are living abroad are women and children; their numbers have doubled since 1980 and, according to estimates, will double again by 2005 to about 70 million people. Including not only those considered refugees according to the narrow definition of the Geneva Convention, which involves crossing borders, but also environmental refugees or even subsistence migrations of poverty refugees moving from the countryside to the slums of the 'giant cities', then the numbers would soon exceed the thousand million mark.[68]

At the end (only in calendar terms) of the 'century of refugees', there was a gaping difference between global dramas in actual refugee movements and Europe's staging of its 'concern' regarding the growing 'migration pressure' worldwide. The history of south–north migration to Europe is less the history of migration movements than of the fear of and defensive responses to them, as has already been discussed; the movements themselves, therefore, will be dealt with only in a closing summary. Emphasis will be placed on late twentieth-century development trends that can be observed in the evolution of migratory events and the forms and routes of south–north migration to 'Fortress Europe'.[69]

Worldwide migratory events in the late twentieth century are driven by long-acting structural tensions and problems that were intensified to different extents by the collapse of the Iron Curtain, along with diverse and mutually reinforcing correlations.

In pride of place for the southern hemisphere is the divide between high population growth and stagnating or even dwindling job opportunities. It is particularly evident in the agrarian crisis resulting from growing scarcity of land, environmental problems, automation of production and world trade influences. As the increasingly impoverished rural population tries to escape the crisis mostly by migrating from the land, the crisis worsens in overcrowded urban immigration areas with inadequate infrastructure, which in turn sets new migratory movements in motion.

World population reports for the 1990s have indicated that the acceleration in global population growth is slowing down slightly, but this change is due primarily to population developments in developed industrial countries. Growth rates in the 'Third World', which is responsible for 97 per cent of worldwide population growth, are still extremely high. This is the case above all in Africa and Asia, where more than half of the world's population growth takes place. The world's population reached the level of about 6,000 million in 1999, and according to estimates by the US Bureau of Census, it might be as high as 9,000 million by around

2050. Projections of the United Nations predict growth from 96.9 million to only 107.2 million for eastern Europe in the period 1992–2025, and from 284.5 million to only 344.5 million for the CIS. In Europe's neighbouring countries to the south-east (western Asia including Turkey but not Iran), on the other hand, the population is estimated to grow from 139.3 million to 286.6 million; and in the six North African countries, from 147.7 million to 280.4 million. This means the population in this region will double from about 287 million to about 567 million people by 2025.

Contrasts in population developments (natural growth and migration) are even more extreme if the calculations and extrapolations are extended over the range of an entire century: for the period from 1950 to 2050, a total growth of 10.5 per cent is estimated for Germany, France, Italy, Spain, the Netherlands and Belgium. For Algeria, Morocco, Tunisia, Egypt, Libya and Turkey, the estimated growth is 457 per cent. Especially in the Afro-Mediterranean zone, a dramatic tension has developed between the disproportionate growth of population and employment opportunities. The starkly contrasting developments in natural population growth between the Euro-Mediterranean and Afro-Mediterranean zones are even more clearly revealed, influencing the (re-)emergence of a new form of Euro-African migratory system in the Mediterranean realm. A projection for sub-Saharan Africa in 1991 concluded that economic growth rates in the next two decades would have to increase threefold in order to keep up with the expected doubling of the size of the labour force – a hopeless proposition.[70]

Moreover, climatic and human environmental destruction was a mobilizing force in many regions of origin. There are currently about 1.6 thousand million people living in environmentally critical zones worldwide. According to statistics of the UN Environmental Programme (UNEP), the living space of about 135 million people is acutely threatened by environmental destruction, especially desertification. Since 1960, the amount of per capita forest area with respect to the world population has declined by a factor of two, to 0.6 hectares; by 2025 it could dwindle further to 0.4 hectares, an area smaller than a football pitch. According to cautious estimates, by 2050 massive migration movements will be triggered when at least 150 million people become 'environmental refugees' due to the greenhouse effect and rising sea levels. In addition to global warming and rising sea levels is the problem of drastically sinking groundwater levels, because at the end of the twentieth century, 260 million hectares of cultivable land had to be irrigated by pumping up groundwater. For this reason, cultivable land in the 'Third World' uses up far more water than is compensated for by precipitation.

These factors force migratory movements not only in arid regions of the 'Third World' and in South-east Asian flood regions. They partly also apply to successor states of the Soviet Union, which have to deal with serious additional burdens in the transformation process, including indifference to environmental issues by the former economic system, one-sided agrarian policies based on monocultures, lasting ground pollution from uncontrolled use of fertilizers and the neglect of infrastructure. General supply shortages, especially of water, energy and food, have created potential for a catastrophe that could suddenly erupt, triggering mass migrations. Since 1989, about 700,000 people have had to leave their homes in the territory of the former USSR because of environmental catastrophes, including, for example, the shrinking of the Aral Sea in Central Asia, radioactive contamination of the nuclear test site in Semipalatinsk (Semey) and the aftermath of the nuclear disaster at Chernobyl.

In addition to the environmental problems that ensue from environmental destruction comes the battle over resources, which are becoming ever scarcer yet are indispensable for life and survival. This includes especially the growing conflicts over inshore waters that extend over borders. Such threatening 'water disputes' over the subsistence basis for hundreds of millions of people can erupt, according to the assessment of development expert Franz Nuscheler, between, for example, Egypt and Sudan over the Nile and between Israel and Jordan over the River Jordan. Other possible areas of conflict involve Turkey and Syria over the Euphrates, India and Pakistan over the Indus, and India and Bangladesh over the Ganges. But even before these tensions break into open conflicts, the scarcity of water resources serves to push up the number of environmental refugees in the 'Third World'.[71]

The global and regional development gap has worsened as a result of disproportionate growth. According to the Human Development Report of the United Nations Development Programme (UNDP), 1.6 thousand million people were living in worse conditions in 1996 than they had been 15 years earlier and the per capita income in 70 'Third World' countries was lower than two decades earlier. The development gap has intensified since the end of the east–west division, encouraged by the release of capital movements, production and market relations in the globalization process. At the same time, the end of the system rivalry reduced willingness for 'development aid' in the broadest sense, as it served not only humanitarian purposes during the Cold War but had been motivated also by power politics. Against this complex background and in conjunction with it, the 1993 world population report of the United Nations Population Fund (UNFPA) assumed that the search for better income options is becoming increasingly overshadowed by subsistence migration in search of work and income.

The globalization process also directly or indirectly influences migratory events themselves in that more and more countries have been incorporated as regions of origin or destination since the 1980s, even those that had been totally cut off by the worldwide system boundaries until the end of the Cold War. The worldwide stripping of bounds in production contexts and market and capital movements also corresponds to a certain lifting of boundaries in migratory events, albeit very limited with respect to specific classes and groups. Images of the comparatively wealthy north and west transported through globally networked media provide not only consumer incentives in the south and east but also migration incentives, not necessarily to head for the supposedly 'golden' west or north but in any case to leave the home regions either temporarily or permanently.

Networking of global transport and communications offers increasing options to carry out such migration incentives – not for the poorest of the poor, however, but primarily for the educated middle class. Above all, the emigration of highly qualified people ('brain drain') accelerates the relative process of impoverishment of the region of origin. In particular young urban middle-class people in the 'Third World' with educational and professional qualifications who are looking for work, for example, are migration potential for intercontinental long-distance migration to Europe. Where they are unable to reach the few migration doors that are open – for example, educational and training migrations to support the elite – they are often forced by European obstacles to in-migration to try to enter the west through asylum applications or illegal means. Their motivation as regards their migration behaviour is related to their image of Europe, in part taken from the media and sometimes unrealistic, and in part a concrete picture gained through schooling and vocational training. This group does stand some chance of being able to finance the usually illegal 'trip' and the attendant costs of the smuggling services. The destitute generally have no options at all, not even as refugees or expellees, as they have neither sufficient information nor the necessary means to cover the 'travel costs'. Talk of 'poverty refugees' is therefore often misleading, because the economic refugees – in the strict sense of this much-abused expression – who arrive in Europe are acting in response to economic and social motivations; they are usually fleeing not because they are impoverished but to avoid poverty. Compared with the social situations in their home regions, they sometimes even come from such high standards of living that their migration could be classified as 'elite migration'.[72]

At the same time, migration is assuming greater and greater diversity worldwide. The proportion of women involved is growing, not only in refugee migrations but also in regular and irregular or illegal labour migration. All in all, globalization of production and labour market structures has created a new class society that is characterized by a global mobility of varying ranges and frequencies: 'Scientists, engineers and managers circulate around the globe as highly remunerated employees of "multis". Migrants with fewer qualifications find employment as low-paid workers in private households or as seasonal labourers in agriculture and construction. At the lower spectrum are the "new helots" of the international division of labour: without rights and exploited, irregular labour migrants and the victims of internationally organized trafficking in women.'[73]

Mobility potential and options separate 'those who can reach every place on earth by plane and without a visa from those who lack the material prerequisites to leave their home and who do not receive a visa out of fear of immigration'. In 1965, for example, citizens of 43 African countries could enter the Federal Republic of Germany without a visa; in 1995, this was possible from only 14. The greater the crush of asylum seekers and refugees, the more restrictive the immigration restrictions.[74] What applies for the 'Third World' as regards the class society and freedom to travel is also true for travellers from the CIS. Poor CIS citizens have little chance of obtaining a visa to the west, in contrast to the members of the group lately referred to as '*novarich*', a neologism combining the Russian *tovarich* (comrade) and *nouveau riche*.

In addition to structural problems, the development gap and the globalization process as forces leading to or supporting migration, other mobilizing factors are the tensions and conflicts – partly from indigenous developments and partly from colonial and post-colonial conflict potential – between population groups in the regions of origin that could lead to migration or flight and expulsion of minorities. As 'ethnic power and distribution struggles', they were partly triggered or intensified by worsening structural problems and by the contest for political power or control of limited resources. In categorizations of 'self' and 'other', however, they were often viewed as being isolated from these contexts as ethnic, religious or cultural conflicts. This applies to the situation in Sudan, for example, where apart from an almost ten-year interruption a civil war between north and south has been raging since 1955. It cannot be considered a regional 'clash of civilizations' between the Arab-Islamic-dominated north and the African-influenced south with its mixture of natural religions and Christianity. The result is that 3–4 million of the roughly 6 million inhabitants of Khartoum are refugees, mostly from the war zones in the south. Yet the same also largely applies for the militant Islamism in North Africa. It is most pronounced and has had the most serious migration consequences in Algeria, having been ignited there in 1991 as a result of political oppression by the military government of the fundamentalist Islamist Front Islamique du Salut (FIS), which was trying to assume power. According to official sources, despite restrictive emigration requirements about 410,000 people found a way to emigrate or flee between 1990 and 1995, including many senior employees and intellectuals.[75]

Such conflicts sometimes have a long history preceding them. In the southern hemisphere, this includes the crisis and conflict potential originally implanted by European colonial rule; in successor states to the Soviet Union, problems resulted from frequently forced mass migrations or 'resettlements' and deportation of entire populations at the time of Stalinism. Such migration-inducing tensions were pushed or unleashed, for one thing, by the retreat of the 'Second' from the 'Third World' after the end of the system rivalry; for another, by the collapse of the Soviet Union and the end of totalitarian control of this tension in the Soviet multi-ethnic empire and its neighbouring countries.

The former colonies, especially in Africa, remained largely alone in coping with post-colonial problems. After the end of the Cold War, many major areas of the 'Third World' lost their economic and strategic interest, especially in Africa. In place of the former missionary legitimization of colonial intervention as a 'cultural mission' in the age of high imperialism, Europe referred to the legitimization of post-colonial non-intervention, noting that Africa has to find its own way to its own future, and that, after all, Europe had had to deal with its own development problems on its way to the modern age. It was often forgotten that Europe had been concerned mostly with its own problems, while Africa and other parts of the former colonial world also had to deal with colonial-induced problems from Europe and their repercussions.[76] As regards the former colonial regions, there was a wide range of factors leading to colonial-induced and post-colonial escalating tensions and conflicts: colonial powers enforced biased preferences and disadvantages for certain population groups, which led to unequal distribution of property, education and social opportunities. Also, colonial borders were drawn without consideration for economic and ethnic structures. Furthermore, the colonial strategy of forced resettlement in the struggle against indigenous liberation movements triggered refugee migrations, further migrations and returns after the end of colonial rule.

These and other problems are part of the background, in Africa for example, to conflicts and tragedies of genocide and mass refugee movements in Burundi, Rwanda (Hutu/Tutsi) and Zaire. These also involved power and distribution battles including ethnic motivations led by rival traditional and new elites, as well as by regional and local 'warlords' with their respective militias and armed bands. These struggles are fomented by highly armed private armies recruited on the free mercenary

330 Europe: A Continent of Immigration

market and other external groups, especially those interested in natural resources (such as diamonds in central Africa). In increasingly chaotic war and civil-war zones, they can reach infernally bestial proportions, as in Congo and Sierra Leone. Wars and civil wars in some African countries have caused the share of refugees in the population to increase to 10–20 per cent. In Malawi, for example, the 1 million refugees from Mozambique represented more than 10 per cent of the population of the host country. After the attempted coup in Burundi in October 1993, about 1 million people fled, mostly to neighbouring Rwanda. Rwanda had had its own serious ethnic conflicts, which had been only superficially resolved, and still had about 900,000 of its own IDPs. At least 500,000 people were murdered in the Hutu massacres of the Tutsi in Rwanda from April to June 1994, and many more were injured and mutilated. Millions of people fled to the supposedly secure south-western part of Rwanda and about 1.6 million fled across the border, especially to Zaire, which was soon faced with its own serious internal conflicts.[77]

In the 1990s civil wars became the most significant driving forces of forced and refugee migrations in the 'Third World'. In the Middle East, in Asia and Latin America, the number of warlike conflicts declined considerably in the 1990s. In Africa the number remained constant from 1992 (14 wars) to 1998 (14 wars). In 1998, 44 per cent of all wars in the world took place in Africa. Research on the causes of war[78] has determined that a stagnating or reverse trend in the development process coincided with the increasing instance of war and the attendant repercussions as migratory movements. In other words, the collapse of economic order and social structures, the establishment of authoritarian regimes or terrorist dictatorships and the resultant dwindling of professional and social life prospects promote migration-readiness among highly qualified people with external contacts and the minimum of means to facilitate emigration or escape.

The subsequent intensification of the already powerful 'brain drain' is forced by the cause-and-effect relation into a vicious cycle, with dire consequences for the 'development process', because any slowdown, stagnation, or even reversal, of the development process gives additional thrust to the migration process. According to the 1992 Human Development Report of the UNDP, Africa lost almost 60,000 executives from mid- and high-level management from 1985 to 1990. Ghana lost about 60 per cent of its physicians in the 1980s. In some fields, 'development aid' degenerates into an absurd cycle of the limited replacement of a far higher number of local specialists who have emigrated by development aid workers from industrial countries that have often directly or indirectly financed the professional qualification of those emigrated specialists.

Intercontinental in-migration to Europe was substantial from a European perspective. Compared with worldwide migration movements, however, it has hitherto been insignificant, despite the noticeable 'deregionalization of migration' in the 'communicative' and 'mobile integration of the world' that is accompanying the globalization process.[79] In Europe – apart from the former colonial countries – this was attributable to the lack of privileged migration relations or bridges in the form of intercontinental migration networks; in the potential regions of origin it was partly caused by a class-specific scarcity of informational and material options. It was also a consequence of exclusion regulations that keep such movements away from the borders of the OECD countries and try to stem them or break them off as soon as they start assuming the character of chain migrations.

In Europe, opinions are divided in the dispute on how to assess the 'migration pressure' from the south. At the heart of the matter are the following questions: whether or not it is even targeting Europe, whether it is inevitable that it will continue to grow, and whether it can be reduced through coordinated, that is, not just European but global intervention ('global governance') to keep the causes of migration in check. It is above all a matter of combating the causes of flight and refugee movements by economic, political and humanitarian efforts, as well as, if necessary, by the means described in UN jargon as 'peace-building', that is, military efforts. In Rwanda such measures were not taken owing to rivalries between France and the United States; in Kosovo, global intervention in the form of the NATO bombing of 1999 initially led, in the absence of a UN mandate, to the further escalation of 'ethnic cleansing'; in September 1999, intervention was initiated in East Timor through the stationing of international peace-keeping forces. In view of the much-debated yet hitherto unfulfilled economic stemming of the causes for flight or migration, Europe faces the 'alternative between lasting high migration pressure or increased employment opportunities in the countries of origin by means of better options for participation in international competition'.[80] Of all conceivable scopes and forms of action, Europe has thus far done the least towards fighting the causes for flight and migration in the regions of origin and the most towards combating refugee migrations to Europe. This is true despite numerous initiatives, appeals and declarations of intent to combat the causes of refugee migration; there have also been concrete plans – which have remained non-binding owing to unclear participation and financing issues – and even resolutions at national, European and UN levels.

All in all, the concept of 'Fortress Europe' is simultaneously both true and false. It is false because Europe has remained open for many immigrants who are wanted at the national level or tolerated on the basis of higher European law or universalist principles. This allows a substantial yet manageable amount of admission. It is true as regards restrictions on immigration and the defensive measures taken to reject unwanted migrants before they cross European borders and enter the jurisdiction of European law and principles. The number of people thus excluded can only be estimated, but it is in any case incomparably higher. Because the unrestricted power of definition regarding whether immigrants are wanted or unwanted lies with the continent of immigration and its countries, the conflict over 'Fortress Europe' remains an issue of splitting hairs. It is definitely the purpose of a fortress to offer protection to those living within from actual or presumed threats from without and to allow entry only to those whom its inhabitants deem to be wanted or in need of protection.

The delimitation of 'Fortress Europe' has left open very few options for entry to immigrants from the 'Third World', and these options simultaneously became tighter and more specific in the 1990s. The legal dimension of migration still includes elite migration, education and training migrations limited to the middle and upper classes and, often overlapping with this, privileged albeit increasingly limited migration relations in the form of post-colonial and 'ethnic' immigration. There is also family reunification following earlier migrations and the ever-more restrictive admission of asylum seekers and refugees. Beyond these legal options for entry there begins the grey area of irregular or illegal immigration and residence.

The definition of in-migrant groups to be accepted under certain conditions, such as asylum seekers, and the specific opening of immigration gates for these groups is the European role in the intercontinental play about chances to immigrate from the 'Third World'. Moreover, there are very limited interests in Europe in opening those gates. The role played by would-be immigrants is to orient themselves to these regulations, that is, to adapt to them through corresponding self-descriptions. The very European question of whether someone is a 'genuine' refugee, for example, can ultimately be reduced to whether the person can credibly show that he or she corresponds to the criteria that the European side has defined as describing acceptable immigrant groups. Whether or not these criteria are in fact important in the person's individual motivation for migration is irrelevant.

Wherever scarce options are available for regular immigration, other means than those intended must be resorted to instead, such as applications for asylum. Apart from quota refugees, the restrictions imposed essentially force everyone involved to play cards with a stacked deck. The restrictions in the asylum law are less a matter of keeping a way open for humanitarianism than a means of securing borders against unwanted immigration. In this context, it has become a common defensive game to deploy arguments about security policy and imminent global threats. The gap between not admitting individual asylum seekers from crisis regions outside Europe and the fear of Europe's decline under the crush of massive chain reactions triggered by such migration is so great, however, that it can be used only for demagogic purposes. As long as the counter-part to defensive measures against refugees from the 'Third World' – that is, combating the causes for flight and migration in the regions of origin – is absent, this defence remains a historical scandal by which future generations will judge Europe's understanding of humanity in the late twentieth and early twenty-first century.

Notes

Preface and Acknowledgements

1 On this, among many others see Bade 1988; Jackson and Page Moch 1996; Matthes (ed.) 1992; Jaritz and Müller (eds) 1988; Hoffmann-Nowotny 1988; Wierlacher (ed.) 1993; Green 1997; Morawska 2003.
2 Bade 1994c.
3 Le Goff 1994; Braudel (ed.) 1989; Duchhardt and Kunz (eds) 1997.
4 On the following, representative for others, see Tilly 1978.
5 Tilly 1990; Hoerder 1997.
6 Brettell 1986; Gabaccia 1996; Page Moch 2003.
7 Page Moch 1997.
8 Hoerder 2002.
9 Kulischer and Kulischer 1932.
10 Kulischer 1948.
11 Hoerder (ed.) 1985; Emmer and Mörner (eds) 1991; Canny (ed.) 1994a; Cohen (ed.) 1995; Holmes (ed.) 1996.
12 Castles and Miller 1998; Santel 1995; Wihtol de Wenden and Tinguy 1995.
13 Nugent 1992; Baines 1995.
14 Hoerder 1988.
15 Marrus 1985.
16 Lucassen 1987.
17 Thomas 1973; Bade (ed.) 1985a; Bade (ed.) 1992; Pooley and Whyte (eds) 1991.
18 Coulmas 1990; Todd 1998; Chambers 1994; Gilroy 1994; Sowell 1996; Cohen 1997; Hear 1998.
19 Page Moch 1992; though no comparison, see also Sassen 1996.
20 Ferenczi 1930, 6.
21 Wingenroth 1959.
22 Rees 1957.
23 See also Zolberg 1987.

Chapter 1: Migration during the Shift from Agrarian to Industrial Societies

1 Gräf and Pröve 1997; Griep and Jäger (eds) 1983.
2 Wilton and Bignamini (eds) 1986; Schubert 1983; Küther 1983.
3 For a few representative examples see Jaritz and Müller (eds) 1988; Page Moch 1992, 22–59; Canny (ed.) 1994a; for a survey see Mieck 1993, 45–52, 72–87.
4 Reinhard et al. 1968, 146–73.
5 Livi Bacci 1999, 11f.
6 Kriedte et al. 1977, 39–57; Leboutte (ed.) 1996; Cerman and Ogilvie (eds) 1994.
7 Schubert 1983; Schubert 1995 (on itinerant trade 335–50); Küther 1983; Mayall 1988; Lucassen 1996.
8 Reininghaus 1993b, 32f., 37f.; Oberpenning 1996, 40–8.
9 For the general background see Lucassen 1987.
10 Kocka 1990b, 144–51.
11 Bade 1982b.
12 Uhlig 1978, 60–87, 122–32 (citation: 60).
13 Walz 1999; Lourens and Lucassen 1999.
14 Page Moch 1992, 30–40, 43–58.
15 On this term see Lucassen 1987; Page Moch 1992, 13–18; Hoerder 1996.
16 Page Moch 1997; Fawcett 1989.
17 On this and the following see Lucassen 1987, 19–41, 95–9.
18 Ibid., 37–9.
19 Lucassen 1988, 80.
20 On this and the following see Lucassen 1987, 107–28; see also Page Moch 1992, 76–88.
21 Lucassen 1994, 161–5, 180–5.
22 On this, often with reference to Lucassen, see esp. Bölsker-Schlicht 1987.
23 Lucassen 1988, 76, 80.
24 Page Moch 1992, 69f.
25 Lucassen 1987, 29–39.
26 The name may come from the East Frisian word *todden*, to lug or to carry, or even the English *toddle*, referring to the short, unsteady steps taken by heavily laden travelling traders.
27 Oberpenning 1996, 114.
28 Lucassen 1987, 52–76; Bölsker-Schlicht 1987, 66–74.
29 Bölsker-Schlicht 1987, 76–94; Henkes 1995.
30 Lünnemann 1992.
31 Lucassen 1994, 165–9.
32 Bossenbroek 1992.
33 Bölsker-Schlicht 1987, 35f.
34 The Dutch *Moffen* is a pejorative term for Germans.
35 Lucassen 1987, 42–51; Bölsker-Schlicht 1987, 62–6.

36 Niedersächsisches Staatsarchiv [State Archives of Lower Saxony] Osnabrück, Rep. 100, Section 220, No. 5, Sheet 230ff.; I would like to thank Dr Susanne Meyer of the Clothmaking Museum in Bramsche for this information.
37 Goinga 1995, 20.
38 Meyer 1991, 189–92; Meyer 1995; Hochstadt 1999, 55–106.
39 For special attention to southern and south central Europe see Fontaine 1996; Maistre et al. 1992; for consideration also of labour migration see Poitrineau 1983; Westerfield 1968; on northern Europe see Rosander 1976; on Italy see Walz 1999; for a general overview see Oberpenning 1996, 37–78.
40 On this and the following see Oberpenning 1996, 40, 48, 66–75.
41 Ibid., 76f.
42 On this and the following: ibid., 48–74; see also Reininghaus (ed.) 1993a.
43 Mertens 1984.
44 Poitrineau 1983; Fontaine 1996.
45 Augel 1971; Schindling 1992; Wennemann 1997, 33–42; Walz 1999.
46 Walter 1993.
47 On the following see Oberpenning 1996, 11, 16, 99f., 107–84, 192–227, 276–9, 339–57, 365–9, 372–5.
48 Blackburn 1997.
49 Fourastié 1969.
50 Kaelble 1997, 8.
51 Bade 1982b.
52 Sombart 1927, 408.
53 Hochstadt 1996, 161.
54 Kaelble 1997, 31f.
55 Hochstadt 1996, 156–61.
56 On Germany see Marschalck 1987; on Europe see Livi Bacci 1999, 126–58.
57 Stürmer 1979, ch. 2.
58 Armengaud 1980, 29; Page Moch 1996, 123.
59 Walle 1979, 139–43.
60 Ó Tuathaigh 1996; Pooley 1995, 66–8.
61 Page Moch 1996, 126f.
62 Bade 1982b.
63 Page Moch 1996, 127f.
64 On this and the following see Matzerath 1983; see also Matzerath 1985.
65 Wehler 1995, 510–15.
66 Page Moch 1992, 126.
67 Fischer 1985, 44.
68 Matzerath 1983, 38, 40f.; Page Moch 1992, 131–43.
69 Page Moch 1996, 128f.
70 Jackson 1997; Hochstadt 1999.
71 Langewiesche 1977, 18f.
72 Lucassen 1987, 196f.; Page Moch 1996, 132f.
73 Pabst 1992, 268.
74 Family history sources are in the possession of the author, who comes from this family.

75 On the following see Kleßmann 1978.
76 The following has been taken from Bade 1980a, 275–80.
77 A derogatory expression in the local slang whose approximate meaning is 'slaving-away Polacks'.
78 Noiriel 1984.

Chapter 2: Migration in Nineteenth- and Early Twentieth-century Europe

1 For the general background see Chatelain 1977; Lucassen 1987, 195–8; Page Moch 1992, 102–43.
2 Cross 1983, 22f.
3 On the following see Lucassen 1987, 186–90.
4 Bade 1984.
5 Holmes 1988.
6 Zimmermann 1996, 150f.
7 On the following see Lucassen 1987, 200–2; Del Fabbro 1996, 30–6; Wennemann 1997, 47–62.
8 On this and the following see Morawska 1989, 246–66.
9 Page Moch 1992, 128.
10 Kleßmann 1978, 70–3.
11 Page Moch 1992, 134.
12 Gruner and Wiedmer 1978, 249–56.
13 Lourens and Lucassen 1999.
14 Kraus 1979, 118f.
15 Page Moch 1992, 121.
16 Kocka 1990a, 362.
17 Holmes 1988, 114–16.
18 Bade 1984, 104.
19 Del Fabbro 1996, 63–82; Wennemann 1997, 75–9.
20 On the following see Bade 1980a, 311–23.
21 Weber 1892, 9f., 40.
22 Riegler 1985a, 135–8.
23 Cited in Bade 1980a, 298.
24 Bade 1984.
25 Rosenberg 1967, 43–5.
26 Bade 1985d, 462.
27 Lucassen 1987, 196f.; Cross 1983, 22, 25.
28 Lucassen 1987, 186.
29 Ibid., 203; Nellemann 1981, 362f.
30 Ferenczi 1930, 21.
31 On the following and for citations see Bade 1982b, 197–205; Bade 1984, 102.
32 Schilling 1988, 77–81.

33   On this and the following see esp. Fremdling 1984b.
34   Schumacher 1968, 232.
35   Cited in Giedion 1994, 161–89.
36   Landes 1976, 137–40.
37   Weber 1975, 293.
38   Bolenz 1996, 17.
39   On the following see Fremdling 1984b, 3–6; Fremdling 1984a.
40   On the following see Gardlund 1955, 233–44; Riegler 1985b; Riegler 1985a, 267–71.
41   Cited in Riegler 1985b, 524.
42   Reinhard 1985, 32–132; Emmer 1988, 17.
43   Slicher van Bath 1986; Wirsching 1992, 152–61; Smith 1947; Emmer 1988, 17f.
44   Canny 1994b, 279; see also Bailyn 1986, 104–6.
45   Moltmann 1986, 107, 113.
46   Cited in ibid., 112.
47   Mittelberger 1756, 13–15.
48   Grubb 1994.
49   Grabbe 1984, 289; Moltmann 1982.
50   Cited in Brinck 1993, 202.
51   Grubb 1987, 584.
52   Brinck 1993, 23f.
53   Cited in Grabbe 1984, 288f.
54   On this see esp. Grubb 1984, 2f.; Wokeck 1999.
55   Moltmann (ed.) 1979, 26.
56   Grubb 1994, 813.
57   On this see the articles by H. Sundhaussen, G. Schödl and D. Brandes in: Bade (ed.) 1992; Beer and Dahlmann 1999.
58   Moltmann (ed.) 1979, 21f., 30–3, 44–119, 335–99.
59   Cited in Grubb 1994, 814.
60   Cited in Grabbe 1984, 289.
61   Cited in ibid., 289f.
62   Moltmann (ed.) 1979, 32.
63   Grubb 1994, 815.
64   Ziegler 1985, 192–228; Wagner 1995, 68–93.
65   On chain migration and networks see Tilly 1990; Brettell 1986.
66   Grubb 1994, 815–24.
67   Page Moch 1992, 152.
68   Kamphoefner 1987, 40–9; Meyer 1995, 195–8.
69   On the following see Körner 1990, 45–7.
70   Kamphoefner et al. (eds) 1991, 27–30; Bretting and Bickelmann, 1991.
71   Hoerder 1996.
72   Körner 1990, 34–7; Puskás (ed.) 1990.
73   Just 1988, 44–61.
74   Bade 1985c, 274f.; Bade 1985d, 459.
75   Kamphoefner 1987, 170–200.

76 Adams 1985, 304f.
77 Willcox (ed.) 1931, 85–7.
78 Kamphoefner 1988, 292–5.
79 Willcox (ed.) 1929, 697.
80 Gould 1980a, 65–74.
81 Nugent 1996, 78.
82 Page Moch 1996, 124.
83 Willcox (ed.) 1929, 82.
84 Baines 1995, 1.
85 Körner 1990, 29.
86 On the following see ibid., 29f.
87 Bade 1985c, 268f.; Körner 1990, 31, 58–60.
88 Baines 1995, 3.
89 Körner 1990, 51f.
90 Meyer 1991, 137.
91 Moltmann (ed.) 1979, 120–87.
92 Canny 1994b, 282.
93 Gould 1980a, 65–74; Wyman 1993.
94 Åkerman 1978, 303.
95 Kulischer and Kulischer 1932, 144f.
96 Page Moch 1992, 149–58; Hoerder 1996, 34–9.
97 Nugent 1992, 44–54; Baines 1986, 213–49, 266–79; Miller 1985.
98 Köllmann 1976, 20.
99 For regional studies see Lubinski 1997; Reich 1997.
100 Cited in Bade 1980a, 306–9.
101 Ibid., 309–11.
102 Morawska 1989, 254; Nugent 1992, 83–94.
103 Nugent 1992, 95–100; Mörner 1985, 35–66; Rosoli 1994, 229–35.
104 Hoerder and Page Moch (eds) 1996; Fertig 2000.
105 Thistlethwaite 1960; for an early model study see Kamphoefner 1988.
106 Körner 1990, 29.
107 Moltmann 1984.
108 Semmel 1961, 513f.
109 Gallagher and Robinson 1970.
110 Hausen 1970, 186–91, 216–24; Albertini 1976, 135–7, 299f., 360; Bley 1968, 167f., 208–12, 263–84; Bald 1970, 35–115; Saunders (ed.) 1984; Emmer (ed.) 1986; Northrup 1995, 104–39; Castles and Miller 1998, 46–50.
111 Hobson 1968, 44.
112 On this and the following see Knorr 1944, 269–349; Semmel 1961, 513–15.
113 Malthus 1798.
114 Cited in Knorr 1944, 279.
115 Semmel 1961, 524f.
116 Bade 1975, 159f., 165, 180.

117 On this and the following see Constantine 1991, 62–78 (citation: 66).
118 House of Commons Health Committee, Third Report, 'Welfare of Former British Child Migrants', 23 July 1998, esp. para. 1, 15, 18, 51, cited in *Der Spiegel* (10 August 1998), 130.
119 Constantine 1991, 77.
120 Wehler 1970a, 112–68, 454–502; Bade 1975, 67–189; Bade 1989b, 180–201.
121 Burgdörfer 1929.
122 Marschalck 1984, 83.
123 Schulze 1994, 150.
124 Eisenstadt 1991.
125 Meßmer 1974, 209f., 215.
126 Bergeron et al. 1969, 201–7.
127 Meßmer 1974, 214; Grandjonc and Werner 1984, 91.
128 Meßmer 1974; Grandjonc 1975.
129 Noiriel 1994, 17, 25; Lademacher 1983, 195–7; Hartig 1984, 46f.; Meßmer 1974, 213.
130 Bergeron et al. 1969, 222–5, 265–70.
131 Noiriel 1994, 19f.
132 Kramer 1988, 235.
133 Grandjonc 1975, 4; Noiriel 1994, 45; Schieder 1963, 110–12.
134 Bergeron et al. 1969, 266, 268.
135 Reiter 1992, 79.
136 On this and the following see Noiriel 1994, 29–42, 51–65; Reiter 1992, 33, 65, 112–15, 193–203.
137 Bonjour 1946, 228.
138 Noiriel 1994, 62f.
139 Morelli 1991, 117; Sande and Valk 1991, 191–204; Bergeron et al. 1969, 222, 267.
140 Sande and Valk 1991, 198–201.
141 Jelavich 1991, 238–45.
142 Reiter 1992, 116; Grandjonc 1975, 10, 15, 19; Meßmer 1974, 226, 232.
143 Cited in Stengers 1975, 158.
144 Ibid., 158–61.
145 On this and the following see Reiter 1992, 31–48, 78, 105–18, 210–13, 228–39.
146 On this and the following see Bonjour 1946, 168–81, 212–24; Reiter 1992, 108–11, 217–27, 236–41.
147 On this and the following see Reiter 1992, 56, 262–72; Sundermann 1997, 36f.; Schulte Beerbühl 1997, 2–13; Lattek 1985, 23, 39f.
148 Cited in Reiter 1992, 259.
149 Cited in Meßmer 1974, 232f.
150 Cited in Sundermann 1997, 36.
151 Meßmer 1974, 231.
152 Wehler (ed.) 1969, 7–42; Bade 1975, 112, 115–18.

153 Oberacker 1961.
154 Reiter 1992, 67, 241.
155 Brubaker 1992, 21–34; see also Bommes 1994.
156 On this and the following see Noiriel 1994, 65–83; Brubaker 1992, 98, 102, 104–10.
157 Bamberger, cited in Noiriel 1994, 61.
158 Brubaker 1992, 105.
159 On this and the following see Brubaker 1992, 114–37 (citation: 115); Bade 1996; Fahrmeir 1997.
160 Just 1988; Maurer 1986.
161 *Sten. Ber. des Dt. Reichstages* [*Stenographic Reports of the German Reichstag*], vol. 290, 153rd Session (28 May 1913), 5276 C; see also Brubaker 1992, 136.
162 Schulte Beerbühl 1997.
163 Noiriel 1994, 76; Holmes 1992, 26, 35, 65–74.
164 Bevan 1986, 70f.; Panayi 1994, 42f., 46; Noiriel 1994, 76.
165 Cited in Noiriel 1994, 75.
166 Ibid., 71, 73f., 77; Brubaker 1992, 110.
167 Caestecker 1998, 81; Noiriel 1994, 72.
168 Bade 1984, 104.
169 Bade 1982b; on this and the following see also Bade 1984; Bade 1981, 26–33, 37f.; Bade 1985d, 461f.
170 Zentrales Staatsarchiv Merseburg [Merseburg Central State Archives], Rep. 87B, no. 116, pp. 7, 11.
171 Zentrales Staatsarchiv Merseburg, Rep. 120, VIII, 1, no. 106, vol. 1, pp. 32f.
172 Zentrales Staatsarchiv Merseburg, Rep. 87B, no. 116, p. 8.
173 Weber 1892; Morawska 1989, 253.
174 *Verhandlungen der Budapester Konferenz* [Proceedings of the Budapest Conference] 1911, 8f., 84; see also Nichtweiss 1959, 200–8.
175 Ferenczi 1930, 17f.
176 Caestecker 1998.

Chapter 3: The Period of the World Wars: Escape, Expulsion, Forced Labour

1 Wehler 1995, 1250.
2 Wingenroth 1959.
3 Nuscheler 1999.
4 On this section see in general Oltmer 1995, chs 6 and 7; Oltmer 1998a, 1998b.
5 Hardach 1987, 66–114.
6 Cornelißen 1997, 46–8.
7 Horne 1985, 57.
8 Chen 1923, 142–58.

9   Freeman 1989, 162.
10 Panayi 1991, 120f.; Holmes 1992, 86–114.
11 On the German example see, in general, Oltmer 1995, 279–432; Oltmer 1998a, 1998b.
12 Wennemann 1997, 177–86; Del Fabbro 1996, 277–82.
13 Bade 1983, 47.
14 Herbert 1990, 97.
15 Passelecq 1928, 389.
16 Herbert 1990, 98.
17 Oltmer 1998b, 152f.
18 Ibid., 161f.
19 Panayi 1988, 4f.; Panayi 1991, 70–98.
20 Speed 1990, 141–53.
21 T. H. Marshall, 'A British Sociological Career', *International Social Science Journal* 25 (1973), 88–100 (here: 89f.); cited in Rieger 1992, 11.
22 Höpken 1996, 4–16; Sundhaussen 1996, 34–7.
23 Leenders 1993, 140.
24 Martin Herzog and Marko Rösseler, 'Der große Zaun. Ein bizarres Kapitel aus der Terrorgeschichte des deutschen Militärs im Ersten Weltkrieg', in *Die Zeit* (14 June 1998), 82.
25 Panayi 1993, 98f.
26 Dyer 1978, 30f.
27 Williams 1972, 266–9.
28 Hoffmann-Holter 1995, 29f.
29 Graf 1974, 395–411; Marrus 1985, 53f.; Levene 1993, 95–8.
30 On this section see in general Oltmer 2001a, 2001b.
31 Ritter 1991, 109; Lucassen 1998.
32 Ferenczi 1930, 6.
33 Thalheim 1930, 47.
34 Ferenczi 1930, 28–40; Willcox (ed.) 1929, 168–75, 192–5, 210–21, 230–3.
35 Bade 1980b, 160–87.
36 Felshtinsky 1982, 336–43.
37 Rosa 1991; Bologna 1997b, 26f.; Bermani 1997, 37–46.
38 Kirk 1956, 109f.
39 Bade 1989a, 320; Thalheim 1926, 28–52, 111–39; Bickelmann 1980, 7–18, 52–107.
40 For the general background see Dowty 1987.
41 Fischer 1987, 37.
42 Woytinsky and Woytinsky 1953, 77.
43 Bade 1980b, 166f.
44 Körner 1990, 62; Cinel 1991, 96–121.
45 Moya 1998, 56.
46 Cinel 1991, 106.
47 For an overview of this and the following see Bade 1980b, 165–8; Kahrs 1993.

48 Bade 1980b, 169f.
49 On this and the following see Singer-Kérel 1991; Cross 1983.
50 Kirk 1956, 105.
51 Ferenczi 1927, 890; on this and the following see Bade 1980b, 167, 171f.
52 Noiriel 1994, 79f.; Kimminich 1994, 186–9.
53 Ladas 1932, 338, 341.
54 Noiriel 1994, 102f.
55 Marrus 1985, 68–74.
56 Sundhaussen 1987, 920f.
57 Bade and Oltmer 1999b, 14f.
58 Fleischhauer and Pinkus 1987, 166–9.
59 Friedmann et al. 1993, 43.
60 On this and the following see Volkmann 1966, 1–9; Schlögel (ed.) 1994; Skran 1994; Marrus 1985; Caestecker and Moore 1998.
61 For an overview see Röder 1992; Krohn et al. (ed.) 1998.
62 Lacina 1982, 75–114.
63 Kühnhardt 1984, 48f.
64 Bernecker 1997, 56–8; Tosstorff 1996.
65 Macura 1978.
66 Kulischer 1948, 264.
67 Fischer 1987, 44f.
68 Newly compiled and expanded according to Kühnhardt 1984, 52f.
69 Kulischer 1948, 255, 257; Panayi 1993, 103f.
70 Remarque 1998, 178.
71 Melville and Steffens 1992, 1103f.; Brandes 1997, 208–12.
72 For a basic overview of this and the following see Streit 1978; Herbert 1997; Herbert (ed.) 1991; see also Dahlmann and Hirschfeld (eds) 1999, part 4.
73 Dohse 1981, 126.
74 Fröbe 1991.
75 Herbert 1997, 1.
76 Wegner 1997, part 5.
77 Dallin 1957, chs 14–20.
78 Zielinski 1995.
79 Benz 1995b.
80 Burgdörfer 1932.
81 Benz 1992, 376f.
82 Aly 1998, 76; see also Aly 1999.
83 For an overview of this and the following see Marrus 1985, 209–40; Hilberg 1973; Benz 1997.
84 Benz (ed.) 1996.
85 Krausnick 1985.
86 For an overview see Benz (ed.) 1995a; Schulze et al. (eds) 1987, esp. parts 1 and 2; Benz 1992; Marrus 1985, 296–345; Frantzioch 1987.
87 Jacobmeyer 1985.
88 Kulischer 1948, 286–92; Ther 1998.

Chapter 4: Migration and Migration Policies in the Cold War

1 On the following see Fassmann and Münz 1996b, 29f.; Münz 1997b, 224, 229f., 233f.; Santel 1995, 64.
2 Heckmann 1992, 66–161.
3 Albertini 1966, 28.
4 Reinhard 1988, 187–204; Reinhard 1990, 133–93.
5 Emmer 1993, 309.
6 Dubois and Miège 1994b, 15, 18; Layton-Henry 1994; Vandermotten and Vanlaer, 1993, 144f.; Obdeijn 1994, 68; Weil 1991, 90–128; Jordi 1995; Thränhardt 1997, 141.
7 Dubois 1994, 214, 218, 232, 241–3.
8 Holmes 1992, 226; Panayi 1997, 133.
9 Bartels 1989; Entzinger and Stijnen (eds) 1990; Smith 1977; Cohen 1987; Noiriel 1996, 77f.; Tribalat 1991; Manfrass 1991, 9–23; Freeman 1979; Ogden 1995, 293.
10 Balibar and Wallerstein 1991; Balibar 1993; Solomos 1993.
11 Solomos 1992, 347–51; Thränhardt 1997, 144; Freeman 1979, 308; Amar and Milza 1990, 96, 129–35; Piper 1998, 33–48; Entzinger 1997, 162–4, 167–9.
12 Fanon 1992; Miles 1992; Layton-Henry 1992.
13 Pilkington 1988; Holmes 1991, 44–64.
14 Twaddle 1994, 35–48; Panayi 1997, 134f.; Holmes 1991, 65–96.
15 Miles and Solomos 1987, 75–110; Emmer 1989, 189f.
16 On the following see Hammar (ed.) 1984; Santel 1995, 54–70; Thränhardt 1997.
17 Hoffmann-Nowotny 1970, 97–140.
18 King 1993c, 26.
19 King 1998a.
20 Steinert 1995, 277–326.
21 For the general picture see Bommes and Halfmann (eds) 1998.
22 Santel 1995, 57.
23 Bade 1983, 73–5, 78; Heckmann 1981, 165–72.
24 Nikolinakos 1973, 98–100.
25 Bade 1994a, 45f.
26 Page Moch 1992, 187.
27 Anwar 1995, 275.
28 Seifert 1994, 13–17; Hollifield 1992, 214–32.
29 Santel 1995, 63; King 1993c, 31f.
30 Cohn-Bendit and Schmid 1992, 122–8.
31 Bade 1994a, 47–9; Werner 1994; Münz et al. 1997, 83–7.
32 Santel and Hollifield 1998.
33 Survey commissioned by the German government, cited in *Süddeutsche Zeitung* (5 August 1999), 6.
34 Zlotnik 1998, 437f.; Münz 1994, 104–6.

35 For the general picture see King and Rybaczuk 1993; Suárez-Navaz 1997; Wihtol de Wenden 1999, 145–56; King et al. (eds) 2000.

36 Nuscheler and Rheims 1996, 30.

37 Santel 1995, 88f.; Rath 1999; Engbersen 1999.

38 Santel 1995, 84–9; Calavita 1994, 310, 315; Montanari and Cortese 1993.

39 Santel 1995, 89–93; Cornelius 1994, 332, 342, 345–50.

40 Santel 1995, 93–5; McLean Petras and Kousis 1988.

41 Sassen 1996, 119–21; Jordan 1999; Engbersen 1999.

42 Hammar 1990.

43 Bommes and Halfmann (eds) 1998; Bommes 1999, 96–147.

44 Esping-Andersen 1993, 21f.; Faist 1998a.

45 Marshall 1950b; Castles and Miller 1998, 244–50.

46 Hollifield 2000.

47 Entzinger 1998; Ring 1998.

48 On the following see Bade 1994a, 38–90; Heckmann 1981, 144–222; Meier-Braun 1988, 10–74; Münz et al. 1997, 35–45, 52–114.

49 Faist 1998a, 157f.; Hoffmann 1990, 61–117; Oberndörfer 1993, 34–77.

50 Pries 1999b; Faist 1999; Glick-Schiller et al. 1999.

51 Müggenburg 1996, 18; Bade 1994a, 175–206; Jasper 1991.

52 Noiriel 1996, 1–44; Hollifield 1992, 124–66; Kastoryano 1996; Brubaker 1992; Weil 1994.

53 Bertillon 1911.

54 On this and the following see Tapinos 1975; Weil 1991, 224–41; Hollifield 1994; Manfrass 1984, 541–73; Page Moch 1992, 184f.

55 Nyström 1997, 88f.

56 Wihtol de Wenden 1998, 224.

57 Weil 1991, 333–79.

58 Wihtol de Wenden 1998, 268f.; Ogden 1993, 106.

59 Wihtol de Wenden 1998, 224–30, 236f.

60 Holmes 1992, 226; Panayi 1997, 132–4, 136.

61 Bade 1994a, 16–28.

62 Ring 1998, 242–9; Westin 1996; Oberndörfer and Berndt 1993, 15f., 31f., 47; Schierup 1992.

63 Muus 1993, 23–55; Entzinger 1997; Entzinger 1998; Penninx 1993; Groenendijk and Heijs 1999; Oberndörfer and Berndt 1993, 16f., 32, 39f.

64 Hoffmann-Nowotny 1995; Wimmer 1998, 211–16.

65 For an overview see Wihtol de Wenden 1999, 99–156.

66 Fassmann and Münz 1996c, 227.

67 Martiniello (ed.) 1995.

68 Dummet 1973, 74–6; Thränhardt 1993, 73–6; Layton-Henry 1992.

69 Wihtol de Wenden 1994, 79; Minkenberg 1998, 97–164.

70 Bade 1996; Bade and Bommes 2000.

71 Thränhardt 1988; Rudolph 1996; Bade 1994a; Cohn-Bendit and Schmid 1992.

72 Soysal 1994; Sassen 1995; Cohen 1997, 169–75; Faist 1998b; Castles 1998; see also note 50.

73   On the following see Santel 1995, 82, 95, 98f., 102, 110–13.
74   Art. 1 of the 1951 Geneva Convention Relating to the Status of Refugees, supplemented by Art. 1 of the 1967 Protocol Relating to the Status of Refugees, cited in Masing 1993.
75   Schneider 1992; Bade 1994a, 92–5.
76   Münz 1997a, 41.
77   Heidemeyer 1994; Ackermann 1995.
78   Münz 1997a, 41f.; Lederer 1997, 273–6.
79   Thränhardt 1994, 55; Thränhardt 1992b, 49–56; Balibar and Wallerstein 1991; Balibar 1993; Piper 1998, 43–8.
80   Gorenflos 1995.
81   Ritter 1990; Werner 1992; Nicholson 1990.
82   EUROSTAT 1994, 118 (Belgium), 128 (Germany), 138 (France), 156 (Britain).
83   Lederer 1997, 295.
84   EUROSTAT 1994, 59; Lederer 1997, 282.
85   On the following see Bade 1994a, 91–147.
86   Elsner and Elsner 1992, 30f.
87   Marx 1988, 148–58 (citation: 155).
88   Santel 1995, 101–6.
89   Bade 1994a, 101.
90   On this and the following see Santel 1995, 95–112, 173–81.
91   Ibid., 100–4 (citation: 178f.).
92   Bade 1994a, 135.
93   Santel 1995, 178f.; Papademetriou 1996, 41.
94   Lederer 1997, 296f.
95   Santel 1995, 95–8, 180f.

Chapter 5: Europe: A Continent of Immigration at the End of the Twentieth Century

1   OCDE/SOPEMI 1997, 29, 142, 144, 230f.; Castles and Miller 1998, 222f., 226f., 230f.; Fassmann et al. 1999; Fassmann and Münz 1996b, 17, 31, 39; Fassmann and Münz 1995, 48–54; Lederer 1997, 40f., 75–81; Peach 1992; White 1993; Anwar 1995, 276f.; Tribalat 1996; Ogden 1993; Leimgruber 1992, 37; Weber 1997b, 9.
2   Rex 1996a, 1996b; Baumann and Sunier (eds) 1995.
3   Santel 1999.
4   Knabe 1997, 53f.; Salt 1992b, 1094f.; Santel 1995, 121f. (citation).
5   Nuscheler 1994, 34–7.
6   Vogeley 1991, 3; Santel 1995, 117f.
7   Cited in Werner 1992, 253; interview with Wolfgang Schäuble, in *Der Spiegel* (1–3 January 1994), 25.
8   Penninx and Muus 1991; Gorenflos 1995, 45–53; Zlotnik 1998, 446–8; Morokvasic 1994; Okólski 1994.

9 Opitz 1994.
10 On this and the following see Bade 1994a, 96f., 109–12, 119–22, 175–206.
11 Bodo Morshäuser, 'Die guten Menschen von Deutschland', in *Die Zeit* (20 August 1993), 32.
12 Lassen and Hughes (eds) 1997.
13 Kauffmann 1999; Renner 1999b.
14 Brochmann 1993.
15 Weber 1998.
16 Meissner et al. 1993, 76f.; Dicke 1994, 101–3; Eichenhofer 1994; Lang 1998.
17 Santel and Hunger 1997, 390–3; Rack 1997, 80f.
18 On this and the following see Santel 1995, 173–227.
19 EUROSTAT 1994; Tomei 1997, 18f., 25; Weil 1998; Hailbronner 1995; Papademetriou 1996, 75–103; Marx 1999, 272–5 (citation); Guild 1998.
20 On this and the following see Wollenschläger 1995; Golini et al. 1993; Marie 1996; Tomei 1997, 31–44, 58–70.
21 Salt 1992a; Redor 1994; Wolter 1997; Sassen 1988.
22 Rhode 1991, 39; Rudolph and Hillmann 1998; Fassmann and Münz 1996b, 27f.
23 Wollenschläger 1994, 197f.; Faist et al. (eds) 1999; Werner 1996.
24 Goodwin-Gill 1996, 199–202, 296–323.
25 International Labour Conference 1999, 103–40; King 1998b; Marie 1996, 181–97.
26 Staring 1998.
27 On this and the following see Miller 1995; Lederer 1999; Renner 1999a; Vogel 1999.
28 Engbersen and van der Leun 1998.
29 Meier-Braun 1998, 22.
30 *Financial Times* (20 February 1990), cited in Overbeek 1995, 29.
31 Lederer and Nickel 1997.
32 Koser 1998; Castles and Miller 1998, 96–101.
33 For a case study see Westin 1998.
34 Marie 1996, 192–201; IOM 1996a.
35 Santel 1995, 111.
36 IOM 1996b, 6, 39.
37 Nyíri 1995.
38 King and Champion 1993, 54f.; Betty and Cahill 1998; Rodríguez et al. 1996; King et al. 1998.
39 Castles and Miller 1998, 274; Frankenberg 1993.
40 Santel 1995, 119; Slany 1993.
41 Brubaker 1995; Fassmann and Münz 1996b, 13f.; Codagnone 1998.
42 On this see the articles by Holm Sundhaussen, Günter Schödl and Detlef Brandes, in Bade (ed.) 1992.
43 As assessed by Nicole Hirschler, who is preparing a doctoral dissertation for the University of Osnabrück on the integration of *Aussiedler* in East Germany.

44 On this and the following see Bade 1994a, 147f., 153–5, 165f.; Bade and Oltmer 1999b, 28f.

45 Dietz and Hilkes 1992; Herwartz-Emden and Westphal 1997, 208–10; Koller 1993; Greif et al. 1999.

46 Dietz 1997; Eckert et al. 1999; Pfeiffer et al. 1998.

47 Mertens 1993, 122–31.

48 Bade and Troen (eds) 1994; Siegel 1998.

49 Luks (ed.) 1988; Lustiger 1988; Friedmann et al. 1993, 46.

50 Mertens 1993, 120–2, 132–8, 185–9; Harris 1999.

51 Aptekman 1993; Doomernik 1997, 77–86; Mertens 1993, 199–203.

52 Mertens 1993, 186f., 216, 221; Harris 1998, 116–38; Jasper et al. 1996, 33, 150, 152f.

53 On this and the following see Oschlies 1993, 10, 12, 16–19, 21–4, 28; Roma National Congress 1995, 81; Blahusch 1994, 12–14, 82–5; Fassmann and Münz 1995, 34–46.

54 Bade 1994a, 185f.; Mutz 1995.

55 Zülch (ed.) 1979; Zimmermann 1989; Frost et al. 1995, 28.

56 Bade 1994a, 129–31; Schubert 1988, 130–8; Lucassen 1996, 35–116; Blahusch 1994, 86–9; Roma National Congress 1995, 81f. (citation).

57 Fassmann and Münz 1996b, 26; Ternon 1996, 294–311.

58 Kussbach 1994, 121.

59 UNHCR 1998; UNHCR 1997, 178f.; Malacic 1994, 207f.; Castles and Miller 1998, 109.

60 Zinn and Rivera 1995; IOM Trafficking Migration Newssheet, no. 16 (September 1997), 2; Santel 1995, 84; IOM 1995; Hear 1998, 119–26.

61 Glenny 1993, 121; Rabehl 1998a, 211–13.

62 'Erasing History: Ethnic Cleansing in Kosovo', Report of the US Department of State, Washington, DC, May 1999, cited in *Süddeutsche Zeitung* (12–13 May 1999), 6.

63 'Kosovo: Rückkehr albanischer Flüchtlinge und Flucht anderer ethnischer Gruppen', in *Migration und Bevölkerung* (August 1999), 1f.

64 Timothy Garton Ash, 'Mündel und Vormünder: Im Kosovo baut die UN einen Staat', in *Süddeutsche Zeitung* (7–8 August 1999), 13.

65 Eric J. Hobsbawm, 'Die neuen Nationalismen. Kosovo I: Der Krieg auf dem Balkan ist das Symptom einer tiefen europäischen Krise', in *Die Zeit* (6 May 1999), 37f.; Dan Diner, 'Ein Schlüsselereignis. Die atlantische Gegenwartskultur setzt auf dem Balkan ein unübersehbares Signal', in *Die Zeit* (10 June 1999), 45f.; Mazower 1998.

66 Opitz 1994; Nuscheler 1999, 284–6; Nuscheler and Rheims 1996, 23; Leisinger 2000, 108f.

67 Powell, 'Rivers of Blood' speech delivered in Walsall, West Midlands, April 1968, cited in Solomos 1993, 67; Raspail 1972; Nicholson 1990; Ritter 1990; Werner 1992.

68 Meier-Braun 1998, 22; Wöhlcke 1992, 16–21; Zolberg et al. 1989, 3–33.

69 On this and the following see Birg 1993, 53–8; Birg 1996, 82–111; Nuscheler 1995, 54–103; Nuscheler 2000; Opitz 1997b, 41–52; Santel 1995, 124–45; Leisinger 2000, 98–224.

70 Opitz 1994, 57f.

71 Nuscheler 1994, 32–4; Meier-Braun 1998, 21; Knabe 1998, 61; Barandat (ed.) 1997.

72 Nuscheler 1994, 32–4; Hoffmann-Nowotny 1991, 31f.; Santel 1995, 167.

73 Castles and Miller 1998, 170–4; Nuscheler 1994, 34 (citation).

74 Santel 1995, 193f.; Santel 1999 (citation).

75 Nuscheler 1994, 32; Huntington 1996; Sintenis 1997, 245–8.

76 Bade and Brötel (eds) 1992; Zolberg et al. 1989, 37–179, 227–57.

77 Ternon 1996, 181–95; Meier-Braun 1998, 22f.

78 Rabehl (ed.) 1998b, 11f., 15.

79 Santel 1995, 153–72.

80 Hönekopp 1993, 69.

Bibliography

Ackermann, Volker (1995), *Der 'echte' Flüchtling: Deutsche Vertriebene und Flüchtlinge aus der DDR 1945–1961*, Osnabrück.

Adams, Willi Paul (1985), 'Die Assimilationsfrage in der amerikanischen Einwanderungsdiskussion 1890–1930', in Klaus J. Bade (ed.), *Auswanderer – Wanderarbeiter – Gastarbeiter. Bevölkerung, Arbeitsmarkt und Wanderung in Deutschland seit der Mitte des 19. Jahrhunderts*, 2 vols, 2nd ed., Ostfildern, vol. 1, pp. 300–20.

Åkerman, Sune (1978), 'Towards an Understanding of Emigrational Processes', in William McNeill and Ruth Adams (eds), *Human Migration: Patterns and Policies*, Bloomington, pp. 287–306.

Albertini, Rudolf von (1966), *Dekolonisation. Die Diskussion über Verwaltung und Zukunft der Kolonien 1919–1960*, Cologne.

Albertini, Rudolf von (1976), *Europäische Kolonialherrschaft 1880–1940*, Zürich.

Aly, Götz (1998), '"Judenumsiedlung". Überlegungen zur politischen Vorgeschichte des Holocaust', in Ulrich Herbert (ed.), *Nationalsozialistische Vernichtungspolitik 1939–1945*, Frankfurt a.M., pp. 67–97.

Aly, Götz (1999), *'Final Solution': Nazi Population Policy and the Murder of the European Jews*, trans. Belinda Cooper and Allison Brown, London and New York.

Amar, Marianne and Milza, Pierre (1990), *L'immigration en France au XXe siècle*, Paris.

Angenendt, Steffen (ed.) (1997), *Migration und Flucht*, Bonn.

Anwar, Muhammad (1995), '"New Commonwealth" Migration to the UK', in Robin Cohen (ed.), *The Cambridge Survey of World Migration*, Cambridge, pp. 274–8.

Aptekman, David (1993), 'Jewish Emigration from the USSR, 1990–1992', *Jews in Eastern Europe* 1, pp. 15–33.

Armengaud, André (1980), 'Population in Europe 1700–1914', in Carlo M. Cipolla (ed.), *The Fontana Economic History of Europe: The Industrial Revolution*, Glasgow, pp. 22–76.

Augel, Johannes (1971), *Italienische Einwanderung und Wirtschaftstätigkeit in rheinischen Städten des 17. und 18. Jahrhunderts*, Bonn.

Bade, Klaus J. (1975), *Friedrich Fabri und der Imperialismus in der Bismarckzeit*, Freiburg i.Br.

Bade, Klaus J. (1980a), 'Massenwanderung und Arbeitsmarkt im deutschen Nordosten von 1880 bis zum Ersten Weltkrieg: überseeische Auswanderung, interne Abwanderung und kontinentale Zuwanderung', *Archiv für Sozialgeschichte* 20, pp. 265–323.

Bade, Klaus J. (1980b), 'Arbeitsmarkt, Bevölkerung und Wanderung in der Weimarer Republik', in Michael Stürmer (ed.), *Die Weimarer Republik – Belagerte Civitas*, Königstein i.Ts., pp. 160–87.

Bade, Klaus J. (1981), 'Arbeitsmarkt, Ausländerbeschäftigung und Interessenkonflikt: Der Kampf um die Kontrolle über Auslandsrekrutierung und Inlandsvermittlung ausländischer Arbeitskräfte in Preußen vor dem Ersten Weltkrieg', *Fremdarbeiterpolitik des Imperialismus* 10, Rostock, pp. 27–47.

Bade, Klaus J. (1982a), 'Altes Handwerk, Wanderzwang und gute Policey: Gesellenwanderung zwischen Zunftökonomie und Gewerbereform', *Vierteljahrschrift für Sozial- und Wirtschaftsgeschichte* 69, pp. 1–37.

Bade, Klaus J. (1982b), 'Transnationale Migration und Arbeitsmarkt im Kaiserreich: Vom Agrarstaat mit starker Industrie zum Industriestaat mit starker agrarischer Basis', in Toni Pierenkemper and Richard Tilly (eds), *Historische Arbeitsmarktforschung*, Göttingen, pp. 182–211.

Bade, Klaus J. (1983), *Vom Auswanderungsland zum Einwanderungsland? Deutschland 1880–1980*, Berlin.

Bade, Klaus J. (1984), ' "Preußengänger" und "Abwehrpolitik": Ausländerbeschäftigung, Ausländerpolitik und Ausländerkontrolle auf dem Arbeitsmarkt in Preußen vor dem Ersten Weltkrieg', *Archiv für Sozialgeschichte* 24, pp. 91–162.

Bade, Klaus J. (ed.) (1985a), *Auswanderer – Wanderarbeiter – Gastarbeiter. Bevölkerung, Arbeitsmarkt und Wanderung in Deutschland seit der Mitte des 19. Jahrhunderts*, 2 vols, 2nd ed., Ostfildern.

Bade, Klaus J. (1985b), 'Einführung: Vom Export der Sozialen Frage zur importierten Sozialen Frage: Deutschland im transnationalen Wanderungsgeschehen seit der Mitte des 19. Jahrhunderts', in Klaus J. Bade (ed.), *Auswanderer – Wanderarbeiter – Gastarbeiter. Bevölkerung, Arbeitsmarkt und Wanderung in Deutschland seit der Mitte des 19. Jahrhunderts*, 2 vols, 2nd ed., Ostfildern, vol. 1, pp. 9–71.

Bade, Klaus J. (1985c), 'Die deutsche überseeische Massenauswanderung im 19. und frühen 20. Jahrhundert', in Klaus J. Bade (ed.), *Auswanderer – Wanderarbeiter – Gastarbeiter. Bevölkerung, Arbeitsmarkt und Wanderung in Deutschland seit der Mitte des 19. Jahrhunderts*, 2 vols, 2nd ed., Ostfildern, vol. 1, pp. 259–99.

Bade, Klaus J. (1985d), 'Vom Auswanderungsland zum "Arbeitseinfuhrland": Kontinentale Zuwanderung und Ausländerbeschäftigung in Deutschland im späten 19. und frühen 20. Jahrhundert', in Klaus J. Bade (ed.), *Auswanderer – Wanderarbeiter – Gastarbeiter. Bevölkerung, Arbeitsmarkt und Wanderung in Deutschland seit der Mitte des 19. Jahrhunderts*, 2 vols, 2nd ed., Ostfildern, vol. 2, pp. 433–85.

Bade, Klaus J. (1988), 'Sozialhistorische Migrationsforschung', in Ernst Hinrichs and Henk van Zon (eds), *Bevölkerungsgeschichte im Vergleich: Studien zu den Niederlanden und Nordwestdeutschland*, Aurich, pp. 63–74.

Bade, Klaus J. (1989a), '"Amt der verlorenen Worte": Das Reichswanderungsamt 1918–1924', *Zeitschrift für Kulturaustausch* 39, no. 3, pp. 312–21.

Bade, Klaus J. (1989b), 'Die "Zweite Reichsgründung" in Übersee: Imperiale Visionen, Kolonialbewegung und Kolonialpolitik in der Bismarckzeit', in Adolf M. Birke and Günther Heydemann (eds), *Die Herausforderung des europäischen Staatensystems*, Göttingen, pp. 183–215.

Bade, Klaus J. (ed.) (1992), *Deutsche im Ausland – Fremde in Deutschland: Migration in Geschichte und Gegenwart*, Munich.

Bade, Klaus J. (1994a), *Ausländer – Aussiedler – Asyl. Eine Bestandsaufnahme*, Munich.

Bade, Klaus J. (ed.) (1994b), *Das Manifest der 60: Deutschland und die Einwanderung*, Munich.

Bade, Klaus J. (1994c), *Homo Migrans: Wanderungen aus und nach Deutschland*, Essen.

Bade, Klaus J. (1996), 'Transnationale Migration, ethno-nationale Diskussion und staatliche Migrationspolitik im Deutschland des 19. und 20. Jahrhunderts', in Klaus J. Bade (ed.), *Migration – Ethnizität – Konflikt*, Osnabrück, pp. 403–30.

Bade, Klaus J. (ed.) (1997), *Fremde im Land: Zuwanderung und Eingliederung im Raum Niedersachsen seit dem Zweiten Weltkrieg*, Osnabrück.

Bade, Klaus J. and Bommes, Michael (2000), 'Migration und politische Kultur', in Klaus J. Bade and Rainer Münz (eds), *Migrationsreport 2000*, Frankfurt a.M.

Bade, Klaus J. and Brötel, Dieter (eds) (1992), *Europa und die Dritte Welt*, Stuttgart.

Bade, Klaus J. and Oltmer, Jochen (eds) (1999a), *Aussiedler: deutsche Einwanderer aus Osteuropa*, Osnabrück.

Bade, Klaus J. and Oltmer, Jochen (1999b), 'Einführung: Aussiedlerzuwanderung und Aussiedlerintegration', in Bade and Oltmer (eds), *Aussiedler: deutsche Einwanderer aus Osteuropa*, Osnabrück, pp. 9–51.

Bade, Klaus J. and Troen, S. Ilan (eds) (1994), *Returning Home: Immigration and Absorption into their Homelands of Germans and Jews from the Former Soviet Union*, Be'er-Sheva.

Bailyn, Bernard (1986), *The Peopling of British North America: An Introduction*, New York.

Baines, Dudley (1986), *Migration in a Mature Economy: Emigration and Internal Migration in England and Wales, 1861–1900*, Cambridge, MA.

Baines, Dudley (1995), *Emigration from Europe, 1815–1930*, Cambridge.

Bald, Detlef (1970), *Deutsch-Ostafrika 1900–1914*, Munich.

Balibar, Étienne (1993), 'Gibt es einen "europäischen Rassismus"?', in Friedrich Balke et al. (eds), *Schwierige Fremdheit. Über Integration und Ausgrenzung in Einwanderungsländern*, Frankfurt a.M., pp. 119–34.

Balibar, Étienne and Wallerstein, Immanuel (1991), *Race, Nation, Class: Ambiguous Identities*, trans. Chris Turner (of Étienne Balibar), London and New York.

Balke, Friedrich et al. (eds) (1993), *Schwierige Fremdheit. Über Integration und Ausgrenzung in Einwanderungsländern*, Frankfurt a.M.

Barandat, Jörg (ed.) (1997), *Wasser – Konfrontation oder Kooperation?*, Baden-Baden.

Bartels, Dieter (1989), *Moluccans in Exile*, Leiden.

Bauböck, Rainer et al. (eds) (1996), *The Challenge of Diversity: Integration and Pluralism in Societies of Immigration*, Aldershot.

Baumann, Gerd and Sunier, Thijl (eds) (1995), *Post-migration Ethnicity*, Amsterdam.

Bausinger, Hermann et al. (eds) (1991), *Reisekultur. Von der Pilgerfahrt zum modernen Tourismus*, Munich.

Beer, Mathias and Dahlmann, Dittmar (eds) (1999), *Migration nach Ost- und Südosteuropa vom 18. bis zum Beginn des 19. Jahrhunderts*, Stuttgart.

Benz, Wolfgang (1992), 'Fremde in der Heimat: Flucht – Vertreibung – Integration', in Klaus J. Bade (ed.), *Deutsche im Ausland – Fremde in Deutschland: Migration in Geschichte und Gegenwart*, Munich, pp. 374–86.

Benz, Wolfgang (ed.) (1995a), *Die Vertreibung der Deutschen aus dem Osten*, Frankfurt a.M.

Benz, Wolfgang (1995b), 'Der Generalplan Ost. Zur Germanisierungspolitik des NS-Regimes in den besetzten Ostgebieten 1939–1945', in Wolfgang Benz (ed.), *Die Vertreibung der Deutschen aus dem Osten*, Frankfurt a.M., pp. 45–57.

Benz, Wolfgang (ed.) (1996), *Dimension des Völkermords. Die Zahl der jüdischen Opfer des Nationalsozialismus*, Munich.

Benz, Wolfgang (1997), *Der Holocaust*, Munich.

Bergeron, Louis et al. (1969), *Das Zeitalter der europäischen Revolution 1780–1848*, Frankfurt a.M.

Bermani, Cesare (1997), 'Odyssee in Deutschland. Die alltägliche Erfahrung der italienischen "Fremdarbeiter" im "Dritten Reich"', in Sergio Bologna et al., *Proletarier der 'Achse'. Sozialgeschichte der italienischen Fremdarbeit in NS-Deutschland 1937 bis 1943*, trans. Lutz Klinkhammer, Berlin, pp. 37–252.

Bernecker, Walther L. (1997), *Spaniens Geschichte seit dem Bürgerkrieg*, 3rd ed., Munich.

Bertillon, Jacques (1911), *La Dépopulation de la France*, Paris.

Betty, Charles and Cahill, Michael (1998), 'Consideraciones sociales y sanitarias sobre los immigrantes britanicos mayores en España', *Migraciones* 3, pp. 83–115.

Bevan, Vaughan (1986), *The Development of British Immigration Law*, London.

Bickelmann, Hartmut (1980), *Deutsche Überseeauswanderung in der Weimarer Zeit*, Wiesbaden.

Birg, Herwig (1993), 'Eigendynamik demographisch expandierender und kontraktiver Bevölkerungen und internationale Wanderungen', in Bernhard Blanke (ed.), *Zuwanderung und Asyl in der Konkurrenzgesellschaft*, Opladen, pp. 25–78.

Birg, Herwig (1996), *Die Weltbevölkerung. Dynamik und Gefahren*, Munich.

Blackburn, David (1997), *The Long Nineteenth Century*, London.

Blahusch, Friedrich (1994), 'Roma-Flüchtlinge in Deutschland', in Roland Schopf (ed.), *Sinti, Roma und wir anderen*, Münster, pp. 73–96.

Blanke, Bernhard (ed.) (1993), *Zuwanderung und Asyl in der Konkurrenzgesellschaft*, Opladen.

Bley, Helmut (1968), *Kolonialherrschaft und Sozialstruktur in Deutsch-Südwestafrika 1894–1914*, Hamburg.

Böcker, Anita et al. (eds) (1998), *Regulation of Migration*, Amsterdam.

Bolenz, Eckhard (1996), 'Wegbereiter der Industrie', in *Die erste Fabrik: Ratingen-Cromford*, Cologne, pp. 12–17.

Bologna, Sergio et al. (1997a), *Proletarier der 'Achse'. Sozialgeschichte der italienischen Fremdarbeit in NS-Deutschland 1937 bis 1943*, trans. Lutz Klinkhammer, Berlin.

Bologna, Sergio (1997b), 'Kontinuität und Zäsur in der Geschichte der italienischen Migrationsarbeit', in Bologna et al., *Proletarier der 'Achse'. Sozialgeschichte der italienischen Fremdarbeit in NS-Deutschland 1937 bis 1943*, trans. Lutz Klinkhammer, Berlin, pp. 17–36.

Bölsker-Schlicht, Franz (1987), *Die Hollandgängerei im Osnabrücker Land und im Emsland. Ein Beitrag zur Geschichte der Arbeiterwanderung vom 17. bis zum 19. Jahrhundert*, Sögel.

Bommes, Michael (1994), 'Migration und Ethnizität im nationalen Sozialstaat', *Zeitschrift für Soziologie* 23, pp. 356–77.

Bommes, Michael (1999), *Migration und nationaler Wohlfahrtsstaat. Ein differenzierungstheoretischer Entwurf*, Wiesbaden.

Bommes, Michael and Halfmann, Jost (eds) (1998), *Migration in nationalen Wohlfahrtsstaaten*, Osnabrück.

Bommes, Michael and Morawska, Ewa (eds) (2003), *Reflections on Migration Research*, Berkeley, forthcoming.

Bonjour, Edgar (1946), *Geschichte der schweizerischen Neutralität*, Basel.

Bossenbroek, Martin (1992), '"Dickköpfe" und "Leichtfüße": Deutsche im niederländischen Kolonialdienst des 19. Jahrhunderts', in Klaus J. Bade (ed.), *Deutsche im Ausland – Fremde in Deutschland: Migration in Geschichte und Gegenwart*, Munich, pp. 249–54.

Brandes, Detlef (1997), 'Von den Verfolgungen im Ersten Weltkrieg bis zur Deportation', in Gerd Stricker (ed.), *Deutsche Geschichte im Osten Europas: Rußland*, Berlin, pp. 131–212.

Braudel, Fernand (ed.) (1989), *Europa: Bausteine seiner Geschichte*, Frankfurt a.M.

Brepohl, Wilhelm (1948), *Der Aufbau des Ruhrvolkes im Zuge der Ost-West-Wanderung: Beiträge zur deutschen Sozialgeschichte des 19. und 20. Jahrhunderts*, Recklinghausen.

Brettell, Caroline B. (1986), *Men who Migrate, Women who Wait: Population and History in a Portuguese Parish*, Princeton.

Bretting, Agnes and Bickelmann, Hartmut (1991), *Auswanderungsagenturen und Auswanderungsvereine im 19. und 20. Jahrhundert*, Stuttgart.

Brinck, Andreas (1993), *Die deutsche Auswanderungswelle in die britischen Kolonien Nordamerikas um die Mitte des 18. Jahrhunderts*, Stuttgart.

Brochmann, Grete (1993), 'Control in Immigration Policies: A Closed Europe in the Making', in Russell King (ed.), *The New Geography of European Migrations*, London, pp. 101–15.

Brubaker, Rogers (1992), *Citizenship and Nationhood in France and Germany*, London and Cambridge, MA.

Brubaker, Rogers (1995), 'Aftermaths of Empire and the Unmixing of Peoples', *Ethnic and Racial Studies* 18, no. 2, pp. 189–218.

Burgdörfer, Friedrich (1929), *Der Geburtenrückgang und seine Bekämpfung. Eine Lebensfrage des deutschen Volkes*, Berlin.

Burgdörfer, Friedrich (1932), *Volk ohne Jugend. Geburtenschwund und Überalterung des deutschen Volkskörpers*, Berlin.

Büsch, Otto and Herzfeld, Hans (eds) (1975), *Die frühsozialistischen Bünde in der Geschichte der deutschen Arbeiterbewegung*, Berlin.

Caestecker, Frank (1998), 'The Changing Modalities of Regulation in International Migration within Continental Europe, 1870–1940', in Anita Böcker et al. (eds), *Regulation of Migration*, Amsterdam, pp. 73–98.

Caestecker, Frank and Moore, Bob (1998), 'Refugee Policies in Western European States in the 1930s', *IMIS-Beiträge*, no. 7, pp. 55–103.

Calavita, Kitty (1994), 'Italy and the New Immigration', in Wayne A. Cornelius et al. (eds), *Controlling Immigration: A Global Perspective*, Stanford, pp. 303–26.

Canny, Nicholas (ed.) (1994a), *Europeans on the Move: Studies on European Migration, 1500–1800*, Oxford.

Canny, Nicholas (1994b), 'In Search of a Better Home? European Overseas Migration, 1500–1800', in Nicholas Canny (ed.), *Europeans on the Move: Studies on European Migration, 1500–1800*, Oxford, pp. 263–83.

Castles, Stephen (1998), 'Globalization and the Ambiguities of National Citizenship', in Rainer Bauböck and John Rundell (eds), *Blurred Boundaries: Migration, Ethnicity, Citizenship*, Aldershot, pp. 223–44.

Castles, Stephen and Kosack, Godula (1973), *Immigrant Workers and Class Structure in Western Europe*, London.

Castles, Stephen and Miller, Mark J. (1998), *The Age of Migration: International Population Movements in the Modern World*, 2nd ed., London.

Cerman, Markus and Ogilvie, Sheilagh C. (eds) (1994), *Proto-Industrialisierung in Europa*, Vienna.

Cesarini, David and Fulbrook, Mary (eds) (1996), *Citizenship, Nationality and Migration in Europe*, London.

Chambers, Iain (1994), *Migrancy, Culture, Identity*, London.

Chatelain, Abel (1977), *Les Migrants temporaires en France de 1800 à 1914*, 2 vols, Lille.

Chen, Ta (1923), *Chinese Migration, with Special Reference to Labor Conditions*, Washington.

Cinel, Dino (1991), *The National Integration of Italian Return Migration, 1870–1929*, Cambridge.

Codagnone, Cristino (1998), 'The New Migration in Russia in the 1990s', in Khalid Koser and Helma Lutz (eds), *The New Migration in Europe*, London, pp. 39–59.

Cohen, Robin (1987), *The New Helots: Migrants in the International Division of Labour*, Aldershot.

Cohen, Robin (ed.) (1995), *The Cambridge Survey of World Migration*, Cambridge.

Cohen, Robin (1997), *Global Diasporas: An Introduction*, London.

Cohn-Bendit, Daniel and Schmid, Thomas (1992), *Heimat Babylon. Das Wagnis der multikulturellen Demokratie*, Hamburg.

Constantine, Stephen (1991), 'Empire Migration and Social Reform 1880–1950', in Colin G. Pooley and Ian D. Whyte (eds), *Migrants, Emigrants and Immigrants*, London, pp. 62–83.

Cornelißen, Christoph (1997), 'Europäische Kolonialherrschaft im Ersten Weltkrieg', in Wolfgang Kruse (ed.), *Eine Welt von Feinden. Der Große Krieg 1914–1918*, Frankfurt a.M., pp. 43–54.

Cornelius, Wayne A. (1994), 'Spain: The Uneasy Transition from Labor Exporter to Labor Importer', in Wayne A. Cornelius et al. (eds), *Controlling Immigration: A Global Perspective*, Stanford, pp. 331–69.

Cornelius, Wayne A. et al. (eds) (1994), *Controlling Immigration: A Global Perspective*, Stanford.

Costa-Lascoux, Jacqueline and Weil, Patrick (eds) (1992), *Logique d'Etats et immigrations*, Paris.

Coulmas, Peter (1990), *Weltbürger. Geschichte einer Menschheitssehnsucht*, Reinbek.

Cross, Gary S. (1983), *Immigrant Workers in Industrial France*, Philadelphia.

Cross, Malcolm (ed.) (1992), *Ethnic Minorities and Industrial Change in Europe and North America*, Cambridge.

Dahlmann, Dittmar and Hirschfeld, Gerhard (eds) (1999), *Lager, Zwangsarbeit, Vertreibung und Deportation. Dimensionen der Massenverbrechen in der Sowjetunion und in Deutschland 1933 bis 1945*, Essen.

Dallin, Alexander (1957), *German Rule in Russia, 1941–1945: A Study of Occupation Policies*, London and New York.

Del Fabbro, René (1996), *Transalpini. Italienische Arbeitswanderung nach Süddeutschland im Kaiserreich 1870–1918*, Osnabrück.

Demuth, Andreas (ed.) (1994), *Neue Ost-West-Wanderungen nach dem Fall des Eisernen Vorhangs?*, Münster.

Deutsche Emigranten in Frankreich – französische Emigranten in Deutschland 1685–1945 (1984), 2nd ed., Munich.

Dicke, Klaus (1994), 'Völker- und europarechtliche Richtlinien zum Schutz zugewanderter Ausländer', in Manfred Knapp (ed.), *Migration im Neuen Europa*, Stuttgart, pp. 97–111.

Dietz, Barbara (1997), *Jugendliche Aussiedler*, Berlin.

Dietz, Barbara and Hilkes, Peter (1992), *Rußlanddeutsche*, Munich.

Dohse, Knuth (1981), *Ausländische Arbeiter und bürgerlicher Staat. Genese und Funktion von staatlicher Ausländerpolitik und Ausländerrecht. Vom Kaiserreich bis zur Bundesrepublik Deutschland*, Königstein i.Ts.

Doomernik, Jeroen (1997), *Going West: Soviet Jewish Immigrants in Berlin since 1990*, Aldershot.

Dowty, Alan (1987), *Closed Borders: The Contemporary Assault on Freedom of Movement*, New Haven and London.

Dubois, Colette (1994), 'L'Épineux dossier des retornados', in Colette Dubois and Jean-Louis Miège (eds), *L'Europe retrouvée. Les migrations de la décolonisation*, Paris, pp. 213–46.

Dubois, Colette and Miège, Jean-Louis (eds) (1994a), *L'Europe retrouvée. Les migrations de la décolonisation*, Paris.

Dubois, Colette and Miège, Jean-Louis (1994b), 'Introduction', in Colette Dubois and Jean-Louis Miège (eds), *L'Europe retrouvée. Les migrations de la décolonisation*, Paris, pp. 9–22.

Duchhardt, Heinz and Kunz, Andreas (eds) (1997), *Europäische Geschichte als historiographisches Problem*, Mainz.

Dummet, Ann (1973), *A Portrait of English Racism*, Harmondsworth.

Dyer, Colin (1978), *Population and Society in Twentieth-century France*, New York.

Eckert, Roland et al. (1999), 'Konflikte zwischen einheimischen und Aussiedlerjugendlichen', in Klaus J. Bade and Jochen Oltmer (eds), *Aussiedler: deutsche Einwanderer aus Osteuropa*, Osnabrück, pp. 191–205.

Eichenhofer, Eberhard (1994), *Internationales Sozialrecht*, Munich.

Eichenhofer, Eberhard (ed.) (1999), *Migration und Illegalität*, Osnabrück.

Eisenstadt, Shmuel Noah (1991), 'Die Konstruktion nationaler Identitäten in vergleichender Perspektive', in Bernhard Giesen (ed.), *Nationale und kulturelle Identität*, Frankfurt a.M., pp. 21–38.

Elsner, Eva-Maria and Elsner, Lothar (1992), *Ausländer und Ausländerpolitik in der DDR*, Berlin.

Emmer, Pieter C. (ed.) (1986), *Colonialism and Migration: Indentured Labour before and after Slavery*, Boston.

Emmer, Pieter C. (1988), 'Der Atlantikhandel – die wirtschaftlichen Beziehungen zwischen den europäischen Siedlungskolonien und den Mutterländern', in Eberhard Schmitt (ed.), *Dokumente zur Geschichte der europäischen Expansion*, vol. 4, Munich, pp. 1–27.

Emmer, Pieter C. (1989), 'Migration und Expansion. Die europäische koloniale Vergangenheit und die interkontinentale Völkerwanderung', *Reformatio* 38, no. 3, pp. 183–91.

Emmer, Pieter C. (1993), '"Wir sind hier, weil ihr dort wart". Europäischer Kolonialismus und interkoloniale Migration', *Concilium* 248, pp. 304–12.

Emmer, Pieter C. and Mörner, Magnus (eds) (1991), *European Expansion and Migration: Essays on the Intercontinental Migration from Africa, Asia, and Europe*, New York.

Engbersen, Godfried (1999), 'The Undocumented Outsider Class: Illegal Immigrants in Rotterdam', in Eberhard Eichenhofer (ed.), *Migration und Illegalität*, Osnabrück, pp. 213–31.

Engbersen, Godfried and van der Leun, Joanne (1998), 'Illegality and Criminality: The Differential Opportunity Structure of Undocumented Immigrants', in

Khalid Koser and Helma Lutz (eds), *The New Migration in Europe*, London, pp. 199–223.

Entzinger, Han B. (1997), 'Multikulturalismus im Wohlfahrtsstaat: Zuwanderungs- und Integrationspolitik in den Niederlanden', in Albrecht Weber (ed.), *Einwanderungsland Bundesrepublik Deutschland in der Europäischen Union*, Osnabrück, pp. 157–78.

Entzinger, Han B. (1998), 'Zu einem Modell der Inkorporation von Einwanderern: das Beispiel der Niederlande', in Michael Bommes and Jost Halfmann (eds), *Migration in nationalen Wohlfahrtsstaaten*, Osnabrück, pp. 105–22.

Entzinger, Han B. and Stijnen, Pieter J. (eds) (1990), *Etnische minderheden in Nederland*, Amsterdam.

Esping-Andersen, Gosta (1993), *The Three Worlds of Welfare Capitalism*, Princeton.

EUROSTAT [European Communities. Statistical Office] (1994), *Asylum-seekers and Refugees: A Statistical Report*, vol. 1: *EU Countries*, ed. European Commission, Luxembourg.

Fahrmeir, Andreas K. (1997), 'Nineteenth-century German Citizenship', *Historical Journal* 40, pp. 721–52.

Faist, Thomas (1998a), 'Immigration, Integration und Wohlfahrtsstaaten. Die Bundesrepublik Deutschland in vergleichender Perspektive', in Michael Bommes and Jost Halfmann (eds), *Migration in nationalen Wohlfahrtsstaaten*, Osnabrück, pp. 147–70.

Faist, Thomas (1998b), *International Migration and Transnational Social Spaces*, Bremen.

Faist, Thomas (1999), 'Developing Transnational Social Spaces: The Turkish-German Example', in Ludger Pries (ed.), *Migration and Transnational Social Spaces*, Aldershot, pp. 36–72.

Faist, Thomas et al. (eds) (1999), *Ausland im Inland: Die Beschäftigung von Werkvertragsarbeitnehmern in der Bundesrepublik Deutschland*, Baden-Baden.

Falga, Bernard et al. (eds) (1994), *Au miroir de l'autre. De l'immigration à l'intégration en France et en Allemagne*, Paris.

Fanon, Frantz (1992), *Les Damnés de la terre*, Paris.

Fassmann, Heinz and Münz, Rainer (eds) (1994), *European Migration in the Late Twentieth Century*, Laxenburg.

Fassmann, Heinz and Münz, Rainer (eds) (1995), *Einwanderungsland Österreich?*, Vienna.

Fassmann, Heinz and Münz, Rainer (eds) (1996a), *Migration in Europa*, Frankfurt a.M.

Fassmann, Heinz and Münz, Rainer (1996b), 'Europäische Migration – ein Überblick', in Heinz Fassmann and Rainer Münz (eds), *Migration in Europa*, Frankfurt a.M., pp. 13–52.

Fassmann, Heinz and Münz, Rainer (1996c), 'Österreich – Einwanderungsland wider Willen', in Heinz Fassmann and Rainer Münz (eds), *Migration in Europa*, Frankfurt a.M., pp. 209–29.

Fassmann, Heinz et al. (1999), '*Arbeitsmarkt Mitteleuropa*'. *Die Rückkehr historischer Migrationsmuster*, Vienna.

Fawcett, James T. (1989), 'Networks, Linkages, and Migration Systems', *International Migration Review* 23, pp. 671–80.

Felshtinsky, Yuri (1982), 'The Legal Foundations of the Immigration and Emigration Policy of the USSR, 1917–1927', *Soviet Studies* 34, no. 3, pp. 327–48.

Ferenczi, Imre (1927), 'Weltwanderungen und Wirtschaftsnot', *Soziale Praxis* 36, pp. 890–4.

Ferenczi, Imre (1930), *Kontinentale Wanderungen und die Annäherung der Völker*, Jena.

Fertig, Georg (2000), *Lokales Leben, atlantische Welt. Die Entscheidung zur Auswanderung vom Rhein nach Nordamerika im 18. Jahrhundert*, Osnabrück.

Fischer, Wolfram (1985), 'Wirtschaft und Gesellschaft Europas 1850–1914', in Wolfram Fischer (ed.), *Handbuch der europäischen Wirtschafts- und Sozialgeschichte*, vol. 5, Stuttgart, pp. 1–207.

Fischer, Wolfram (1987), 'Wirtschaft, Gesellschaft und Staat in Europa 1914–1980', in Wolfram Fischer (ed.), *Handbuch der europäischen Wirtschafts- und Sozialgeschichte*, vol. 6, Stuttgart, pp. 10–221.

Fleischhauer, Ingeborg and Pinkus, Benjamin (1987), *Die Deutschen in der Sowjetunion*, Baden-Baden.

Fontaine, Laurence (1996), *History of Pedlars in Europe*, Cambridge.

Fourastié, Jean (1969), *Die große Hoffnung des 20. Jahrhunderts*, 2nd ed., Cologne.

Frankenberg, Günter (1993), 'Zur Alchimie von Recht und Fremdheit. Die Fremden als juridische Konstruktion', in Friedrich Balke et al. (eds), *Schwierige Fremdheit. Über Integration und Ausgrenzung in Einwanderungsländern*, Frankfurt a.M., pp. 41–67.

Frantzioch, Marion (1987), *Die Vertriebenen*, Berlin.

Freeman, Gary P. (1979), *Immigrant Labor and Racial Conflict in Industrial Societies: The French and British Experience 1945–1975*, Princeton.

Freeman, Gary P. (1989), 'Immigrant Labour and Racial Conflict: The Role of the State', in Philip E. Ogden and Paul E. White (eds), *Migrants in Modern France: Population Mobility in the Late Nineteenth and Twentieth Centuries*, London, pp. 160–76.

Fremdling, Rainer (1984a), 'Der Puddler – zur Sozialgeschichte eines Industriehandwerkers', in Ulrich Engelhardt (ed.), *Handwerker in der Industrialisierung*, Stuttgart, pp. 637–65.

Fremdling, Rainer (1984b), 'Die Rolle ausländischer Facharbeiter bei der Einführung neuer Techniken im Deutschland des 19. Jahrhundert', *Archiv für Sozialgeschichte* 24, pp. 1–47.

Friedmann, Alexander et al. (1993), *Eine neue Heimat? Jüdische Emigrantinnen und Emigranten aus der Sowjetunion*, Vienna.

Fröbe, Rainer (1991), 'Der Arbeitseinsatz von KZ-Häftlingen und die Perspektive der Industrie, 1943–1945', in Ulrich Herbert (ed.), *Europa und der 'Reichseinsatz'. Ausländische Zivilarbeiter, Kriegsgefangene und KZ-Häftlinge in Deutschland 1938–1945*, Essen, pp. 351–83.

Frost, Michael et al. (1995), 'Weltweite Nation und nationale Minderheit: Sinti und Roma als Probe auf die innere und äußere Verträglichkeit des vereinigten

Deutschlands', in Joachim S. Hohmann (ed.), *Sinti und Roma in Deutschland*, Frankfurt a.M., pp. 21–32.

Gabaccia, Donna (1996), 'Women of the Mass Migrations: From Minority to Majority, 1820–1930', in Dirk Hoerder and Leslie Page Moch (eds), *European Migrants: Global and Local Perspectives*, Boston, pp. 90–111.

Gallagher, John and Robinson, Ronald (1970), 'Der Imperialismus des Freihandels', in Hans-Ulrich Wehler (ed.), *Imperialismus*, Cologne, pp. 183–200.

Gardlund, Torsten (1955), *Industrialismens samhälle*, Stockholm.

Gestrich, Andreas et al. (eds) (1995), *Ausweisung und Deportation. Formen der Zwangsmigration in der Geschichte*, Stuttgart.

Giedion, Siegfried (1994), *Die Herrschaft der Mechanisierung*, Hamburg.

Gilroy, Paul (1994), *The Black Atlantic: Modernity and Double Consciousness*, London.

Glenny, Misha (1993), *The Rebirth of History: Eastern Europe in the Age of Democracy*, 2nd ed., London.

Glick-Schiller, Nina et al. (1999), 'From Immigrant to Transmigrant: Theorising Transnational Migration', in Ludger Pries (ed.), *Migration and Transnational Social Spaces*, Aldershot, pp. 73–105.

Goinga, Klaus (1995), *Auf den Spuren der Tödden*, Ibbenbüren.

Golini, Antonio et al. (1993), 'A General Framework for the European Migration System in the 1990s', in Russell King (ed.), *The New Geography of European Migrations*, London, pp. 67–82.

Goodwin-Gill, Guy S. (1996), *The Refugee in International Law*, Oxford.

Gorenflos, Walter (1995), *Keine Angst vor der Völkerwanderung*, Hamburg.

Gould, J. D. (1980a), 'European Inter-continental Emigration. The Road Home: Return Migration from the U.S.A.', *Journal of European Economic History* 9, pp. 41–112.

Gould, J. D. (1980b), 'European Inter-continental Emigration: The Role of "Diffusion" and "Feed Back"', *Journal of European Economic History* 9, pp. 267–315.

Grabbe, Hans-Jürgen (1984), 'Das Ende des Redemptioner-Systems in den Vereinigten Staaten', *Amerikastudien/American Studies* 29, no. 3, pp. 277–96.

Graf, Daniel W. (1974), 'Military Rule Behind the Russian Front, 1914–1917', *Jahrbücher für Geschichte Osteuropas* 22, n.s., pp. 390–411.

Gräf, Holger Thomas and Pröve, Ralf (1997), *Wege ins Ungewisse. Reisen in der Frühen Neuzeit, 1500–1800*, Frankfurt a.M.

Grandjonc, Jacques (1975), 'Die deutsche Binnenwanderung in Europa 1830–1848', in Otto Büsch and Hans Herzfeld (eds), *Die frühsozialistischen Bünde in der Geschichte der deutschen Arbeiterbewegung*, Berlin, pp. 3–20.

Grandjonc, Jacques and Werner, Michael (1984), 'Deutsche Auswanderungsbewegungen im 19. Jahrhundert (1815–1914)', *Deutsche Emigranten in Frankreich* 1984, pp. 82–115.

Green, Nancy L. (1997), 'The Comparative Method and Poststructural Structuralism', in Jan Lucassen and Leo Lucassen (eds), *Migration, Migration History, History*, Bern, pp. 57–72.

Greif, Siegfried et al. (1999), 'Erwerbslosigkeit und beruflicher Abstieg von Aussiedlerinnen und Aussiedlern', in Klaus J. Bade and Jochen Oltmer (eds), *Aussiedler: deutsche Einwanderer aus Osteuropa*, Osnabrück, pp. 81–106.

Griep, Wolfgang and Jäger, Hans-Wolf (eds) (1983), *Reisen und soziale Realität am Ende des 18. Jahrhunderts*, Heidelberg.

Groenendijk, Kees and Heijs, Eric (1999), 'Einwanderung, Einwanderer und Staatsangehörigkeitsrecht in den Niederlanden 1945–1998', in Ulrike Davy (ed.), *Politische Integration der ausländischen Wohnbevölkerung*, Baden-Baden, pp. 105–46.

Grubb, Farley (1984), 'The Disappearance of Organized Markets for European Immigrant Servants in the United States', *Social Science History* 18, no. 1, pp. 1–30.

Grubb, Farley (1987), 'Morbidity and Mortality on the North Atlantic Passage: Eighteenth-century German Immigration', *Journal of Interdisciplinary History* 17, no. 3, pp. 565–85.

Grubb, Farley (1994), 'The End of European Immigrant Servitude in the United States', *Journal of Economic History* 54, no. 4, pp. 794–824.

Gruner, Erich and Wiedmer, Hans-Rudolf (1978), *Arbeiterschaft und Wirtschaft in der Schweiz 1880–1914*, Zürich.

Guild, Elspeth (1998), 'Competence, Discretion and Third Country Nationals: The European Union's Legal Struggle with Migration', *Journal of Ethnic and Migration Studies* 24, no. 4, pp. 613–25.

Hailbronner, Kay (1995), 'Perspektiven einer europäischen Asylrechtsharmonisierung nach dem Vertrag von Maastricht', in Michael Piazolo and Klaus Grosch (eds), *Festung oder offene Grenzen? Entwicklung des Einwanderungs- und Asylrechts in Deutschland und Europa*, Munich, pp. 73–109.

Hammar, Tomas (ed.) (1984), *European Immigration Policy*, Cambridge.

Hammar, Tomas (1990), *Democracy and the Nation State: Aliens, Denizens and Citizens in a World of International Migration*, Aldershot.

Hardach, Gerd (1987), *The First World War, 1914–1918*, trans. Peter and Betty Ross, Harmondsworth.

Harris, Paul (1998), 'Jewish Immigration to the New Germany', in Dietrich Thränhardt (ed.), *Einwanderung und Einbürgerung in Deutschland*, Münster, pp. 105–47.

Harris, Paul (1999), 'Russische Juden und Aussiedler', in Klaus J. Bade and Jochen Oltmer (eds), *Aussiedler: deutsche Einwanderer aus Osteuropa*, Osnabrück, pp. 247–63.

Hartig, Irmgard A. (1984), 'Französische Emigranten in Deutschland zur Zeit der Revolution und Napoleons', *Deutsche Emigranten in Frankreich* 1984, pp. 46f.

Hausen, Karin (1970), *Deutsche Kolonialherrschaft in Afrika. Wirtschaftsinteressen und Kolonialverwaltung in Kamerun vor 1914*, Zürich.

Hear, Nicholas van (1998), *New Diasporas: The Mass Exodus, Dispersal and Regrouping of Migrant Communities*, Seattle.

Heckmann, Friedrich (1981), *Die Bundesrepublik: Ein Einwanderungsland?*, Stuttgart.

Heckmann, Friedrich (1992), *Ethnische Minderheiten, Volk und Nation*, Stuttgart.

Heidemeyer, Helge (1994), *Flucht und Zuwanderung aus der SBZ/DDR 1945–1961*, Düsseldorf.

Heinelt, Hubert (ed.) (1994), *Zuwanderungspolitik in Europa*, Opladen.

Henkes, Barbara (1995), *Heimat in Holland. Duitse Dienstmeisjes 1920–1950*, Amsterdam.

Herbert, Ulrich (1990), *A History of Foreign Labor in Germany, 1880–1980: Seasonal Workers/Forced Laborers/Guestworkers*, trans. William Templer, Ann Arbor.

Herbert, Ulrich (ed.) (1991), *Europa und der 'Reichseinsatz'. Ausländische Zivilarbeiter, Kriegsgefangene und KZ-Häftlinge in Deutschland 1938–1945*, Essen.

Herbert, Ulrich (1997), *Hitler's Foreign Workers: Enforced Foreign Labour in Germany under the Third Reich*, trans. William Templer, Cambridge.

Herwartz-Emden, Leonie and Westphal, Manuela (1997), 'Die fremden Deutschen: Einwanderung und Eingliederung von Aussiedlern in Niedersachsen', in Klaus J. Bade (ed.), *Fremde im Land: Zuwanderung und Eingliederung im Raum Niedersachsen seit dem Zweiten Weltkrieg*, Osnabrück, pp. 167–212.

Hilberg, Raul (1973), *The Destruction of the European Jews*, New York.

Hinrichs, Ernst and van Zon, Henk (eds) (1988), *Bevölkerungsgeschichte im Vergleich: Studien zu den Niederlanden und Nordwestdeutschland*, Aurich.

Hobson, John A. (1968), *Imperialism: A Study*, London.

Hochstadt, Steve (1996), 'The Social Economic Determinants of Increasing Mobility in 19th-century Germany', in Dirk Hoerder and Leslie Page Moch (eds), *European Migrants: Global and Local Perspectives*, Boston, pp. 141–69.

Hochstadt, Steve (1999), *Mobility and Modernity: Migration in Germany, 1820–1989*, Ann Arbor.

Hoerder, Dirk (ed.) (1985), *Labor Migration in the Atlantic Economies*, Westport, CT.

Hoerder, Dirk (1988), 'Arbeitswanderung und Arbeiterbewußtsein im atlantischen Wirtschaftsraum', *Archiv für Sozialgeschichte* 28, pp. 391–425.

Hoerder, Dirk (1996), 'Migration in the Atlantic Economies', in Dirk Hoerder and Leslie Page Moch (eds), *European Migrants: Global and Local Perspectives*, Boston, pp. 21–51.

Hoerder, Dirk (1997), 'Segmented Microsystems and Networking Individuals: The Balancing Functions of Migration Processes', in Jan Lucassen and Leo Lucassen (eds), *Migration, Migration History, History*, Bern, pp. 73–84.

Hoerder, Dirk (2002), *Cultures in Contact: World Migration in the Second Millennium*, Durham, NC.

Hoerder, Dirk and Page Moch, Leslie (eds) (1996), *European Migrants: Global and Local Perspectives*, Boston.

Hoffmann, Lutz (1990), *Die unvollendete Republik. Zwischen Einwanderungsland und deutschem Nationalstaat*, Cologne.

Hoffmann-Holter, Beatrix (1995), *'Abreisendmachung'. Jüdische Kriegsflüchtlinge in Wien 1914 bis 1923*, Vienna.

Hoffmann-Nowotny, Hans-Joachim (1970), *Migration. Ein Beitrag zu einer soziologischen Erklärung*, Stuttgart.

Hoffmann-Nowotny, Hans-Joachim (1988), 'Paradigmen und Paradigmenwechsel in der sozialwissenschaftlichen Wanderungsforschung', in Gerhard Jaritz and Albert Müller (eds), *Migration in der Feudalgesellschaft*, Frankfurt a.M., pp. 21–42.

Hoffmann-Nowotny, Hans-Joachim (1991), 'Weltmigration – eine soziologische Analyse', in Walter Kälin and Rupert Moser (eds), *Migrationen aus der Dritten Welt*, 2nd ed., Bern, pp. 29–40.

Hoffmann-Nowotny, Hans-Joachim (1995), 'Switzerland: A Non-immigration Immigration Country', in Robin Cohen (ed.), *The Cambridge Survey of World Migration*, Cambridge, pp. 302–7.

Hohmann, Joachim S. (ed.) (1995), *Sinti und Roma in Deutschland*, Frankfurt a.M.

Hollifield, James F. (1992), *Immigrants, Markets, and States: The Political Economy of Post-war Europe*, Cambridge, MA.

Hollifield, James F. (1994), 'Immigration and Republicanism in France: The Hidden Consensus', in Wayne A. Cornelius et al. (eds), *Controlling Immigration: A Global Perspective*, Stanford, pp. 143–75.

Hollifield, James F. (2000), 'Immigration and the Politics of Rights: The French Case in Comparative Perspective', in Michael Bommes and Andrew Geddes (eds), *Welfare and Immigration*, London, pp. 109–33.

Holmes, Colin (1991), *A Tolerant Country? Immigrants, Refugees, and Minorities in Britain*, London.

Holmes, Colin (1992), *John Bull's Island: Immigration and British Society 1871–1971*, London.

Holmes, Colin (ed.) (1996), *Migration in European History*, 2 vols, Cheltenham.

Holmes, Madelyn (1988), *Forgotten Migrants: Foreign Workers in Switzerland before World War I*, London and Toronto.

Hönekopp, Elmar (1993), 'Das Haupteinwanderungsland Europas sollte sich den Realitäten stellen', *Die Mitbestimmung*, no. 10, pp. 65–9.

Höpken, Wolfgang (1996), 'Flucht vor dem Kreuz? Muslimische Emigration aus Südosteuropa nach dem Ende der osmanischen Herrschaft', *Comparativ* 6, pp. 1–24.

Horne, John (1985), 'Immigrant Workers in France during World War I', *French Historical Studies* 14, pp. 57–88.

Huntington, Samuel P. (1996), *The Clash of Civilizations: Remaking of World Order*, New York.

Hutter, Franz-Josef et al. (eds) (1999), *Menschen auf der Flucht*, Opladen.

Immigrantes, Trabajadores, Ciudadanos. Una Vision de las Migraciones desde España (1999), ed. Colectivo Ioè, Valencia.

International Labour Conference, 87th Session (1999), *Migrant Workers*, Geneva.

IOM (1995), *Profiles and Motives of Potential Migrants from Albania*, Budapest.

IOM (1996a), *Trafficking in Women to Italy for Sexual Exploitation*, Budapest.

IOM (1996b), *CIS Migration Report*, Geneva.

Jackson Jr, James (1997), *Migration and Urbanization in the Ruhr Valley, 1821–1914*, Atlantic Highlands, NJ.

Jackson Jr, James and Page Moch, Leslie (1996), 'Migration and the Social History of Modern Europe', in Dirk Hoerder and Leslie Page Moch (eds), *European Migrants: Global and Local Perspectives*, Boston, pp. 52–69.

Jacobmeyer, Wolfgang (1985), *Vom Zwangsarbeiter zum heimatlosen Ausländer. Die Displaced Persons in Westdeutschland 1945–1951*, Göttingen.

Jaritz, Gerhard and Müller, Albert (eds) (1988), *Migration in der Feudalgesellschaft*, Frankfurt a.M.

Jasper, Dirk (1991), 'Ausländerbeschäftigung in der DDR', in Marianne Krüger-Potratz (ed.), *Anderssein gab es nicht: Ausländer und Minderheiten in der DDR*, Münster, pp. 151–89.

Jasper, Willi et al. (1996), 'Jüdische Emigranten aus der ehemaligen Sowjetunion in Deutschland', in Willi Jasper et al. (eds), *Russische Juden in Deutschland*, Weinheim, pp. 24–207.

Jelavich, Barbara (1991), 'The Polish Emigration, 1831–1871: The Challenge to Russia', *Les migrations politiques* 1991, pp. 238–45.

Jordan, Bill (1999), 'Undocumented Brazilian Workers in London', in Eberhard Eichenhofer (ed.), *Migration und Illegalität*, Osnabrück, pp. 177–93.

Jordi, Jean Jacques (1995), *1962: l'arrivée des Pieds-Noirs*, Paris.

Just, Michael (1988), *Ost- und südosteuropäische Amerikaauswanderung 1881–1914*, Stuttgart.

Kaelble, Hartmut (1997), 'Der Wandel der Erwerbsstruktur in Europa im 19. und 20. Jahrhundert', *Historical Social Research* 22, no. 2, pp. 5–28.

Kahrs, Horst (1993), 'Die Verstaatlichung der polnischen Arbeitsmigration nach Deutschland in der Zwischenkriegszeit', in Eberhard Jungfer et al. (eds), *Arbeitsmigration und Flucht*, Berlin and Göttingen, pp. 130–94.

Kamphoefner, Walter D. (1987), *The Westfalians: From Germany to Missouri*, Princeton.

Kamphoefner, Walter D. (1988), 'Umfang und Zusammensetzung der deutsch-amerikanischen Rückwanderung', *Amerikastudien/American Studies* 33, no. 3, pp. 291–308.

Kamphoefner, Walter D., Helbich, Wolfgang and Sommer, Ulrike (eds) (1991), *News from the Land of Freedom: German Immigrants Write Home*, trans. Susan Carter Vogel, Ithaca and London.

Kastoryano, Riva (1996), *La France, l'Allemagne et leurs immigrés*, Paris.

Kauffmann, Heiko (1999), 'Menschenrechte, Asyl und Abschiebehaft in Deutschland', in Franz-Josef Hutter et al. (eds), *Menschen auf der Flucht*, Opladen, pp. 215–31.

Kimminich, Otto (1994), 'Minderheiten, Volksgruppen, Ethnizität und Recht', in Klaus J. Bade (ed.), *Das Manifest der 60: Deutschland und die Einwanderung*, Munich, pp. 180–97.

King, Russell (ed.) (1993a), *Mass Migration in Europe: The Legacy and the Future*, Chichester.

King, Russell (ed.) (1993b), *The New Geography of European Migrations*, London.

King, Russell (1993c), 'European International Migration 1945–1990', in Russell King (ed.), *The New Geography of European Migrations*, London, pp. 19–39.

King, Russell (1998a), 'From Guestworkers to Immigrants: Labour Migration from the Mediterranean Periphery', in David Pinder (ed.), *The New Europe: Economy, Society, and Environment*, Chichester, pp. 263–79.

King, Russell (1998b), 'Post-Oil Crisis, Post-Communism: New Geographies of International Migration', in David Pinder (ed.), *The New Europe: Economy, Society, and Environment*, Chichester, pp. 281–304.

King, Russell and Champion, Tony (1993), 'New Trends in International Migration in Europe', *Geographical Viewpoint* 21, pp. 45–56.

King, Russell and Rybaczuk, Krysia (1993), 'Southern Europe and the International Division of Labour: From Emigration to Immigration', in Russell King (ed.), *The New Geography of European Migrations*, London, pp. 175–206.

King, Russell et al. (1998), 'International Retirement Migration in Europe', *International Journal of Population Geography* 4, no. 2, pp. 91–111.

King, Russell et al. (eds) (2000), *Eldorado or Fortress? Migration in Southern Europe*, London.

Kirk, Dudley (1956), *Europe's Population in the Interwar Years*, Princeton.

Kleger, Heinz (ed.) (1997), *Transnationale Staatsbürgerschaft*, Frankfurt a.M.

Kleßmann, Christoph (1978), *Polnische Bergarbeiter im Ruhrgebiet 1870–1945*, Göttingen.

Knabe, Bernd (1997), 'Migration in und aus Osteuropa', in Steffen Angenendt (ed.), *Migration und Flucht*, Bonn, pp. 51–9.

Knabe, Bernd (1998), '"Neue Völkerwanderung" aus Osteuropa?', in Karl-Heinz Meier-Braun and Martin Kilgus (eds), *Migration 2000 – Perspektiven für das 21. Jahrhundert*, Baden-Baden, pp. 53–69.

Knorr, Klaus E. (1944), *British Colonial Theories, 1570–1850*, Toronto (repr. 1968).

Kocka, Jürgen (1990a), *Arbeitsverhältnisse und Arbeiterexistenzen. Grundlagen der Klassenbildung im 19. Jahrhundert*, Bonn.

Kocka, Jürgen (1990b), *Weder Stand noch Klasse. Unterschichten um 1800*, Bonn.

Koller, Barbara (1993), 'Aussiedler nach dem Deutschkurs. Welche Gruppen kommen rasch in Arbeit?', *Mitteilungen aus der Arbeitsmarkt- und Berufsforschung* 26, pp. 207–22.

Köllmann, Wolfgang (1976), 'Bevölkerungsgeschichte 1800–1970', in Hermann Aubin and Wolfgang Zorn (eds), *Handbuch der deutschen Wirtschafts- und Sozialgeschichte*, vol. 2, Stuttgart, pp. 9–50.

Körner, Heiko (1990), *Internationale Mobilität der Arbeit. Eine empirische und theoretische Analyse der internationalen Wirtschaftsmigration im 19. und 20. Jahrhundert*, Darmstadt.

Koser, Khalid (1998), 'Out of the Frying Pan and into the Fire: A Case Study of Illegality amongst Asylum Seekers', in Khalid Koser and Helma Lutz (eds), *The New Migration in Europe*, London, pp. 185–98.

Koser, Khalid and Lutz, Helma (eds) (1998), *The New Migration in Europe*, London.

Kramer, Lloyd S. (1988), *Threshold of a New World: Intellectuals and the Exile Experience in Paris, 1830–1848*, Ithaca and London.

Kraus, Antje (1979), 'Arbeiteralltag auf einer Großbaustelle des neunzehnten Jahrhunderts', *Hamburger Jahrbuch für Wirtschafts- und Gesellschaftspolitik* 24, pp. 109–20.

Krausnick, Helmut (1985), *Hitlers Einsatzgruppen*, Frankfurt a.M.

Kriedte, Peter et al. (1977), *Industrialisierung vor der Industrialisierung. Gewerbliche Warenproduktion auf dem Land in der Formationsperiode des Kapitalismus*, Göttingen.

Kritz, Mary M. et al. (eds) (1983), *Global Trends in Migration*, New York.

Krohn, Klaus-Dieter et al. (eds) (1998), *Handbuch der deutschsprachigen Emigration 1933–1945*, Darmstadt.

Kühnhardt, Ludger (1984), *Die Flüchtlingsfrage als Weltordnungsproblem*, Vienna.

Kulischer, Alexander and Kulischer, Eugen (1932), *Kriegs- und Wanderzüge. Weltgeschichte als Völkerbewegung*, Berlin.

Kulischer, Eugen M. (1948), *Europe on the Move: War and Population Changes, 1917–47*, New York.

Kussbach, Erich (1994), 'Situation und Perspektiven der österreichischen Migrationspolitik', in Andreas Demuth (ed.), *Neue Ost-West-Wanderungen nach dem Fall des Eisernen Vorhangs?*, Münster, pp. 110–40.

Küther, Carsten (1983), *Menschen auf der Straße. Vagierende Unterschichten in Bayern, Franken und Schwaben in der zweiten Hälfte des 18. Jahrhunderts*, Göttingen.

Lacina, Evelyn (1982), *Emigration 1933–1945*, Stuttgart.

Ladas, Stephen P. (1932), *The Exchange of Minorities: Bulgaria, Greece and Turkey*, New York.

Lademacher, Horst (1983), *Geschichte der Niederlande*, Darmstadt.

Landes, David S. (1976), *The Unbound Prometheus: Technological Change and Industrial Development in Western Europe from 1750 to the Present*, Cambridge.

Lang, Gernot (1998), 'Zu den Rechtswirkungen des Vertrags von Amsterdam auf den Rechtsstatus der Drittstaatsangehörigen', *Zeitschrift für Ausländerrecht und Ausländerpolitik* 18, no. 2, pp. 59–67.

Langewiesche, Dieter (1977), 'Wanderungsbewegungen in der Hochindustrialisierungsperiode. Regionale, interstädtische und innerstädtische Mobilität in Deutschland 1880–1914', *Vierteljahrschrift für Sozial- und Wirtschaftsgeschichte* 64, no. 1, pp. 1–40.

Lassen, Nina and Hughes, Jane (eds) (1997), '*Safe Third Country' Policies in European Countries*, Copenhagen.

Lattek, Christine (1985), 'Die Emigration der deutschen Achtundvierziger in England', in Gottfried Niethard (ed.), *Großbritannien als Gastland und Exilland für Deutsche im 19. und 20. Jahrhundert*, Bochum, pp. 22–47.

Layton-Henry, Zig (1992), *The Politics of Immigration: Immigration, 'Race' and 'Race' Relations in Post-war Britain*, Oxford.

Layton-Henry, Zig (1994), 'Britain the Would-be Zero-immigration Country', in Wayne A. Cornelius et al. (eds), *Controlling Immigration: A Global Perspective*, Stanford, pp. 273–95.

Leboutte, René (ed.) (1996), *Proto-industrialisation*, Geneva.

Lederer, Harald W. (1997), *Migration und Integration in Zahlen*, Bamberg.

Lederer, Harald W. (1999), 'Typologie und Statistik illegaler Zuwanderung nach Deutschland', in Eberhard Eichenhofer (ed.), *Migration und Illegalität*, Osnabrück, pp. 53–70.

Lederer, Harald W. and Nickel, Axel (1997), *Illegale Ausländerbeschäftigung in der Bundesrepublik Deutschland*, Bonn.

Leenders, Marij (1993), *Ongenode gasten. Van traditioneel asielrecht naar immigrantiebeleid, 1815–1938*, Hilversum.

Le Goff, Jacques (1994), *Das alte Europa und die Welt der Moderne*, Munich.

Leimgruber, Walter (1992), *Impact of Migration in the Receiving Countries: Switzerland*, Geneva.

Leisinger, Klaus M. (2000), *Die sechste Milliarde. Weltbevölkerung und nachhaltige Entwicklung*, Munich.

Levene, Mark (1993), 'Frontiers of Genocide: Jews in the Eastern War Zones, 1914–1920 and 1941', in Panikos Panayi (ed.), *Minorities in Wartime*, Providence, RI, and Oxford, pp. 83–117.

Livi Bacci, Massimo (1999), *The Population of Europe: A History*, trans. Cynthia De Nardi Ipsen and Carl Ipsen, Oxford.

Lourens, Piet and Lucassen, Jan (1999), *Arbeitswanderung und berufliche Spezialisierung. Die lippischen Ziegler im 18. und 19. Jahrhundert*, Osnabrück.

Lubinski, Axel (1997), *Entlassen aus dem Untertanenverband. Die Amerika-Auswanderung aus Mecklenburg-Strelitz im 19. Jahrhundert*, Osnabrück.

Lucassen, Jan (1987), *Migrant Labour in Europe 1600–1900: The Drift to the North Sea*, London.

Lucassen, Jan (1988), 'Quellen zur Geschichte der Wanderungen, vor allem der Wanderarbeit, zwischen Deutschland und den Niederlanden vom 17. bis zum 19. Jahrhundert', in Ernst Hinrichs and Henk van Zon (eds), *Bevölkerungsgeschichte im Vergleich: Studien zu den Niederlanden und Nordwestdeutschland*, Aurich, pp. 75–89.

Lucassen, Jan (1991), *Dutch Long Distance Migration: A Concise History 1600–1900*, Amsterdam.

Lucassen, Jan (1994), 'The Netherlands, the Dutch, and Long Distance Migration in the Late Sixteenth to Early Nineteenth Centuries', in Nicholas Canny (ed.), *Europeans on the Move: Studies on European Migration, 1500–1800*, Oxford, pp. 153–91.

Lucassen, Jan (1995), 'Labour and Early Modern Economic Development', in Jan Lucassen and Karel Davids (eds), *A Miracle Mirrored: The Dutch Republic in European Perspective*, Cambridge, pp. 367–409.

Lucassen, Jan and Lucassen, Leo (eds) (1997), *Migration, Migration History, History*, Bern.

Lucassen, Jan and Penninx, Rinus (1997), *Newcomers, Immigrants and their Descendants in the Netherlands 1550–1993*, Amsterdam.

Lucassen, Leo (1996), *Zigeuner. Die Geschichte eines polizeilichen Ordnungsbegriffes in Deutschland 1700–1945*, Cologne.

Lucassen, Leo (1998), 'The Great War and the Origins of Migration Control in Western Europe and the United States (1880–1920)', in Anita Böcker et al. (eds), *Regulation of Migration*, Amsterdam, pp. 45–72.

Luks, Leonid (ed.) (1988), *Der Spätstalinismus und die 'jüdische Frage'*, Cologne.

Lünnemann, Sigrid (1992), 'Binnenländer als Hochseefischer. Die maritime Wanderarbeit aus dem Kreis Vechta im 19. Jahrhundert', Master's thesis, Osnabrück.

Lustiger, Arno (1988), *Rotbuch: Stalin und die Juden*, Berlin.

McLean Petras, Elizabeth and Kousis, Maria (1988), 'Returning Migrant Characteristics and Labor Market Demand in Greece', *International Migration Review* 22, no. 4, pp. 586–608.

McNeill, William and Adams, Ruth (eds) (1978), *Human Migration: Patterns and Policies*, Bloomington.

Macura, Milos (1978), 'Population in Europe 1920–1970', in Carlo M. Cipolla (ed.), *The Fontana Economic History of Europe*, vol. 5, 2nd ed., Glasgow, pp. 1–87.

Maistre, Chantal et al. (1992), *Colporteurs et marchands savoyards dans l'Europe des XVIIe et XVIIIe siècles*, Annecy.

Malacic, Janez (1994), 'Labour Migration from Former Yugoslavia', in Heinz Fassmann and Rainer Münz (eds), *European Migration in the Late Twentieth Century*, Laxenburg, pp. 207–20.

Malthus, Thomas R. (1798), *An Essay on the Principle of Population as it Affects the Future Improvement of Society*, London.

Manfrass, Klaus (1984), 'Ausländerpolitik und Ausländerproblematik in Frankreich', *Francia* 11, pp. 527–78.

Manfrass, Klaus (1991), *Türken in der Bundesrepublik. Nordafrikaner in Frankreich*, Bonn.

Mantelli, Brunello (1992), '*Camerati del lavore*'. I lavoratori italiani emigrati nel Terzo Reich nel periodo dell'Asse 1938–1943*, Florence.

Marie, Claude-Valentin (1996), 'L'Union Européenne face aux déplacements de populations', *Revue Européenne des Migrations Internationales* 12, no. 2, pp. 169–209.

Marks, Schula and Richardson, Peter (eds) (1984), *International Labour Migration*, London.

Marrus, Michael R. (1985), *The Unwanted: European Refugees in the Twentieth Century*, New York and Oxford.

Marschalck, Peter (1984), *Bevölkerungsgeschichte Deutschlands im 19. und 20. Jahrhundert*, Frankfurt a.M.

Marschalck, Peter (1987), 'The Age of Demographic Transition: Mortality and Fertility', in Klaus J. Bade (ed.), *Population, Labour and Migration in 19th- and 20th-century Germany*, Leamington Spa, pp. 15–33.

Marshall, Thomas H. (1950a), *Citizenship and Social Class and Other Essays*, Cambridge.

Marshall, Thomas H. (1950b), 'Citizenship and Social Class', in Thomas H. Marshall, *Citizenship and Social Class and Other Essays*, Cambridge, pp. 10–85.

Marshall, Thomas H. (1992), *Bürgerrechte und soziale Klassen: Zur Soziologie des Wohlfahrtsstaats*, ed., trans. and with an intro. by Elmar Rieger, Frankfurt a.M.

Martiniello, Marco (ed.) (1995), *Migration, Citizenship and Ethno-national Identities in the European Union*, Aldershot.

Marx, Reinhard (1988), 'Die Definition politischer Verfolgung in der Bundesrepublik Deutschland', in Dietrich Thränhardt and Simone Wolken (eds), *Flucht und Asyl*, Freiburg i.Br., pp. 148–58.

Marx, Reinhard (1999), 'Flüchtlingsschutz oder Menschenrechtsschutz?', in Franz-Josef Hutter et al. (eds), *Menschen auf der Flucht*, Opladen, pp. 265–81.

Masing, Johannes (1993), 'Genfer Flüchtlingskonvention und Art. 16 Abs. 2 Satz 2 Grundgesetz', in Bernhard Blanke (ed.), *Zuwanderung und Asyl in der Konkurrenzgesellschaft*, Opladen, pp. 239–58.

Matthes, Joachim (ed.) (1992), *Zwischen den Kulturen? Die Sozialwissenschaften vor dem Problem des Kulturvergleichs*, Göttingen.

Matzerath, Horst (1983), 'Grundstrukturen städtischer Bevölkerungsentwicklung in Mitteleuropa im 19. Jahrhundert', in Wilhelm Rausch (ed.), *Die Städte Mitteleuropas im 19. Jahrhundert*, Linz, pp. 25–46.

Matzerath, Horst (1985), *Urbanisierung in Preußen 1815–1914*, Stuttgart.

Maurer, Trude (1986), *Ostjuden in Deutschland 1918–1933*, Hamburg.

Mayall, David (1988), *Gypsy-travellers in 19th-century Society*, Cambridge.

Mazower, Mark (1998), *Dark Continent: Europe's Twentieth Century*, New York.

Meier-Braun, Karl-Heinz (1988), *Integration oder Rückkehr? Zur Ausländerpolitik des Bundes und der Länder, insbesondere Baden-Württembergs*, Mainz.

Meier-Braun, Karl-Heinz (1998), 'Die Neue Völkerwanderung', in Karl-Heinz Meier-Braun and Martin Kilgus (eds), *Migration 2000 – Perspektiven für das 21. Jahrhundert*, Baden-Baden, pp. 12–28.

Meier-Braun, Karl-Heinz and Kilgus, Martin (eds) (1998), *Migration 2000 – Perspektiven für das 21. Jahrhundert*, Baden-Baden.

Meissner, Doris M. et al. (1993), *Internationale Migration: Herausforderungen einer neuen Ära*, Bonn.

Melville, Ralph and Steffens, Thomas (1992), 'Die Bevölkerung', in Gottfried Schramm (ed.), *Handbuch der Geschichte Rußlands*, vol. 3: *1856–1945*, Stuttgart, pp. 1009–1193.

Mertens, Jozef (1984), *De vier dorpen van de Bank van Pelt (16de–17de eeuw). Bijdrage tot de kennis van de Loonse Kempen en van de teutenhandel*, Overpelt.

Mertens, Lothar (1993), *Alija. Die Emigration der Juden aus der UdSSR/GUS*, Bochum.

Meßmer, Beatrix (1974), 'Die politischen Flüchtlinge im 19. Jahrhundert', in André Mercier (ed.), *Der Flüchtling in der Weltgeschichte*, Bern and Frankfurt a.M., pp. 209–39.

Meyer, Susanne (1991), *Schwerindustrielle Insel und ländliche Lebenswelt: Georgsmarienhütte 1856–1933*, Münster.

Meyer, Susanne (1995), 'In-migration and Out-migration in an Area of Heavy Industry: The Case of Georgsmarienhütte, 1856–1870', in Dirk Hoerder and Jörg Nagler (eds), *People in Transit: German Migrations in Comparative Perspective, 1820–1930*, Cambridge, MA, pp. 177–99.

Mieck, Ilja (1993), 'Wirtschaft und Gesellschaft Europas von 1650 bis 1850', in Wolfram Fischer (ed.), *Handbuch der europäischen Wirtschafts- und Sozial-geschichte*, vol. 4, Stuttgart, pp. 1–233.

Les Migrations politiques en Europe aux XIXième et XXième siècles (1991), Rome.

Miles, Robert (1992), 'Racism: The Evolution of a Debate about a Concept in Changing Times', in Dietrich Thränhardt (ed.), 'Europe – A New Immigration Continent: Policies and Politics since 1945', *Comparative Perspective*, Münster, pp. 75–104.

Miles, Robert and Solomos, John (1987), 'Migration and the State in Britain', in Charles Husband (ed.), *'Race' in Britain*, London, pp. 75–110.

Miller, Kerby A. (1985), *Emigrants and Exiles: Ireland and the Irish Exodus to North America*, New York and Oxford.

Miller, Mark J. (1995), 'Illegal Migration', in Robin Cohen (ed.), *The Cambridge Survey of World Migration*, Cambridge, pp. 537–40.

Minkenberg, Michael (1998), *Die neue radikale Rechte im Vergleich: USA, Frankreich, Deutschland*, Wiesbaden.

Mittelberger, Gottlieb (1756), *Gottlieb Mittelbergers Reise nach Pennsylvanien im Jahr 1750 und Rückreise nach Teutschland im Jahr 1754*, Frankfurt a.M.

Moltmann, Günter (ed.) (1979), *Aufbruch nach Amerika. Friedrich List und die Auswanderung aus Baden und Württemberg 1816/17*, Tübingen.

Moltmann, Günter (1982), 'Das Risiko einer Seereise. Auswanderungsbedingun-gen im Europa-Amerika-Verkehr in der Mitte des 19. Jahrhunderts', in Heinz Duchhardt and Manfred Schlenke (eds), *Festschrift für Eberhard Kessel zum 75. Geburtstag*, Munich, pp. 182–211.

Moltmann, Günter (1984), 'Auswanderung als Revolutionsersatz?', in Michael Salewski (ed.), *Die Deutschen und die Revolution*, Göttingen, pp. 272–97.

Moltmann, Günter (1986), 'The Migration of German Redemptioners to North America, 1720–1820', in Pieter C. Emmer (ed.), *Colonialism and Migration: Indentured Labour before and after Slavery*, Boston, pp. 105–22.

Monferrini, Mario (1987), *L'emigrazione italiana in Svizzera e Germania nel 1960–1975*, Milan.

Montanari, Armando and Cortese, Antonio (1993), 'Third World Immigration in Italy', in Russell King (ed.), *Mass Migration in Europe: The Legacy and the Future*, Chichester, pp. 275–92.

Morawska, Ewa (1989), 'Labor Migrations of Poles in the Atlantic World Econ-omy, 1880–1914', *Comparative Studies in Society and History* 31, pp. 237–72.

Morawska, Ewa (2003), 'Sociology and History of Immigration', in Michael Bommes and Ewa Morawska (eds), *Reflections on Migration Research*, Berke-ley, forthcoming.

Morelli, Anne (1991), 'Belgique, terre d'accueil? Rejet et accueil des exilés politiques en Belgique de 1830 à nos jours', in *Les Migrations politiques* 1991, pp. 117–28.

Mörner, Magnus (1985), *Adventurers and Proletarians: The Story of Migrants in Latin America*, Paris and Pittsburgh.

Morokvasic, Mirjana (1994), 'Pendeln statt auswandern. Das Beispiel Polen', in Mirjana Morokvasic and Hedwig Rudolph (eds), *Wanderungsraum Europa*, Berlin, pp. 166–87.

Morokvasic, Mirjana and Rudolph, Hedwig (eds) (1994), *Wanderungsraum Europa*, Berlin.

Moya, Jose C. (1998), *Cousins and Strangers: Spanish Immigrants in Buenos Aires, 1850–1930*, Berkeley.

Müggenburg, Andreas (1996), *Die ausländischen Vertragsarbeitnehmer in der ehemaligen DDR*, Berlin.

Münz, Rainer (1994), 'Bevölkerung und Wanderung in Europa', in Klaus J. Bade (ed.), *Das Manifest der 60: Deutschland und die Einwanderung*, Munich, pp. 102–17.

Münz, Rainer (1997a), 'Phasen und Formen der europäischen Migration', in Steffen Angenendt (ed.), *Migration und Flucht*, Bonn, pp. 34–47.

Münz, Rainer (1997b), 'Woher – wohin? Massenmigration im Europa des 20. Jahrhunderts', in Ludger Pries (ed.), *Transnationale Migration*, Baden-Baden, pp. 221–43.

Münz, Rainer et al. (1997), *Zuwanderung nach Deutschland*, Frankfurt a.M.

Mutz, Gerd (1995), 'Die gesellschaftliche Produktion von sozialer und kultureller Fremdheit in der Medienöffentlichkeit', in Joachim S. Hohmann (ed.), *Sinti und Roma in Deutschland*, Frankfurt a.M., pp. 116–75.

Muus, Philip J. (1993), *Migration, Immigration and Policy in the Netherlands*, Geneva.

Nellemann, George (1981), 'Polish Rural Workers in Denmark', *Folk* 23, pp. 359–86.

Nicholson, William (1990), *Der Marsch. Aufbruch der Massen nach Europa*, Rosenheim.

Nichtweiss, Johannes (1959), *Die ausländischen Saisonarbeiter in der Landwirtschaft der östlichen und mittleren Gebiete des Deutschen Reiches. Ein Beitrag zur Geschichte der preußisch-deutschen Politik von 1890–1914*, Berlin.

Nikolinakos, Marios (1973), *Politische Ökonomie der Gastarbeiterfrage*, Reinbek.

Noiriel, Gérard (1984), *Longwy: Immigrés et Prolétaires, 1880–1980*, Paris.

Noiriel, Gérard (1994), *Die Tyrannei des Nationalen. Sozialgeschichte des Asylrechts in Europa*, Lüneburg.

Noiriel, Gérard (1996), *The French Melting Pot*, Minneapolis.

Northrup, David (1995), *Indentured Labor in the Age of Imperialism, 1834–1922*, Cambridge.

Nugent, Walter (1992), *Crossings: The Great Transatlantic Migrations, 1870–1914*, Bloomington.

Nugent, Walter (1996), 'Demographic Aspects of European Migration Worldwide', in Dirk Hoerder and Leslie Page Moch (eds), *European Migrants: Global and Local Perspectives*, Boston, pp. 70–89.

Nuscheler, Franz (1994), 'Migration und Konfliktpotential im Jahr 2000', in Carsten Tessmer (ed.), *Deutschland und das Weltflüchtlingsproblem*, Opladen, pp. 29–38.

Nuscheler, Franz (1995), *Internationale Migration. Flucht und Asyl*, Opladen.

Nuscheler, Franz (1999), 'Ein Ende des "Jahrhunderts der Flüchtlinge"?', in Franz-Josef Hutter et al. (eds), *Menschen auf der Flucht*, Opladen, pp. 283–94.

Nuscheler, Franz (2000), 'Bevölkerung und Migration', in Ingomar Hauchler et al. (eds), *Globale Trends 2000*, Frankfurt a.M., pp. 101–19.

Nuscheler, Franz and Rheims, Birgit (1996), 'Migration und Sicherheit', unpublished manuscript, Duisburg.

Nyíri, Pál D. (1995), 'From Settlement to Community', in Maryellen Fullerton et al. (eds), *Refugees and Migrants: Hungary at a Crossroads*, Budapest, pp. 191–235.

Nyström, Kenneth (1997), 'France and its Aliens', in Hans-Åke Persson (ed.), *Encounters with Strangers: The European Experience*, Lund, pp. 85–126.

Obdeijn, Herman (1994), 'Vers les bords de la mer du Nord. Les retours aux Pays-Bas induits par la décolonisation', in Colette Dubois and Jean-Louis Miège (eds), *L'Europe retrouvée. Les migrations de la décolonisation*, Paris, pp. 49–74.

Oberacker, Carlos H. (1961), *Carlos von Koseritz*, São Paulo.

Oberndörfer, Dieter (1993), *Der Wahn des Nationalen. Die Alternative der offenen Republik*, Freiburg i.Br.

Oberndörfer, Dieter and Berndt, Uwe (1993), *Einwanderungs- und Eingliederungspolitik als Gestaltungsaufgaben*, Gütersloh.

Oberpenning, Hannelore (1996), *Migration und Fernhandel im 'Tödden-System'. Wanderhändler aus dem nördlichen Münsterland im mittleren und nördlichen Europa des 18. und 19. Jahrhunderts*, Osnabrück.

OCDE/SOPEMI (1997), *Tendances des migrations internationales*, annual report 1996, Paris.

Ogden, Philip E. (1993), 'The Legacy of Migration: Some Evidence from France', in Russell King (ed.), *Mass Migration in Europe: The Legacy and the Future*, Chichester, pp. 101–17.

Ogden, Philip E. (1995), 'Labour Migration to France', in Robin Cohen (ed.), *The Cambridge Survey of World Migration*, Cambridge, pp. 289–96.

Okólski, Marek (1994), 'Alte und neue Muster: Aktuelle Wanderungsbewegungen in Mittel- und Osteuropa', in Mirjana Morokvasic and Hedwig Rudolph (eds), *Wanderungsraum Europa*, Berlin, pp. 133–48.

Oltmer, Jochen (1995), *Bäuerliche Ökonomie und Arbeitskräftepolitik im Ersten Weltkrieg*, Sögel.

Oltmer, Jochen (1998a), 'Arbeitszwang und Zwangsarbeit. Kriegsgefangene und ausländische Zivilarbeitskräfte im Ersten Weltkrieg', in Rolf Spilker and Bernd Ulrich (eds), *Der Tod als Maschinist. Der industrialisierte Krieg 1914–1918*, Bramsche, pp. 96–107.

Oltmer, Jochen (1998b), 'Zwangsmigration und Zwangsarbeit: Ausländische Arbeitskräfte und bäuerliche Ökonomie im Deutschland des Ersten Weltkriegs', *Tel Aviver Jahrbuch für deutsche Geschichte* 27, pp. 135–68.

Oltmer, Jochen (2001a), 'Migration and Public Policy in Germany, 1918–1939', in Larry E. Jones (ed.), *Crossing Boundaries*, Providence, RI, and Oxford, pp. 50–69.

Oltmer, Jochen (2001b), *Migration als Obsession. Studien zu Wanderungsgeschehen und Wanderungspolitik in der Weimarer Republik*, postdoctoral dissertation (*Habilitation*), Osnabrück.

Opitz, Peter J. (1994), 'Weltproblem "Migration"', in Carsten Tessmer (ed.), *Deutschland und das Weltflüchtlingsproblem*, Opladen, pp. 43–62.

Opitz, Peter J. (ed.) (1997a), *Der globale Marsch. Flucht und Migration als Weltproblem*, Munich.

Opitz, Peter J. (1997b), 'Das Flucht- und Migrationsgeschehen seit dem Ende des Zweiten Weltkriegs', in Peter J. Opitz (ed.), *Der globale Marsch. Flucht und Migration als Weltproblem*, Munich, pp. 15–55.

Oschlies, Wolf (1993), *Asylbewerber aus dem Karpastenbogen. Versuch über Geschichte, Gegenwart und soziale Problem der Zigeuner Rumäniens*, Cologne.

Ó Tuathaigh, M. A. G. (1996), 'The Irish in Nineteenth-century Britain', in Colin Holmes (ed.), *Migration in European History*, 2 vols, Cheltenham, vol. 1, pp. 51–75.

Overbeek, Henk (1995), 'Towards a New International Migration Regime', in Robert Miles and Dietrich Thränhardt (eds), *Migration and European Integration*, London, pp. 15–36.

Pabst, Wilfried (1992), 'Subproletariat auf Zeit: deutsche "Gastarbeiter" im Paris des 19. Jahrhunderts', in Klaus J. Bade (ed.), *Deutsche im Ausland – Fremde in Deutschland: Migration in Geschichte und Gegenwart*, Munich, pp. 263–8.

Page Moch, Leslie (1992), *Moving Europeans: Migration in Western Europe since 1650*, Bloomington.

Page Moch, Leslie (1996), 'The European Perspective: Changing Conditions and Multiple Migrations, 1750–1914', in Dirk Hoerder and Leslie Page Moch (eds), *European Migrants: Global and Local Perspectives*, Boston, pp. 115–40.

Page Moch, Leslie (1997), 'Dividing Time: An Analytical Framework for Migration History Periodization', in Jan Lucassen and Leo Lucassen (eds), *Migration, Migration History, History*, Bern, pp. 41–56.

Page Moch, Leslie (2003), 'Gender and Migration Research in the Age of Mass Migration, 1870–1914', in Michael Bommes and Ewa Morawska (eds), *Reflections on Migration Research*, Berkeley, forthcoming.

Panayi, Panikos (1988), 'The Lancashire Anti-German Riots of May 1915', *Manchester Region History Review* 2, pp. 3–11.

Panayi, Panikos (1991), *The Enemy in our Midst: Germans in Britain during the First Word War*, Providence, RI, and Oxford.

Panayi, Panikos (1993), 'Refugees in Twentieth-century Britain', in Vaughan Robinson (ed.), *The International Refugee Crisis*, Basingstoke, pp. 95–112.

Panayi, Panikos (1994), *Immigration, Ethnicity and Racism in Britain, 1815–1945*, Manchester.

Panayi, Panikos (1997), 'The Evolution of British Immigration Policy', in Albrecht Weber (ed.), *Einwanderungsland Bundesrepublik Deutschland in der Europäischen Union*, Osnabrück, pp. 123–37.

Papademetriou, Demetrios G. (1996), *Coming Together or Pulling Apart? The European Union's Struggle with Immigration and Asylum*, Washington.

Passelecq, Fernand (1928), *Déportation et travail forcé des ouvriers et de la population civile de la Belgique occupée (1916–1918)*, Paris and New Haven.

Peach, Ceri (1992), 'Urban Concentration and Segregation in Europe since 1945', in Malcolm Cross (ed.), *Ethnic Minorities and Industrial Change in Europe and North America*, Cambridge, pp. 112–36.

Penninx, Rinus (1993), 'Einwanderungs- und Minoritätenpolitik der Niederlande', in Friedrich Ebert Foundation (ed.), *Partizipationschancen ethnischer Minderheiten*, Bonn, pp. 77–105.

Penninx, Rinus (1996), 'Immigration, Minorities, Policy and Multiculturalism in Dutch Society since 1960', in Rainer Bauböck et al. (eds), *The Challenge of Diversity: Integration and Pluralism in Societies of Immigration*, Aldershot, pp. 187–206.

Penninx, Rinus and Muus, Philip J. (1991), 'Nach 1992. Migration ohne Grenzen?', *Zeitschrift für Bevölkerungswissenschaft* 17, no. 2, pp. 191–207.

Pfeiffer, Christian et al. (1998), *Ausgrenzung, Gewalt und Kriminalität im Leben junger Menschen*, Hannover.

Piazolo, Michael and Grosch, Klaus (eds) (1995), *Festung oder offene Grenzen? Entwicklung des Einwanderungs- und Asylrechts in Deutschland und Europa*, Munich.

Pilkington, Edward (1988), *Beyond the Mother Country: West Indians and the Notting Hill White Riots*, London.

Piper, Nicola (1998), *Racism, Nationalism, and Citizenship: Ethnic Minorities in Britain and Germany*, Aldershot.

Poitrineau, Abel (1983), *Remues d'hommes: Essai sur les migrations montagnardes en France aux XVIIe et XVIIIe siècles*, Paris.

Pooley, Colin G. (1995), 'The Role of Migration in the Development of Ethnic Minorities in European Cities *c.*1850–1940', in Hugo Soly and Alfons K. L. Thijs (eds), *Minderheden in Westeuropese Steden*, Brussels and Rome, pp. 55–72.

Pooley, Colin G. and Whyte, Ian D. (eds) (1991), *Migrants, Emigrants and Immigrants*, London.

Pries, Ludger (ed.) (1997), *Transnationale Migration*, Baden-Baden.

Pries, Ludger (ed.) (1999a), *Migration and Transnational Social Spaces*, Aldershot.

Pries, Ludger (1999b), 'New Migration in Transnational Spaces', in Ludger Pries (ed.), *Migration and Transnational Social Spaces*, Aldershot, pp. 1–35.

Puskás, Julianna (ed.) (1990), *Overseas Migration from East-Central and Southeastern Europe, 1880–1940*, Budapest.

Rabehl, Thomas (1998a), 'Daten und Tendenzen des Kriegsgeschehens', in Thomas Rabehl (ed.), *Das Kriegsgeschehen 1998*, Opladen, pp. 211–20.

Rabehl, Thomas (ed.) (1998b), *Das Kriegsgeschehen 1998*, Opladen.

Rack, Peter (1997), 'Bekämpfung der illegalen Beschäftigung', in Friedrich Ebert Foundation (ed.), *Neue Formen der Arbeitskräftezuwanderung und illegalen Beschäftigung*, Bonn, pp. 77–81.

Raspail, Jean (1972), *Le Camp des saints*, Paris.

Rassismus und Migration in Europa (1992), Hamburg.

Rath, Jan (1999), 'The Informal Economy as Bastard Sphere of Social Integration: The Case of Amsterdam', in Eberhard Eichenhofer (ed.), *Migration und Illegalität*, Osnabrück, pp. 117–35.

Redor, Dominique (1994), 'Les migrations de spécialistes hautement qualifiés entre l'Europe centrale et l'Union Européenne', *Revue d'etudes comparatives Est-Ouest* 3, pp. 161–78.

Rees, Elfan (1957), *Century of the Homeless Man*, New York.

Reich, Uwe (1997), *Aus Cottbus und Arnswalde in die Neue Welt. Amerika-Auswanderung aus Ostelbien im 19. Jahrhundert*, Osnabrück.

Reinhard, Marcel R. et al. (1968), *Histoire générale de la population mondiale*, 3rd ed., Paris.

Reinhard, Wolfgang (1985/1988/1990), *Geschichte der europäischen Expansion*, vols 2, 3, 4, Stuttgart.

Reininghaus, Wilfried (ed.) (1993a), *Wanderhandel in Europa*, Dortmund.

Reininghaus, Wilfried (1993b), 'Wanderhandel in Deutschland', in Wilfried Reininghaus (ed.), *Wanderhandel in Europa*, Dortmund, pp. 31–45.

Reiter, Herbert (1992), *Politisches Asyl im 19. Jahrhundert. Die deutschen politischen Flüchtlinge des Vormärz und der Revolution von 1848/49 in Europa und den USA*, Berlin.

Remarque, Erich Maria (1998), *The Night in Lisbon*, trans. Ralph Manheim, New York.

Renner, Günter (1998), *Ausländerrecht in Deutschland*, Munich.

Renner, Günter (1999a), 'Grenzen legaler Zuwanderung: das deutsche Recht', in Eberhard Eichenhofer (ed.), *Migration und Illegalität*, Osnabrück, pp. 41–51.

Renner, Günter (1999b), 'Von der Rettung des deutschen Asylrechts', *Zeitschrift für Ausländerrecht und Ausländerpolitik* 19, no. 5, pp. 206–17.

Rex, John (1996a), 'The Potentiality for Conflict Between National and Minority Cultures', in John Rex, *Ethnic Minorities in the Modern Nation State*, London, pp. 149–67.

Rex, John (1996b), 'Ethnic and Class Conflict in Europe', in John Rex, *Ethnic Minorities in the Modern Nation State*, London, pp. 187–99.

Rey, Annette (1997), *Einwanderung in Frankreich 1981 bis 1995*, Opladen.

Rhode, Barbara (1991), *East–West Migration/Brain-drain*, Brussels.

Rieger, Elmar (1992), 'T. H. Marshall: Soziologie, gesellschaftliche Entwicklung und die moralische Ökonomie des Wohlfahrtsstaates', in Thomas H. Marshall, *Bürgerrechte und soziale Klassen: Zur Soziologie des Wohlfahrtsstaats*, Frankfurt a.M., pp. 7–32.

Riegler, Claudius H. (1985a), *Emigration und Arbeitswanderung aus Schweden nach Norddeutschland 1868–1914*, Neumünster.

Riegler, Claudius H. (1985b), 'Transnationale Migration und Technologietransfer: das Beispiel der schwedisch-deutschen Arbeitswanderung von Technikern und Ingenieuren vor dem Ersten Weltkrieg', in Klaus J. Bade (ed.), *Auswanderer – Wanderarbeiter – Gastarbeiter. Bevölkerung, Arbeitsmarkt und*

Wanderung in Deutschland seit der Mitte des 19. Jahrhunderts, 2 vols, 2nd ed., Ostfildern, pp. 506–26.

Ring, Hans (1998), 'Einwanderungspolitik im schwedischen Wohlfahrtsstaat', in Michael Bommes and Jost Halfmann (eds), *Migration in nationalen Wohlfahrtsstaaten*, Osnabrück, pp. 239–49.

Ritter, Gerhard A. (1991), *Der Sozialstaat*, 2nd ed., Munich.

Ritter, Manfred (1990), *Sturm auf Europa. Asylanten und Armutsflüchtlinge. Droht eine neue Völkerwanderung?*, Munich.

Rocha Trindade, Maria Beatriz (1973), *Immigrés Portugais*, Lisbon.

Röder, Werner (1992), 'Die Emigration aus dem nationalsozialistischen Deutschland', in Klaus J. Bade (ed.), *Deutsche im Ausland – Fremde in Deutschland: Migration in Geschichte und Gegenwart*, Munich, pp. 345–53.

Rodríguez, Vicente et al. (1996), *European Retirement Migration to the Costa del Sol (Spain)*, Madrid.

Roma National Congress (1995), 'Zur Situation der Roma in Europa und Deutschland seit der Wiedervereinigung', in Joachim S. Hohmann (ed.), *Sinti und Roma in Deutschland*, Frankfurt a.M., pp. 77–83.

Rosa, Luigi de (1991), 'Italian Emigration in the Post-unification Period, 1861–1971', in Pieter C. Emmer and Magnus Mörner (eds), *European Expansion and Migration: Essays on the Intercontinental Migration from Africa, Asia, and Europe*, New York, pp. 157–78.

Rosander, Göran (1976), 'Peddling in the Nordic Countries', *Ethnologia Europaea 9*, pp. 123–71.

Rosenberg, Hans (1967), *Große Depression und Bismarckzeit*, Berlin.

Rosoli, Gianfausto (1994), 'Italian Emigration to Brazil', in Lydio F. Tomasi et al. (eds), *The Columbus People: Perspectives in Italian Immigration to the Americas and Australia*, New York, pp. 229–35.

Rudolph, Hedwig (1996), 'Die Dynamik der Einwanderung im Nichteinwanderungsland Deutschland', in Heinz Fassmann and Rainer Münz (eds), *Migration in Europa*, Frankfurt a.M., pp. 161–81.

Rudolph, Hedwig and Hillmann, Felicitas (1998), 'The Invisible Hand Needs Visible Heads: Managers, Experts and Professionals from Western Countries in Poland', in Khalid Koser and Helma Lutz (eds), *The New Migration in Europe*, London, pp. 60–84.

Salt, John (1992a), 'Migration Processes Among the Highly Skilled in Europe', *International Migration Review 29*, pp. 484–505.

Salt, John (1992b), 'The Future of International Labor Migration', *International Migration Review 29*, pp. 1077–1111.

Sande, Anton van de and Valk, Hans de (1991), 'Italian Refugees in the Netherlands during the Restauration 1815–1830', *Les Migrations politiques 1991*, pp. 191–204.

Santel, Bernhard (1995), *Migration in und nach Europa*, Opladen.

Santel, Bernhard (1999), 'Freizügigkeit, Wohnbürgerschaft und staatsbürgerliche Inklusion in Deutschland und den Vereinigten Staaten', in Axel Schulte and Dietrich Thränhardt (eds), *Internationale Migration und freiheitliche Demokratien*, Münster, pp. 101–34.

Santel, Bernhard and Hollifield, James F. (1998), 'Erfolgreiche Integrationsmodelle? Zur wirtschaftlichen Situation von Einwanderern in Deutschland und den USA', in Michael Bommes and Jost Halfmann (eds), *Migration in nationalen Wohlfahrtsstaaten*, Osnabrück, pp. 123–45.

Santel, Bernhard and Hunger, Uwe (1997), 'Gespaltener Sozialstaat, gespaltener Arbeitsmarkt. Die Etablierung postwohlfahrtsstaatlicher Einwanderungspolitiken in Deutschland und in den Vereinigten Staaten', *Soziale Welt* 48, no. 4, pp. 379–96.

Sassen, Saskia (1988), *The Mobility of Labor and Capital: A Study in International Investment and Labor Flow*, New York.

Sassen, Saskia (1995), *Losing Control? Sovereignty in an Age of Globalisation*, New York.

Sassen, Saskia (1996), *Migranten, Siedler, Flüchtlinge. Von der Massenauswanderung zur Festung Europa*, Frankfurt a.M.

Saunders, Kay (ed.) (1984), *Indentured Labour in the British Empire, 1834–1920*, London.

Schieder, Wolfgang (1963), *Anfänge der deutschen Arbeiterbewegung. Die Auslandsvereine im Jahrzehnt nach der Julirevolution von 1830*, Stuttgart.

Schierup, Carl-Ulrik (1992), 'Konstruktion und Krise des schwedischen Multikulturalismus', in *Rassismus und Migration in Europa*, pp. 163–73.

Schilling, Heinz (1988), *Aufbruch und Krise. Deutschland 1517–1648*, Berlin.

Schindling, Anton (1992), 'Bei Hofe und als Pomeranzenhändler: Italiener im Deutschland der Frühen Neuzeit', in Klaus J. Bade (ed.), *Deutsche im Ausland – Fremde in Deutschland: Migration in Geschichte und Gegenwart*, Munich, pp. 287–94.

Schlögel, Karl (ed.) (1994), *Der große Exodus. Die russische Emigration und ihre Zentren 1917 bis 1941*, Munich.

Schneider, Hans-Peter (1992), 'Das Asylrecht zwischen Generosität und Xenophobie. Zur Entstehung des Artikels 16 Absatz 2 Grundgesetz im Parlamentarischen Rat', *Jahrbuch für Antisemitismusforschung*, pp. 217–36.

Schubert, Ernst (1983), *Arme Leute, Bettler und Gauner im Franken des 18. Jahrhunderts*, Neustadt a.d. Aisch.

Schubert, Ernst (1988), 'Mobilität ohne Chance: Die Ausgrenzung des fahrenden Volkes', in Winfried Schulze (ed.), *Ständische Gesellschaft und soziale Mobilität*, Munich, pp. 113–64.

Schubert, Ernst (1995), *Fahrendes Volk im Mittelalter*, Bielefeld.

Schulte Beerbühl, Margrit (1997), 'Aus Fremden werden Bürger: Staatsangehörigkeit und Immigration in Großbritannien, 1660–1844/70', unpublished manuscript.

Schulze, Hagen (1994), *Staat und Nation in der europäischen Geschichte*, Munich.

Schulze, Rainer et al. (eds) (1987), *Flüchtlinge und Vertriebene in der westdeutschen Nachkriegsgeschichte*, Hildesheim.

Schumacher, Martin (1968), *Auslandsreisen deutscher Unternehmer 1750–1851 unter besonderer Berücksichtigung von Rheinland und Westfalen*, Cologne.

Seifert, Wolfgang (1994), 'Berufliche und ökonomische Mobilität ausländischer Arbeitnehmer', in Heinz Werner and Wolfgang Seifert, *Die Integration ausländischer Arbeitnehmer in den Arbeitsmarkt*, Nuremberg, pp. 7–84.

Semmel, Bernhard (1961), 'The "Philosophical Radicals" and Colonization', *Journal of Economic History* 21, pp. 513–25.

Siegel, Dina (1998), *The Great Immigration: Russian Jews in Israel*, Providence, RI.

Simon, Rita and Brettell, Caroline B. (eds) (1986), *International Migration: The Female Experience*, Totowa, NJ.

Singer-Kérel, Jeanne (1991), 'Foreign Workers in France, 1891–1936', *Ethnic and Racial Studies* 14, pp. 279–93.

Sintenis, Monique (1997), 'Nordafrika', in Peter J. Opitz (ed.), *Der globale Marsch. Flucht und Migration als Weltproblem*, Munich, pp. 241–56.

Skran, Claudena M. (1994), *Refugees in Interwar Europe: The Emergence of a Regime*, Oxford.

Slany, Krystyna (1993), 'Emigration from Central and Eastern Europe since the Early Fifties till the Late Eighties', *Polish Sociological Review* 104, no. 4, pp. 355–86.

Slicher van Bath, Bernhard (1986), 'The Absence of White Contract Labour in Spanish America during the Colonial Period', in Pieter C. Emmer (ed.), *Colonialism and Migration: Indentured Labour before and after Slavery*, Boston, pp. 19–31.

Smith, Abbot E. (1947), *Colonists in Bondage*, Chapel Hill.

Smith, David J. (1977), *Racial Disadvantage in Britain*, Harmondsworth.

Solomos, John (1992), 'Politische Sprache und Rassendiskurs. Britische Aspekte eines Problems', *Rassismus und Migration in Europa*, pp. 346–58.

Solomos, John (1993), *Race and Racism in Britain*, 2nd ed., London.

Sombart, Werner (1927), *Die deutsche Volkswirtschaft im 19. Jahrhundert und im Anfang des 20. Jahrhunderts*, 7th ed., Berlin.

Sori, Ercole (1978), *L'emigrazione italiana dall'unità alla seconda guerra mondiale*, Bologna.

Sowell, Thomas (1996), *Migrations and Cultures: A World View*, New York.

Soysal, Yasemin (1994), *Limits of Citizenship: Migrants and Postnational Membership in Europe*, Chicago.

Speed III, Richard B. (1990), *Prisoners, Diplomats, and the Great War*, New York.

Stahl, Heinz-Michael (1982), *Perspectivas da Emigraçao Portuguesa para a C.E.E. 1980–1990*, Lisbon.

Staring, Richard (1998), '"Scenes from a Fake Marriage": Notes on the Flip-side of Embeddedness', in Khalid Koser and Helma Lutz (eds), *The New Migration in Europe*, London, pp. 224–41.

Steinert, Johannes-Dieter (1995), *Migration und Politik. Westdeutschland – Europa – Übersee 1945–1961*, Osnabrück.

Stengers, Jean (1975), 'Die Bedingung für eine sozialistische Betätigung der Deutschen in Brüssel', in Otto Büsch and Hans Herzfeld (eds), *Die frühsozialistischen Bünde in der Geschichte der deutschen Arbeiterbewegung*, Berlin, pp. 157–61.

Streit, Christian (1978), *Keine Kameraden. Die Wehrmacht und die sowjetischen Kriegsgefangenen 1941–1945*, Stuttgart.

Stürmer, Michael (1979), *Herbst des Alten Handwerks. Zur Sozialgeschichte des 18. Jahrhunderts*, Munich.

Suárez-Navaz, Liliana (1997), 'Political Economy of the Mediterranean Rebordering: New Ethnicities, New Citizenships', in Douglas Klusmeyer and Sophie H. Pirie (eds), *Membership, Migration and Identity*, Stanford, pp. 174–200.

Sundermann, Sabine (1997), *Deutscher Nationalismus im englischen Exil. Zum sozialen und politischen Handeln der deutschen Kolonie in London 1848– 1871*, Paderborn.

Sundhaussen, Holm (1987), 'Griechenland von 1914 bis zur Gegenwart', in Wolfram Fischer (ed.), *Handbuch der europäischen Wirtschafts- und Sozialgeschichte*, vol. 6, Stuttgart, pp. 916–45.

Sundhaussen, Holm (1996), 'Bevölkerungsverschiebungen in Südosteuropa seit der Nationalstaatswerdung', *Comparativ* 6, pp. 25–40.

Tapinos, George (1975), *L'Immigration étrangère en France, 1945–1973*, Paris.

Ternon, Yves (1996), *Der verbrecherische Staat. Völkermord im 20. Jahrhundert*, Hamburg.

Tessmer, Carsten (ed.) (1994), *Deutschland und das Weltflüchtlingsproblem*, Opladen.

Thalheim, Karl C. (1926), *Das deutsche Auswanderungsproblem der Nachkriegszeit*, Jena.

Thalheim, Karl C. (1930), 'Gegenwärtige und zukünftige Strukturwandlungen in der Wanderungswirtschaft der Welt', *Archiv für Wanderungswesen* 3, pp. 41– 7.

Ther, Philipp (1998), *Deutsche und polnische Vertriebene. Gesellschaft und Vertriebenenpolitik in der SBZ/DDR und in Polen 1945–1956*, Göttingen.

Thistlethwaite, Frank (1960), 'Migration from Europe Overseas in the Nineteenth and Twentieth Centuries', in *XIe Congrès International des Sciences Historiques, Stockholm 1960*, report V, Stockholm, pp. 32–60.

Thomas, Brinley (1973), *Migration and Economic Growth: A Study of Great Britain and the Atlantic Economy*, Cambridge.

Thränhardt, Dietrich (1988), 'Die Bundesrepublik Deutschland – ein unerklärtes Einwanderungsland', *Aus Politik und Zeitgeschichte* 10, no. 6, pp. 3–13.

Thränhardt, Dietrich (ed.) (1992a), 'Europe – A New Immigration Continent: Policies and Politics since 1945', *Comparative Perspective*, Münster.

Thränhardt, Dietrich (1992b), 'Introduction', in Dietrich Thränhardt (ed.), 'Europe – A New Immigration Continent: Policies and Politics since 1945', *Comparative Perspective*, Münster, pp. 13–73.

Thränhardt, Dietrich (1993), 'Die neuen Minderheiten in Europa: Marginalisierung, Klientelisierung, Bürgerrechte', *Interkulturelle Studien* 21, pp. 73–9.

Thränhardt, Dietrich (1994), 'Die weltweiten Wanderungsprozesse in komparativer Sicht', in Andreas Demuth (ed.), *Neue Ost-West-Wanderungen nach dem Fall des Eisernen Vorhangs?*, Münster, pp. 34–59.

Thränhardt, Dietrich (1997), 'Zuwanderungspolitik im europäischen Vergleich', in Steffen Angenendt (ed.), *Migration und Flucht*, Bonn, pp. 137–53.

Tilly, Charles (1978), 'Migration in Modern History', in William McNeill and Ruth Adams (eds), *Human Migration: Patterns and Policies*, Bloomington, pp. 48–72.

Tilly, Charles (1990), 'Transplanted Networks', in Virginia Yans-McLaughlin (ed.), *Immigration Reconsidered*, New York and Oxford, pp. 79–95.

Todd, Emmanuel (1998), *Das Schicksal der Immigranten: Deutschland, USA, Frankreich, Großbritannien*, Hildesheim.

Tomei, Verónika (1997), *Europäische Migrationspolitik zwischen Kooperationszwang und Souveränitätsansprüchen*, Bonn.

Tosstorff, Reiner (1996), 'Spanische Flüchtlinge nach dem Ende des Bürgerkriegs', *Archiv für die Geschichte des Widerstandes und der Arbeit*, pp. 181–208.

Tribalat, Michèle (1991), *Cent ans d'immigration. Étrangers d'hier, Français d'aujourd'hui*, Paris.

Tribalat, Michèle (1996), *De l'immigration à l'assimilation. Enquête sur les populations d'origine étrangère en France*, Paris.

Troyano Pérez, José Fernando (1998), *Los otros emigrantes. Alteridad e immigración*, Malaga.

Twaddle, Michael (1994), 'British Nationality Law, Commonwealth Immigration and the Ending of the British Empire', in Colette Dubois and Jean-Louis Miège (eds), *L'Europe retrouvée. Les migrations de la décolonisation*, Paris, pp. 35–48.

Uhlig, Otto (1978), *Die Schwabenkinder aus Tirol und Vorarlberg*, Innsbruck.

UNHCR (1997), *The State of the World's Refugees 1997–98*, Oxford and New York.

UNHCR (1998), Refugees and Others of Concern to UNHCR. 1997 Statistical Overview, Geneva.

Vandermotten, Christian and Vanlaer, Jean (1993), 'Immigrants and the Extreme-right Vote in Europe and in Belgium', in Russell King (ed.), *Mass Migration in Europe: The Legacy and the Future*, Chichester, pp. 136–55.

Verhandlungen der Budapester Konferenz betreffs Organisation des Arbeitsmarktes (1911), 7 and 8 October 1910, Leipzig.

Vogel, Dita (1999), 'Illegale Zuwanderung nach Deutschland und soziales Sicherheitssystem', in Eberhard Eichenhofer (ed.), *Migration und Illegalität*, Osnabrück, pp. 73–90.

Vogeley, Dieter (1991), *Massenansturm aus dem Osten? Ursachen und Auswirkungen der Ost-West-Migration*, Bonn.

Volkmann, Hans-Erich (1966), *Die russische Emigration in Deutschland 1919–1929*, Würzburg.

Wagner, Reinhardt W. (1995), *Deutsche als Ersatz für Sklaven. Arbeitsmigration aus Deutschland in die brasilianische Provinz São Paulo 1847–1914*, Frankfurt a.M.

Walle, Etienne van der (1979), 'France', in W. R. Lee (ed.), *European Demography and Economic Growth*, London, pp. 123–43.

Walter, Rolf (1993), 'Träger und Formen des südwestdeutschen Wanderhandels in historischer Perspektive', in Wilfried Reininghaus (ed.), *Wanderhandel in Europa*, Dortmund, pp. 101–15.

Walz, Markus (1999), *Italienische Zinngießer in Rheinland-Westfalen*, doctoral dissertation, Osnabrück.

Weber, Albrecht (ed.) (1997a), *Einwanderungsland Bundesrepublik Deutschland in der Europäischen Union*, Osnabrück.

Weber, Albrecht (1997b), 'Einwanderungsland Bundesrepublik Deutschland in der Europäischen Union', in Albrecht Weber (ed.), *Einwanderungsland Bundesrepublik Deutschland in der Europäischen Union*, Osnabrück, pp. 9–28.

Weber, Albrecht (1998), 'Möglichkeiten und Grenzen europäischer Asylrechtsharmonisierung vor und nach Amsterdam', *Zeitschrift für Ausländerrecht und Ausländerpolitik* 18, no. 4, pp. 147–52.

Weber, Max (1892), *Die Verhältnisse der Landarbeiter im ostelbischen Deutschland*, Leipzig.

Weber, Wolfhard (1975), 'Industriespionage als technologischer Transfer in der Frühindustrialisierung Deutschlands', *Technikgeschichte* 42, pp. 287–305.

Wegner, Bernd (1997), *Hitlers politische Soldaten: die Waffen-SS 1933–1945*, 5th ed., Paderborn.

Wehler, Hans-Ulrich (ed.) (1969), *Friedrich Kapp. Briefe 1843–1884*, Frankfurt a.M.

Wehler, Hans-Ulrich (1970a), *Bismarck und der Imperialismus*, 4th ed., Munich.

Wehler, Hans-Ulrich (ed.) (1970b), *Imperialismus*, Cologne.

Wehler, Hans-Ulrich (1995), *Deutsche Gesellschaftsgeschichte*, vol. 3, Munich.

Weil, Patrick (1991), *La France et ses étrangers. L'aventure d'une politique de l'immigration de 1983 à nos jours*, Paris.

Weil, Patrick (1994), 'Immigration, nation et nationalité: regards comparatifs et croisés', *Revue Française de Science Politique* 44, no. 2, pp. 308–26.

Weil, Patrick (1998), *The Transformation of Immigration Policies: Immigration Control and Nationality Laws in Europe*, San Domenico.

Wennemann, Adolf (1997), *Arbeit im Norden. Die Italiener im Rheinland und Westfalen des späten 19. und frühen 20. Jahrhunderts*, Osnabrück.

Werner, Heinz (1994), 'Integration ausländischer Arbeitnehmer in den Arbeitsmarkt – Deutschland, Frankreich, Niederlande, Schweden', in Heinz Werner and Wolfgang Seifert, *Die Integration ausländischer Arbeitnehmer in den Arbeitsmarkt*, Nuremberg, pp. 85–187.

Werner, Heinz (1996), 'Befristete Zuwanderung von ausländischen Arbeitnehmern. Dargestellt unter besonderer Berücksichtigung der Ost-West-Wanderungen', *Mitteilungen aus der Arbeitsmarkt- und Berufsforschung* 29, no. 1, pp. 36–53.

Werner, Heinz and Seifert, Wolfgang (1994), *Die Integration ausländischer Arbeitnehmer in den Arbeitsmarkt*, Nuremberg.

Werner, Jan (1992), *Die Invasion der Armen. Asylanten und illegale Einwanderer*, Munich.

Wertheimer, Jack (1987), *Unwelcome Strangers: East European Jews in Imperial Germany*, New York.

Westerfield, Ray Bert (1968), *Middlemen in English Business, particularly between 1660 and 1760*, 2nd ed., New York.

Westin, Charles (1996), 'Equality, Freedom of Choice and Partnership: Multicultural Policy in Sweden', in Rainer Bauböck et al. (eds), *The Challenge of*

Diversity: Integration and Pluralism in Societies of Immigration, Aldershot, pp. 207–25.

Westin, Charles (1998), 'On Migration and Criminal Offence: Report on a Study from Sweden', *IMIS-Beiträge*, no. 8, pp. 7–29.

White, Paul (1993), 'Immigrants and the Social Geography of European Cities', in Russell King (ed.), *Mass Migration in Europe: The Legacy and the Future*, Chichester, pp. 65–82.

Wierlacher, Alois (ed.) (1993), *Kulturthema Fremdheit. Leitbegriffe und Problemfelder kulturwissenschaftlicher Fremdheitsforschung*, Munich.

Wihtol de Wenden, Catherine (1994), 'The French Debate: Legal and Political Instruments to Promote Integration', in Heinz Fassmann and Rainer Münz (eds), *European Migration in the Late Twentieth Century*, Laxenburg, pp. 67–79.

Wihtol de Wenden, Catherine (1998), 'Einwanderung im Wohlfahrtsstaat: das Beispiel Frankreich', in Michael Bommes and Jost Halfmann (eds), *Migration in nationalen Wohlfahrtsstaaten*, Osnabrück, pp. 223–37.

Wihtol de Wenden, Catherine (1999), *L'Immigration en Europe*, Paris.

Wihtol de Wenden, Catherine and Tinguy, Anne de (1995), *L'Europe et toutes ses migrations*, Brussels.

Willcox, Walter F. (ed.) (1929/1931), *International Migrations*, vols 1, 2, New York.

Williams, John (1972), *The Home Fronts: Britain, France and Germany 1914–1918*, London.

Wilton, Andrew and Bignamini, Ilaria (eds) (1986), *Grand Tour: The Lure of Italy in the Eighteenth Century*, London.

Wimmer, Andreas (1998), 'Binnenintegration und Außenabschließung. Zur Beziehung zwischen Wohlfahrtsstaat und Migrationssteuerung in der Schweiz', in Michael Bommes and Jost Halfmann (eds), *Migration in nationalen Wohlfahrtsstaaten*, Osnabrück, pp. 199–222.

Wingenroth, Carl D. (1959), 'Das Jahrhundert der Flüchtlinge', *Außenpolitik* 10, no. 8, pp. 491–9.

Wirsching, Andrea (1992), 'Von der freien Lohnarbeit zur Sklaverei: Die Ausbildung der karibischen Plantagengesellschaft', in Thomas Beck et al. (eds), *Kolumbus' Erben. Europäische Expansion und überseeische Ethnien im ersten Kolonialzeitalter, 1415–1815*, Darmstadt, pp. 145–64.

Wöhlcke, Manfred (1992), *Umweltflüchtlinge. Ursachen und Folgen*, Munich.

Wokeck, Marianne (1999), *Trade in Strangers: The Beginnings of Mass Migration to North America*, University Park, PA.

Wollenschläger, Michael (1994), 'Die Gast- und Wanderarbeiter im deutschen Arbeitsrecht', *Recht der Arbeit* 47, no. 4, pp. 193–209.

Wollenschläger, Michael (1995), 'Ein europäisches Asylrecht in der Tradition europäischer Rechtskultur', in Michael Piazolo and Klaus Grosch (eds), *Festung oder offene Grenzen? Entwicklung des Einwanderungs- und Asylrechts in Deutschland und Europa*, Munich, pp. 12–34.

Wolter, Achim (1997), *Globalisierung der Beschäftigung. Multinationale Unternehmen als Kanal der Wanderung Höherqualifizierter innerhalb Europas*, Baden-Baden.

Woytinsky, W. S. and Woytinsky, E. S. (1953), *World Population and Production*, New York.

Wyman, Mark (1993), *Round-trip to America: The Immigrants Return to Europe, 1880–1930*, Ithaca.

Ziegler, Béatrice (1985), *Schweizer statt Sklaven. Schweizerische Auswanderer in den Kaffee-Plantagen von São Paulo 1852–1866*, Stuttgart.

Zielinski, Bernd (1995), *Staatskollaboration. Vichy und der Arbeitskräfteeinsatz im Dritten Reich*, Münster.

Zimmermann, Clemens (1996), *Die Zeit der Metropolen. Urbanisierung und Großstadtentwicklung*, Frankfurt a.M.

Zimmermann, Michael (1989), *Verfolgt, vertrieben, vernichtet. Die national-sozialistische Vernichtungspolitik gegen Sinti und Roma*, Essen.

Zinn, Dorothy Louise and Rivera, Annamaria (1995), 'Notes on a Displaced Womanhood: Albanian Refugee Women in Southern Italy', *Anthropology of East Europe Review* 13, no. 1, pp. 23–9.

Zlotnik, Hania (1998), 'International Migration 1965–96: An Overview', *Population and Development Review* 24, no. 3, pp. 429–68.

Zolberg, Aristide (1987), 'International Migration Policies in a Changing World System', in William McNeill and Ruth Adams (eds), *Human Migration: Patterns and Policies*, Bloomington, pp. 241–86.

Zolberg, Aristide et al. (1989), *Escape from Violence: Conflict and the Refugee Crisis in the Developing World*, New York.

Zülch, Tilman (ed.) (1979), *In Auschwitz vergast, bis heute verfolgt. Zur Situation der Roma (Zigeuner) in Deutschland und Europa*, Reinbek.

Index

Index 385

iron and steel industry, 78–9; *see also* coal and steel industry

Iron Curtain: Cold War, 281, 282; collapse of, 165, 275, 291–2, 297, 301, 304, 324; east–west migration, 283; immigration, 276

irregular employment: ethnicity, 236–7; France, 249–50; gender differences, 327–8; informal sector, 295; Italy, 237–8, 295; tourists, 263, 268; women, 305

Islam: Balkans, 178; Christianity, 225, 328; Front Islamique du Salut, 329; Greece, 199; integration, 243; Muslim headscarf issue, 261

Israel, 300, 306, 309–10

Israeli–Arab Six Days' War, 307

Italy, 11–12; Albanian refugees, 318; asylum seekers, 269, 275; Christian Democrats, 217; colonial migration, 222; colonialism, 118, 187; cross-border migration, 40; emigrants, 112–13, 144, 185, 187, 194, 220, 253, 278; fascist, 203; Friuli, 63; illegal immigrants, 237–8; as immigration country, 293; industrialization, 34; inflation, 182; internal migration, 56; irregular employment, 237–8, 295; labour migrants, 227, 248, 258, 293; labour migration, 52, 56–8, 70; Libya, 119, 187; North Africans, 293; overseas emigration, 112–17; political manipulation, 217; protectionism, 186–7; refugees, 133, 137, 139, 140–2; Roma, 322; seasonal labour migrants, 113, 238, 293; south–north migration, 235; United States of America, 37

itinerant traders, 2, 4, 21; companies, 22; cottage industries, 25; France, 24; fruit dealers, 24–5; Germany, 25–6; households, 21; income levels, 30–1; indirect dealers, 26; licenses, 31; regional specialization, 23–6; roots, 20–1; seasonal labour migrants, 21–2; *Tödden* system, 14, 28; work brigades, 24, 25

Jackson, James H., 44

Japanese contract workers, 120

Jews, 211–12, 223; attacks against, 308; Britain, 154, 203; CIS, 309, 310; deportation, 181, 211, 212–13, 307; emigrants, 93, 300–1; Israel, 306, 309–10; Nazi Germany, 202–3; novels about diaspora, 203; refugees, 309, 310; Russian, 154, 181, 200–1, 211–12; Soviet Union, 300–1, 306–10; transit migration, 152–3, 202–3; United States of America, 93, 300; urban settlement, 310

July Monarchy, 133, 135–6

July Revolution, 132, 133, 134, 135

jus sanguinis, 151–2, 241

jus soli, 144, 151–2, 155, 241, 245, 277

Kádár regime, 266

Kapp, Friedrich, 88, 146, 147

Kennan, George F., 166–8

Kenya, 119

Khorev, Boris, 283

Khrushchev, Nikita, 307

Kipling, Rudyard, 125

Kleßmann, Christoph, 48

Kohl, Helmut, 286

Köllmann, Wolfgang, 37, 39

Körner, Heiko, 97, 99, 114

Koselleck, Reinhart, 131

Koseritz, Karl von, 147

Kosovo: Albanians, 320, 321; International Protectorate, 322; NATO, 321, 331; refugees, 320, 321–3; Roma, 320, 322

Kosovo Liberation Army, 320

Kossuth, Lajos, 146

Ku Klux Klan, 188

Kühn Report, 244

Kulischer, Alexander, xi, 103

Kulischer, Eugen M., xi, 103, 204–5

Kurds, 233, 268

Labour and Socialist International, 197

labour contracts, 160, 231–2

labour force transfer, 232

labour market: agriculture, 35, 64–5, 162–3; chain migration, 8–9; colonial service, 118–19; France, 155; gender differences, 21; Germany, 164, 284; globalization, 328;

peat cutting, 14, 15–16, 18–19
pedlars, 20, 22, 23, 24, 28, 30
perfume industry, 70
pewterers, 5
Philadelphia, 88–9
Philippines, 237, 239
plantations, 82, 83, 109, 120
Po plain, 9, 11
Poepenmärkte (people markets),
  Netherlands, 15
'Polack', 51
Poland: agriculture, 162–3; asylum
  seekers, 265; coal and steel industries,
  111; cross-border migration, 40;
  deportation, 206, 211; emigration, 93,
  110, 144, 185, 194; ethnic Germans,
  303, 304; France, 51–2, 69;
  Germanization policies, 211;
  Germany, 62–3, 172, 173–4, 207, 267;
  Hitler–Stalin pact, 212; immigration,
  301; Jews, 200, 211; labour migration,
  48, 58, 60, 62–3, 69, 111, 156, 161,
  163, 172, 173–4, 207, 267; Mazurs,
  59; overseas migration, 109–12; re-
  established, 182; refugees, 133–4, 137,
  140–2, 205, 267; resettlement, 210,
  216; returnees, 111–12; seasonal
  labour migrants, 67–8, 70, 110, 111;
  transit migration, 152–3, 298;
  unemployment, 283; uprising, 270;
  wage levels, 293
political asylum, 130–2, 235, 273
political manipulation, 217
political refugees, 130–2, 134; Belgium,
  137–9; Britain, 142–5, 146, 153–4;
  exile, 147; extradition, 138–9; France,
  132–6; non-Jewish, 203; Switzerland,
  140–2; United States of America,
  142
Pollard, J. J., 307
population growth, 2, 37, 39, 114–15,
  217; agrarian society, 36; employment,
  13, 324; Euro-Mediterranean zone,
  234–5; France, 37–8, 42, 193–4, 228;
  global, 324–5; industrialization, 37,
  116; Nazi Germany, 129; Netherlands,
  37, 42; predictions, 325; Ruhr valley,
  41; Third World, 324
ports, 88–9, 96

Portugal: asylum seekers, 269, 275;
  Brazil, 82; colonialism, 118;
  emigration statistics, 185, 220; foreign
  nationals, 238–9; labour migrants,
  227, 248, 249, 258; post-colonial
  migration, 223; unemployment, 223;
  women, 249
post-colonial migration, 222, 223, 270,
  281, 329
potato blight, 105
potato farms, 9
Potsdam Conference, 215
poverty, 32, 318, 327
poverty refugees, 268, 272
Powell, Enoch, 224, 225, 323
Prague Spring, 266, 270
prepaid tickets, 90, 108
Principe, 223
prisoners of war: forced labour, 175;
  France, 171; Germany, 172, 174–5,
  206–10, 215–16; Hague Convention,
  172; living conditions, 174, 175;
  working conditions, 174–5
pro-asylum seekers demonstrations, 286
Prognos institute, 284
proletariat: industrial, 35; migration, xii,
  33, 53, 81, 113–14, 166
prostitution, 297, 328
protectionism: First World War, 182;
  France, 193–7; Germany, 191–3;
  interwar, 184; Italy, 186–7; labour
  market, 154–5, 164, 191–7;
  nationalism, 148–9
Provence, 9, 11
Prussia: agricultural crisis, 107; anti-
  Polish defence policy, 68, 130, 157–9,
  160, 164, 192; brokerage, 159, 161;
  compulsory military service, 96;
  compulsory return, 158; foreign
  labour laws, 158; German Customs
  Union, 91; labour contracts, 160;
  labour migration records, 55; labour
  policies, 40; licences for itinerant
  traders, 31; recruitment areas, 159;
  registration, 158, 160–1; Ruhr Poles,
  47–52, 58; Russian troops, 180–1;
  seasonal labour migrants, 67–8; Trade
  and Tariff Act, 91; urbanization, 42,
  43; *see also* Germany